TREMBLING IN THE BALANCE:
The Chesapeake and Ohio Canal During the Civil War

by
Timothy R. Snyder

Blue Mustang Press

Boston, Massachusetts

First printing

Cover image by Thomas Nast, *New York Illustrated News*, Nov. 11, 1861, Courtesy of Enoch Pratt Library, Baltimore, Md.

ISBN: 978-1-935199-12-0
PUBLISHED BY BLUE MUSTANG PRESS
www.bluemustangpress.com
Boston, Massachusetts

Printed in the United States of America

TREMBLING IN THE BALANCE:
The Chesapeake and Ohio Canal During the Civil War

by
Timothy R. Snyder

for my parents,
who on summer vacations took me and my brother
to many out-of-the-way forts and historical sites,
often to the chagrin of our sisters

RE-OPENING OF THE C. AND O. CANAL

The Water's boiling through the locks, with many a whirl and prank;
The tow-boat lifts like yeasty bread, and swings against the bank.
The captain takes a view of things, across the cabin door;
The bow-man stands with folded arms, the tow-boy's on the shore.
The skipper calls with such a voice, as *skipper* should employ;
To start his engine on the shore, three mules, a whip and boy.
The driver jumps a button off; but mends it with a stick,
Whispers the tow-boy's gentle oath and gives the mule a kick.
The tow-line straitens with a snap, and scatter its mimic spray;
The captain's hand is on the helm, the tow-boat's under way.

April 2, 1860
Williamsport

–Hagerstown Herald of Freedom and Torch Light,
April 4, 1860

TREMBLING IN THE BALANCE:
THE CHESAPEAKE AND OHIO CANAL DURING THE CIVIL WAR

CONTENTS

A NOTE ON MAPS, PHOTOS AND ILLUSTRATIONS

All of the maps, photographs and illustrations used in this book were produced during or very near to the Civil War period. The maps are from the Library of Congress's Civil War Maps collection. While an occasional flaw can be discerned on a particular map, these maps also depict features that existed during the war but which have faded from modern memory, such as the location of fords, ferries and obscure towns. Additionally, it is my hope that the character and authenticity of period maps will add to legitimacy of the narrative.

MAPS

TABLES

PHOTOS AND ILLUSTRATIONS

PREFACE

The story of the Chesapeake and Ohio Canal during the Civil War is a tale of a company's struggle to operate a transportation line in one of the country's major theaters of war. The canal's position along Maryland's southern border with Virginia left it in a unique position to experience the war first-hand, and indeed records show that the company was drawn into the conflict within days after the surrender of Fort Sumter. Except perhaps for books on the railroads, there are very few accounts of how a nineteenth-century company responded to the challenge of conducting business in a region that experienced so much of the war. An examination of the canal company during this period allows readers to see how the company responded to the many threats it faced, including the seizure and destruction of its property, military interference in its operations, and a chronic shortage of operating funds. Existing records are such that on some occasions the reader can determine how the canal company responded to a challenge—such as a Confederate invasion—on nearly a day-to-day basis, providing a glimpse into the operations of a company during the Civil War that few other accounts provide.

Because Maryland was a border state, the canal company was beset with additional problems inherent in a state whose citizens had divided political loyalties and in a nation that was determined to tolerate no infidelity. An assessment of the canal company during this period shows that indeed the company faced a difficult ordeal in meeting the Federal government's demand for unconditional loyalty from its officers and employees, a test that the canal company was ultimately unable to meet.

In short, a look at the C&O Canal during the Civil War provides a unique window into the operations of the company at a time of great national peril and explains how the company survived the war in spite of being on the verge of bankruptcy as the conflict dawned. It will also show that the canal indeed played a significant part in sustaining the Union war effort, a role that rivaled that of its old adversary, the Baltimore and Ohio Railroad

Company. The canal company's survival set the stage for a period of significant growth in the decade that followed the conflict, growth that helped propel the Industrial Revolution.

§

I was born and raised just outside of Williamsport, Maryland, the approximate mid-point of the Chesapeake and Ohio Canal, and the town that the National Park Service describes as the one that most retains the look of a canal town. The house in which I was raised was only about one-half mile from the old waterway "as the crow flies." I spent a great deal of time on the canal as a child and young adult—camping, fishing, hiking, running, and biking.

The history of Washington County, Maryland, is rich in itself, extending back well beyond the Civil War period. Anyone who passes through the region will note the many historical markers posted along roadsides, describing events from the French and Indian War, the Revolutionary period, and of course the Civil War. Over the years the markers mounted along the canal at Falling Waters, Dam Number 5, McCoys Ferry, and other locations—placed there by the Civil War Centennial Commission—drew my attention and provoked questions. What, for example, was the relationship between the canal company and the U.S. government during the war? Was the canal company loyal, disloyal or indifferent? How similar or dissimilar was its experience to that of its old rival, the B&O Railroad Company? Did it fail to play a significant role in the conflict altogether? As a graduate student in history at Shippenburg (Pa.) University, I attempted to answer some of these questions in my master's thesis. Urged on by my thesis committee chairman, John Quist, and by John Frye, the director of the Western Maryland Room at the Washington County Library in Hagerstown, Md., I continued to research the topic after my graduation. In doing so, I was pleased and excited to find a wealth of additional primary sources. This book is the product of my extended research, which entirely supersedes my original thesis in both volume and focus.

In addition to the above named individuals, I would like to acknowledge and thank the following people: David Godshalk and Kim Klein who served on my thesis committee at Shippensburg University; Harlan Unrau and Tom Clemens, both of whom read early drafts of this manuscript and offered many useful suggestions; and Robert J. Kapsch and Karen Gray who read later drafts and provided much helpful advice. Karen, in particular, saved me from not a few errors, especially in the prologue. Steve French supplied me not only with encouragement, but with a few primary documents. In addition to the above, I would like to thank Virginia Rasbold Williams, James I. Robertson, Jr., Richard Sommers, John Pezzullo, Tom Hayes, Brad Forbush, Ted Alexander, Gary Petrichick and Curt Gaul. I also extend many thanks to my publisher, Walter Chalkley, and the staff at Blue Mustang Press. Walter has both a personal and professional interest in the canal and jumped at the opportunity to publish this book. I would also like to thank Linda, Tyler and Christian, for their patience and understanding during my many hours of travel, research and writing.

Because of the contributions of those individuals mentioned above, this is a better book; I, of course, I take full responsibility for all errors and omissions

Timothy R. Snyder
Hagerstown, Md.

February 13, 2011

TREMBLING IN THE BALANCE:
The Chesapeake and Ohio Canal During the Civil War

by
Timothy R. Snyder

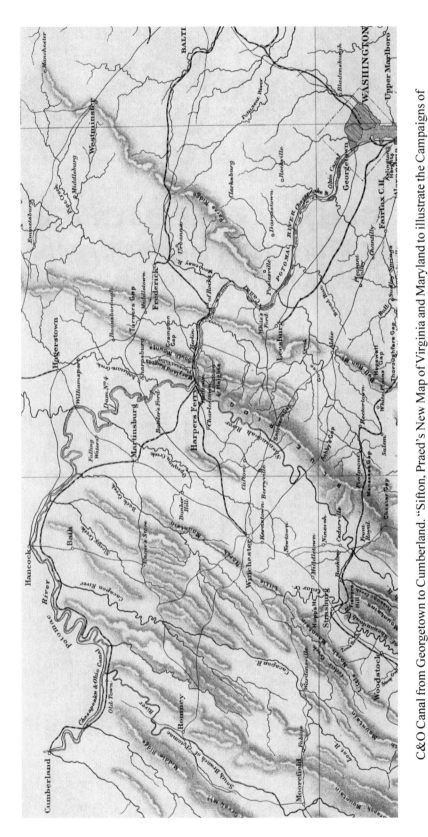

C&O Canal from Georgetown to Cumberland. "Sifton, Praed's New Map of Virginia and Maryland to illustrate the Campaigns of 1861 to 1864," (1912). Source: Library of Congress, Geography and Map Division

PROLOGUE

THE MOST FORTUNATE INCIDENT IN MY LIFE:
THE CHESAPEAKE AND OHIO CANAL TO 1860

When the construction of the Chesapeake and Ohio Canal began in 1828, it was but one of a series of efforts over the previous eighty years to improve transportation and trade along the Potomac River. Long before the first European settlers arrived in the seventeenth century, the Potomac was utilized by Native Americans as a means of travel and trade. Frederick Gutheim, in his 1949 classic, *The Potomac*, from the Rivers of America series, noted: "The very name Potomac in the Algonkin tongue is a verbal noun meaning 'something brought,' and as a designation for a place 'where something is brought,' or, more freely, 'trading place.'"[1]

Colonists to North America likewise utilized the Potomac for transportation purposes. In 1749 the English government chartered the Ohio Company, an enterprise that was organized to participate in the lucrative fur trade with Native Americans of the Ohio River Valley. In 1750 the company built a storehouse on the west bank of Wills Creek (present-day Cumberland, Maryland) and another two years later opposite Wills Creek on the Virginia side of the Potomac. To facilitate trade, the company's agents built a road from Wills Creek to the Monongahela River in Pennsylvania, where another storehouse was constructed. The company utilized the Potomac River to transport goods from above the fall line—the point where the upland region meets the coastal plain, characterized by steep waterfalls and rapids—to the company's storehouses on the upper Potomac.

In 1754 conflict erupted between England and France over control of territory in the Ohio River Valley. In that year the French took possession of the Ohio Company's unfinished fort at the forks of the Ohio River (present-day Pittsburgh, Pennsylvania). This event led directly to English General Edward Braddock's campaign to retake the fort. Although Braddock's expedition was a failure, a portion of the supplies his quartermasters' had acquired from Maryland and Pennsylvania were sent to a storehouse at Conococheague (present-day Williamsport, Maryland) and then up the Potomac River to Fort Cumberland.

Following the American Revolution, there was interest in improving the river as a trade and transportation route, which George Washington had long advocated. As a young surveyor, soldier, and owner of western lands, the future president had become familiar with the upper Potomac and was convinced that the river was the most practical route to the west. Additionally, Washington believed that improvement of the Potomac would help unite the eastern seaboard with the western frontier of the young nation. He advocated the linkage of the river with the tributaries of the Ohio River via short land portages, thereby establishing a complete transportation route from east to west.

In 1785 the Potomac Company was formed with George Washington as president. It was charted by Virginia and Maryland, overcoming the opposition of merchants and politicians in Baltimore who were loath to promote the growth of rival ports at Georgetown and Alexandria, Virginia. The Potomac Company was authorized to improve the navigation of the Potomac to the highest point that permanent navigation could be maintained. At a minimum, it was expected that the company would make river improvements to Fort Cumberland, which would provide a connection to Braddock's Road that led to the tributaries of the Ohio River. The company built short skirting canals around falls and rapids and removed obstructions from the river channel. It also made improvements to many of the major tributaries of the Potomac. In the end, however, the Potomac Company was burdened with substantial debt and had not improved the river enough to meet the terms of its charter. The tolls collected did not even pay the interest on its debts. By 1819 all efforts to extend navigation came to a standstill. In the remaining years of its existence, the company would only have enough resources to maintain its existing works.

After the Virginia Board of Public Works was created in 1816, it subsequently made the first known suggestion that a complete still-water canal could be built to link the Potomac with the waters of the Ohio. In 1820 its engineer, Thomas Moore, conducted a survey and reported that a continuous canal to the coal banks above Cumberland could be completed for $1,114,300. Moore suggested, however, that only $18,000-$20,000 more would be needed by the existing Potomac Company to finish its improvements of the river. But with the Erie Canal in the midst of construction, interest was focused on the creation of a competing still-water canal rather than on finishing the Potomac Company's river improvements. The following year officials from Virginia and Maryland formed a joint committee to determine if the still-extant Potomac Company had met the terms of its charter. It quickly found that it had not, and that its financial resources were scant. In 1822 another survey of the river was made to the mouth of the Savage River above Cumberland. It determined that a complete canal could be built to that point for $1,574,954.

Efforts to find support for the canal project proceeded to the state legislatures. Virginia passed an act of incorporation in 1823. Maryland did not charter the canal company due to the continuing opposition from merchants and public officials in Baltimore. Public support for the canal was mounting in Maryland, however. Western Maryland, which would lie adjacent to the proposed canal, would benefit greatly once the project was completed. Its representatives exerted pressure on the legislature to charter the company. In addition, the Erie Canal was nearing completion and Pennsylvania had begun a series of public works, all of which engendered fears in Maryland and Virginia that a share of the western trade might elude them.

In 1823 proponents of the canal called for a convention of supporters to meet in Washington. The convention resolved to support the construction of a canal to the Ohio River and ultimately to Lake Erie. The 212-mile canal was estimated to cost $2,750,000. Resolutions and a charter were drawn and submitted to the U.S. Congress and to the legislatures of Virginia, Maryland, Pennsylvania, and Ohio.

The efforts met with success. Virginia passed the charter in early 1824. Although Maryland initially failed to pass it for the usual reasons, its support was obtained at a subsequent session when the state was granted the right to build a branch canal to Baltimore. Congress passed the charter in March 1825. Pennsylvania also passed it, albeit with many conditions. The company's charter required it to complete 100 miles of construction within five years. In 1826 the U.S. Engineers conducted a survey of the proposed canal route to Lake Erie, divided into eastern, middle and western sections. It estimated that the entire canal would cost $22,375,428, well above earlier estimates. The eastern section alone was anticipated to cost $8,177,081. Such high estimates dampened the enthusiasm of all but the most ardent canal advocates. In 1826 canal proponents quickly organized a second convention to revive interest in at least the eastern portion of the project. It convinced President John Quincy Adams to fund another survey from Cumberland to tidewater that would be conducted by experienced canal engineers from the now-completed Erie. That survey concluded that a canal could be built between those points for $4,479,347.

The new estimate gave impetus to canal advocates, and the company quickly organized. Stock subscriptions were taken: the United States subscribed to $1,000,000, Maryland to $500,000, Washington to $1,000,000, and Georgetown and Alexandria to $250,000 each. In June 1828 the company's first president, Charles Fenton Mercer, and directors were elected. Two weeks later, at a lavish ceremony, President John Quincy Adams broke the soil, which officially commenced construction of the canal. Before breaking the ground he proclaimed: "I regard this event the most fortunate incident in my life." When he put the spade to soil it immediately struck the root of a tree, which foreshadowed subsequent construction difficulties. The Potomac Company, which only grudgingly came to the conclusion that the construction of the Chesapeake and Ohio Canal would fulfill its original objective, surrendered its charter to the canal company in August 1828.[2]

Unfortunately for the new canal company, the only practicable route for the waterway was within the Potomac River Valley itself, which was quite narrow and restricted by steep cliffs in several places. The potential problems that could result from these conditions were not given serious consideration in any of the surveys. As a result, wrote George Washington Ward, the canal was built on the "very margin of the river—sometimes partly in the channel—thus exposing the works to the full force of the frequent and violent freshets in the Potomac Valley." Throughout its history the canal company would repeatedly experience problems that resulted from the unique geography of the river valley and the limitations of nineteenth-century engineering technology.[3]

The construction phase was one of great frustration to the canal company. Initially there was a shortage of laborers, and thus agents were sent to Great Britain and other European countries to obtain workers. The company paid for their passage to America in exchange for a fixed term of service. However, the Irish workers in particular—faced with difficult working conditions—tended to be insubordinate and prone to fighting, and many ran off before their terms of indenture had expired. Sickness and disease also spread amongst the workers, which resulted in scores of dead and the loss of many weeks of work. Due to the problems it experienced with indentured servants, the company's board of directors declined to purchase slaves for use as laborers. An examination of run-away slave ads from this period, however, shows that contractors hired by the canal company used slave labor. Additionally, evidence suggests that in the Antebellum period the canal was utilized by runaway slaves as both a destination where men could find work and earn money, and as a means of escape to Pennsylvania. In "Narrative of James Curry, A Fugitive Slave," Curry writes of escaping from his master's plantation in North Carolina, crossing the Potomac at Alexandria, Virginia, and traveling up the canal towpath to Williamsport, at which point he moved north to Hagerstown and then into Pennsylvania ultimately bound for Canada.[4]

Despite labor difficulties, twenty miles of the canal had been completed by 1830. The next year the first section of the canal—totaling just over twenty-two miles between Georgetown and Seneca—was completed and boating began in earnest. Trade was mostly agricultural, and the company continued to use the Potomac Company's locks until the end of the year.

The canal company also experienced legal problems with the Baltimore and Ohio Railroad Company, which hindered the work of building the canal. The construction of one of the earliest American railroads—considered an unproven experiment by many—had begun on the same day as the canal company's ground-breaking ceremony. The railroad had also planned to build its line through the narrow river valley from Point of Rocks to Cumberland, and then westward until it reached its ultimate destination at Wheeling, Virginia. In 1828 a court granted the canal company an injunction to stop the B&O from building on property over which it claimed prior authority to plot its right-of-way. The B&O subsequently filed suit against the canal company. Eventually, after four years of hearings and court-ordered surveys, the canal company's claim to build through the river valley was affirmed. Political and financial pressures compelled the canal company to permit joint construction of the railroad and canal from Point of Rocks to Harpers Ferry—at the confluence of the Potomac and Shenandoah rivers—in exchange for a subscription of 2,500 shares of its stock by the B&O Railroad.

During the four years it took to resolve the issue, both lines could continue construction only to Point of Rocks, which delayed the westward construction of the waterway. Additionally, the costly legal battle and the expense of land condemnation had drained the canal company of it financial resources. Lastly, the 1828 election of Andrew Jackson, who opposed Federal support of public works projects, eliminated any chance of further aid from the U.S. government.

During the construction phase violence occasionally erupted between Irish and German laborers and between factions of rival Irish workers. Between 1834 and 1840, at least ten episodes of violence occurred. On five occasions the Maryland Militia was dispatched to the canal to restore order. In 1834 President Jackson sent Federal troops to the canal near Williamsport to quell violence and unrest among Irish workers, the first such intervention of U.S. troops in a labor disturbance in the nation's history.[5]

In 1834 Maryland rescued the canal from its financial woes. It subscribed to stock for $125,000, and the next year issued bonds to provide a $2 million loan to the company. In 1836 it passed a bill that issued bonds for an additional $3 million stock subscription. However, the latter bonds proved difficult to sell following the Panic of 1837. In 1839 the state subscribed to an additional $1,375,000 in stock. The company also obtained private loans. In 1834, 1837–1838, 1839, and 1840–1841 the company issued its own script—promissory notes payable with interest upon maturation—that allowed it to maintain construction. The market value of the script varied wildly depending upon the company's prospects for future success.

The expense of construction materials, labor, land, and repairs of completed sections caused by periodic floods continued to put financial stress on the company. By 1843 the company was again short of funds and had only completed the canal to Dam Number 6 west of Hancock. Additionally, the twelve-year time limit to complete the canal to Cumberland, specified in the company's charter, had expired in 1840. Once more Maryland bailed the company out of its troubles. In 1844 it authorized the canal company to issue $1,700,000 in preferred bonds on the mortgage of the company's revenue after it received guarantees from shippers for 195,000 tons of canal trade for five years. Poor financial conditions and uncertainty caused by the Mexican War resulted in weak demand for the bonds, which again slowed construction.

By 1842, the tolls the company had collected from its primarily agricultural trade were barely enough to maintain the 135 miles of the canal already in operation. To gain a larger share in the coal trade, in 1843 the canal company reached an agreement with the B&O Railroad in which the latter agreed to transport coal to the Virginia side of Dam Number 6, where it was boated over to Maryland and transferred to the canal. The railroad, however, later argued that as a feeder of goods to the canal, completion of the waterway to Cumberland was unnecessary. In reality, little coal was transferred to the canal by this method and the canal company countered the railroad's argument by reminding the Maryland legislature that if it ever expected to recoup any of its investment in the waterway, completion of the canal to Cumberland was paramount. To encourage further agricultural commerce, in 1848 the canal company reduced tolls on fertilizer transported up the canal.

The company experienced costly delays completing the Paw Paw Tunnel, located thirty miles west of Hancock. To save building five miles of canal along a meandering section of the Potomac that was a part of the Paw Paw Bends, the company elected to build a tunnel of 3,118 feet through a rocky ridge. Company officials anticipated that construction of the tunnel would take two years. Although the company successfully bored through the ridge in 1839, in the next decade work on the tunnel was suspended for four years. When work resumed, completion of the tunnel was more costly and more time-consuming than the company had anticipated, continuing intermittently over a period of twelve years. In the end, the Paw Paw Tunnel was considered one of the engineering marvels of the canal.

In its push to complete the last 50 miles of the waterway to Cumberland, the company permitted inferior construction on the western portion of the waterway, which included the use of wood-lined rubble-stone locks rather than the ashlar masonry technique that it utilized in previous lock construction. It delayed the construction of lock houses and determined that Lock Number 65 was unnecessary. After considering a number of possible locations for the proposed Dam Number 7, engineers determined that construction of the dam was not only not feasible, but not essential. The decision to not build the dam would have a detrimental affect on maintaining an adequate volume of water in the canal between Dam numbers 6 and 8. The canal was completed and officially opened for navigation—twenty-two years after construction began—with an October 10, 1850, ceremony at Cumberland. It had reached the Queen City eight years after the B&O Railroad had done so. The limitations of early railroad technology and a more direct route to port, however, would provide the canal company with some competitive advantages over its rival. Estimates for canal's total construction cost range from just over $11 million to almost $14 million, an overrun of from $6.5–9.5 million.[6]

The additional investment Maryland provided to see the canal to completion, combined with state sponsorship of other public works, caused a widespread backlash across the state. Heavy indebtedness and high taxation were blamed on these expenditures. As a result, in 1843 the General Assembly passed a law that authorized the state to sell its interest in five public works projects, including the Chesapeake and Ohio Canal. Although Maryland would not undertake a serious effort to dispose of its canal stock before the Civil War, at the Constitutional Convention of 1850 the state delegates adopted a new constitution that forbade future General Assemblies from involving the state in additional sponsorship of internal improvement projects. The new constitution also prohibited the legislature from using the proceeds from existing public works and associated taxes except to pay state debt and interest. These provisions were a clear sign to the canal company that it could expect no further aid from Maryland.[7]

When completed, the canal extended for 184.5 miles from the mouth of Rock Creek in Georgetown (within the boundary of the District of Columbia), which was located just below the fall line, to Wills Creek in Cumberland, Maryland. Rock Creek was dammed to create a canal basin along which wharves and warehouse facilities were constructed. Little Falls, located about four miles above Georgetown, marks the end of a series of falls, rapids, and swift water, below which the Potomac become a tidal estuary. About fourteen miles from Georgetown is the head of Great Falls, where the river passes over a steeper series of rapids and falls. At one point the elevation drops seventy-six feet in less than a mile. From east to west, the canal passed along the southern border of Montgomery, Frederick, Washington, and Allegany counties in Maryland. In Montgomery County the river passes through the piedmont, an upland region of rolling ridges and fertile valleys between the tidewater plain and the mountains. In Frederick County the river valley slices through the Catoctin Mountain ridge and then through South Mountain and smaller ridges that are part of the northern extension of the Blue Ridge Mountains. Most of Washington County is a part of a broad valley known in the north as the Cumberland Valley. To the south, the valley is drained by the Shenandoah River and is thus known as the Shenandoah Valley. In western Washington County and in Allegany County a series of great ridges and mountains emerge—Cove Ridge, Tonoloway Ridge, Sideling Hill, Town Hill, Martin Mountain, and Collier Mountain—through and around which the river flows from Cumberland. At the western terminus, a complex system of canal basins was created, drawing water from behind Dam Number 8 that was built across the Potomac just below the mouth of Wills Creek. Like at the eastern terminus, wharves and warehouses were built along the basins to facilitate canal trade. Boatyards and shops were also established in Cumberland and the surrounding region to supply and serve the needs of boatmen and merchants. Railroad tracks were constructed to the basins as well, providing a direct connection to the coal fields that lie to the west of Cumberland.

From Georgetown to Little Falls, the canal channel was excavated to its most extensive dimension, varying from 70–80 feet in width at the surface and from 7–8 feet in depth. Between Little Falls and Harpers Ferry the canal channel was approximately 6 feet deep, 60 feet wide at the surface, and 48 feet wide at the bottom. As the canal construction progressed beyond Harpers Ferry, however, the width of the canal generally diminished in size, becoming as narrow as 50 feet at the surface and at some places only 30 feet at the bottom.[8]

Cumberland.

The canal basin at Cumberland. *Our Whole Country; or, The Past and Present of the United States, Historical and Descriptive,* by John Warner Barber, (1861), 593.

    The company built 74 lift locks to overcome an elevation change of 605 feet from Georgetown to Cumberland. The waterway included 11 stone aqueducts that carried the channel over the largest tributaries of the Potomac. The longest aqueduct, which carried the canal over the Monocacy River, was 516 feet long and included 7 arches, and, along with the Paw Paw Tunnel, was considered one of the company's most significant engineering achievements. Approximately 230 culverts led small creeks, streams, and roads under the canal. The company built 6 dams in the Potomac to impound water for diversion into the canal, and it utilized a dam at Harpers Ferry that the government had built to power its rifle-works. It also provided for 2 stretches of slackwater navigation—both in Washington County—to bypass areas where rocky ridges came right to the river's edge. Instead, boats entered the river into the pool formed behind Dam numbers 4 and 5. Big Slackwater—the longest distance of navigation outside of the canal channel—was just over 3 miles. The company also constructed 3 river locks—at Edwards Ferry, Harpers Ferry, and Shepherdstown—that allowed boats to trade with towns in Virginia by navigating across the Potomac. In addition to these features, in 1843 the Alexandria Canal Company completed the 1,100-foot Potomac Aqueduct above Georgetown to link Virginia's Alexandria Canal to the Chesapeake and Ohio Canal, which provided boatmen with access to a deepwater port at Alexandria.

For a short period of time the Chesapeake and Ohio Canal also established a connection across Washington, D.C., to the western end of the Washington City Canal that terminated at the Eastern Branch of the Potomac (Anacostia River). Pierre Charles L'Enfant, who designed the nation's capital, had envisioned a canal running from tidewater at Tiber Creek below the capitol to the Eastern Branch, at one point diverging into two distinct channels: an eastern channel at James Creek and a western channel just above the mouth of the river adjacent to the Navy Yard. A number of early efforts failed to raise funds needed to begin construction. In 1809, however, Congress chartered a company that was able to raise enough money to begin the work the following year. Delayed by the British invasion of Washington in 1814, the two and one-quarter mile Washington City Canal was completed in 1815. In 1828 the Chesapeake and Ohio Canal Company agreed to extend its waterway to a basin that the city would construct at the mouth of Tiber Creek. In 1831 the municipal authorities of Washington bought the old canal and began to deepen and widen it. The C&O Canal Company began construction on the extension—known as the Washington Branch—the following year and completed it in 1833. Unfortunately for both canals, the tides from both the Potomac and Eastern Branch regularly deposited silt in the Washington City Canal and, as a result, it was not widely used. After the C&O reached Cumberland, Washington's official again undertook work to restore the City Canal. However, continual problems with silting and low bridges across the C&O Canal in Georgetown reduced traffic on the Washington Branch. Additionally, the completion of the Potomac Aqueduct in 1843 provided a more viable option for boatmen to reach tidewater.

By the time of the Civil War the Washington City Canal and the Washington Branch of the C&O Canal were not regularly utilized. In fact, the sewers of Washington, D.C., emptied into the City Canal and businesses used it as a dumping ground. Acidic waste from the burning of coal gas, for example, was deposited in the old waterway. On July 29, 1863, during the Gettysburg Campaign, military engineers brought a convoy of pontoon bridge material from Berlin to Washington, first over the C&O and then into the Washington City Canal. In the latter canal the convoy became stuck in shallow water, which required the engineers accompanying it to get into the water to free the boats. One man wrote that afterwards his feet swelled from exposure to contaminated water in the Washington City Canal.[9]

The primary competitor to the Chesapeake and Ohio Canal was the Baltimore and Ohio Railroad. Early railroads faced many technological difficulties that would only be overcome in the last quarter of the nineteenth century. To move heavy freight, railroads required bigger and heavier freight cars and consequently more powerful engines. Additionally, to handle heavier payloads, railroads needed to develop stronger iron rails, couplers and more reliable breaks. Because of these mid-Nineteenth Century technological limitations, by the time of the Civil War canals had a competitive advantage over railroads in transporting heavy cargo. In fact, it was thought that railroads were most appropriately utilized to transport passengers and light freight, while canals were the best means by which to move heavy cargo.

The B&O Railroad did have several advantages over the canal as a freight carrier, however. It had reached the Ohio River at Wheeling and developed a more significant two-way trade than did the waterway. Both carriers established connections to the coal fields in western Maryland, but the railroad also had more access to coal fields in western Virginia. The B&O also had rail connections to both Baltimore and Washington, although at the latter city its terminus was located inland on the east side rather than on the waterfront. Additionally, the B&O's line to Washington followed an

No. 573.—AQUEDUCT BRIDGE, GEORGETOWN, D. C.,
Looking toward Washington.

The canal at Georgetown. Note the Potomac Aqueduct, middle right. Source: Library of Congress, Prints and Photographs Division

indirect route, requiring a trip to Relay House outside of Baltimore before it began to travel south toward the capital over the Washington Branch. Other northern railroads brought coal—largely anthracite—to the eastern seaboard, but any that was transported to Baltimore or Washington did so over the rails of the B&O through junctions north of Baltimore. The railroad also established regular passenger service over the rails. Prior to the war packet boats provided passenger on the canal, but these lines were short-lived and largely unprofitable, with the exception of a service from Georgetown to Harpers Ferry.

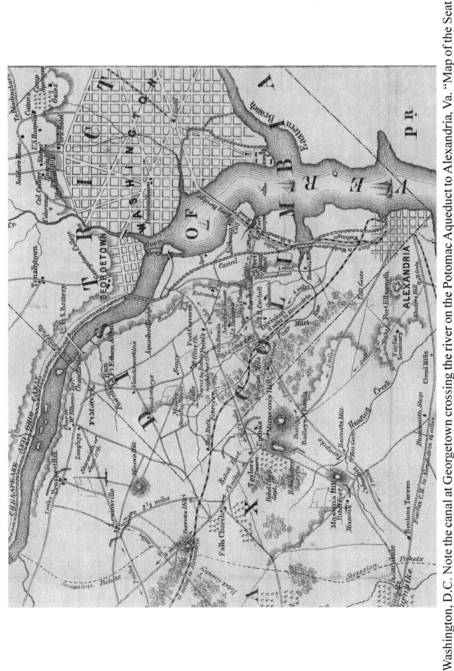

Washington, D.C. Note the canal at Georgetown crossing the river on the Potomac Aqueduct to Alexandria, Va. "Map of the Seat of War Showing the Battles of July 18th, 21st & Oct. 21st 1861,' by A. Hoen & Co. (1861). Source: Library of Congress, Geography and Map Division

Other transportation lines in Maryland were more often than not feeders to the canal rather than competitors. Canal transportation gave farmers and merchants access to markets in Georgetown, Washington, and Alexandria, Virginia, and other port cities via coastal vessels.

The eastern extension of the National Road, known as the Baltimore Pike, was utilized by shippers to send goods from the road to the canal, particularly at Cumberland, Hancock, and Hagerstown, cities where the road was closest to the waterway. Agricultural products from the lower Shenandoah Valley in Virginia—taking advantage of the macadamized Shenandoah Valley turnpike—were also sent across the Potomac by ferry for transshipment via canal.

In 1841 the Franklin Railroad, which ran between Chambersburg, Pennsylvania, and Hagerstown, Maryland, was completed. Four years earlier the Maryland General Assembly had authorized the extension of the Franklin from the Mason-Dixon Line to connect with the canal within one-half mile of Williamsport and with the B&O within seven miles of Hagerstown. Financial problems and the B&O's inability to build its line in the Potomac River Valley beyond Harpers Ferry prevented the Franklin from pursuing a junction with either carrier. Just prior to the Civil War the Franklin Railroad was carrying light freight from Pennsylvania to Hagerstown, such as lumber, livestock and manufactured goods. Although it is likely that shippers sent some of these goods to the canal at Williamsport—only about seven miles away—for transshipment to eastern markets, records are not extant to show the volume that was transferred from the Franklin to the waterway.[10]

With arrival of the canal at Cumberland in 1850, coal soon became the waterway's primary article of transport. Coal from western Maryland was a high-grade bituminous (soft coal) variety. In the marketplace it was called "Cumberland Coal," although it was mined west and southwest of Cumberland in the Georges Creek Valley between Dans and Big Savage mountains. Cumberland Coal found ready markets in eastern port cities, including Philadelphia, New York, and Boston. In 1860 coal officials noted that the Cunard steamship line would pay higher prices for Cumberland Coal over lesser quality bituminous coals. The officials also stated that the boilers of European steamers running out of New York were specifically adapted for the use of Cumberland Coal. In Philadelphia and New York the primary competition to Cumberland Coal was Broad Top Coal, a lesser quality bituminous variety from Broad Top, Pennsylvania. In Boston, the rival coals were Sydney and Pictou, bituminous coals from Nova Scotia, both of which were imported duty-free. Anthracite (hard coal) from Pennsylvania, the officials also noted, was gaining an increasing share of the market, especially for use in American-built steamships.[11]

By the outbreak of the Civil War there were at least seventeen mining companies operating in western Maryland. The largest coal producer was the Cumberland Coal and Iron Company. Other large producers were the Frostburg Coal Company, the Hampshire Coal and Iron Company, the American Coal Company, and the Borden Mining Company. The last named company along with the American Coal Company, C. E. Detmold (later renamed the Central Coal Company), and the Cumberland Coal and Iron Company, used the canal most frequently. Two rail lines delivered coal from the mines to the canal; one was owned by the Cumberland Coal and Iron Company, and the second was the Cumberland and Pennsylvania Railroad. The Baltimore and Ohio, which received coal via the Georges Creek Railroad, also transported the article to the canal at Cumberland from its Piedmont Station, located opposite the mouth of Georges Creek.[12]

The tonnage of coal shipped on the waterway increased steadily in the years before the Civil War. In 1850, the year the canal reached Cumberland, only 7,956 tons were shipped, but the next year the total transported jumped to 82,690 tons. By 1859, 300,743 tons were shipped, constituting eighty-six percent of all goods sent down the canal. In 1860 maintenance and weather-related problems reduced coal shipments to 283,249 tons, but this amount was still eighty-five percent of all goods shipped down the canal. Other leading products sent down the canal were limestone, flour, wheat, and corn. Articles sent up the canal were dwarfed by those sent east, but the most significant products were fertilizers, salt, plaster, and flour.[13]

During the decade before the Civil War several problems emerged that remained throughout the company's history. Weather caused the most serious trouble. In 1852 the worst flood in the recorded history of the Potomac River struck the canal. The company spent about $100,000 on repairs and lost three to four months of navigation. Summer droughts hindered navigation in 1853, 1854 and 1855. High water in the winter of 1857 brought blocks of ice raging down the river. Three additional floods that spring caused extensive damage, particularly to Dam numbers 4 and 5, the affects of which would linger into the next decade.

The company made several efforts to respond to the weather-related difficulties. To protect against low water caused by summer droughts, in 1856 the company installed a steam pump near the mouth of the South Branch of the Potomac, one of the proposed sites of the un-built Dam Number 7. The pump was designed to move 2,500 cubic feet of water per minute. The company also raised and strengthened the river side of the canal. To raise funds to repair flood damage, the company sold toll certificates to shippers. The certificates were purchased in advance at a discount, thereby allowing the canal company to raise money while providing shippers with a discount on future tolls.[14]

Intense competition with rival transportation lines also hurt the canal. Although in 1835 the canal company had reached an agreement with the B&O railroad to build a tracking path across the river alongside the railroad bridge at Harpers Ferry, in 1841 the B&O tore down the path even though the canal company had paid for its construction. Until the railroad company rebuilt the tracking path, the B&O set the rate to carry goods across its bridge at fifty cents a ton, well above what was allowed in its charter and in violation of the agreement between railroad and canal that permitted the construction of the bridge. After the tracking path had been rebuilt, the railroad charged shippers rates that made transportation on the canal unprofitable. Such heated competition and questionable practices by the railroad created an environment in which the canal company was compelled it to keep tolls low to prevent any further loss of business to the railroad, which suppressed the company's profitability.

The influence of politics in the operation of the canal also emerged in the pre-war period. Although Maryland had become the majority shareholder in 1836, only once since then had the state used political considerations to select company officials. Beginning in 1852, however, the practice was revived and utilized throughout the 1850s and into the early 1860s. In effect, positions on the canal company's Board of Directors were used to reward the friends and supporters of the political party that controlled the Commission of Public Works, a popularly elected body that was charged with overseeing the state's investment in public works. The directors, in turn, often rewarded party loyalists with jobs on the canal. Since its completion, critics of the canal found this practice a convenient scapegoat to assign blame for most of the canal's problems. In reality, politics had much less influence on the canal's financial problems than did construction cost overruns, legal battles with the B&O Railroad, competitive pressures, the cost of land, and certainly reoccurring droughts and floods, the last of which regularly wrecked a portion of the waterway.

In the immediate pre-war period, Dam numbers 4 and 5 (below and above Williamsport) were a continual drain on the canal company's financial resources. The 1857 floods swept away portions of both dams, including five hundred feet of Dam Number 5. With the dams in disrepair, the company had no means to impound the water that was needed to maintain the water level from the damaged dam down to the next inlet. To fill the breeches, the company installed heavy wooden cribs filled with stone that were sheeted with planks and anchored to the riverbed. The structures were only intended to serve temporarily until the company could build permanent masonry dams. Additional freshets in 1857 damaged the temporary dams. In his message to the General Assembly at the commencement of the 1858 legislative session, Maryland Governor T. Watkins Ligon provided an overview of the canal company's difficulties, adding: "The company now heavily encumbered with debt, appears to be without sufficient means, or credit, properly to prosecute the work, and its heavy losses and repeated disasters seem to have dampened the ardor and destroyed the hopes of the warmest friends of this great but most unfortunate enterprise." Ligon recommended that the General Assembly provide for the sale of the canal to a private company.[15]

The canal company let contracts to replace Dam Number 4 in 1856 and Dam Number 5 in 1857, but cost overruns and high water caused delays. In 1859 heavy floods caused a breach in Dam Number 4 and carried away much of the new masonry. Again, temporary repairs were made to permit the resumption of boating. In his June 4, 1860 report to the stockholders, company President James Fitzpatrick noted that the amount spent to install and maintain the temporary dams would have been more than enough to have completed masonry dams at both locations.[16]

Prior to the war the company's financial condition was dismal. From January 1859 through May 1860, expenses exceeded revenue by $66,086. Of the company's $301,903 total expenses during this period, sixty-three percent was for repair work. About one-half of that expended on repairs was for work on the two dams. In his June 4, 1860 report to the stockholders, Fitzpatrick noted glumly: "The current expenses on the line of the Canal for the past year have been unusually large, exceeding those of any former year for the ordinary maintenance of the Canal, and as far as I have ascertained from the present condition of the Canal, there does not appear to have been improvements made or advantages obtained to correspond with the excess of expenditures."[17]

In the pre-war years the company began to accumulate a large floating debt, defined by the company as debt payable from the first available funds after the payment of current expenses, necessary improvements, and repairs. Through June 1, 1860, the company owed $57,334 to merchants and contractors for services and supplies. In addition, company agents had issued $31,355 in toll certificates in lieu of cash. Other floating debt—including arrearage of the salaries of company officers and interest and principal on short-term loans obtained from the coal companies—amounted to over $9,000. These expenses were exclusive of unpaid interest on the company's old construction and repair bonds. In fact, interest due to the state of Maryland on the company's $2 million loan had ballooned to $7.9 million during the twenty-five years since the funds were authorized. Writing of the issuance of toll certificates against the future revenues of the company, Fitzpatrick noted: "This was the last act of hopeless bankruptcy, exhausting to-day, the sole means of existence to-morrow."[18]

At the beginning of the 1860 legislative session, Maryland Governor Thomas Holliday Hicks, like Ligon before him, recommended that the General Assembly permit the sale of the canal to a private enterprise. He pointed out that in other states internal improvements were constructed with public funds and then sold to private investors who operated them successfully.[19]

Virginia's legislature was also concerned with the fate of the canal. In the late 1840s the state had guaranteed bonds worth $500,000 for the completion and repair of the canal. In January 1860 the Virginia Senate debated a resolution that requested Maryland's General Assembly to enact legislation to relieve the company of its debt. The resolution also would have directed Virginia's attorney general to proceed to Annapolis to represent the Old Dominion's interests in the Maryland General Assembly. In early 1861, at the height of the secession crisis, Virginia Governor John Letcher reminded his state's legislature that the state had been paying the interest on the canal company's bonds and might soon become responsible for the full principal should the company default on its debt. He recommended legislation to protect Virginia's interests.[20]

During Maryland's 1860 legislative session, an effort was made to address the canal's hardship. The company's bondholders were nervous as a result of the canal's failing financial condition and their representatives met with legislators to urge passage of a bill that would save the waterway from bankruptcy. The bondholders, like other critics of the canal during this period, believed that mismanagement due to political interference was the primary cause of the canal's difficulties. A bill was introduced that would have transferred control of the canal to the bondholders, but it failed passage in the House of Delegates after getting the approval of the Senate.[21]

Despite the gloomy financial picture, Fitzpatrick and the board of directors were hopeful that the natural growth of trade and uninterrupted navigation would improve the company's financial condition. In light of the company's need for revenue to maintain the canal, in 1860 the president and board suspended temporarily the acceptance of toll certificates, to which the coal companies, the largest holders of the certificates, submitted. On June 9, 1860, the company contracted with a firm to complete the work of rebuilding Dam Number 4 as a permanent masonry structure. It had hoped to complete the work on Dam Number 5 as well, but lacked the means to do so. Instead, the company planned to finish the second dam in the summer of 1861.[22]

In 1860 a leak at or near Dam Number 6, combined with a summer drought, brought navigation to another standstill. The July 19 *Cumberland Civilian and Telegraph* expressed the frustration of its readers: "The Canal is the main artery through which the current of our monetary life is made to flow, and its good condition is essential to the prosperity of all the interests of Allegany county. Cannot something be done by which to secure to us the Canal, as a reliable channel for the conveyance of our products to market? Must it ever remain in its present unfortunate condition?"[23]

Over the summer of 1860 a rumor circulated that Maryland's Commission of Public Works would demand that the canal company's board of directors raise the toll on coal so as to prevent "injurious competition" with the B&O Railroad; if the directors refused, the Commission would replace them with others who would do so. The rumor caused great concern along the canal, especially in Allegany County. On August 10 concerned citizens of Allegany County—many associated with the coal trade—met in convention, drafted resolutions, and wrote a letter to both the Commission of Public Works and the canal company's board. The delegates explained that the existing rate of toll was set several years earlier to develop the coal trade and promote a market for it at tidewater. The Convention noted that the coal trade on the canal had been growing steadily until the 1857 freshets seriously damaged the waterway, which "threw it into a worse condition than it was in before, and from which it has never since recovered." Once the coal trade on the canal was thriving, the company hoped to fully restore the waterway, pay its debts, and make some return to the state on its investment.[24]

The convention was incredulous that the Commission saw the canal as a threat to the B&O Railroad. Referring to the waterway, the convention wrote: "A bankrupt company, whose work is greatly out of order . . . is not likely to be an injurious competitor, with a company like the Baltimore and Ohio Railroad Company, in the height of prosperity, making large profits and declaring regular dividends."[25]

The convention pointed out that coal sent by canal provided only a negligible financial advantage to the waterway. It submitted a table that showed that a ton of coal transported to market at Philadelphia or New York cost nineteen and one-half cents less per ton by canal, but the delegates explained that the railroad was liable for additional expense to which the waterway was not subject. On the canal, damage to coal by loss, theft, fire, accident, or other causes was the responsibility of the shipper since the waterway was only a highway or avenue to market. The railroad, on the other hand, was fully responsible for damage to coal in its custody. Additionally, coal sent on the railroad was handled less frequently and consequently suffered less breakage than that sent by canal. As a result, it could command higher prices.[26]

The convention warned that increasing tolls on coal would cause significant unemployment in western Maryland and would not accrue to the advantage of the B&O. It pointed out that the coal companies would be forced to seek an additional outlet to market, perhaps via Bedford, Pennsylvania, thereby taking much of the trade out of state. Hiking the toll would also serve to increase demand for bituminous coal from the mines at Broad Top, Pennsylvania. Instead, the convention recommended that the Commission force the B&O to lower its freight charges since it was making significant profit on the trade, reportedly $1.01 per ton.[27]

Lastly, the convention complained about the tactics used by the B&O to maintain its regional dominance as a coal carrier. It related that the railroad refused to transport coal from some mining companies unless it was sent to the B&O at Piedmont, Virginia, rather than to the canal at Cumberland, even though the latter route was the shortest avenue to market. Additionally, the B&O charged thirty-five cents more to move coal from Piedmont Station to the canal at Cumberland than it did to send the same coal over its rails to Baltimore.[28]

Late in 1860 the weather caused additional hardship for the canal. A November flood caused damage to the guard bank and towpath at Dam Number 4 and washed away the Virginia abutment of Dam Number 5. The Guard bank below Dam Number 8 at Cumberland was also damaged. Additionally, in December Lock Number 21 above Great Falls partially collapsed, the high water of the previous month having undermined it.[29]

On the eve of the Civil War the Chesapeake and Ohio Canal Company was in a dire condition. The company had a large floating debt due to its employees, contractors, merchants, and banks. In addition, it owed significant sums of interest and principal on its loans and bonds for the construction and repair of the canal. Several significant structures vital to the operation of the canal, particularly Dam numbers 4 and 5, needed major work. Lastly, after regular interruptions to navigation, shippers had gradually lost confidence in the canal as a reliable means of transportation.

HARPER'S FERRY, VIRGINIA.

Pre-war illustration of Harpers Ferry from the Maryland shore. Note the canal in the foreground. *Harper's Weekly,* May 4, 1861. Source: author's collection.

Beginning October 16, 1859, the canal witnessed the so-called "spark" that ignited the Civil War. On that day John Brown and his followers left the Kennedy farmhouse in Maryland and crossed the railroad bridge that passed over the canal and the Potomac to Harpers Ferry. Eventually, Brown, his men, and hostages took refuge in a brick firehouse, which was soon surrounded by gun-toting citizens and local military companies. At one point Brown requested that Colonel Edward Shriver, commander of a three-company battalion of the Maryland Militia, permit him safe passage to canal Lock Number 33 opposite Harpers Ferry, where he promised to release his hostages and then fight for his escape. The request was denied and the next day U.S. Marines under the command of Col. Robert E. Lee stormed the building and ended the raid.[30]

With the arrival of the Civil War, the continued operation of the canal was threatened. Its location on Maryland's southern border—literally between the Union and Confederacy—left it vulnerable to damage from opposing armies. Given the company's precarious financial and physical condition on the eve of the conflict, it seemed probable that open warfare would put the canal out of existence, if not from the physical destruction of its works, then surely from utter bankruptcy. The waterway emerged from the conflict intact and viable, however, and it experienced its most profitable period in the decade that followed the war.

How it did so is a remarkable story.

Pre-war photo of lower town Harpers Ferry and Maryland shore. Note the canal in the upper middle. Source: National Park Service.

CHAPTER 1

TIMES AIN'T AS THEY USED TO WAS:
JANUARY–JUNE 1861

Despite its tenuous financial condition, on the eve of the Civil War the Chesapeake and Ohio Canal Company was optimistic about the upcoming boating season. Over the winter of 1860-61 it had completed several repairs and improvements to the waterway. The most significant was the long-delayed work to Dam Number 4, where a contractor had finished replacing the temporary crib structure with a masonry dam. In February the *Williamsport Ledger* reported that the completion of the dam, "so long looked for, and so long deferred, will, we have no doubt, be received by all parties interested in the welfare of the Canal with feelings of unmingled joy." The company had also repaired a culvert below the dam and restored Lock Number 21 above Great Falls, the last of which had partially collapsed near the end of the preceding year. At Dam Number 5 the company had installed a temporary crib on the Virginia side to replace the abutment washed out by the November 1860 flood, and it had tightened the cribs of the existing dam.[1]

Others factors bode well for the upcoming season. The coal companies of western Maryland were pleased to learn that on February 6 the canal's board of directors had voted against raising tolls on coal and agreed to accept toll certificates as long as its financial resources permitted. Additionally, the Thirty-Sixth Congress had passed a new tariff on coal due to take effect on April 1, imposing a duty of one dollar per ton on bituminous coal mined abroad—the same type mined in western Maryland—and fifty cents per ton on other overseas coals. The March 14 *Cumberland Civilian and Telegraph* noted that the new tariff would effectively limit the market to domestic coals.[2]

The boating season opened on March 15. For the next three or four weeks all seemed well along the canal. By April 9 over 400 boats, loaded with more than 45,000 tons of coal, had left Cumberland for eastern ports. Then, as if a portent of the coming war, heavy rains began to fall in the Potomac River Valley. The river left its banks, subsided, and then rose again. By mid-April high water had caused breaks in the towpath near Seneca and Williamsport. It was estimated that navigation would be suspended for a month before the canal company could complete repairs.[3]

While the canal company suffered breaks in its line, the nation itself broke into two. After the election of Abraham Lincoln in November 1860 the states of the deep South began to secede from the Union, led by South Carolina on December 20, 1860, and followed by Mississippi, Florida, Alabama, Georgia, Louisiana, and Texas. The states of the upper South and Arkansas showed more willingness to compromise and remained in the Union throughout the winter and early spring. On April 12 the Confederate bombardment of Fort Sumter began and two days later the garrison surrendered. On April 15 Lincoln called for seventy-five thousand three-month volunteers to put down the rebellion, which caused the remaining southern states to secede. On April 17 Virginia passed an ordinance of secession and referred it to its citizens for referendum. The next day Virginia militia marched toward the Federal arsenal and rifle works at Harpers Ferry, Virginia, where a handful of United States soldiers set fire to the cache of weapons and workshops, then fled for the military base at Carlisle, Pennsylvania. The flood-damaged canal sat just north of Harpers Ferry on the Maryland side of the Potomac.

On April 18 the war came to Maryland as the first volunteers passed through Baltimore on their way to Washington. Violence erupted the following day when secessionist sympathizers assaulted the Sixth Massachusetts Volunteers while they attempted to pass through the city. Four soldiers and at least twelve citizens were killed and scores more were wounded. In the days that followed, the railroad bridges north of Baltimore were burned to prevent more troops from coming to Baltimore. At the request of Maryland's governor Thomas Holliday Hicks and Baltimore's mayor George W. Brown, Lincoln agreed to send no more troops through Baltimore; instead, a water route around the city was established. Troops embarked on ships at Perryville, Maryland—near where the Susquehanna River flows into Chesapeake Bay—and steamed down the bay to Annapolis, where on April 22 U.S. volunteers under the command of Brig. Gen. Benjamin F. Butler established a foothold in Maryland. Butler was placed in command of the military Department of Annapolis and opened an unbroken transportation route to Washington. On May 5 his troops occupied Relay House, the railroad junction of the Baltimore and Ohio, where the Washington Branch departed for the capital and the Main Stem led, ironically, directly through Harpers Ferry. He occupied Federal Hill in Baltimore on May 13.

During the "Secession Winter" Governor Hicks had resisted great pressure from southern sympathizers to convene the General Assembly, which was not due to meet again until 1862. After the events of mid-April, however, Hicks relented and called the legislature into extra session. He directed the body to assemble at Frederick—located in Unionist western Maryland, fifty-seven miles from Annapolis—in order to provide the legislators with an opportunity to deliberate apart from Butler's troops. Both houses of the General Assembly declared, however, that they had no authority to decide if Maryland should secede, but their published views showed a pronounced sympathy with the South. When the first extra session ended on May 14, the legislature declared the war and presence of Federal troops in Maryland unconstitutional, and it called for the recognition of the Confederacy as an independent nation.[4]

It was against this backdrop of violence and political uncertainty that the canal company sought to make repairs to its flood-damaged works and resume navigation. By a cruel confluence of circumstances, the entire 184.5-mile-long canal was located between the Southern forces that gathered in Virginia and the Northern volunteers streaming through Maryland to Washington. The canal was positioned quite literally between the armies and it was not long before it was drawn into conflicts along the border.

§

Grain merchant Charles F. Wenner lived in Berlin in Frederick County, Maryland, located along the Potomac. He owned a warehouse and two canal boats that he used to transport grain to Georgetown. At noon on April 24, as one of his laden boats prepared to depart, a group of horsemen from Virginia rode up and demanded that he turn over the boat and its cargo to them, by the authority of the commanding officer at Harpers Ferry. Wenner protested and demanded to inspect the men's orders. While a soldier was dispatched to the Ferry to obtain the orders, the remaining men, under the command of Col. William S. H. Baylor, took charge of the boat and moved it six miles down the canal to Point of Rocks. Over Wenner's protests, the Confederates began to unload the grain, sending a portion over the bridge to Virginia and loading the remainder into Baltimore and Ohio Railroad cars for transportation to Harpers Ferry. The soldier who had been sent to obtain a copy of the orders from Harpers Ferry returned with additional men, but no orders.[5]

Wenner wrote two letters to Sheriff Michael H. Haller of Frederick County, demanding protection of his property, and he visited the sheriff in person on April 25. On April 27 Haller provided Governor Hicks with copies of Wenner's notes and described the merchant's confrontation with the soldiers: "Mr. Wenner . . . stated that he gave some resistance, until the officers ordered the soldiers to fire after a minute's notice; and that they refused to give him one of his mules to go home with; and while loading the grain on the cars, he insisted on the grain being weighed by the Agent of the Baltimore and Ohio Railroad Company, that he might seek redress, which was denied him by the officer, who stated that he might go to Harper's Ferry to see it weighed. He also stated they took from him grain to feed near one hundred horses without weighing or measuring."[6]

Hicks had also become aware of another border transgression committed by the troops from Virginia. On April 20, only two days after the Confederates had occupied Harpers Ferry, troops had crossed the river to Sandy Hook and searched the homes of citizens for arms from the arsenal. Hicks referred both incidents to the General Assembly, which was still in session in Frederick. On May 2 the Committee on Federal Relations, chaired by Severn Teackle Wallis, reported that it was unlikely that Virginia's troops would violate the homes of Marylanders again. The committee had learned that the garrison at Harpers Ferry had recently come under the command of an officer from the regular army, Col. Thomas J. Jackson (who would soon be known as "Stonewall"), whom they expected to enforce strict military discipline. The committee found the seizure of the canal boat more troubling. It suggested that additional confrontations were likely to occur unless the two states came to some arrangement to avoid future incidents. The General Assembly appointed a commissioner, Outerbridge Horsey of Frederick County, to investigate the disturbance. Horsey was a distiller whose father had been U.S. Senator from Delaware and whose mother was the daughter of former Maryland Governor Thomas Sim Lee. The legislature authorized Horsey to enter into negotiations with Virginia's authorities to ensure that Marylanders and their property were protected from the actions of Virginia's military forces, to obtain compensation for damages already incurred, and to preserve friendly relations between the two states.[7]

At his meeting with Horsey, Virginia Governor John Letcher expressed concern about the border strife and appointed a representative to investigate the incidents along with Maryland's delegate. Although on May 1 Hicks had rebuffed an overture of cooperation from Letcher, Virginia's governor continued to view Maryland as a potential ally and declined to entertain suggestions that Virginia troops invade its northern neighbor for any reason. Hicks also wrote to Letcher, protesting against the actions of Virginia's troops. Letcher replied that he had directed Col. Jackson to restrain those under his command from "all acts of violence and lawlessness" and to provide him with a report of the incidents Hicks had described. In a May 6 report, Jackson claimed that if any outrages were committed by the troops stationed at Harpers Ferry, the acts were perpetrated before he had taken command. He added: "Since I have been in command, I have strictly observed your Excellency's instructions touching the relations to be maintained towards the State of Maryland, and feel assured that no just complaint can be made." Jackson did discover one instance in which troops had been allowed to cross over to Maryland to recover arms if the citizens who held the weapons would turn them over voluntarily. Jackson also told Letcher that he had found record of a command issued by the previous post commander who had ordered the detention of canal boats under the presumption that they were transporting provisions to Washington, but that he had countermanded that order and since then no boats had been detained. On May 8 Hicks also informed President Lincoln of the border violations, although the president, whose first concern was for the defense of

Washington, took no immediate steps to defend Maryland from incursions by Confederate troops from Harpers Ferry.[8]

By mid-May, the House of Delegates placed two other issues on Horsey's agenda. Residents of Sharpsburg, Maryland, had complained that the Confederates had occupied Maryland Heights, the mountain eminence opposite Harpers Ferry, and had burned the timber. Additionally, citizens from Montgomery County petitioned Hicks for protection of their grain sent over the canal. After another investigation by the two state representatives, Confederate officials assured Horsey that the timber on Maryland Heights had caught fire accidentally. Governor Letcher told him that the occupation of the mountain was temporary and that Virginia would compensate any party who suffered damages. With regard to the other issue, Horsey learned that a mill owner on Seneca Creek used the canal to supply the government with flour. The petitioners were the mill owner's neighbors who feared that Confederate troops would damage the mill because of his ties with the government. Maryland's commissioner concluded that the Confederates had not actually molested the mill or canal at Seneca. Regarding his investigation of the threats against the canal, Horsey wrote:

> Your commissioner may be permitted to remark that the people
> of the western counties of the State adjacent to the canal are much
> interested in preserving from molestation the trade along its lines of
> navigation, and he has been particularly solicitous in removing all
> obstacles which threatened it. While the bed of the canal is on the
> soil of Maryland, the damns [sic] which furnish it with water are
> dependent on the protection of the Virginia authorities, and while
> they have manifested no disposition to withdraw their guardianship,
> and leave them liable to the depredations of malignant persons,
> your commissioner had deemed it his duty to guard against as far as
> possible such a contingency, and he indulges in a well founded
> confidence that the material interests of this great State work will
> not be seriously jeopardized.[9]

In the meantime, a five-member advisory council recommended unanimously to Governor Letcher that Virginia pay for Wenner's grain, although it determined that nothing additional should be paid for the detention of the boat or for transportation costs and tolls. On June 4 Charles F. Wenner received $1,693.75 in compensation from Virginia.[10]

For a period of about six weeks the hostilities along the upper Potomac were defused by diplomacy between Maryland and Virginia. Soon, however, conditions along the border began to deteriorate beyond the control of the two states, and soon the Confederates would stop canal navigation altogether.

§

Before long the outbreak of hostilities between the sections reached into the internal management of the canal. On May 2 the stockholders of the Chesapeake and Ohio Canal Company—controlled by the state of Maryland—removed President James Fitzpatrick from his post without comment. Local newspapers reported that he had resigned. On January 10, 1861 Fitzpatrick had served as a delegate from Allegany County to a "Conference of the Counties" held in Baltimore, which was formed to pressure governor Hicks to convene the General Assembly, that, in turn, would establish a sovereign convention to consider Maryland's secession from the Union. Months later, on October 11, 1861, a coal company official informed canal company director Lawrence J. Brengle that Fitzpatrick was one of the most prominent "opponents of the Government" in Allegany County. Director Alfred Spates was selected to fill the position for one month, until the next meeting of the stockholders. Spates would remain president of the company throughout the war.[11]

The forty-nine year-old Spates, a native of Montgomery County, Maryland, had clerked in shops in Georgetown and Baltimore. He later married and returned to Montgomery County as proprietor of the Washington Hotel. In 1848 he moved to Cumberland to work for Horace Resley, clerk of the court in Allegany County, who had also been a contractor engaged in constructing the canal. In 1853 Spates was appointed deputy clerk of the circuit court in Allegany County and was later employed by attorney J. Phillip Roman. Spates was first appointed to the canal company's board of directors in July 1859. Upon his elevation to the presidency, the *Cumberland Civilian and Telegraph* wrote: "We consider the appointment of Mr. Spates a most excellent one, as he will bring to the office an energy and business tact which has seldom been found." Canal associates often addressed Spates as "colonel," a reference to his rank as lieutenant colonel in the Fiftieth Regiment, Maryland Militia, a post he assumed March 4, 1861. He quickly developed a reputation for the enormous energy he exerted on behalf of the company.[12]

In early May the entire canal was back in working order following the flooding of the previous month. On May 6 Alfred Spates was optimistic that coal shipments from Cumberland would be resumed, but only "if we have no trouble in Virginia." By mid-month, word of the border strife near Harpers Ferry and uncertainty at the port of Alexandria, Virginia, reached Cumberland. On May 13 Spates wrote: "The coal companys [sic] are not willing to boat on account of the troubles along the line by the Virginia people and at Alexandria. I cannot tell what we are to do. The canal is now in order, yet we will have no boating as things now stand."[13]

Unbeknownst to Spates and the canal company, from the beginning of the war the Confederates identified the waterway as a potential Union supply line. As such, it was subject to Confederate strategic plans, including acts of sabotage. The company had to endure these assaults until either the Confederates evacuated their positions along the Potomac or until the Union army arrived to provide protection. It would be weeks before either condition would be in effect.

Robert E. Lee, commander of Virginia's state forces and a resident of northern Virginia, was no stranger to the canal. On May 6 he informed Jackson that the Union government might move against Harpers Ferry via either the Baltimore and Ohio Railroad or the Chesapeake and Ohio Canal. He ordered his subordinate to watch both carriers and authorized him to destroy the railroad bridge at Harpers Ferry and obstruct navigation on the waterway if hostile troops were approaching. The general also suggested that Jackson make arrangements with sympathetic Marylanders to destroy the railroad bridge over the Monocacy River and let the water out of the canal if the Federal army attempted to use either carrier.[14]

Confederate General Robert E. Lee. Source: Library of Congress, Prints and Photographs Division

Jackson undertook an aggressive defense of Harpers Ferry that included the occupation of Maryland soil at Maryland Heights and Point of Rocks. Lee urged the colonel to avoid provocative acts and admonished him for posting troops in Maryland, but he was still concerned that the Union army might make military use of the canal. In a May 10 letter to Jackson he wrote: "I have already suggested to you the probability of the use of the canal as a means of carrying ordnance and munitions from

Confederate General Thomas J. "Stonewall" Jackson. Source: Library of Congress, Prints and Photographs Division

Washington to use against you. In that event it would be well to cut the supply dams to prevent its use."[15]

Jackson interfered repeatedly with boating despite instructions from Lee and Letcher to avoid confrontation unless Union forces actually attempted to make use of the canal. He posted sentinels on the canal towpath in Maryland and required boatmen to obtain permits to take their boats past Harpers Ferry. One permit was published in the May 23, 1861 *Baltimore American and Commercial Advertiser*: "Alexander Dent has permission to remove his family from Sandy Hook to Montgomery county, Maryland, on canal boat E. Reid, without molestation, the said boat to return empty. By order of Colonel Jackson. J. W. Massie, Aid." Confederate military activity in the vicinity and their restrictions on boating caused fear and uncertainty among the boatmen, which brought navigation to a near-standstill. Canal Company records show that in May its agents collected only $657 in tolls at all points on the waterway, and in June only $206; in comparison, the company collected over $16,000 in only two weeks of boating in March.[16]

On May 27 Alfred Spates visited Harpers Ferry to meet Brig. Gen. Joseph E. Johnston, the Confederate commander who on May 24 had replaced Jackson. Spates hoped to persuade Johnston to allow canal boats to pass the town. While there he learned that Turner Ashby's cavalrymen had blasted rock onto the tracks of the B&O and into the nearby canal at Point of Rocks. On the same day Spates explained to the company's general superintendent: "I visited Harper's Ferry to-day for the purpose of knowing if Coal or other Boats could pass. I find it will be impossible for any Boats to pass the Ferry, or the Point of Rocks. The rock that has been thrown down at the Point, would not stop the Canal, but other rocks will also be thrown down, and Boats cannot pass."[17]

To confront the Confederates at Harpers Ferry, by late-May Union troops were gathering in Chambersburg, Pennsylvania, under command of the sixty-nine-year-old Maj. Gen. Robert Patterson. On April 27 General-in-Chief Winfield Scott had appointed him to head the Department of Pennsylvania. Patterson had served in the Mexican War and was engaged in milling and railroading before Pennsylvania Governor Andrew Gregg Curtin tapped him to lead the state's volunteers. Patterson was responsible for

BOLMAN'S ROCK.

Bollmans Rock at Point of Rocks. *The Pictorial Field Book of the Civil War in the United States of America*, vol 1, by Benson J. Lossing (1874), 521.

Confederate General Joseph E. Johnston. Source: Library of Congress, Prints and Photographs Division

Union General-in-Chief Winfield Scott. Library of Congress, Prints and
Photographs Division

forwarding the first Federal troops to Washington in response to Lincoln's
call for seventy-five thousand troops. On May 24, after the capital had
been sufficiently garrisoned and Baltimore secured, Scott directed Patterson
to send troops toward Cumberland, Hagerstown, and Frederick to threaten
Harpers Ferry and support the Union sentiment in western Virginia. The
reopening of trade and communication on the railroad and canal, which the
Confederates at Harpers Ferry would soon cut off entirely, would become
an important objective of Patterson's advance against the Ferry.[18]

Union Maj. General Robert Patterson. Library of Congress, Prints and
Photographs Division

The Confederates, on the other hand, were determined to deny
Patterson the means to cross the Potomac. Beginning in late May skirmishes
broke out between the Confederates and Union home guard companies
from Sharpsburg, Williamsport, and Clear Spring in Washington County,
Maryland. On June 1 the Confederates attempted to capture a ferry boat
opposite Williamsport, which resulted in a brisk exchange of fire. The
conflict—coupled with inactivity on the canal—drew the ire of the

Hagerstown Herald of Freedom and Torch Light, which on June 5 wrote that the fight "created intense excitement all along the Maryland side of the river, and aroused the people to a firm determination to defend themselves from the aggressions and outrages of the Rebels, who have seized the Canal and deprived these people of all means of livelihood."[19]

On June 7 the lead brigade of Patterson's force, commanded by Col. George Henry Thomas, advanced thirteen miles south to Greencastle, Pennsylvania. With a confrontation imminent, Johnston took steps to impede the Federal advance and organized raids against the railroad and canal. On June 9 the Confederates destroyed turnpike bridges over the river at Point of Rocks and Berlin. On June 11 a correspondent of the *Philadelphia Public Ledger* described additional acts of sabotage between Harpers Ferry and Sharpsburg: "They have been busy for the past few nights cutting out the dams, sinking the ferry scows . . . breaking up the small boats, setting lumber afloat and doing everything else they can think of likely to annoy the advancing force and delay their crossing the river." In early June the Confederates cut sluices in the canal near Harpers Ferry, which drained the water and grounded a number of boats. Additionally, they burned about twenty-five canal boats and destroyed two locks in the vicinity.[20]

Beginning on June 8 the Confederates attempted to destroy Dam numbers 4 and 5 near Williamsport, which were defended by local home guard companies. A correspondent of the Philadelphia *Public Ledger* described the events at Dam Number 5:

At dam No. 5, eight miles above Williamsport, a company of rebels, about seventy in number, attempted to blow up the dam, in order to prevent the Government from making use of it for the transporting of troops and to ruin the canal, thus preventing the forwarding of provisions. They made their appearance on the dam about eight o'clock on Saturday [June 8] morning, and succeeded in discharging one blast, when they were fired upon by the Union men from the Maryland side. . . . Word was then sent to Clear Springs [sic] and Williamsport, when a detachment of the Home Guards from each place was detailed to protect the dam. A two-story brick [house], used by the lock tenders, and the only dwelling on this side of the river, was immediately taken possession of, port holes were made, and everything arranged to defend themselves; while the rebels posted themselves in a stone mill below the dam, and also in a brick house above the dam. . . . Others [on the Maryland side] secreted themselves behind a ledge of rocks, elevated about 100 feet above the lock tender's post. Firing continued all day from both sides, resulting in the loss of one rebel, who was seen to fall from the rocks towards the river. It was renewed on Sunday without any damage, but yesterday matters took a change. Becoming emboldened by the random firing of the day before, the rebels ventured from the hiding places when two of them were shot, one of them being seen to fall from his horse by your correspondent. The firing was again renewed this morning.[21]

In the early evening of June 10 news arrived that the Confederates were attempting to put another powder charge into Dam Number 5, but the Clear Spring Home Guard drove them away. On the same day, southern troops attempted to strike Dam Number 4, but were unable to damage the new masonry dam. The Confederates had crossed the river at the latter dam, however, and then destroyed the guard lock and threw large rocks into the channel to obstruct navigation. They also attempted to destroy canal boats and seize flour from mills before the Sharpsburg Home Guard drove them back across the river.[22]

The damage to the canal caused great consternation to those who earned their livelihood from the waterway or used it to obtain goods. A correspondent to the June 12 *Frederick Examiner* lamented: "We presume there is no remedy for these 'vandal' acts—Virginia can't pay, and the other Secession States won't while their tory sympathisers [sic] here justify every act of Treason regardless of the life and property of the citizens. . . . The citizens along the line of the Canal are much excited and greatly outraged."[23]

During the first eight weeks of the war life in Williamsport—an important port city located at the approximate mid-point of the canal—was tense and uncertain. In late May Jackson sent a full regiment of troops opposite Williamsport, from which a guard was posted to watch the ferry landing directly across from the town. In addition to the Confederate raids on the ferry and the nearby dams, southern pickets were observed daily and threats and skirmishes with the local home guard were common. The

June 5 murder of a local secessionist in Williamsport, coupled with the Federal advance to Greencastle two days later, only increased the tensions between the two sides. On June 8 the Unionists at Williamsport observed that the number of southern pickets had been increased and that the sentinels were more active than usual. The Confederates also shouted across the river that they intended to exact revenge for the murder. On June 11 a correspondent of the *Baltimore American* wrote: "The Unionists are alarmed at Williamsport, and are fearful of an attack to-night. The Confederate pickets have boasted over the Potomac that they intend to cross the river to-night and burn the [canal] boats and the town. Great alarm prevails." Men from nearby Hagerstown went to reinforce the town and the home guard increased the number of pickets on duty. In the evening of the same day the correspondent reported: "All quiet in Williamsport, if living in a shiver of fear can be called quiet. Every night we expect to get shelled, and every night 'nobody's hurt.'"[24]

On June 13, as Johnston began to make preparations to evacuate Harpers Ferry, the Confederates made a final attempt to disable Dam Number 4. Newspapers reported that men with dark lanterns were spied on the Virginia side, attempting to drill blasting holes in the solid rock that formed the southern abutment of the dam. The Sharpsburg Home Guard, reinforced by a company of forty-five riflemen from nearby Boonsboro, Maryland, engaged the southern soldiers in a sharp exchange. A newspaper reported that four Virginians were wounded while they bored at the rock.[25]

Alfred Spates was greatly distressed at the damage done to the canal during the first month of his presidency. While the sides were exchanging shots at Dam Number 4, he crossed the river under a flag of truce and demanded to be taken to Harpers Ferry to meet with Johnston. The Confederates furnished Spates with a twelve-man escort that delivered him to the general. He pleaded with Johnston to stop the destruction of canal company property, pointing out that the canal was owned by Maryland and as such should be exempt from seizure and destruction. Johnston replied that canal property belonged to all northern states engaged in the war and that he had been ordered to destroy everything of value to the Union. On June 13 Spates informed the company office in Georgetown that four locks had been destroyed, a number of boats burned and "much other damage done . . . . A grate [sic] destruction to the Canal and Canal interests has been made by the Virginians."[26]

Western Marylanders were particularly offended by the assaults against the canal. Unlike the B&O Railroad, which passed through Virginia territory, the canal was located entirely on Maryland soil. In addition, while the railroad carried an extensive passenger business and could easily be utilized to move troops, the canal was almost exclusively a freight line. In mid-June a Williamsport correspondent of the *Baltimore American* wrote that the damage inflicted to the canal "has done more for the Union sentiment in this quarter than any other act that has transpired thus far. Many who were hitherto ready to justify any act of the Southern Confederacy are now bold and earnest in the condemnation of that act of vandalism." After the Confederate assaults against the nearby dams, on June 12 the *Hagerstown Herald of Freedom and Torch Light* wrote: "It is clearly the duty of every loyal citizen in the county to rally to the defence [sic] and protection of the property of the Canal Company. —The Canal cost the State of Maryland many millions of dollars, its trade and commerce are the life arteries of our people, and they must defend it at all hazards and every cost until the Government can relieve them"[27]

The Maryland General Assembly was still in extra session in Frederick while the attacks on the canal ensued, and many members thought that the actions of Virginia's troops violated Maryland's sovereignty. The legislators recalled the promise that Governor Letcher had made to Outerbridge Horsey as a result of the Confederate occupation of Maryland Heights. On June 19 the General Assembly passed the following resolution:

Whereas the Legislature has been informed that the southern troops are now destroying the Dams, Locks, Canal Boats, and other property belonging to the Chesapeake and Ohio Canal Company, and to individuals doing business on the Canal; and,

Whereas our commissioner to the Governor of Virginia, in his report to the Legislature, informs us that the Governor of Virginia was understood to say, "that if, at any time, the military forces of Virginia should trespass, or temporarily occupy the soil of Maryland, it could only be justified by the pressing exigency of a military necessity, in defense and protection of her own soil from threatened or actual invasion, and certainly with no hostile intent towards the citizens of the State of Maryland, and that any and all damages to persons or property, consequent upon such occupation should be fully and liberally compensated;" therefore,

Resolved by the General Assembly of Maryland, That Maryland will rely upon the honor of Virginia for full recompense for all property destroyed by said troops.

The General Assembly requested that Governor Hicks forward a copy of the resolution to Letcher.[28]

At about 5:00 A.M. on June 14 the Confederates at Harpers Ferry destroyed the railroad bridge over the Potomac and other public property in town. The next morning the army left Harpers Ferry for Winchester. Patterson's troops approached the Potomac just as the Confederates were completing the destruction of property in and near Harpers Ferry—too late to prevent any of the damage.[29]

§

Two other Union commands were given responsibility to protect portions of the canal to the east and west of Patterson. On June 6 the general ordered Col. Lewis Wallace and the Eleventh Indiana Zouaves to establish a camp at Cumberland, the western terminus of the waterway, which was located in his Department of Pennsylvania. In May the Confederates had destroyed a number of railroad bridges below Cumberland. Patterson directed Wallace to watch the remaining bridges east of Cumberland and to arrest anyone plotting sabotage against the railroad or canal.[30]

On June 8 General-in-Chief Scott ordered Col. Charles P. Stone to lead an excursion up the Potomac west of Washington—known as the Rockville Expedition—that would serve as either a diversion from or cooperation with Patterson's advance against Harpers Ferry. This little-known advance, which began two days later, placed the first Federal pickets at the fords and ferries above Washington and allowed for the resumption of navigation on a portion of the waterway. One of Stone's three columns advanced up the canal towpath to Great Falls and Seneca Creek, using two canal boats for supplies and provisions. Stone posted units at Great Falls, Seneca Creek, Edwards Ferry, Conrads Ferry and other points along the river in Montgomery County.[31]

Confederate Colonel Eppa Hunton, commanding at Leesburg, had learned from informants that the Federal army was loading canal boats at Georgetown with supplies and munitions. In response, General Lee ordered Hunton to destroy the canal company's dams in the Potomac or the Monocacy Aqueduct. Destroying either would have involved much labor-intensive and time-consuming work, however. Instead on June 12 Hunton sent a party across the river at Edwards Ferry. The Confederates intended to break the canal, but the lockkeeper let the water out instead, which satisfied the raiders. The next day Stone informed Scott's adjutant: "Sufficient water can at any time be let in to float out canal-boats in case of our desiring it." He also reported that his men had gained control of the canal to within six miles of Edwards Ferry.[32]

Stone's guardianship of the Chesapeake and Ohio Canal also helped him gain the support of local inhabitants. Following the raid, Brig. Gen. Joseph K. F. Mansfield, commander of the Department of Washington and nominally Stone's commanding officer, directed the colonel to protect the canal and restore boating. Although in doing so the colonel was insuring the operation of what would become an important coal carrier and military supply line, it also aided the citizens who lived near the waterway by reopening an avenue to markets for their goods. Stone wrote from Poolesville on June 17, "the canal is absolutely necessary to the well-being of this neighbor-hood—one of the best small-grain districts in the state. It is now suffering for want of means of transportation, and the appearance of troops here has had an excellent effect." Stone reported that water could be let into the canal a few miles above Edwards Ferry, which, he noted, would aid the local community in forwarding goods to market and the army in sending supplies to his command. He sent an officer out to inspect the canal above his position. The Confederates began fortifying positions south of the river, however, which prevented Stone from using the canal to Edwards Ferry. Instead the colonel received supplies and munitions over the waterway to Seneca Creek, then by wagon over local roads to his headquarters.[33]

Harpers Ferry after Confederate evacuation. Note dry canal in foreground. Source: Library of Congress, Prints and Photographs Division

Stone eventually extended his pickets to Nolands Ferry in Frederick County, covering about thirty miles of riverfront. On June 19 he sent a scout up the river to Harpers Ferry and learned with certainty that the Confederates had abandoned the town. With a large Confederate garrison no longer in the vicinity of the waterway, Stone took steps to put the canal in order. On June 20 he wrote the War Department that the canal company would begin work immediately, which was expected to take ten days to complete. Confederate scouts and pickets still patrolled the southern bank of the river, however, and the canal company took no immediate steps to repair the canal.[34]

Stone urged the army to send a force to occupy Point of Rocks because communication across the river was ongoing and he feared that the Confederates would cross and destroy the canal and railroad. On June 29 he informed Mansfield that between Point of Rocks and Harpers Ferry "the railroad and canal are not safe for a single night, and yet, I cannot with anything like prudence detach a force for guarding the line unless strengthened for the purpose." He proposed that if he was reinforced with two more regiments, he could occupy the entire line of the river from Georgetown to Harpers Ferry.[35]

On June 30, instead of being reinforced, Scott ordered Stone to join Patterson in Virginia. The colonel was, however, concerned about leaving the Edwards Ferry region without troops. The next day he wrote Scott's adjutant: "It will be with serious misgivings that I leave this horseshoe of the river unguarded, for I shall expect to learn that the enemy have crossed immediately on my leaving, and doubtless the canal will be destroyed, as well as large amounts of grain." Stone fears were unfounded as the Confederates were more concerned about Union advances in Virginia to the east and west than to contemplate raids at Edwards Ferry. Over the next week Stone and his command advanced up the river for a rendezvous with Patterson.[36]

§

Maj. Gen. George Cadwalader, who commanded the First Division in Patterson's force, moved out of Greencastle on June 15 and arrived at

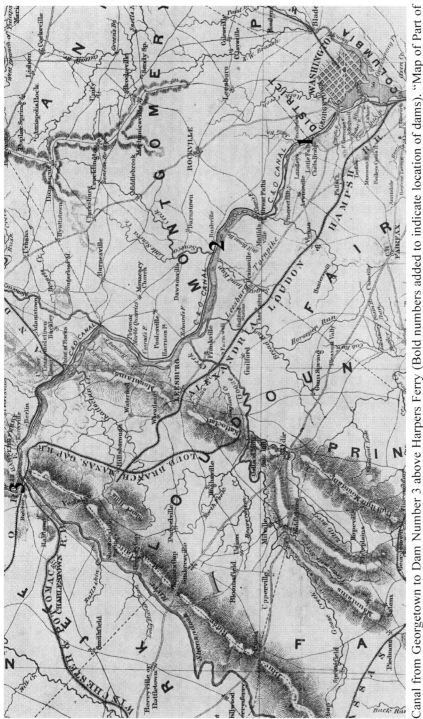

Canal from Georgetown to Dam Number 3 above Harpers Ferry (Bold numbers added to indicate location of dams). "Map of Part of Virginia, Maryland and Delaware," by E. & G. W. Blunt (1861). Source: Library of Congress, Geography and Map Division

Williamsport on the same day. The next day Cadwalader's men, singing camp songs and under the cover of two pieces of artillery posted on the bluffs, forded the four feet-high Potomac at Williamsport. By the time Patterson arrived in Hagerstown he received positive information that the Confederates had abandoned Harpers Ferry. In light of this, he planned to advance toward Winchester and predicted that the railroad and canal would be back in operation in a week. With the advance of the Federal army, the spirits of local Unionists along the river were lifted. On June 14 a resident of Berlin wrote naively: "I can say that our District will welcome the Federal troops with a great deal of hospitality when they arrive, and indeed many are impatient to see them on our railroad and canal, as the two great works are to be resumed very soon, and business will flourish as formerly."[37]

The repair of the railroad and canal would have to wait, however. On June 16 General-in-Chief Scott ordered Patterson to send all cavalry, artillery, and all infantry from the regular army to Washington. Afterwards, when Confederate horsemen where observed returning to Martinsburg and Harpers Ferry, Patterson withdrew his troops back to Maryland. He complained loudly and persistently about the troops he had lost and requested replacements. Nevertheless, on June 25 Scott ordered Patterson to cross the river and engage the Confederates, hoping to prevent Johnston's army from crossing the Blue Ridge Mountains and reinforcing the Confederates at Manassas Junction.[38]

On July 2, under the cover of Doubleday's artillery posted on the bluffs above the river, the First Division again prepared to cross the Potomac.

§

During the first three months of the war, canal navigation had come to a virtual halt. In May the company collected only about four-percent of the tolls it had taken in March in only two weeks of boating; in June the company collected just over one-percent of March's total. In its June 4, 1861, *Thirty-third Annual Report*, the president and directors noted with irony: "The general condition of the Canal for navigation at this time is believed to be better than it has been for some years past, and a fair business for the season could be done, but for the political agitations of the country, by which business has been prostrated, transportation rendered uncertain and precarious, and subject to frequent delays, if not seizures by the contending parties on the banks of the Potomac, and unless there be an early removal of the seat of war, it is feared that a general suspension of the transportation on the Canal, for the season, will occur."[39]

The interruption of boating caused wholesale coal dealers to seek the product elsewhere. The *U.S. Railroad Mining Register* reported that "the obstructions put in the way of deliveries from the Cumberland region by the secessionists . . . have diminished the Cumberland coal trade, and diverted orders from Maryland to Broad Top."[40]

The trade in flour, the second most plentiful article sent down the canal before the war, was also harmed by the near-suspension of navigation. The May 31 *Middletown Valley Register* noted that millers along the Potomac in Washington County were not purchasing any more wheat out of concern that the Confederates might cross the river and seize it. Additionally, flour that had been previously sent to market over the canal was instead put on the Franklin Railroad at Hagerstown for transportation Harrisburg, Pennsylvania, and then to markets in Baltimore, Philadelphia, and New York. The May 29 *Hagerstown Herald of Freedom and Torch Light* noted: "Thus, the Canal trade has been prostrated and ruined by the 'big riot' in Virginia."[41]

Other businesses along the canal were affected by the war as well. The Pioneer Cotton Factory in Georgetown rented water power from the canal to run its spinning machines. On June 20 the owner of the factory requested that the company release him from the terms of his water-rent agreement because cotton was so scarce and high-priced that he could not make goods profitably.[42]

Life along the canal had changed irrevocably as a result of the war. On June 26, Andrew K. Stake, the canal company's general superintendent, wrote from Williamsport in the midst of Cadwalader's camp: "Nothing but soldiers, baggage, waggons [sic], camps, guns, pistols, and swords meets our gaze here, wherever we go. They have pretty nearly eaten up everything we have. I hope they will get away soon." On June 11 a Williamsport correspondent of the *Baltimore American and Commercial Advertiser* quipped: "Times ain't as they used to was."[43]

CHAPTER 2

DAMN THE HATS IN SUMMER, DAM NO. 5 IN WINTER:
JULY–DECEMBER, 1861

By the early summer of 1861 the canal was still in disrepair. The company was eager to begin repairs, but the opposing armies were posted on either side of the Potomac. Nonetheless, it was optimistic that Patterson's anticipated advance into Virginia would drive the Confederates far enough away from the river to enable it to restore navigation.

At 4:00 A.M. on July 2, 1861, for the second time Patterson's command began to cross the Potomac at Williamsport. Several miles from the ford the Federal army engaged the Confederates in the Battle of Falling Waters. In the half-hour fight, Patterson's larger army swept the Confederates under Jackson off the field. On July 4 Patterson occupied Martinsburg, Virginia. On July 8 Stone's expedition forded the river at Williamsport and joined Patterson, followed by other reinforcements over the next several days. With Patterson no longer on Maryland soil, on July 5 General-in-Chief Scott ordered Col. John R. Kenly's First Maryland Infantry from Baltimore to Washington County. Kenly was directed to protect the canal between Dam numbers 4 and 5 and as much above and below the dams as possible.[1]

With Patterson finally south of the Potomac, the general-in-chief was concerned about the pending offensive against the Confederates at Manassas Junction. On July 13 Scott wrote Patterson that if he was not strong enough to defeat the southern troops under Johnston, to at least engage in demonstrations that would prevent him from crossing the Blue Ridge and reinforcing the Confederates at Manassas. If Johnston retreated toward Strasburg en route to Manassas, Scott directed Patterson to advance toward Alexandria, transporting his heavy supplies on the canal protected by a small detachment on the Maryland side. In mid-July Patterson sent engineers O.E. Babcock and John Newton to Harpers Ferry to prepare it to become his new supply base. The engineers oversaw some repairs to the canal, prepared an entrance to the river ford, and established a ferry to Maryland.[2]

By mid-July Patterson realized that the enlistments of his ninety-day volunteers were due to expire soon, which made it hazardous to attack the Confederates at Winchester. On July 17 he asked Scott if he should instead establish camp at Harpers Ferry or withdraw to Maryland. On July 18 Scott shot back: "I have certainly been expecting you to beat the enemy. If not, to hear that you have felt him strongly, or, at least, had occupied him by threats and demonstrations. . . . Has he not stolen a march and sent re-enforcements toward Manassas Junction?" Patterson claimed to have kept the Confederates occupied with "threats and reconnaissances," but, in fact, Johnston had stolen a march—rather a train ride—and arrived at Manassas by rail in time to participate in the subsequent Confederate victory. As a result of Johnston's escape from the Valley, Patterson's commission was allowed to expire.[3]

Although Patterson had failed to prevent Johnston from re-enforcing the Confederate army at Manassas, his second move into Virginia had cleared large bodies of southern soldiers from the Potomac above and below Harpers Ferry, which permitted the canal company to assess damages and arrange for repairs. On July 6 General Superintendent Andrew K. Stake reported that the damages to the canal were not as serious as anticipated. The stout masonry structures and the stubborn defense put up by local home guard companies had helped save the canal from significant damage. Stake thought that it was futile to attempt repairs, however, because the waterway could be attacked at any time. He relayed a rumor that the Confederates were planning to destroy Dam Number 6 above Hancock, and added, "all along the river there are still seen bands of strolling soldiers shooting at and in every way anoying [sic] those upon this side."[4]

Nevertheless, the company soon put repair crews to work. By July 10 it had restored the canal from Georgetown to Harpers Ferry. On the same day the *Frederick Examiner* estimated that it would require another month to complete the repairs to Cumberland. In order to pay for the work, the company consolidated the positions of paymaster, general superintendent, and chief engineer into the office of the president, with no increase in salary, which was expected to result in yearly savings of over $5,000. The engineer's position was terminated retroactively to May 10, while the general superintendent's post was due to fold on August 10. On July 18 the *Cumberland Civilian and Telegraph* praised Spates, writing "he has acted with the greatest energy, perseverence [sic] and efficiency since his accession to his present responsible position."[5]

In July the Federal government began to take an active part in protecting the canal from further attacks by the Confederates. In mid-July local newspapers reported that Scott had agreed to provide military protection to the entire canal. On July 21, Patterson, who was at Harpers Ferry waiting to be relieved, placed the Third Wisconsin Volunteers on the canal, "which parties have lately attempted to destroy." Three days later Spates wrote that Patterson had ordered protection of the canal from Williamsport to Cumberland, which Spates hoped would allow him to complete repairs to the upper half of the waterway. In addition, on July 19 Francis "Frank" Thomas, western Maryland's representative in the Special Session of Congress, obtained authorization from the secretary of war to raise four home guard regiments. These regiments, which would be designated the Potomac Home Brigade, Maryland Volunteers, were approved specifically to protect the canal and loyal citizens along the Potomac from the Monocacy River to the western boundary of the state. Soldiers were to be recruited from loyal citizens on both sides of the river. A cavalry battalion was also subsequently approved and raised.[6]

Thomas, a native of Frederick County who had moved to Allegany County (present-day Garrett County), Maryland, was a politician of national stature in the first half of the nineteenth century. He was elected to the Maryland House of Delegates in 1822, 1827 and 1829, and to the United States House of Representatives from 1831 to 1841. From 1839 to 1840, while he served in Congress, he also was president of the canal company. In 1841 he was elected governor of Maryland. Soon after he assumed the governorship, his marriage to Sallie Campbell Preston McDowell, the daughter of Virginia Governor James McDowell, ended in divorce and caused him great embarrassment. He questioned his wife's chastity in a pamphlet that he personally placed on the desks of all members of the U.S. Congress. His public marital difficulties and his decision to increase taxes to finance Maryland's public debt resulted in his defeat for a second term as governor. Contemporaries alluded that his public humiliation had cost him the Democratic presidential nomination. After his divorce, a biographer wrote, "a morbid sentiment took possession of his mind which crushed the impulse of ambition within him, and caused him to withdraw from public life." Thomas retreated to his farm in western Maryland where, except for sitting as a delegate to the state Constitutional Convention of 1850, he lived as a virtual recluse.[7]

With the sectional difficulties and outbreak of the Civil War, Thomas's political passions came to life again. With a sense of moral indignation, he emerged from his mountain home and began to give fiery speeches on behalf of the Union. Will Lowdermilk, in *History of Cumberland*, wrote: "When the news of his country's danger reached him all the slumbering statesman was aroused. The strong spirit of former years came upon him. Like some weird, hoary prophet of old, he came down from his mountain retreat and, suddenly appearing in the streets of Cumberland, sounded the alarm of patriotism, and pleaded with the people to stand by the Union, the Constitution, and the laws. It seemed as if one had arisen from the dead."[8]

Thomas represented Maryland's three western counties (Frederick, Washington, and Allegany) in Congress throughout the war. During his tenure he repeatedly proved himself to be a strong friend of the canal, the railroad, and the mining companies of western Maryland, upon which so many of his constituents earned their livelihoods. When he succeeded in getting authorization to raise a home guard unit to protect the waterway, it was but one of many efforts he would make on behalf of the canal company. In fact, the July 10, 1861, *Frederick Examiner* reported that it was as a result of Thomas's intercession with Scott that the general had agreed to place the canal under the protection of the army so that the repairs could be completed.[9]

On July 25 Maj. Gen. Nathaniel P. Banks relieved Patterson. Banks, a former Congressman and governor of Massachusetts, assumed command of the newly created Department of the Shenandoah, which included Washington and Allegany counties and any area of Virginia occupied by his army. Among his responsibilities was the defense of the canal within his department. He initially occupied Harpers Ferry, but his ninety-day volunteers continued to depart, and by early August his army was reduced by about half. On August 13 Scott authorized Banks to withdraw all but a small guard from Maryland Heights and Harpers Ferry and to post the remainder of his command on either side of the Monocacy River to watch the river crossings and protect the canal between Point of Rocks and Harpers Ferry.[10]

Following minor victories in western Virginia, in late July Scott called Maj. Gen. George B. McClellan to Washington to head the Military Division of the Potomac, later reorganized as the Department of the Potomac. On August 11 McClellan ordered Charles P. Stone, who had been promoted to brigadier general, to Poolesville to command a corps of observation from Point of Rocks to Seneca, a distance of about 22 miles. He was directed to observe the river and defend the fords against raids until reserves could be called forward. His command filled the gap between Banks's division to the west and the brigades of Brig. Gen. George McCall and Col. William F. Smith who commanded troops in the vicinity of Great Falls and Chain Bridge. A day after his arrival, the Confederates fired on a passing canal boat. Stone, who was aware of the significance of the canal to the army and to local economy, would continue to prove himself a strong friend of those who depended upon the waterway.[11]

Efforts to get the canal back in order continued. By early August the company had completed repairs to Dam Number 6, about ten miles above Hancock. Two significant difficulties remained. A heavy rockslide had occurred near the Paw Paw Tunnel, where the company had a forty five-man force at work removing the rocks from the canal bed. Five miles further west a thirty five-man crew was working to repair a culvert that the Confederates had destroyed in early July. Alfred Spates, now wearing the hats of engineer and general superintendent in addition to president, was onsite overseeing repairs. To protect the canal against future raids, he met with Virginians on the opposite shore. Although the terms of the understanding are unknown, on August 13 Spates wrote Walter S. Ringgold: "I am satisfied no further trouble will take place on the canal by the Virginians. I have made an agreement with them in this section—the canal can now be worked with all ease in my judgment. I have come on up the line making repairs as I come without the least trouble on earth from the Virginians in any way."[12]

Chain Bridge over the Potomac above Georgetown. Note the canal in the foreground. Source: Source: Library of Congress, Prints and Photographs Division

By the end of August the company completed the final repairs to the canal and navigation between Cumberland and Georgetown resumed for the first time in about four months. The main stem of the Baltimore and Ohio Railroad was still in disrepair and would remain so until late winter of the next year. During this period the canal was the only direct link with the coalfields of western Maryland. The break in both carriers had placed a hardship not only on the residents of Washington, Baltimore, and other northern cities who depended on Cumberland Coal, but on the U.S. Navy whose burgeoning steam fleet was charged with the blockade of southern ports. Cumberland Coal was renowned for its "smokeless" quality and was ideally suited for use by steam vessels.[13]

At the end of August canal boats began to take on coal at Cumberland. Within two weeks trade was brisk and boats were regularly leaving the western terminus "ladened [sic] with the 'black diamonds.'" After overseeing repairs, Alfred Spates came to the western terminus to facilitate the resumption of navigation. The *Civilian and Telegraph* reported that the repairs cost $11,000 and that Spates had paid for it out of his own means.[14]

As canal boats began their voyage east, picket fire across the river occurred with greater frequency. On September 4 the Confederates opposite Great Falls lobbed shells at the Federal encampment on the Maryland side of the river. The company commander of the Washington (New Orleans) Light Artillery reported that his batteries fired several rounds of solid shot at unnamed canal structures, which dislodged several stones. At the end of the month, other Confederate bombardments occurred at Great Falls and Seneca. In addition, between late August and September, skirmishes took place across the river at or near Point of Rocks, Berlin, Sandy Hook, Shepherdstown, and Oldtown. On September 11 the sides were exchanging fire near Shepherdstown when an unsuspecting canal boat passed and the unfortunate boatman was mortally wounded.[15]

Marylander Harry Gilmor was one of the southern sharpshooters who harassed canal traffic when navigation resumed. He wrote the following in his post-war memoir:

While encamped near Morgan's Springs, parties, of which I was generally one, would be sent frequently to the Potomac for the purpose of blockading the canal on the Maryland side, by which immense supplies of coal and provisions were brought to the capital. We would go down before daylight, conceal ourselves behind rocks or trees, or in some small building, and, when the sun was up, not a soldier or boat could pass without our taking a crack at them, and generally with effect, for we were all good shots. We became a perfect pest to them, and many an effort was made in vain to dislodge us; but we could not be found, for every day we were in a new spot, miles apart.[16]

In September Confederate cavalryman Turner Ashby, stationed near Halltown, Virginia, offered to lead a contingent across the river to stop navigation on the canal. He noted that only two Union regiments were guarding the canal in that region, John Geary's Twenty-eighth Pennsylvania at Point of Rocks and Samuel Leonard's Thirteenth Massachusetts at Sandy Hook. A third regiment—Kenly's First Maryland at Williamsport—was too far away to render assistance. On September 19 Confederate Assistant Adjutant General Robert H. Chilton wrote Ashby: "The destruction of the canal and railroad have been cherished objects, and a disappointment at the failure of all past attempts to effect them has been proportionate to the importance attached to their achievement." He advised Ashby to attempt to destroy the Monocacy Aqueduct since it would be almost impossible to repair during the war.[17]

For unknown reasons, Ashby decided to strike the canal at another point. On September 26 his cavalry and Virginia militia units broke camp in a driving rain and proceeded to Dam Number 4, below Williamsport. The men arrived at the dam at dawn, but the heavy rain prevented them from moving their artillery into position over the soft ground. Instead they fired a few rounds at the Union encampments on the Maryland side of the river. Ashby stayed in the area to await another opportunity to assault the dam and word of his objective spread to local newspapers. On October 9 Ashby's men fired artillery rounds at the aqueduct over Antietam Creek, located below Sharpsburg, but he was unable to damage it. Continued rain and high water on the Potomac likely prevented him from making additional attempts against the canal. Responding to intelligence that the Union army was moving troops and supplies toward the Shenandoah Valley, on

November 10 Confederate President Jefferson Davis lamented: "The failure to destroy his communications by the Baltimore and Ohio Railroad and by the Potomac Canal has left him in possession of great advantages for that operation."[18]

In order to promote trade on the canal, in August Alfred Spates wrote to Montgomery Blair, a Marylander and the postmaster general in the Lincoln administration. His letter suggested "certain measures for the encouragement of trade on the border of the canal." On August 16, however, Lincoln had signed legislation that prohibited commerce with the states in rebellion. Spates's letter was referred to Banks, who acknowledged that the canal president's ideas had merit, but apologized that the newly passed "no intercourse doctrine" prevented him from implementing the suggestions. The legislation exempted regions of Virginia west of the Alleghany Mountains, but the entire canal bordered regions of the Old Dominion that had a significant Confederate presence. Although the canal had always engaged in trade with Virginia via river locks and the Potomac Aqueduct, the new law limited almost all wartime commerce to that moving east and west.[19]

Union military officers were also concerned that some canal trade might be diverted to the Confederacy. On September 2 Kenly informed Banks that a large quantity of salt was being shipped from Georgetown to Williamsport and Hancock. Kenly allowed the shipments to proceed to Williamsport, where his headquarters was located, but intended to interdict any destined to Hancock for fear of it falling into Confederate hands. He acknowledged his actions would inconvenience Unionists in that region, but was unwilling to risk that cargoes might be sent south. Banks had also ordered him to impose restrictions on public use of the canal towpath. Kenly acknowledged that local citizens were using it as a highway.[20]

In October the canal played a small role in two military engagements along the Potomac. A. H. Herr, a Unionist who owned a mill on Virginius Island in the Shenandoah River at Harpers Ferry, invited Federal soldiers to cross the river and take the grain stored in his mill. On an earlier occasion Union troops had disabled the mill to prevent the Confederates from using it. Local citizens were impressed to tote sacks of wheat to wagons that were waiting to transport the grain to a boat in the river. Most of the grain was removed October 14-15. Early on October 17 Federal pickets were

Thomas Nast illustration of soldiers coming down canal in two boats. *New York Illustrated News,* Nov. 11, 1861. Source: Enoch Pratt Library, Baltimore, Md.

driven back to Harpers Ferry by a Confederate force of about six hundred men commanded by Ashby. A general engagement ensued until mid-day, when Col. Geary sent reinforcements and artillery across the river, which helped to drive the Confederates away. Casualties were light on both sides. About 15,000 bushels of grain were brought to the Maryland shore where it was transferred to canal boats and sent to Georgetown. Millers later ground it into 3,100 barrels of flour for government use.[21]

The second engagement involved Stone's command in Montgomery County. On October 20 McClellan directed Stone to observe Confederates activities in the vicinity of Leesburg and suggested that a "slight demonstration" might distract the enemy from a Federal reconnaissance near Dranesville, Virginia. Stone created the diversion by sending troops across the river at Edwards Ferry. The soldiers elicited no response from the Confederates and were withdrawn. Suspecting that the Confederates might have abandoned Leesburg, Stone ordered his own reconnaissance. He directed troops to cross the river three miles above Edwards Ferry and follow a footpath up the heights, known as Ball's Bluff, toward Leesburg. Due to unexpected delays, the scouting expedition was not conducted until after nightfall. In the darkness the party thought that it had spied an enemy camp within a mile of Leesburg. Stone ordered a raiding party to cross the river and attack the encampment at daybreak, then return to Maryland unless it could find a position that it could hold against superior numbers until reinforced. Soldiers lifted boats from the canal to the river to augment the expedition's means of crossing the Potomac. The next morning the expedition failed to find the Confederate camp, but decided to stay on the Virginia side of the river until reinforced.[22]

Col. Edward Baker, U.S. Senator from Oregon and personal friend of Abraham Lincoln, was given command of the troops that had ascended the bluff. Baker personally supervised the lifting of what was described as a large ferryboat from the canal to the river, although more likely it was a packet boat. By the time Baker arrived on the field, the Union force had skirmished with the Confederates and had fallen back. A subsequent Confederate attack resulted in the death of Baker and the wounding of another officer. A retreat to the riverbank quickly ensued. In the confusion that followed, the largest boat, overloaded with desperate men, sank. Two

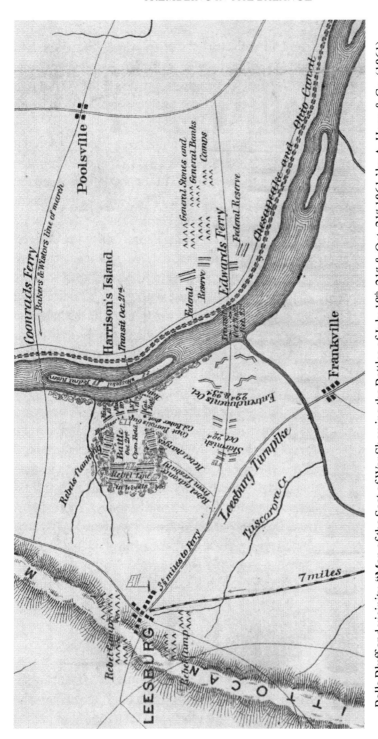

Balls Bluff and vicinity. "Map of the Seat of War Showing the Battles of July 18th, 21st & Oct. 21st 1861," by A. Hoen & Co. (1861). Source: Library of Congress, Geography and Map Division

skiffs that had been used to transport the men across the river had disappeared. Many men tried to swim to safety in the rain-swollen Potomac and drowned or were shot by the Confederates from the bluff. About two hundred Union soldiers were killed and over five hundred captured in the Battle of Ball's Bluff.[23]

While the raiding party was crossing the river, Stone ordered a second reconnaissance to divert attention from the first and to scout the area between Edwards Ferry and Leesburg. This expedition crossed the river and advanced along the road to Leesburg. When it became apparent that the Battle of Ball's Bluff had gone against him, Stone began to make preparations to withdraw the second party. McClellan, however, ordered Stone to not withdraw the troops. Seven boats and two repair scows were seized from the canal and transferred to the river to ferry additional soldiers across. Two days later McClellan ordered the withdrawal of the second expedition from Virginia. Lumbermen and boatmen from the First Minnesota Infantry were detailed to pole the boats across the high, wind-swept river, aided by contingents from the First Maryland Infantry and two other regiments. Despite the adverse conditions, by the morning of October 24 the entire expedition was returned to Maryland without loss.[24]

On October 26 ambulances and medical attendants stood by on the banks of the canal at Georgetown to receive the wounded from Ball's Bluff. The medical personnel later learned that the wounded were hospitalized in Poolesville. Oliver Wendell Holmes, Jr., a future Supreme Court justice, was one of the wounded at Ball's Bluff. He was initially taken to a field hospital on Harrisons Island, and then ferried to the Maryland shore. In his diary, Holmes wrote that attendants put him and other wounded in the hold of a canal boat where they were nearly killed when one of the hatches fell through. After a short stay at a hospital in Poolesville, Holmes and about forty sick and injured soldiers from Bank's division were transported to Georgetown in canal boats and taken to local hospitals.[25]

§

The Battle of Ball's Bluff was a serious embarrassment to the government. Although the numbers engaged were not large, and the Confederate victory had little military significance, the Union defeat helped

THE CIVIL WAR IN AMERICA: RETREAT OF THE FEDERALISTS AFTER THE FIGHT AT BALL'S BLUFF, UPPER POTOMAC, VIRGINIA.—FROM A SKETCH BY OUR SPECIAL ARTIST.

Union Retreat from Balls Bluff. *Illustrated London News*, Nov. 23, 1861. Courtesy of "The Civil War in America from the Illustrated London News": A Joint Project by Sandra J. Still, Emily E. Katt, Collection Management, and the Beck Center of Emory University.

launch the congressional Joint Committee on the Conduct of the War. This investigative body conducted hearings to determine why the Union war effort was languishing. The committee investigated both the defeat at Ball's Bluff and Patterson's campaign against Harpers Ferry. Eventually the committee caught up with Stone and undermined his career [see Chapter 3].[26]

After a summer of no boating and the expense of completing repairs, the canal company's finances were abysmal. Some company employees were threatening to quit unless they received overdue wages. On October 1 the president and board of directors decided to suspend the acceptance of toll certificates and require that shippers pay all tolls in cash. When shippers protested, the company agreed to permit them to pay one-quarter tolls due in certificates, three-quarters in cash.[27]

Significant trade occurred on the canal during September and October, which relieved some financial pressure on the company. In the former month over 22,000 tons of coal left port at Cumberland and over $10,500 was collected in tolls. In October over 30,000 tons of coal were shipped from Cumberland and over $17,700 in tolls were collected, both of which were the highest monthly totals of 1861. In an October 21 letter to Ringgold, the Cumberland toll collector noted that about one-half of the boats had discharged their coal west of Georgetown, primarily at Sandy Hook. The railroad bridge at Harpers Ferry had not yet been replaced and in the meantime the B&O had erected two horse-powered derricks along the canal at Sandy Hook. The coal companies then contracted with boatmen to bring coal to the town over the canal, at which point the railroad company transferred coal from canal boats to railcars. The railroad company eventually erected enough derricks to transfer coal to fifty cars in one day. It also forwarded lumber, crossties, and gas coal from Newburg and Fairmont in western Virginia over the canal to Sandy Hook, then to Baltimore and other points via rail.[28]

The autumn rains continued, however, and on November 2, after over twenty-four hours of heavy rain, the river left its banks and swept over vulnerable portions of the canal. The Twelfth Indiana Infantry was on duty along the Potomac in Washington County during the deluge. In his journal, Sergeant William S. Hemphill described what happened at Dam Number 4:

The water raised [sic] so rapidly that it became necessary to call in
the guard at, and below the dam. The rise was about twenty feet,
the canal below the dam being entirely submerged, while the dam
itself could only be distinguished in the mad rush of water, by the
abutements [sic] and a slight depression where the foaming flood
dashed over the breast of the dam which in ordinary stages is ten or
twelve feet high. It was a grand and terrific sight, the waters foaming
and boiling threatening to tear everything before it. So fierce was
the flood that toward evening it was deemed necessary to call in the
guard that was stationed at the Guard Lock. On going to their relief
it was found that the guard had taken refuge with the family at the
Lock, and all were upstairs, the lower floor being some three feet
under water. A boat was procured and all were safely removed to
safer quarters.[29]

In Cumberland, the water washed through the lower portion of the
town, destroyed property, and carried away buildings. Property damage in
the city was estimated at $50,000. The affects of the flood was so great
that the public and military authorities on both sides of the Potomac thought
it likely that the canal would remain closed for the balance of the year.[30]

In dealing with the flood damage, the canal company found allies in
Generals Stone and Banks. On November 5 Stone informed Banks that
there were five breaks in the canal within the boundaries of their commands.
Stone put one hundred soldiers to work repairing three breaches within his
lines, and Banks's men repaired the other two. To evaluate other damage
and arrange for its repair, Stone gave Spates a pass that allowed him to go
beyond picket lines.[31]

The flooding of early November again strained the company's
finances. To address the problem, the company began to hold loaded boats
until their tolls for the previous month were paid. Shippers had requested
that the company accept half of tolls due in certificates, but on November 3
Spates wrote Ringgold that to do so would bring navigation to a standstill.
A week later the president and directors agreed to let the mining companies
pay their tolls on the last day of the month, but warned that failure to make
payment would result in the company seizing boats and selling the cargoes

The canal at Sandy Hook. *Harper's Weekly*, Aug. 10, 1861. Source: author's collection.

to liquidate unpaid tolls. In late November the company decided to suspend payment of interest due on a bank debt.[32]

On November 18, after the floodwater had receded, Charles Mynn Thruston, the mayor of Cumberland and newly appointed brigadier general of volunteers, wrote letters to two canal officials and ordered them to make repairs to the waterway between Hancock and Cumberland. He claimed authority from a verbal order given by Stone through a messenger. Thruston, a sixty-three-year-old native of Kentucky, had entered the U.S. Military Academy in 1813 and a year later was commissioned lieutenant of artillery. He had served at Governor's Island, New York, and helped to erect fortifications until the close of the War of 1812. He was later assigned to garrison duty in Maryland, Connecticut, and Virginia, and filled various staff positions connected with the artillery branch. In 1835–36 he served as acting adjutant-general of the Florida army in the Seminole War before he resigned and retired to a farm in Cumberland. Thruston had also served as an officer in the Maryland Militia and in 1839 had led the state forces that quelled violence between rival Irish factions engaged in the construction of the canal. He was also involving in banking and mining in Allegany County.[33]

Alfred Spates resented Thruston's interference in canal affairs. It is obvious that the men, both Cumberland residents, held mutual animosities. Even the canal separated the men. Thruston had been an early backer of the canal. In 1840 he and two other Allegany County residents traveled to Annapolis to memorialize the state legislature for aid to complete the construction of the canal to Cumberland. In the years that followed, political control of the canal had turned Thruston against it. On November 20, 1861, when Thruston informed the War Department that he had ordered repair of the flood-damaged canal, he added: "The Chesapeake and Ohio Canal has never been any thing but a means of reward to State Politicians, and therefore, has always been inefficiently managed. The President of the Canal Co. has not, so far as I can learn, been heard from or of, since the freshet of the 2nd inst." He further recommended that the government take charge of the canal and place an army officer in command with the power to dismiss employees at will. He concluded: "It [the canal] will then become for the first time a useful improvement."[34]

Two months earlier Spates and other colleagues had become involved in a quiet campaign to insure that Thruston was not appointed brigadier general of the Potomac Home Brigade, the unit charged with protecting the canal in western Maryland. On September 24 recruiting officer Daniel Blocher suggested to the First Regiment's lieutenant colonel that Representative Francis Thomas ask Spates to raise a regiment for the brigade. Blocher wrote: "If Col. S. [Spates] can be engaged as . . . suggested and the whole matter be left in his hands, Col. Thruston will never be the Brig. Gen. of the Pot. Home Brigade. I believe if he [Thruston] were appointed to-day that in less than a fortnight Spates and every prominent officer on the line [of the canal] would be under arrest—and I think Spates feared this—hence he is interested in arresting this thing." Earlier in the month Thomas had asked Lincoln not to appoint a brigadier general to command the brigade until he could meet with the president. Late in September Spates was in Washington where he met with Thomas, Lt. Gen. Scott, and Postmaster General Blair. It is very likely that Spates was lobbying Thomas and the administration to prevent Thruston from being appointed to the command. Of Spates's meeting in Washington, Blocher wrote: "The whole matter has been postponed for a time, and that he [Spates] has a hope that things will yet turn out right." Ultimately, the regiments of the Potomac Home Brigade never served together in the same brigade, perhaps as a result of Spates's efforts.[35]

Although the Union army stationed along the length of the canal helped to protect it from Confederate raids and flood damage, it also subjected company property to seizure and misuse by Federal soldiers. Additionally, the army often transported troops and supplies on the waterway without paying tolls and interfered with the duties of canal officials. On October 5, for example, a supervisor on the Monocacy Division wrote the company office: "I am very much annoyed with the soldiers taken our boates [sic] & wheelbarrows & doing what they please & often times won't let us pass on the line to see to it." On November 11 he informed the company that the army had taken possession of his repair scow and sunk it, and that soldiers had taken his ice-breaking boat to transport cannon and had damaged it as well.[36]

Late in the year the company prepared to file a claim against the government for services it had provided to the army and for damages and losses it had sustained since the beginning of the war. On November 20 the company filed a claim for $5,190 with Brig. Gen. Stewart Van Vliet, quartermaster of the Army of the Potomac. Spates enclosed an affidavit that was endorsed by Postmaster Blair. The company requested $500 for the transportation of troops and stores during Stone's June 1861 expedition up the Potomac; $300 for transportation rendered to Generals Patterson and Banks; $200 for use of company houses at Sandy Hook; $600 for three houses destroyed by the soldiers of the Thirteenth Massachusetts; $2,400 for three house boats used by the troops and "rendered valueless;" $500 for damages incurred to scows and ice breakers; $450 for the hire of fifty men for six days, at $1.50 per day, and $240 for the hire of twenty horses and carts for six days, at $2.00 per day, as ordered by the engineer officer Babcock.[37]

On November 30 Van Vliet referred the matter to Montgomery C. Meigs, the quartermaster general of the army. Prior to the war Meigs worked on a number of engineering projects for the army, including the extension of the U.S. Capitol and the design of the dome that would sit atop the structure. He also was in charge of the construction of the Washington Aqueduct, which carried water from the Potomac to Washington, D.C. After the series of destructive floods in the Potomac in 1857, Meigs had assisted the canal company in making temporary repairs to Dam numbers 4 and 5.[38]

Van Vliet wrote Meigs that Spates was anxious to be paid and had made a new account for $1,490 "covering a portion of the items embraced in the original account." It is unclear if Spates intended the new account to replace the earlier one or serve as a partial payment toward the original claim. Regardless, the company was in great need of cash to pay its employees and make repairs to the canal as a result of the November flooding. Van Vliet recommended that Meigs pay the claim, although he could not verify that it was correct. The quartermaster general took no immediate action on the claim, however.[39]

Picket duty along the Potomac provided a wide range of experiences to the soldiers involved. Some thought it laborious, uneventful, and boring. Others were enamored with the beauty of the Potomac River Valley. During periods of inactivity Union soldiers fished, hitched rides on passing canal boats, and swam in the canal. In the winter, some northern soldiers wrote home and asked their parents to send their ice skates. At other times rifle and artillery fire across the river made it a frightening and dangerous experience. During the fall of 1861 the pickets on both sides of the Potomac became so well acquainted at places that an informal truce was called, particularly at Edwards Ferry. Small parties of soldiers met in the middle of the river to exchange handshakes, camp gossip, newspapers, and whiskey. When friendly units of pickets were replaced with new troops, the crack of a rifle was often heard again until the fresh soldiers learned the etiquette in place along the river. In November Brig. Gen. Alpheus S. Williams, who commanded Federal pickets at Muddy Branch, three miles below Seneca Creek, wrote that Confederate soldiers were clearly visible on the Virginia side of the river, but he could walk along the towpath with as much ease as he could on New York's Erie Canal.[40]

By the end of November the company was finishing repairs to the canal. With the B&O Railroad still in disrepair west of Harpers Ferry, the November 20 *Frederick Examiner* noted the good news and added, "this is specially important, as the supply of bituminous coal is nearly exhausted and there are no other means of obtaining it." In early December boats began to take on coal in Cumberland. A company official reported that by December 7, 2,584 tons of coal had been shipped. About seventy-percent of the coal had been unloaded at Sandy Hook for transfer to the B&O, the remainder at Georgetown. With the resumption of navigation, General Banks informed McClellan's chief of staff that he expected about 1,000 tons of coal a day would be transported to the latter city.[41]

Following the Confederate victory in the First Battle of Bull Run, rumors were afoot that Maryland's secessionists were emboldened and planned to foment an uprising. Before the General Assembly could meet again, in mid-September about thirty suspected disloyal members of the legislature and its staff were arrested in Annapolis, Baltimore, and other places. Then in the November state elections, Unionist candidate Augustus

W. Bradford was elected governor and the Union Party gained control of the legislature, which put an end to such concerns for good.[42]

As a stockholder in the B&O Railroad and the C&O Canal, Maryland's financial interests were threatened by the ongoing war. On December 4 the outgoing governor, Thomas Holliday Hicks, addressed the matter before the General Assembly, which he had called into extra session following the electoral triumph of the Union Party. "The condition of the Baltimore and Ohio railroad and of the Chesapeake and Ohio canal requires action on your part," he told the legislature. "The reopening of these great works to traffic and travel is of immense importance not only to the people directly, but as bearing on the future of our financial resources." Although the canal was then just beginning to resume navigation, in reality there was little the legislature could do to assist either line. Both carriers would have benefited from a general Union military advance into Virginia that would have placed each behind a secure line of defense. The canal could have used additional state investment in order to provide much needed cash, but there was little political will in the legislature to sink more money into a "nonproductive investment," as defined by the state comptroller of the treasury.[43]

Following the Unionist victory in the state elections and numerous Confederate attempts to destroy the canal, Alfred Spates offered the Federal army military use of the waterway in exchange for better protection. On November 24 he wrote to McClellan—who had succeeded Scott as general-in-chief—and pointed out that the canal offered great facilities for the transportation of agricultural products, coal, and military supplies. He suggested that the army move supplies from the west over the B&O Railroad to Cumberland and then transfer the goods to the canal for shipment directly to Washington. For the army to take advantage of canal transportation, however, Spates wrote "it is desirable and essential that proper protection of the works, and facilities for transportation, should be given by the United States." He noted that military restrictions on boating, such as forbidding navigation at night and detaining boats at will during the day, had nearly doubled the amount of time necessary for a boat to traverse the canal. He also asked McClellan to return company property that the army had taken. The following day Spates wrote a similar letter to Quartermaster General

Meigs, suggesting that the waterway would be of great value to transport troops and supplies from the west. He also asked the quartermaster to pay the company's recent claim for tolls and damages.[44]

On December 6 McClellan responded to Spates's request by appointing Brig. Gen. Charles P. Stone military supervisor of the canal. The appointment of a military supervisor did not signify an outright seizure of the canal by the army. Although McClellan ordered Stone to protect the canal and help keep it in repair, he directed that Alfred Spates was to remain in charge of day-to-day operations. In actuality, the canal company was fortunate to have the vigilant and sympathetic Stone appointed to the post. He had spent six months posted along the canal, was familiar with its operations, and had come to the canal's assistance on several occasions. Additionally, he was aware of the waterway's importance to the army and the regions it served. Local reaction to Stone's appointment was positive. The December 12 *Cumberland Civilian and Telegraph* wrote: "This desirable result has been brought about through the indefatigable exertions of Mr. Spates, who has been unceasing in his efforts to keep the Canal open."[45]

On December 11 Stone assumed his new duties and ordered all officers who commanded lines of pickets along the canal to provide assistance to the company. The following day he asked Spates for a list of employees and their duties, and an estimate of the number and types of boats and animals that were required in each division in order to keep the waterway open during the winter. He also asked for a list of the points where it was important that canal boats discharge their cargoes so that he could remove the restrictions that prevented the transportation of goods to Maryland's interior. On December 12 Stone wrote Spates that he soon expected the defense of the river to be strong enough to permit the company to begin work on Dam Number 5, and that he was readying small steamers to keep the waterway free from ice.[46]

With the main stem of the B&O Railroad still broken and barges of coal beginning to move on the canal, Jackson at Winchester planned the first of four raids against the canal near Williamsport. He would be opposed by troops in Banks's division, headquartered in Frederick, to whom on November 28 McClellan had given responsibility to protect the canal from

76

Union Maj. Gen. George B. McClellan. Source: Library of Congress, Prints and Photographs Division.

Union Brig. Gen. Charles P. Stone, military supervisor of the canal. Source: Library of Congress, Prints and Photographs Division.

the Monocacy River to Cumberland. At Williamsport, Col. Samuel Leonard commanded that line of pickets that protected the river from the mouth of Antietam Creek to Hancock.[47]

In early December Jackson sent a small force under Ashby to destroy Dam Number 5. Included in the expedition were two companies from the Stonewall Brigade, Ashby's cavalry, two batteries, and a Virginia militia force commanded by Brig. Gen. James H. Carson. The Confederates approached the dam in the afternoon of December 6 and exchanged fire with the pickets from the First Virginia (U.S.) Infantry. The Federal pickets were reinforced, but the firing quickly died out and all remained quiet throughout the rest of the day and night.[48]

At about 4:00 P.M. the following day the Confederates advanced in force toward the dam. The southern troops opened fire opposite a ferry crossing near Four Locks and commenced a cannonade of the dam and nearby buildings, which destroyed a home near the river and drove Union pickets from their hiding places in the canal lock house, barns, and other buildings. On the Maryland side, additional men were sent to the dam and the ferry crossing. Local citizens took arms and joined in the defense of the dam. Most of the Union troops formed behind a fence on a bluff that overlooked the river. The Federals troops had no artillery to answer the Confederate batteries. By nightfall the artillery fire ended, but at the ferry, musketry fire continued into the night. After a lull, at 9:00 P.M. the Confederates resumed fire to cover a work party that was attempting to cut the cribbing of the dam. Other workmen attempted to dig a trench around the abutment in order to divert the river around the dam. By 11:00 P.M. Union pickets clearly heard the sounds of the axes and spades and commenced fire upon the work party. The detail withdrew and Confederate infantry moved into position on the heights that overlooked the river, returning fire at the flash of Union guns until about 2:00 A.M. After the firing had died out, soldiers from the Second Virginia Infantry taunted the Union soldiers to resume the fight, calling them "free negroe scoundrels" and "negroe stealers," but the Federals withheld their fire.[49]

At daylight on December 8 Confederate artillery again opened at the dam and the ferry. A barn was struck and set afire and the canal tollhouse was riddled with shot and shell. Sources estimated that over 200 artillery rounds had been fired in the first two days of the engagement. Overnight Colonel Leonard had dispatched Company C of Thirteenth Massachusetts from Williamsport to the dam via canal boat. The next day a party of Massachusetts sharpshooters, armed with long-range Enfield rifles, took positions behind the dam's abutment and returned fire across the river. "Crack! went all the other rifles of our 'fighting Company C,' as it is called," wrote one Bay State rifleman, "and we kept it up, as fast as we could load and fire, until the enemy retreated and hid behind trees, houses, stones, &c." Other Federal units blazed away at the southern troops from the bluff overlooking the dam. Heavy Union fire and strong defensive positions forced Ashby to abandon the enterprise. After dark the Confederates retrieved their guns and fired a few parting artillery rounds across the river before they withdrew.[50]

Some Confederates, such as W. Morton Brown of the Rockbridge Artillery, were convinced that the Union soldiers had drained water from the canal and were using it as a breastwork. On January 17, 1862, he wrote: "The sense of personal danger was decidedly stronger to my mind on this occasion than at Masassas. They had some hundred of sharp shooters in the canal—which formed an admirable breastwork & protection from cannon as well as from small arms." It appears that the Confederates mistook the space occupied by Union sharpshooters behind the abutment of the dam for the canal channel itself.[51]

On December 9 Jackson informed the Confederate Secretary of War that although Union sharpshooters had prevented his men from damaging the dam, he planned to make another attempt. Two days later Jackson gave Ashby command of another small expedition that he sent to Dam Number 4 below Williamsport, about twenty-three miles from Dam Number 5. In the early morning rifle fire was exchanged near Shepherdstown and in mid-morning the pickets of the Twelfth Indiana spotted the Confederates opposite the dam. The southerners soon opened a heavy cannonade and advanced a raiding party with boats a mile above the dam opposite the guard lock, but the Union soldiers drove them back. Another Confederate detachment advanced near a gristmill below the dam, but again strong Federal fire from a rifle pit forced them to retire.[52]

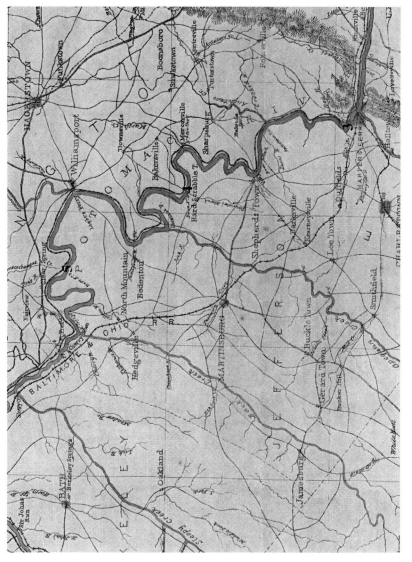

Canal from Dam Number 3 to Dam Number 5 (Bold numbers added to indicate location of dams). "Portions of the Military Departments of Virginia, Washington, Middle & the Susquehanna." (1863). Source: Library of Congress, Geography and Map Division.

UNSUCCESSFUL ATTEMPT OF THE CONFEDERATE TROOPS TO DESTROY DAM NO. 5, NEAR WILLIAMSPORT, MD.

From a Sketch by Captain Harry Brogt.

Jackson attempts to Destroy Dam Number 5. *Frank Leslie's Illustrated Newspaper*, Jan. 18, 1862, reprinted in *The Soldier in Our Civil War*, edited by Paul Fleury Mottelay. (1884), 197.

After a period of inactivity the Indiana troops began to think the Confederates had departed. An officer ordered a captain to take a small squad across the river and determine if the southern troops had indeed withdrawn. Soon after the party crossed to Virginia about one hundred Confederate cavalry emerged from the woods and captured them. An Indiana soldier wrote: "The captain was a general favorite with all the men in camp and his capture seemed to make them perfectly fearless. They left their rifle pits and poured volley after volley into the ranks of the enemy. . . . The men, who were under fire for the first time, stood bravely up to their work, and soon became cool as veterans, taking as deliberate aim as if hunting squirrels in their home woods." The Confederates quickly withdrew out of range. Union reinforcements were called forward, but the next day the Indiana soldiers learned that the southerners had withdrawn with their prisoners.[53]

Once again, Federal riflemen had frustrated Jackson's design on the canal company's dams. On December 14 Jackson wrote Johnston: "I have made two attempts to prevent navigation on the canal, but have not thus far succeeded." Jackson was still not about to give up on the endeavor. He wrote that he may use the boats to cross the Potomac if needed, "but my desire is to complete the work commenced on the dam [number 5]." This time, Jackson planned to personally supervise the destruction of the dam.[54]

On December 16 Jackson advanced from Winchester to Martinsburg with the entire Stonewall Brigade, Ashby's cavalry and Carson's militia. The following day after nightfall the Confederates arrived at Dam Number 5. A party of Irishmen—facetiously called the "dam detail," and fortified by a whiskey ration—went down to the Virginia end of the dam and began to cut the cribs. They were not discovered until just before dawn when they were driven from the dam and took refuge in nearby Colston's Mill. In order to cover the work at the dam, Jackson had sent Carson's militia to Falling Waters where they skirmished with Federal pickets and made demonstrations as if they intended to cross the river, including backing the wagons that carried the boats to the river's edge. At night the militia kept a large number of campfires burning to convince the Federal troops that a large force was opposite Williamsport. Like six months earlier, the town was rife with rumors that the Confederates would cross the river and attack the town.[55]

During the night of the eighteenth—all work to disable the dam was conducted at night—the Confederates erected a stone barricade to protect the work party; the only danger was going to and from the dam. A soldier from the Thirteenth Massachusetts wrote that a brisk exchange of fire was kept up through the night. At daybreak the Federals discovered the barricade. Massachusetts soldiers went down river and found a location from which they could bring fire upon the workers and soon drove the southerners from the dam and into the millhouse.[56]

The following day, December 19, skirmishing at the dam and at Falling Waters resumed. When Leonard realized that the threat against Williamsport was a ruse, he dispatched artillery to the dam and drove the Confederates from the mill. An artillery duel commenced with Jackson's gunners who were throwing shells into a stone barn that concealed Federal sharpshooters. At one point the Union guns found the range of the southern battery and put the gunners to flight. No amount of cajoling by Jackson could convince the men to come out from their hiding places and retrieve their guns. As the Confederates moved more cannon forward a gunner wrote that several men were lined up behind a large tree, dodging shot to the left and right. The Federals eventually ceased their fire, and the Confederates withdrew from the river.[57]

A lull in the fighting at the dam commenced in the afternoon. The boys of the Thirteenth Massachusetts found time to relax and take a hearty meal with a local Unionist. One of them wrote: "We had just reached headquarters when intelligence was received from our pickets at Little Georgetown . . . that the rebels had appeared opposite in strong force, numbering as many as three regiments; that they had yelled across the river that they should cross that night at all odds, asking if 'we didn't want some more Bull Run soup.'" The skirmishing continued there until 9:00 that evening. While fire was exchanged near Little Georgetown, a party of Federal troops crossed the river at Dam Number 5 and burned the millhouse. When the Confederates returned at dusk to resume their work on the dam, they found that the burning mill provided too much light and made it unsafe for the work party to approach the dam.[58]

On December 20 Jackson "yankeed the yankees." After another artillery duel, Jackson decoyed the Federals into believing that he intended to cross the river. In sight of the Union troops he sent his boats—"Old Jack's fleet," his men called them—upriver toward Little Georgetown. The Federal artillery and nearly all the infantry followed and left Jackson's men with an evening to work on the dam in relative safety. At some point in the night the workers heard the sound of timber breaking and assumed that they had made a significant breach. On December 21, Jackson left the river.[59]

Jackson was convinced that he had significantly damaged the dam. On December 24 he wrote to Johnston's adjutant: "There is reason to believe that the recent break in Dam No. 5 will destroy any vestiges of hope that might have been entertained of supplying Washington with Cumberland coal by the Chesapeake and Ohio Canal, and consequently their only prospect of procuring coal must be the Baltimore and Ohio Railroad." The following day Johnston wrote to a staff officer in Richmond to emphasize the importance of preventing the repair of the B&O since it was believed that the canal had been disabled. "No one understands this subject better than the President [Jefferson Davis]," he added. The damage Jackson's men had inflicted on the canal was not enough to stop navigation, however. The day after his departure, Banks reported that canal boats were moving in both directions.[60]

When Jackson learned that navigation on the canal had resumed, on January 1 he sent a small party back to Dam Number 5. Ashby again led the force, which was composed of his cavalry, two pieces of artillery, five companies of infantry, and some of the militia. The expedition spent two additional nights at the dam, widening the breach.[61]

During the third week of December Alfred Spates asked an officer on duty near the dam for permission for a work party to cross the river and begin repairs. The officer was concerned that some of the workers might be secessionist sympathizers and denied the request. Col. Leonard had expected Spates to begin repairs, but was unsure when he intended to start the work.[62]

Confederate President Jefferson Davis. Source: Library of Congress, Prints and Photographs Division.

Confederate Cavalry officer Turner Ashby. Source: Library of Congress, Prints and Photographs Division.

The Federal army may have caused more enduring harm to the canal in December than Jackson. With the growth of the coal trade, shippers had found it more efficient to ship as large a quantity of coal over the canal as possible. As a result, over the years the size of the boats on the canal increased. Navigation through Georgetown, however, was problematic. The waterway could not easily accommodate the largest class of boats because they drew such a large draft of water that when unburdened of their cargo they had difficulty ascending under several of the bridges of the city. Only by filling the hold of the boats with water or by lowering the water level in the canal could empty boats return. One solution was to utilize the Potomac Aqueduct to take coal and other products to the wharves at Alexandria for transportation along the eastern seaboard. The Federal army, though, saw the aqueduct as one of three potential routes that the Confederates could use to invade Washington (the other two were the Long Bridge in Washington and the Chain Bridge three miles above Georgetown).

In December the army seized the aqueduct and prepared to turn it into a military bridge to supply Union troops who occupied northern Virginia. In a postwar report on the defenses of Washington, Brig. Gen. John G. Barnard, the chief engineer in the Army of the Potomac, wrote:

> Though a certain service could have been rendered by the canal in the transportation of military supplies to Alexandria, this utility was insignificant weighed against the importance of having a second permanent and secure bridge connecting Washington with the Virginia shore. . . . Accordingly, early in the winter of 1861–62, the water was shut off from the aqueduct and its trough converted into a double-track wagon-road, the floor being overlaid with 4-inch planks and long inclines, on trestles, forming connections with the roads on either side.[63]

The canal company bitterly opposed the confiscation of the Potomac Aqueduct. Not only did its seizure deny the company the opportunity to directly supply the Federal army that occupied northern Virginia, but also denied it access to the deepwater port of Alexandria. Additionally, because all boats traveling to Georgetown now had to unload at the wharves there, and because the largest boats had difficulty ascending the canal under the bridges of Georgetown, it caused great inconvenience and delays for the boatmen. Due to the opposition of the canal company and some within the Army of the Potomac, Barnard wrote that other options were considered, including the construction of a bridge of boats across the river. All were ruled out as impractical, however.[64]

Work on converting the aqueduct to a bridge took about a month, beginning in early December, and it opened for military traffic in January 1862. The Federal army maintained possession of the "aqueduct bridge," as it was commonly called, throughout the war. To defend this potential invasion route, the army built three forts at the southern end of the aqueduct. Fort Corcoran was the largest and was supported on either side by Forts Haggerty and Bennett. Three wooden blockhouses and a rifle trench were also constructed. In addition, the southern end of the aqueduct was eventually enclosed by a stockade fence with a gate.[65]

§

The first year of the war was a difficult one for the canal company. Tolls collected were over $110,000 less than in 1860 and goods shipped decreased by about 202,000 tons. Expenses exceeded revenues by nearly $30,000. During the year the flour trade declined by 36 percent, while the coal trade fell by 58 percent. Merchants lamented the disruption of the coal trade by both railroad and canal. The January 1, 1862, *Baltimore American and Commercial Advertiser* noted that local manufacturers were forced to use more expensive coal from Pennsylvania and had come to the "universal acknowledgment that our Cumberland Coal is superior to any other Bituminous Coal they are now compelled to use."[66]

In its Thirty-Fourth Annual Report the company's president and directors noted that damage to the canal by military operations was not very significant, but nevertheless the war's affect on business was disastrous. Of those factors that suppressed navigation, the board identified the proximity of the armies to the Potomac, restrictions in navigation imposed by the Union Army, and the frequent detention of boats. It noted that revenues were less than any year since the canal reached Cumberland in 1850. The report pointed out that the canal had only been in operation for one month

Potomac Aqueduct, seized by the U.S. Army and converted into the "Aqueduct Bridge." Source: Library of Congress, Prints and Photographs Division.

before the first freshet stopped navigation. When the company completed repairs hostilities had begun and there was almost no navigation on the canal until September. From then until the close of navigation in December there were occasional interruptions in navigation caused by high water. Decreased revenues did not permit any improvements to the canal and prevented the company from completing routine maintenance chores, which undermined the future viability of the canal.[67]

On a brighter note, with the appointment of Stone as military supervisor, the army had taken responsibility for protecting the waterway. Many canal officials hoped that this, coupled with a general military advance, would remove the canal from the scene of conflict and permit the resumption of unimpeded navigation in the next year. Little did these officials know that the canal company would experience an even more difficult boating season in 1862.

By the end of 1861 Charles E. Davis, Jr., and the Thirteenth Massachusetts Infantry had spent nearly its entire five months of service picketing the Potomac and protecting the canal. After a hot summer followed by a cold winter under the fire of Jackson's men, he summed up his regiment's service: "It was d[am]n the hats in summer, and Dam No. 5 in winter."[68]

CHAPTER 3

RED TAPE OR UTTER INDIFFERENCE:
JANUARY–MAY 1862

For the canal company, 1862 opened much as 1861 closed: with Jackson on the Potomac threatening a Federal army north of the river, the canal between the two. With the Confederates poised along the river, and the mid-Atlantic in the midst of a deep cold snap, there was no prospect of an early resumption of boating on the Chesapeake and Ohio Canal.

On January 1 Jackson had left Winchester and advanced toward the Potomac again. Three days later his men took Bath (now Berkeley Springs, West Virginia), causing the Union soldiers who had held the town to flee across the river. Turner Ashby and the final expedition to Dam Number 5 rejoined the Confederate army an hour after the town had been seized. That evening Jackson moved opposite Hancock, Maryland, and lobbed artillery rounds into the town, in retaliation, he later wrote, for Union bombardment of Shepherdstown on an earlier occasion.[1]

Union Brig. Gen. Frederick W. Lander hurried to Hancock to confront Jackson. Banks cabled his post commanders to determine if they had rope and boats that the aggressive Lander had requested to enable him to cross the river. At Poolesville, Brig. Gen. Willis A. Gorman, in command for the temporarily absent Stone, put three thousand feet of cable and two flatboats in the canal for Hancock, but ice in the waterway opened leaks in the boats. At Sandy Hook, the post commander placed twelve-hundred feet of cable, three scows, and several skiffs into the canal. The boats had advanced only two miles above Harpers Ferry before they became locked in the ice. An ice breaker was ordered to clear the channel but was slow in arriving due to the rapidly forming ice.[2]

At Hancock, Jackson sent Turner Ashby across the river under a white flag. A letter from the general demanded the surrender of the town under the threat of a cannonade. Lander replied: "Colonel Ashby, give my

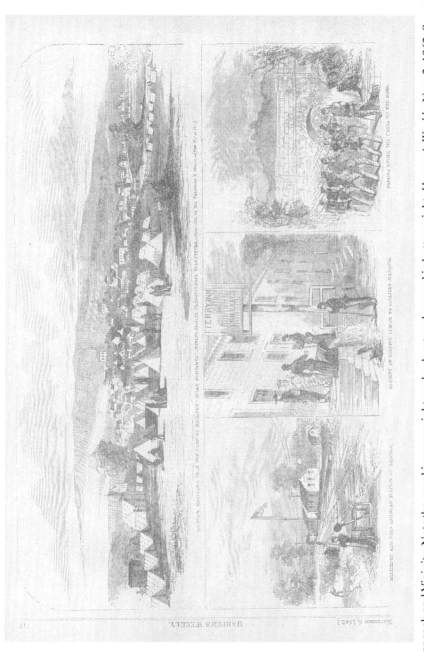

Hancock and Vicinity. Note the canal in upper right, and culvert under canal in bottom right. *Harper's Weekly*, Nov. 2, 1862. Source: author's collection.

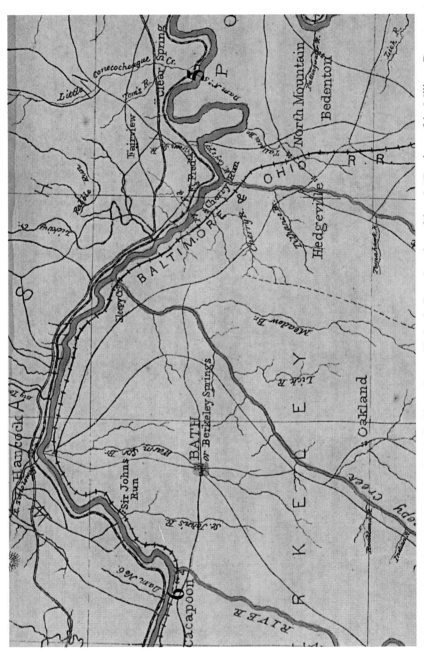

Canal from Dam Number 5 to Dam Number 6. (Bold numbers added to indicate location of dams). "Portions of the Military Departments of Virginia, Washington, Middle & the Susquehanna," (1863). Source: Source: Library of Congress, Geography and Map Division.

compliments to General Jackson and tell him to bombard and be damned!"
After a moment, Lander reconsidered and wrote a more polite refusal. In a
January 5 telegram to Banks, Lander explained that, although outnumbered
and ill-supplied, he intended to fight Jackson because he had 1,000 rifles in
a canal boat that was locked in the ice and he had no transportation to
remove them to safety. After the Confederate commander allowed time for
private citizens to depart, an artillery exchange commenced. Local diarist
James Ripley Smith wrote that about one-hundred rounds were exchanged
before nightfall. The following day Jackson observed that reinforcements
had reached Lander and he decided not to risk his command when the
actual object of his expedition was to free Romney, Virginia, from Federal
occupation. He quietly withdrew and resumed his difficult winter campaign
to Romney.[3]

Union Brig. Gen. Frederick W. Lander. Source: Library of Congress, Prints and
Photographs Division.

Union Brig. Gen. Alpheus S. Williams. Source: Library of Congress, Prints and Photographs Division.

Lander, meanwhile, personally directed the Federal evacuation of Romney and dispersed Confederate outposts at Moorefield and Bloomery Gap in Virginia. On February 20 Lander begged permission to attack Jackson at Winchester. For supply, he explained that the railroad had recently been repaired between Hancock and Cumberland, he had established a ferry service across the Potomac, and he had built a good wagon road along the canal towpath to Cumberland. The pugnacious Lander never got the opportunity to attack Jackson. On March 2 he died from complications of a wound he had received at Edwards Ferry in October of the preceding year.[4]

On January 8 Union Brig. Gen. Alpheus S. Williams arrived at Hancock to relieve Lander. Before long about 6,000 Union soldiers occupied the small canal town, taking up all the free space in homes, churches, and public buildings. When three new regiments arrived without winter tents, Williams assigned some of them to quarters in the field, while he gave the fortunate ones quarters in barns and canal boats that were laid up for the winter. Sick and wounded Union soldiers were housed in local churches and public buildings until, in late March, they were put into canal boats and taken to Williamsport for ground transportation to hospitals in Hagerstown.[5]

Edwards Ferry also heard the frequent boom of the cannon in early 1862. On February 25 Southern artillerists took direct aim at the canal, firing at a canal storehouse and the nearby lock. In early March a round struck a canal boat in the lock at Edwards Ferry.[6]

§

In the election of the preceding year, one-half of Maryland's four-person Commission of Public Works was on the ballot. Two new commissioners were elected, Edward Shriver from the district that comprised the northern counties (from Allegany to Harford) and Frederick Fickey from the Baltimore city district, both of whom were strong Unionists. As was typically the case, a change in the Commission meant a change in the directorate of the canal company.[7]

On January 30, 1862, the Commission of Public Works selected a slate of candidates to present to the stockholders of the C&O Canal Company. Although the commissioners chose Alfred Spates to continue as president, they appointed an entirely new board of directors, one which the *Cumberland Civilian and Telegraph* described as "a strong Directory." Those selected were the Borden Mining Company's resident agent and general superintendent, Albert C. Greene of Allegany County, a Rhode Island native; Lewis Watson and Henry W. Dellinger of Washington County; former company president Lawrence J. Brengle of Frederick County; Charles Abert of Montgomery County; and Joseph Bradley of Washington, D.C. Maryland, which owned a majority of the company's stock, ensured the election of the candidates presented.[8]

The new board met on February 12 and continued to eliminate and consolidate positions to address the company's financial difficulties. The position of treasurer was abolished and the secretary, Walter S. Ringgold, was selected to fill both positions with the aid of a clerk, at a savings of $800. The new board also returned to the traditional practice of hiring six experienced division superintendents to oversee long sections of the canal. The 1860 board had established an administration that consisted of eighteen supervisors who oversaw smaller sections of the canal, some of whom had little or no experience with the waterway. The new board hired Horace Benton as superintendent of the Georgetown Division, which extended from the eastern terminus to Dam Number 2 below Seneca Creek. It offered the Monocacy Division, from Dam Number 2 to Dam Number 3 above Harpers Ferry, to John Cameron. He declined the appointment and George W. Spates, a cousin of Alfred, was appointed in his stead. The board assigned the Antietam Division, from Dam Number 3 to Dam Number 4 below Williamsport, to Levin Benton. It allotted the Williamsport Division, from Dam Number 4 to Dam Number 5 above Williamsport, to Jacob B. Masters. It appointed Thomas Hassett superintendent of the Hancock Division, which extended from Dam Number 5 to Dam Number 6 above Hancock. The board gave the superintendence of the Cumberland Division, from Dam Number 6 to the western terminus, to Lloyd Lowe. The company anticipated savings of $8,000 as a result of the reorganization. In addition, the board selected new toll collectors at Cumberland, Hancock, and Williamsport.[9]

The new division superintendents were indeed experienced canal officials. As late as 1860 Horace Benton, Levin Benton, and Lloyd Lowe were superintendents of the divisions they were subsequently reassigned to. Prior to the war Jacob B. Masters owned a canal transportation company at Williamsport. Thomas Hassett, an Irish immigrant, was a millwright and carpenter who in 1860 had done extensive work to Dam Number 5. George W. Spates had served as supervisor on portions of the Georgetown and Monocacy divisions. In addition to their experience, most of the new superintendents had strong Union credentials, a quality coveted by the new directors. With one exception, these superintendents served throughout the remainder of the war.[10]

§

During the winter and early spring, canal company officials were concerned about the condition of Dam Number 5. Jackson's repeated expeditions against the dam had indeed damaged the structure, although it was not significant enough to completely drain the water impounded behind it. The high water level of the autumn had also masked the damage. When the river dropped, however, officials worried that the dam would not hold back enough water to completely fill the canal. The company had been willing to undertake repairs almost immediately, but Col. Leonard was concerned about the loyalty of the workers while Kenly feared for the men's safety from the Confederates.[11]

In late January a winter freshet swept down the Potomac River Valley that further weakened Dam Number 5 and caused additional damage to the waterway. On January 31 the *Middletown Valley Register* wrote that the flood had caused breaks in the canal at Cumberland, Little Orleans (sixteen miles above Hancock), one just above Hancock, and two below Hancock. At Dam Number 5, the damage inflicted by the Confederates a month earlier was worsened and the abutment on the Virginia side weakened by the high water. At Dam Number 4, a stretch of the bank was washed away and part of the masonry at the stop lock had been undermined and fell into the river. The newspaper estimated that the company needed 25 days to repair the damage at a cost of $12–$15,000, also suggesting that the government should help restore the canal for the benefit of the army.[12]

After the flood waters receded, Banks ordered Colonel Leonard at Williamsport to instruct canal company officials to make immediate repairs and added that the government would be responsible for the wages of the workers. He also ordered Leonard to help the company with the work. As a result, on February 6 Leonard ordered the Twelfth Indiana Infantry at Sharpsburg to assist with the repairs. With the flooded river between them and the Confederates, the Indiana soldiers thought that they had a break from the rigors of winter picket duty. To their indignation, Sgt. William S. Hemphill wrote in his diary, the soldiers were soon "playing at building canal." He explained: "It is deemed necessary by the powers that rule that the men who have been almost constantly on duty, exposed to the stress of winter for four months, should, in addition to guarding this important point, spend the time, which should be devoted to rest, in repairing the damages. 'Put the Hoosiers at it, for they will work,' appears to be the motto."[13]

Other maintenance problems hindered the company during the winter. In late February a large break opened in the towpath of the canal in Montgomery County. The March 4 *Washington Evening Star* wrote that the eighty foot wide breach occurred two miles above Georgetown. Because the guard lock above was not closed immediately, the running water eroded the embankment down to its foundation. Repairs were expected to take one to two weeks.[14]

The bondholders of the canal were nervous as a result of the war-related impediments to navigation and the flood damage of early 1862. On March 6 a banking house wrote to Governor Bradford and suggested that the state lease the canal to a third party who could operate it profitably. The bank blamed the canal's difficulties on political interference and warned that the state may become responsible for the entire debt of the canal. It pointed out that a bill had been introduced in the state legislature that authorized the state to lease the canal, and they urged the governor to support it. Nothing came of the measure, however.[15]

Early in 1862 Spates's dispute with Brig. Gen. Charles M. Thruston came to a head. Over the winter Spates had seen a copy of Thruston's November 18, 1861, letter to the War Department, in which the general had suggested that Spates had been derelict in his duties after the freshet of that month. Thruston had also written that in Spates's absence he had assembled a work force and repaired a section of the canal at his own expense. On January 8 Spates refuted his adversary's claims to Secretary of War Cameron. He wrote that during the time in question, he was busy overseeing repairs between Georgetown and Monocacy so that the army could forward supplies. After these had been completed, he proceeded up the line to Cumberland and insured that any necessary work was completed, and that he—not Thruston—had paid for the repairs. Spates then got to the nub of the matter: "The truth is this man Thruston has become a source of annoyance not only to the management of the canal by meddling with the employees there on—under assumed military authority—but to the people of this section of country generally arising from his old age and dissipated habits." Spates asked that the government relieve Thruston from his duties and revoke his commission.[16]

On the same day Spates wrote to the Postmaster General Blair. His tirade against the general was even less retrained. He informed Blair that all of Thruston's property in Cumberland was rented to the government, and that the general's son, attorney George A. Thruston, had found a profitable business getting people released from military custody through the influence of his father. Spates concluded, "the Thrustons are very strong Union men besides getting rich out of the Government."[17]

Spates's letters ignited a small investigation by the War Department. Copies of the letters were sent directly to General Stone for his account of Thruston's role in repairing the canal the previous year. On February 3 Stone replied that after the freshet of November 1861 he had sent a quartermaster up the canal to purchase forage and determine what damages had occurred to the waterway. Stone wrote that he supposed the quartermaster had requested Thruston to order the repair of the canal under his name.[18]

Thruston's imperious nature and his pecuniary ties to the government spread to the Senate Committee on Military Affairs and the Militia that had the responsibility to confirm his nomination as brigadier general. Thruston soon learned of the complaints against him from the committee chairman, and on February 26 he tendered his resignation to the secretary of war while denying the allegations. The next day Lincoln withdrew the nomination. Adding to his humiliation, in May Thruston was defeated in his bid to be reelected mayor of Cumberland. In the following months, Thruston learned that Alfred Spates had been working behind the scenes to undermine his appointment. In the following year the former general would get his revenge.[19]

In the winter of 1862, yet another general stationed along the Potomac had problems with the War Department. At about midnight on February 8 Stone was arrested upon suspicion of disloyalty. The Joint Committee on the Conduct of the War had their sights on Stone during the winter of 1861–62. The leading members of the committee were Republicans of the radical stripe. In December 1861 the committee began investigating the disastrous Battle of Ball's Bluff. Witnesses were deposed, including those who held grudges against the general. The committee was especially interested in testimony that questioned the loyalty of the Stone, who was a Democrat. The committee was very concerned that Stone had allowed letters to cross the Potomac, had met with Confederates opposite his position, and had allowed the enemy to construct forts without resistance. Stone, who was not allowed to see the transcripts of those who testified against him, explained that McClellan had given him permission to meet with the Confederates under a flag of truce; that the letters he had permitted to cross the river were mostly to and from prisoners of war; and that it was a useless exercise to bombard unmanned earthworks.[20]

Actually, Stone's concern for navigation on the canal contributed to his decision not to contest the construction of Southern earthworks. In a December 23 letter to McClellan, Stone wrote that Confederate Brig. Gen. Daniel H. Hill had threatened to fire on passing canal boats if Stone's men struck the homes of citizens while firing on Hill's entrenchments. In a January 17, 1862 letter to his commanding officer, Hill acknowledged that his threat had prevented Stone from bombarding his fortifications. Stone ordered additional artillery to protect the canal and later testified that he had always intended to bombard the entrenchments once they were manned, but his decision to hold his fire permitted barges of coal and other material to move along the canal.[21]

The removal of Stone was a great loss to the canal company. No other Union general had such a long tenure of service along the Potomac and none was more aware of the importance of the canal to the government and the local economy. His diligent picketing of the river had also denied the Confederates an opportunity to seriously undermine the canal despite explicit orders to do so. The Confederates did indeed have a high opinion of Stone due to his attention to detail and gentlemanly manner, not for sympathy to their cause. On January 17—before the arrest—Hill also wrote: "I can perceive no diminution of Stone's force. He has at least 1,700 men on post every moment from Point of Rocks to Edwards Ferry, or 5,100 on sentry duty. . . . I have never in my life seen such a chain of sentinels. They are evidently very solicitous about the canal."[22]

Meanwhile, Representative Francis Thomas was working behind the scenes to obtain an improved outlet to the river at Georgetown for the canal company. On February 15 he met with new secretary of war Edwin

M. Stanton to discuss the army's seizure of the Potomac Aqueduct. Two days later he asked that the war department appropriate $6,000 so that the company could raise the bridges and market house over the canal in Georgetown by four feet, which would allow the largest boats access to the Rock Creek basin and its tidal lock to the Potomac. Stanton referred Thomas's letter to Quartermaster General Meigs who in turn ordered civil engineer Edward Frost to examine the bridges in question. Frost determined that there were actually eight bridges across the canal that were too low by one to four feet. Four of these were stone bridges. Frost had reviewed a copy of an 1852 report by Charles B. Fisk, former chief engineer of the canal company, who had estimated that the bridges of Georgetown could be raised for $10,000, or for $6,000 if temporary measures were adopted. Fisk's estimate did not include the cost for raising the market house, which Frost thought could be completed for an additional $500. On March 11 Meigs replied to Stanton: "There is no question of the great interests injuriously affected by this condition of the bridges, and interruption of communication across the aqueduct. The removal of these obstructions would lower the price of coal in the city of Washington, and thus be an advantage of the government (which is a consumer at the navy yard) as well as to the people." Meigs also pointed out that Fisk's 1852 estimate could not be completed then, ten years later, for less than twenty-five percent more than the original estimate, or approximately $12,500. Meigs was not and would never become sympathetic toward the plight of the canal. In his letter to Stanton he concluded: "Considering, however, that this interruption, which is a military necessity, is more than compensated to the canal by the protection which the military operations . . . have afforded to other portions of the canal which have been saved from destruction by the Rebels only by the operations of the army of the Potomac, it does not appear to me that the government is under obligations to make other compensation for the use of the aqueduct as a military bridge."[23]

Nearly two months after Thomas first broached the topic with Stanton, the secretary decided that he could not appropriate funds without the approval of Congress. Thomas took up the matter in the House Committee on Military Affairs, of which he was a member, that subsequently passed a motion that requested the secretary of war to submit copies of all papers related to the seizure of the aqueduct, an estimate of when the army would release the structure, and by what route canal boats could proceed to the Washington docks, the Navy Yard, and to Alexandria. On April 21 Stanton submitted the requested documents to the House, where the committee began to craft a piece of legislation that would improve the navigation of the canal through the eastern terminus.[24]

Since his election a year earlier, Thomas had undertaken significant work in Congress to provide protection to both the B&O Railroad and the canal and to promote trade on each carrier. The June 5 *Cumberland Civilian and Telegraph* praised his efforts: "The importance of these two thoroughfares to our people . . . cannot be overrated. . . . But few know or have any idea of the difficulties which had to be surmounted, in order to obtain even a partial protection to these great works, but the energy, coupled with the influence with which Gov. Thomas was able to urge the claims of his constituents, and indeed of the whole State, to have some protection given to our great works, enabled him to succeed, when any other man would have entirely failed."[25]

As spring approached, Alfred Spates wrote a letter to Stanton seeking the removal of restrictions on navigation and the return of company property. He wrote that the revenue of the company had been so reduced that he had used some of his personal resources to make necessary repairs. Since the meddlesome Thruston had resigned his commission and the army had arrested the helpful and sympathetic Stone, Spates saw a leadership void along the canal and offered to fill it himself. He proposed to conduct the affairs of the canal on behalf of the government as an "executive officer."[26]

Spates was also concerned about military inference in the daily operations of the canal. In late February he wrote letters to Banks and McClellan in which he offered to provide his personal assistance to either general in any future military movement along the river. Spates was then attempting to repair the break in the canal near Georgetown, but was stymied because officers of the Quartermaster's Department had begun to repair the canal themselves and would not permit him to attend to the work. On March 8 he informed McClellan's chief of staff that if changes were not made "the canal will be useless in less than six months." In a March 15 letter to Quartermaster General Meigs, Spates wrote: "There can be no question of the fact that those now acting for the Government do not understand the management of the canal." He asked that the army "*concede* the entire management of the canal on the part of the Government to me." He pointed out that the Quartermaster's Department was repairing the breach above Georgetown for a cost of almost $4,000 over eighteen days while the company could have made the repairs in twelve days at a cost of $1,800.[27]

Meigs, in turn, wrote to Col. D. H. Rucker to determine why the army was making repairs to the canal that the company could perform more quickly and at less expense. On March 22 Rucker replied: "I am unable to say who is in charge of the Chesapeake & Ohio Canal, at this time as I do not recollect to have seen any order or notice on the subject." Although Brig. Gen. John Sedgwick had taken command of Stone's division upon the latter's arrest, he was not assigned to supervise the affairs of the canal. In fact, McClellan did not appoint another officer to the post, which caused confusion among the officers who served along the Potomac. Rucker wrote that after the break in the canal near Georgetown, he was unable to ascertain who was responsible to make repairs, and, since the army needed the waterway from Georgetown to Edwards Ferry, he ordered a subordinate to make the repairs and keep an account of the cost. He pointed out that the repairs were delayed by wet weather and the constant passing of military wagons and troops along the towpath.[28]

On March 27 Spates penned another letter to Stanton, again asking the army to release company property and remove boating restrictions. Toward the end of the letter he got to the root of his problem with the army: "Between Washington and Cumberland . . . all officers assume to have power to give orders on the canal, (while no two orders agree,) ignoring all other orders heretofore given, including the order of the Secretary of War . . . of December 6, 1861. The conflict is so great that even now, in many places, the canal is not navigable, neither will permission be given by the officers for the proper repairs to be made." He noted that the government's recent seizure of canal boats had caused the company a loss of at least $1,000 per day. He again requested appointment as an "executive officer" with responsibility for the canal and included a letter of recommendation from Ward Hill Lamon, marshal of the District of Columbia and President

Lincoln's former law partner. The government took no immediate action on Spates's requests.[29]

Over the winter of 1861–1862 the Federal government made plans to complete repairs to the B&O Railroad and reestablish a supply line to the west. The railroad company could not undertake the work, however, unless troops were in position in northwestern Virginia to provide protection to the work crews. Accordingly, in early December 1861 McClellan had sent engineers to Harpers Ferry and Williamsport to evaluate each site as a possible location for a bridge. In doing so, the army continued to view the resources of the canal as open to its confiscation and use. On December 7 engineer officer Babcock recommended that the army build a bridge supported by canal boats near Dam Number 3. He noted that the boats could be locked into the river and anchored in place, and access to the bridge would be via the canal towpath. At Williamsport, Babcock recommended that the army construct a bridge upon two flatboats that were commonly found on the canal. On December 26 Babcock revised his plans. At Harpers Ferry he recommended that the army build a bridge supported by canal boats one hundred yards upriver from the destroyed railroad bridge. He estimated that the 800-foot long bridge would require twenty-five to thirty canal boats. Babcock had also recently met with B&O President John W. Garrett who had offered to bring to Sandy Hook sixty canal boats in his company's possession. Babcock dropped his recommendation for Williamsport and instead suggested that the army use flatboats to expand the ferry service available at the town.[30]

After having received the recommendations of the engineers, General Banks, who was responsible for protecting the work parties, decided to build two bridges at the Ferry. He first planned to build a temporary pontoon bridge over the river that the lead units of his army would cross to take positions to defend the construction of a permanent canal-boat bridge. The second bridge was necessary because the pontoon bridge was not large enough to allow teams to draw artillery and supply wagons across, although the soldiers could initially draw them across by hand. After both bridges were built the army would be in position to defend the reconstruction of the railroad bridge, expected to take two weeks to complete.[31]

On February 7 Babcock had ordered Williamsport Division Superintendent Masters to prepare his division for boating—which was still disabled following the winter freshet—so that the canal boats intended for the bridge at Harpers Ferry could pass. Masters restored the division in ten days for boats drawing no more than four feet of water, which was sufficient to pass the empty boats to Sandy Hook. Masters later wrote that the army had promised to pay for the repairs but had moved away before it had done so.[32]

McClellan arrived at Sandy Hook to oversee the construction of the bridges and consult with Banks. On February 26 he informed Stanton that the pontoon bridge had been "splendidly" constructed by the engineers, and that 8,500 infantry, eighteen guns, and two squadrons of cavalry had crossed and occupied Bolivar Heights, immediately west of Harpers Ferry, and Loudoun Heights, just east of the Shenandoah River, while additional troops occupied Maryland Heights. Other units were expected to cross the next day, when the engineers would begin construction of the canal-boat bridge.[33]

The following day McClellan immediately ran into problems. He explained: "Next morning the attempt was made to pass the canal-boats through the lift-lock, in order to commence at once the construction of a permanent bridge. It was then found for the first time that the lock was too small to permit the passage of boats, it having been built for a class of boats running on the Shenandoah Canal, and too narrow by some four or six inches for the canal-boats. . . . I thus suddenly found myself unable to build the permanent bridge." The news did not sit well with the Lincoln administration. Stanton asked the general if he could make the lock large enough to accommodate the boats, to which McClellan replied that the railroad bridge could be repaired in less time than it would take to enlarge the lock. Work soon began on the railroad bridge, which was completed on March 18, and by the end of the month traffic resumed on the main stem of the B&O Railroad. To supply the commands defending the work parties, the army established a supply line via the canal to Sandy Hook, then across the Potomac to a mill in the mouth of the Shenandoah River. Meanwhile, a wisecrack quickly passed through the administrative departments of government. It was said that McClellan's plan to first build a canal-boat bridge had died of "lock-jaw."[34]

Following the clash of the ironclads at Hampton Roads, Virginia, in March 1862, the Federal government looked to the resources of the C&O Canal to help defend the capital. On March 8, 1862, the new Confederate ironclad *Merrimack* (renamed the C.S.S. *Virginia*) emerged from dry dock, and in the ensuing battle she damaged and disabled three wooden ships of the U.S. Navy. The next morning the news reached Washington and threw Lincoln's cabinet into a panic. Stanton was particularly alarmed. He feared that the *Virginia* would destroy every ship in the U.S. fleet, steam up the Potomac and bombard Washington and disperse the government. She might then move up the coast and ransom New York and Boston. Some Federal officials wondered if the ironclad could ascend the Potomac given the added weight of the iron plating, but no one knew the ship's draft of water. Capt. John. A. Dahlgren, the commandant of the Washington Navy Yard, suggested that the government block the channel of the Potomac River as a precaution. A meeting of cabinet and military officials followed. Gideon Welles, the secretary of the navy, believed that the heavy armor of the *Virginia* would prevent her from passing over Kettle Bottom Shoals, a five-mile length of shallow water in the lower Potomac near the mouth of the Wicomico River that forms the boundary between Maryland's Charles and St. Mary's counties. After Welles left the meeting, and at the insistence of Stanton, it was agreed to proceed with measures to obstruct the channel of the river. McClellan, Dahlgren, and Meigs were charged with the task. Dahlgren was given the chore of determining where to place the obstructions and to acquire the tugs. Meigs was responsibile for obtaining the vessels that the Navy would scuttle in the river. He looked to the Chesapeake and Ohio Canal.[35]

The army had already acquired a small fleet of fifty-nine canal boats collected by the quartermaster's department for the abandoned canal-boat bridge project at Harpers Ferry. Meigs had these boats drawn to Georgetown and directed the army to load them with stone. He also ordered quartermasters on the upper Potomac to seize another lot of boats, although it is likely these boats were obtained to supplement McClellan's transportation for his pending offensive. On March 10 a canal company official at Williamsport reported that one hundred-three empty canal boats had passed the town in the control of military authorities who would not accept waybills.[36]

Dahlgren consulted with river pilots at the Navy Yard and determined that a vessel drawing twenty-two feet of water could pass up the Potomac to within one hundred yards of the U.S. Arsenal situated at the confluence of the Potomac and the Eastern Branch (Anacostia) rivers, only about three miles from the U.S. Capitol. He recommended that the army prepare heavy artillery at points along the lower Potomac, and that they prepare to scuttle canal boats at Kettle Bottom Shoals, below Smith's Point, and at Mattawoman Creek, the latter two sites located in Charles County, Maryland. By the evening of March 9 two steam tugs, each with eight ballasted canal boats in tow, were prepared to depart. Then early on March 10 Gideon Welles ordered Dahlgren to cease all preparations. Stanton had gone over Welles's head by insisting that the navy obstruct the river. Only recently had the Confederates withdrawn their batteries from the south shore of the river. Welles was reluctant to inhibit navigation on the river again, especially since the government had learned that the Federal ironclad *Monitor* had arrived at Hampton Roads on March 9 and fought the *Virginia* to a draw. Welles had a conference with Lincoln and it was agreed that the preparations would continue, but that no obstruction would be placed in the river until it was known with certainty that the ironclad was approaching the Potomac. In total, thirty-one canal boats were transported to the lower Potomac to await orders, all but one ballasted with plaster or stone.[37]

Later that spring, after the *Monitor* had neutralized the *Virginia*, Lincoln noted the long line of canal boats moored in the river at Georgetown, without weapons or means of propulsion. He playfully referred to them as "Stanton's Navy" and joked that the boats were "as useless as the paps of a man to a suckling child."[38]

With the southern bank of the Potomac freed of the Confederates and the C.S.S. *Virginia* confined to Norfolk harbor, on March 17 McClellan's long anticipated campaign against Richmond via the York-James Peninsula got underway. Later that year Brig. Gen. Steward Van Vliet, McClellan's quartermaster, wrote that of the 405 vessels used to transport the army, ninety were barges. Most likely about one-half of the barges were canal boats from the C&O Canal. Of the 162 boats seized by the army from the canal, on March 24 Ringgold noted that only about one-half had been sent "down the river." Of these approximately 81 boats sent to the lower Potomac, 31 were later located at Liverpool Point in Charles County for blockading the Potomac, leaving about 50 that likely were used to transport McClellan's army to the Peninsula. Van Vliet and other officers made numerous references to the canal boats in the transport fleet. The chief commissary officer later reported that his department used 41 barges and canal boats. Engineering material, mortars, and ordnance were also shipped in canal boats. The army devised a means to transport artillery and teams by lashing two canal boats together at a distance of twelve feet apart and then placing planks over both boats to create a deck 40 feet wide and 45 feet long, large enough to transport a battery of artillery while drawing only four feet of water. At high tide the boats were run ashore and a bridge was built to solid ground. Canal boats were used to build wharves by running barges and canal boats ashore at high water and then planking them over. Many of the boats were kept on the Peninsula until August 26, when the last of the army was withdrawn. Records show that at least some canal boats on the Peninsula were burned by the retreating Union forces to prevent them from falling into Confederate hands.[39]

To an undetermined degree, the canal was utilized to supply and provision McClellan's army on the Peninsula. With the opening of the entire canal in mid-April quartermaster Flagg contracted with canal boatmen to forward grain and forage from western Maryland to Georgetown. The canal boats locked into the river at Georgetown and were towed by tugs to Alexandria, where the material was forwarded to the Peninsula.[40]

The seizure of canal boats was a source of great frustration to the canal company. About 250 boats plied the waterway during the typical boating season and the government had seized sixty-five percent of them. With the mining companies ready to ship coal, on March 20 Director Greene wrote to the canal company office to determine what Spates was doing to obtain the release of the boats. Ringgold replied that the president was working on the problem, but the government had given no assurances that it would release them. On April 1 Greene noted that the number of canal boats available to the coal companies had "sadly diminished," but that with "uninterrupted navigation" the canal company might still earn its largest revenue ever from the coal trade.[41]

The company continued to have trouble with the Federal army stationed along the canal. In March the Cumberland Division superintendent reported that government teamsters had damaged a canal wall and had removed the railings from the Evitts Creek Aqueduct to allow wagons to pass. In addition, two pivot bridges near Cumberland were damaged by Union troops. During the same month the Monocacy Division superintendent wrote that tools from the carpenter's and blacksmith's shops had been stolen, and he could only locate one company repair scow, which the army was using as a ferry on the river.[42]

With their claim against the government from November 1861 still unsettled, in the spring the company began to gather information with which to make a further claim for unpaid tolls and damages to the waterway from September 1861 to April 1862. On February 3, 1862, Brig. Gen. Alpheus S. Williams had appointed a board of survey to evaluate claims against the government that resulted from the Federal occupation of Hancock the previous month. The canal company had submitted a $198.50 claim, which was the value of equipment and building material seized or destroyed by Federal troops stationed at Dam Number 6. In denying the claim, the board explained that the government's use of the canal indirectly compensated the company for the damage. This decision foreshadowed all of the company's future dealing with the government over its war loses.[43]

On April 15 Spates sent a new claim to Secretary Stanton with an itemized list of damages and losses that totaled $75,391.96. The claim included $4,000 for the use of and damage inflicted to fourteen lock houses and $8,700 for the destruction of three company houses, three houseboats, ten scows, and three ice boats. The company claimed $19,000 for the difference between tolls collected in March and April 1862 and the same months of previous year, resulting from "the seizure and detention of the boats by the United States for army purposes." The largest item, totaling $43,691.96, was for the difference between tolls collected over the last four months of 1861 and those collected over the same period of 1860. The company attributed the loss in revenue to "belligerent operations and the restrictions imposed by the officers of the United States army on the trade of the canal." As with the previous claim, the government took no immediate action on new one.[44]

In the early spring, labor difficulties also threatened the resumption of navigation. On April 7 Greene informed the company office that there were rumors of a strike amongst the boatmen. He added: "All the Coal Companies are willing to pay an advance on previous rates, but the demands of the boatmen . . . are altogether inadmissible – we could not compete with the Penna. Coals. The Penn. RR Co. has reduced their charges upon Broad Top 30 [cents] per ton expressly to head off Maryland coal." Several days later, however, Greene wrote that the misunderstanding with the boatmen had been cleared up. Because both the B&O Railroad and the canal had been disabled for much of the previous twelve months, many miners were in a desperate condition and needed to resume work.[45]

By early April western Maryland's coal companies were anxious to ship coal, although the canal company was still struggling to complete repairs caused by the freshet of the past winter, especially at Dam Number 5 and the guard bank at Dam Number 4. On April 11 Greene informed the company office that the small number of canal boats was "really alarming." He proposed that the Maryland Commission of Public Works, Governor Bradford, and the canal company make a unified effort to seek the release of the canal boats from Secretary Stanton, especially since many of the boats were moored along the river at Georgetown. He wrote: "The want of them [the boats] is ruin, not only to the Canal Co., but to the poor laborers of this county [Allegany] who have been nearly a year out of work." He wrote that the Pennsylvania coal companies were "moving heaven and earth" to maintain and expand the coal trade they had acquired the previous summer when both the B&O and C&O were in disrepair. At the canal company's lowest point during the war, Greene warned: "The very existence of the Canal is trembling in the balance. The boats in Govt. hands number nearly, if not greater, *one hundred* – and they *cannot possibly* be replaced this season. Neither the capital nor the courage to undertake it can be found. I cannot comprehend why the authorities at Washington continue to hold the boats so persistently when they appear to have absolutely *no* use for them. If the boats were actually and indispensibly [sic] necessary to the Govt. we should submit, but it does not appear that anything stronger than red tape, or utter indifference keep them where they are." He concluded that if the facts were presented to Stanton, the government would surely release the boats, "to retain them would look as if the Govt. itself had joined the Pennsylvania conspirators to crush out and destroy the Maryland coal trade at one blow."[46]

The company sought aid in Congress from Francis Thomas. Alfred Spates sent him an itemized list of fifty-nine canal boats that the army had seized in February, identifying the boat name, owner, date seized, value of the boat and furniture, and where the boats were last located. There is no record of a similar list of the one hundred and three boats that the army had seized in March.[47]

U.S. Representative, Francis "Frank" Thomas. Source: Library of Congress, Prints and Photographs Division.

Albert C. Greene, C&O Canal Director and Borden Mining Company Agent and Resident Superintendent. Source: *History of Western Maryland, vol. 1*, by J. Thomas Scharf (c1882).

In mid-April Spates's efforts to obtain release of company property through the quartermaster's department began to bear fruit. On April 15 Meigs, concerned about the stagnant canal trade and its affect on military supply, advised President Lincoln that no public interest would be harmed by surrendering the idle boats. He also recommended that the army pay for any boats that the army was unable to return as well as those that had been destroyed. Stanton concurred with Meig's recommendation and issued an order that released all but thirty-six boats. On April 16 the canal company received informal word that the government would surrender immediately twenty-four boats held at Georgetown. Some forty to fifty boats had already been released, but army officers had again requisitioned them to transport stores to Alexandria. The company was assured that these would be unloaded and released "at once."[48]

Greene, however, was uncertain that the government would give up the boats. On April 19 he informed Ringgold: "I shall only be satisfied when I see them [the boats] arriving at Cumberland. I reason this way–the Govt. must have had some object in seizing the boats in the first place, but as the boats (or the far greater part of them) have never been used at all, it is difficult to see what reason exists for their present release that has not existed all along when they refused to do it." Greene's cynicism was well founded. The government only released about fifty of the approximately one hundred-sixty canal boats that it had seized.[49]

The canal boats that Stanton had retained were soon transported down the Potomac. With the retreat of the Confederates from their advanced positions in northern Virginia, Union forces moved into the interior of Virginia. By April 20 McDowell's force reached Falmouth, opposite Fredericksburg, but found that southern troops had destroyed the bridges across the Rappahannock River. In late April the Navy transported about forty canal boats down the Potomac and up the Rappahannock to Fredericksburg. In early May the army converted the boats into a bridge across the Rappahannock. In late June, however, a tremendous storm broke up and carried away the canal-boat bridge.[50]

Stanton's April 21 General Orders No. 44 formally ordered military officials to release the canal company's boats. It also went a long way toward removing the influence of army officers in the day-to-day affairs of the canal, as Spates had long requested:

All the lock-houses, boats, scows, and other property belonging to the Chesapeake and Ohio Canal Company on the line of said canal, now held, used, or occupied by the United States officers or troops, will be forthwith given up and restored to the president of the said company. All officers of the Army will respect Alfred Spates, esq., as president of the said company, and are hereby prohibited from interfering in any manner with him in the management of the canal; but are directed to give him such aid and assistance as is consistent with the good of the service in keeping it in repair and

Bridge over the Rappahannock River, made from boats seized from the C&O Canal. Courtesy of Marc and Beth Storch.

removing all restrictions which have been imposed upon the boats navigating the said canal. The president of the said canal company is authorized to give all passes that may be required to be used on the canal, subject to the approval of the commander of the district.[51]

The May 1 *Cumberland Civilian and Telegraph* noted that Stanton's order was "highly complimentary" to Alfred Spates. It added: "We may now expect the Canal interests to revive. As there must be a great scarcity throughout the country of that kind of Coal furnished by this region."[52]

On April 8 Williamsport Division Superintendent Jacob B. Masters reminded the company of the condition of Dam Number 5. High water and other hindrances to navigation had distracted the company from the damage to the dam that the Confederates had inflicted in the winter, which was exacerbated by flooding. Masters explained that there were several ways that the repairs could be made, including building on the foundation of the old cribs or by closing the space between the partially completed stone dam and the abutment of the old dam. He suggested that the company begin to acquire the necessary building material. On May 5 the company board met and authorized Alfred Spates to borrow up to $2,000 toward the repair of the structure. Later in the month the president visited the dam and purchased timber for the work. Upon inspection of the structure, Spates discovered that the abutment of the dam on the Virginia side was in such bad condition that it needed to be rebuilt entirely. The company had constructed the abutment in November 1860 to serve temporarily after a freshet had washed out the old structure. Additional freshets and the Confederate attempts to destroy the dam forced the company to replace it sooner than their resources would have permitted.[53]

In late May former company general superintendent Andrew K Stake and his business partner William Simms proposed to build a stone abutment at Dam Number 5 by September 1 for $12,000. They also offered put in an additional crib to repair the damage made by the Confederates, and to construct a culvert to carry water to Colston's Mill on the Virginia shore. The canal company board subsequently approved the contract and directed Spates to give his personal supervision to the work.[54]

As the canal company completed repairs and opened for navigation in mid-April, the weather again intervened. At first the company watched anxiously as the water in the canal dropped due to the leaky dams, but a spring freshet followed and halted boating. Frustration reigned in the mining region and along the canal. The articulate Greene expressed it best in an April 29 letter to Ringgold:

> The concurrence of circumstances against the resumption of Canal Trade this Spring are positively infernal. Not only is the Canal deprived of Revenue but the [coal] trade itself is imperilled [sic] by these untoward events. I have great fears that the largest and most important buyers of coal will despair of getting any thing from us this year – and contract with the Broad Top people, who are straining everything to retain their footing in market, acquired last year. . . . Rely upon it—very much depends upon our being able to deliver coal early in May.[55]

May 1862 closed with Banks's troops retreating across the Potomac at Williamsport pursued by Jackson. Lincoln, who feared that Jackson might cross the river and threaten Washington, ordered Maj. Gen. John C. Fremont's army to converge on Jackson from the west, a portion of McDowell's army to threaten Jackson from the east, and Banks to resume the offensive from the north. Jackson was forced to beat a hasty retreat away from the Potomac to avoid the converging armies, which may have saved the canal and railroad from his designs.[56]

§

The first months of 1862 constituted one of the lowest periods in the history of the canal company. Navigation that usually resumed in early March was delayed by about six weeks due to a serious February flood that caused significant damage that the company did not have resources to repair, except with stop-gap, temporary measures. High water in April interrupted the already late opening of the canal. Additionally, the seizure of over one-half of the boats plying the canal and the removal of the Potomac Aqueduct as an outlet also significantly limited trade.

Through May 1862 the collection of tolls was greatly reduced. Although the company had endeavored to keep the canal, or portions of it, open during the winter using small steamers to break the ice, the weather

Williamsport in June 1862 as Banks prepares to cross the Potomac. Note the canal boat in middle right. *Frank Leslie's Illustrated Newspaper*, July 5, 1862. Source: author's collection.

and maintenance problems permitted only limited boating. The president and board of directors noted that tolls collected through the end of May 1862 totaled only $18,500, less than one month's usual tally. Coal shipped during this period totaled only about 25,260 tons.[57]

There were several reasons for optimism, however. The government had returned about fifty canal boats and removed the restrictions that had hampered navigation. It had also officially acknowledged Spates as the president of the canal, ordered the army not to interfere with his duties, and directed the troops to assist him. The company noted that about 150 boats were available, and adding in new boats being built, 30,000 tons of coal could be shipped monthly with uninterrupted navigation. The Potomac River was also largely free of the Confederates; McClellan had the largest southern force tied up defending Richmond while parts of two separate Union armies had forced Jackson to flee from the river and hoped to trap and destroy his army in the Shenandoah Valley.[58]

Jackson would slip through the trap, however, and before the summer was over the Confederates would come back to the Potomac in force.

CHAPTER 4

THINGS ARE IN AN AWFUL CONDITION:
JUNE–DECEMBER 1862

In June 1862 the canal company was beset with additional weather-related problems. The third freshet of the year struck early in the month and caused breaks in both the Williamsport and Antietam divisions. On the latter division a repair scow was swept through a breach and broke up in the river. Company officials initially reported that it would take two to three weeks to restore navigation, but the work lagged into mid-summer.[1]

The heavy rains of early spring affected the entire mid-Atlantic region, including the Pennsylvania coal regions, flooding mines and washing out railroad structures. On June 12 Albert C. Greene wrote Ringgold that the flood damage in Pennsylvania had caused coal buyers to reconsider Cumberland Coal. He urged the canal company to expedite repairs and recommended that Spates oversee the work in person so that he could inspire the men with "some portion of his own exuberant energy." The high water had also damaged the B&O's bridge over the Potomac at Harpers Ferry again. Greene saw an opportunity for the canal to be the lone supplier of Cumberland Coal for a time.[2]

The repair work continued to languish, however. After a spring of limited boating, following a year of reduced navigation, the canal company was bereft of resources and unable to obtain credit. On June 21 Greene wrote Ringgold that "it is a thousand pities that we are not in condition to meet the demand." In response to its lack of cash, on June 26 the company suspended the acceptance of toll certificates. Seeing the opportunity to supply coal without competition slipping away, western Maryland's mining companies sent a large number of laborers down the canal to assist the company in repairing breaks in the line.[3]

Despite the late spring freshet, in the early summer the rains stopped abruptly. Several of the company's river dams were not tight enough to hold back substantial volumes of water, and before long the water level in the canal began to drop. In July a significant leak was discovered in Dam Number 6 above Hancock, which helped account for the low water on that division. Superintendent Thomas Hassett had, however, been ordered to help with the repairs at Dam Number 5 on the Williamsport Division—twenty-seven miles away—when the leak was discovered. On July 19 he wrote Ringgold that if he had been permitted to attend to his own division, the leak at Dam Number 6 might never have occurred. Additionally, his laborers at Dam Number 5 had quit work because they were owed one month's pay. The superintendent wrote that if the company would not send him money to pay his workers, he intended to quit as well. In early August Hassett was overseeing the work at Dam Number 6 and was having trouble obtaining laborers. The board had decided that workers must be obtained "at any price," and Greene urged him to hire men from the idle boat crews in the vicinity.[4]

Boating on the canal was greatly reduced in both June and July. In the former month the company collected less than $4,000 in tolls and in the latter month just over $7,000. Through the first week of June, only about 33,000 tons of coal had been shipped on the canal for the entire season, which would have been a good month's business before the war. The poor condition of the canal—as a result of floods, droughts, and inadequate maintenance—were mostly to blame, but shippers were also becoming weary of sending articles over the canal after more than a year of constantly interrupted navigation.[5]

On August 14 the *Civilian and Telegraph* reported that the water in the canal was so low that a boat could only transport one-half of its capacity. If there was no significant rain, the newspaper predicted that navigation would be suspended. The company's steam pump at the mouth of South Branch, which pumped river water into the canal in lieu of Dam Number 7, was also "entirely out of order." On August 11 Greene summed up eight months of frustration: "There has been no real through navigation on the canal this year—that is, no boat, I believe has been able to make a round trip without detention."[6]

Poor management also caused some of the problems. On 5 May the board of directors had passed a resolution that required the division superintendents to inform the company clerk and the toll collectors at Georgetown and Cumberland of any stoppage in navigation, the cause of the delay, and when boating would likely be resumed. On August 12 Greene complained to Ringgold that the superintendents were not promptly reporting suspensions in navigation, which resulted in the coal companies and the railroads having crews on duty at Cumberland awaiting the arrival of boats that never appeared. He also wrote that the superintendents were not doing repair and maintenance chores to the canal while boating was suspended. Greene warned: "One thing is *certain*, unless there is a speedy reform in the management of the Canal, *I* will be out of it. I have no idea of being disgraced by mismanagement I am powerless to remedy." He suggested that the board summon the superintendents to Georgetown to answer for their conduct.[7]

Army officers stationed along the river also began to complain about the condition of the waterway. On August 28 Capt. Robert C. Bamford, post commander at Point of Rocks, informed the company that sediment had accumulated in the canal, two bridges needed repair, and the towpath itself was in need of work. He also wrote that Monocacy Division Superintendent George Spates was using carpenters as laborers, but paying them carpenters' wages. The absence of a general superintendent and engineer almost certainly contributed to maintenance and repair problems on the canal. The general superintendent had responsibility to arrange for and oversee the repairs of the entire canal, guided by the engineer's recommendations. For financial reasons, in August 1861 the positions of engineer and general superintendent were rolled into the office of the president. It seems that Alfred Spates could not attend to his duties as president and provide as much oversight to the division superintendents as was needed. In addition, available records suggest that he had no engineering experience. In the absence of direct oversight, some of the division superintendents, particularly his cousin George Spates, were lax in carrying out their responsibilities. The poor physical condition of the canal resulting from long-term financial difficulties, repeated assaults by high water and droughts, and damage from military operations, were equally to blame, however.[8]

Bamford also complained that George Spates employed men who were southern sympathizers. He wrote that several employees on the division were "beyond all doubt disloyal, one to my certain knowledge, & I do not feel *safe* to have him or such other men either passing through the lines." Bamford was also suspicious of two lockkeepers and another employee. He asked the company to remove the superintendent "in order to clear up the disloyal element on the canal."[9]

To conduct business in a border state like Maryland, the canal company had to confront the likelihood that some of its employees were sympathetic to the South. On April 9 the B&O Railroad, operating in Maryland as well, officially resolved not to employ persons of known disloyalty. Although the canal company did not make a similar announcement in the spring, on April 4 a former supervisor had accused the new board of replacing him because he was a Democrat. As a result of the charges made by Bamford, however, on September 4 Ringgold replied: "It is the earnest desire as it is the duty of the Board to see that no disloyal person is employed in any part of the work under their charge." Instead of dismissing George Spates, the company asked Bamford to provide "distinct charges" of disloyalty and supply the names of suspicious employees and witnesses who could verify treasonous statements. Because of the subsequent Confederate invasion of Maryland, Bamford did not respond to Ringgold's request and George Spates remained in his post.[10]

Meanwhile in Congress, Francis Thomas and the Committee on Military Affairs crafted a bill, House Resolution No. 542, "A bill for the relief of the Chesapeake and Ohio Canal Company," to pay for raising the bridges and market house over the canal through Georgetown. On June 23 the bill was approved by the committee and referred to the Committee of the Whole House on the State of the Union. The bill encountered some difficulty, but was not without support. On July 12 Representative Abraham B. Olin of New York stated that although the army's seizure of the aqueduct was a military necessity, the government should pay for raising the bridges and market house because it had seized private property. He suggested another reason why he supported the bill: "I understand that really the whole expenditure would benefit the Government as much, at least, as it would the canal company, by affording facilities for the transportation of Government supplies, especially coal, of which the Government is a very large consumer at the navy-yard." The bill wound its way slowly through the House, but when the session ended it still had not passed.[11]

On August 3 McClellan's army, which Lee had pushed around the Peninsula and away from Richmond, was withdrawn to Washington. The last Federal troops left Fort Monroe at the tip of the Peninsula on August 26. The men were transported to Aquia Creek and Alexandria to aid Maj. Gen. John Pope's newly created Army of Virginia. On August 30 Pope was defeated at the Second Battle of Bull Run. The demoralized Union armies then returned to the defenses of Washington. With the withdrawal of McClellan's army from the Peninsula and the defeat of Pope, Lee went on the offensive and took his men into Maryland. In order to meet the crisis, Lincoln turned to McClellan, who despite his deficiencies on the battlefield, was a superb organizer and still held the allegiance of the troops. McClellan immediately began melding the two Federal armies. The Chesapeake and Ohio Canal would play an important role in the ensuing campaign. In fact, the destruction of Federal supply lines was a secondary objective of the Confederate invasion.[12]

§

From September 1 the Confederates were observed in large numbers on the southern bank of the Potomac near Edwards Ferry, from which location their artillery fired on passing canal boats. McClellan, drawing on his experience along the river in 1861, wrote: "The shelling of the canal-boats is an old amusement of the rebels; it is probably a pretty strong proof that they do not intend to cross at Edwards Ferry." McClellan was right on that point—on September 4 the main body of the Confederate force crossed the river at Whites Ford, located about three miles below the Monocacy River in Montgomery County, Maryland. Scattered Confederate units also crossed the Potomac at a number of higher fords.[13]

After crossing the Potomac at Whites Ford, the Confederates had to find a way to get the army across the canal. While some of the men passed through a culvert under the canal, the southern soldiers also built a bridge across a nearby lock to pass their wagons. Brig. Gen. Daniel H. Hill wrote that after his men had crossed the river on the fourth, that evening and the next day were spent in destroying a lock and tearing out the banks of the canal, not only to damage the waterway, but to pass their artillery and wagons without having to build additional bridges. His men destroyed the twenty foot-long culvert over the Little Monocacy River. Lockkeeper Thomas Walter tried to talk Hill out of blowing up Lock Number 27 and the nearby Monocacy Aqueduct. Nevertheless, the Confederates damaged the lock and would have destroyed the aqueduct, but were unable, Hill wrote, "for the want of powder and tools." The Confederates also intercepted a number of boats coming down the waterway, their captains entirely ignorant of the invasion. Col. John B. Gordon's men seized a boat loaded with flour and bacon. Others bought a boatload of melons for Confederate script, which the men shared with General Jackson and his staff who proceeded to have a picnic along the canal.[14]

With the invasion of Maryland underway, McClellan expressed concern for the Federal garrison at Harpers Ferry, commanded by Col. Dixon S. Miles. If the Confederates moved between it and the Army of the Potomac in Washington, Miles's command would be isolated with no prospect of being reinforced. Maj. Gen. Henry W. Halleck, who replaced McClellan as general-in-chief of the army on July 23, insisted that Miles defend the post. As a result, Miles sat helplessly as the Confederates began to cross the river between him and McClellan's army. On September 6 the colonel ordered a subordinate at Berlin to hold out as long as possible and then fall back to Sandy Hook. He added: "Make the captains of the canal-boats bring their boats back to this place [Sandy Hook] before the enemy should get them and burn them. If they are loaded with grain (corn and oats) have them brought back anyhow; we want it."[15]

By September 7 all of Lee's army had crossed the Potomac. On September 11 a newspaper correspondent visited the river where the Confederates had crossed:

> The line of the Chesapeake and Ohio Canal, for the distance of twelve miles, presents a scene of desolation which sufficiently attests the malignity of the Rebels and their emissaries. Commencing five miles below Monocacy, continuing up a mile beyond the Point of Rocks, in crossing, they tapped the canal at five different places.

Several flood-gates were hewn to pieces, and from the hights [sic] above large boulders of rocks were dislodged and thrown into the basin. An attempt was made to blow up the beautiful aqueduct at Monocacy, but it did not succeed. For the present, from 20 to 25 miles of the canal are rendered useless. It will take considerable time to repair the damages, and in the mean time boats can proceed only between Georgetown and Seneca. . . . The canal basin is perfectly dry in many places between those points, and where the water remains it is not more than a foot deep.

The correspondent also related that the Confederates had rolled the carcasses of dead horses into the canal and cut trees so that they fell across the waterway. On September 6 General Lee informed Jefferson Davis that canal navigation had been stopped and that his army would endeavor to break the Baltimore and Ohio Railroad.[16]

The port of Georgetown, although distant from the path of the invaders, almost immediately felt the closure of the canal. On September 12 the *Washington Evening Star* reported that "canal navigation is suspended beyond a point twenty miles from here—that is, at Seneca Dam. From that point up, for from thirty to forty miles, there is no water in the canal. . . . This suspension of navigation with the up country of course cuts off arrivals of flour and grain from the fine grain-growing country in Maryland and Virginia lying near the Potomac. The market here, therefore, is very unsettled." As a result, supplies of various grains were limited and prices had begun to rise. The newspaper added that the coal trade was cut off entirely and might remain so for the rest of the year.[17]

The Confederates moved to Frederick and encamped around the town while Lee devised his plans. On September 9 he ordered Brig. Gen. John G. Walker to return to the mouth of the Monocacy River and destroy the aqueduct. Walker's command arrived at the Monocacy in the evening of the same day and drove away Federal pickets who had been posted at the aqueduct by Miles. The sturdy aqueduct proved to be a more stubborn foe than Miles's men. Walker wrote: "The attempted work of destruction began, but [so] admirably was the aqueduct constructed and cemented that it was found to be virtually a solid mass of granite. Not a seam or crevice could be discovered in which to insert the point of a crow-bar, and the only

SEPTEMBER 14, 1861.]

HARPER'S WEEKLY.

583

AQUEDUCT OF THE CHESAPEAKE AND OHIO CANAL, AT THE MOUTH OF THE MONOCACY—PRESENT POSITION OF GENERAL BANKS'S ARMY.

The Monocacy Aqueduct survived a number of Confederate attempts to destroy it. *Harper's Weekly*, Sept. 14, 1861. Source: author's collection.

resource was blasting. But the drills furnished to my engineer were too dull and the granite too hard." His mission a failure, Walker planned to rejoin Lee. Before he could do so he received orders from the general to cooperate with Jackson in the capture of Harpers Ferry.[18]

Lee's famous Special Order No. 191 divided his army into a number of parts, which would have made it vulnerable if the Union Army were in position to attack. While the main Confederate army was to proceed toward Hagerstown, Maj. Gen. James P. Longstreet's Corps was to halt at Boonsboro, with Walker's division to cross the Potomac at Point of Rocks, and the divisions commanded by Maj. Gen. Lafayette McLaws and Maj. Gen. Richard H. Anderson detached to Maryland Heights. Jackson was directed to cross back into Virginia near Sharpsburg, destroy the B&O Railroad at Martinsburg, then move toward Harpers Ferry from the west. He would have overall command of the divisions of Walker, McLaws, and Anderson, all of whom would move to surround the Federal garrison at Harpers Ferry. Maj. Gen. Daniel Harvey Hill was detached from Jackson's Corps to serve as the army's rear guard at Boonsboro.[19]

By September 13 McLaw's men had taken Maryland Heights and occupied Sandy Hook. The next day he moved artillery atop the mountain and joined in the artillery bombardment of Harpers Ferry. Walker threatened the town from Loudoun Heights, while Jackson threatened it from the west. On September 15 the garrison at Harpers Ferry surrendered, although 1,500 Federal cavalrymen had escaped across a pontoon bridge in the night. During the movements against Harpers Ferry, the Confederates cut the canal at Knoxville and Weverton, three and two miles below Harpers Ferry respectively, and also damaged a lock at the latter site.[20]

Meanwhile, McClellan led his army from Washington to meet the invasion and was fortuitous enough to find a copy of Lee's plans. Discovering that his adversary's army was widely dispersed, McClellan moved swiftly toward the mountain passes. On September 14 the Union army forced the Confederates from the passes in the Battle of South Mountain. The following day, as the Union garrison at Harpers Ferry surrendered to Jackson, McClellan's army advanced into Washington County.

On September 17 the bloody Battle of Antietam was fought to a tactical draw. To help repel the invasion, Pennsylvania Governor Andrew G. Curtin sent state militia to Maryland. In the heat of battle, McClellan ordered militia cavalry units to Williamsport to prepare the bridge over the canal for destruction. Union and Confederate riflemen had skirmished across the river there, and destroying the bridge would make it more difficult for Lee to send reinforcements across at Williamsport that might subsequently attack the Union army from the flank or rear. The militia piled hay and fence rails on the bridge and awaited orders to strike the match. A number of local farmers pleaded with the officers not to burn the bridge because without it they would have no access to their fields between the river and canal. Before long, the order to burn the bridge arrived and the structure was set aflame. The troops also attempted to destroy the Conococheague Aqueduct at Williamsport, perhaps to deny the Confederates access to a ford above it. Like its sister aqueduct over the Monocacy, the structure stood up to the assault and suffered only minor damages. The militia also burned a number of canal boats to prevent the Confederates from crossing the canal over them and to ensure that the southerners did not take the coal the vessels held. The next day the armies at Antietam braced for a renewal of hostilities that never came. That evening Lee made preparations to cross back to Virginia at Blackfords Ford below Shepherdstown.[21]

The ford quickly became clotted with troops attempting to get across the river. A day before the battle Lee had ordered artillery chief William Nelson Pendleton, who was in charge of the ford's defenses, to either build a bridge over the canal or tear down the banks to allow easy access to the river crossing. Despite his work, passage across the ford was slow. Topographer Jedediah Hotchkiss wrote that on the Virginia side the egress from the ford was via a narrow road with a bluff both above and below, which contributed to the languid passage. Late on September 18 Hotchkiss found the road to the ford on the Maryland side jammed with horses, wagons, and ambulances, and the river and Virginia shore were in a similar condition. He watched some wagons slide into the dry canal as a result of the press to get to the river.[22]

When the Federals discovered that the Confederates were withdrawing from the field, Maj. Gen. Fitz-John Porter's Fifth Corps moved to the river to harass them. An artillery duel soon commenced between the two sides. Porter deployed skirmishers and sharpshooters on the river banks and in the canal, supported by additional troops and artillery on the heights above the Potomac. Pendleton wrote that fire from Federal sharpshooters posted behind the canal bank was "an evil not slightly trying," and that in the early evening "their infantry at the canal breastwork was much increased, and the crack of their sharpshooters became a continuous roll of musketry." Late in the day several Federal units emerged from the dry canal and forded the river. They advanced up the bluff and established defensive positions, which caused a panic among some of the Confederate pickets, but Porter withdrew the men after an hour. Early the next day Porter sent more units across the river toward Shepherdstown, but Stonewall Jackson sent Maj. Gen. A.P. Hill's division and two others back to the ford.[23]

Lt. Col. Joshua Lawrence Chamberlain and the Twentieth Maine received their "baptism of fire" at the Battle of Shepherdstown. On September 20 his regiment was ordered to secure the ford at the mill dam (which he incorrectly identified as Dam Number 4). Before long the regiment was ordered to ford the river to support the Union force on the Virginia side. Although Federal artillery shelled the opposite shore over their heads and the southern troops sent balls splashing all around them, the Maine soldiers reached the opposite shore. They formed in line, but were then ordered back to the Maryland side after Federal officers realized that the Confederates greatly outnumbered the Union force. After they returned to the Maryland shore, six companies of the Twentieth Maine joined other Federal units in the canal.[24]

A.P. Hill's men drove the rest of Federals back across the river in great confusion and with much loss to the One Hundred-Eighteenth Pennsylvania Volunteers. A soldier in the Twenty-Second Massachusetts Infantry, who fled back across the river under fire, wrote that the Confederates "appeared upon the bluff, and commenced firing at the struggling men in the water. The bullets hissed and spit about us, the shells still shrieked and made their hideous music over our heads. Berdan's Sharpshooters with other troops were lying in the dry bed of the Chesapeake and Ohio Canal, and gave us comfort and aid by firing also over our heads."[25]

To create a diversion and hold another important ford while the main Confederate force passed back into Virginia, on September 19 cavalry brigades under James Ewell Brown "Jeb" Stuart and Wade Hampton crossed the river at another point and then came back into Maryland at

Williamsport. After the horsemen chased away Federal pickets, they discovered that the bridge over the canal had been destroyed. In quick order, the cavalrymen built a makeshift road that passed under the Conococheague Aqueduct. The men then took up positions on the ridges above the town. The following day the Confederates fought a daylong skirmish with Federal troops and the Pennsylvania militia who had been called forward to assist. During the night of September 20 the Confederates withdrew to Virginia. The road that Stuart had built under the aqueduct was maintained by the canal company and used by local citizens for six months until the superintendent replaced the bridge over the canal in March 1863.[26]

Damage to the canal as a result of the Confederate invasion was significant. On the Monocacy Division the Confederates had cut the canal banks in several places and the running water had eroded the towpath twenty-five feet in depth, thirty feet in width, and over eighty feet in length. The water had also washed out the bottom of the canal fifteen feet deep, thirty feet wide, and one-hundred feet in length. About a mile below the Monocacy River, the southern troops had also blasted Lock Number 27 and damaged the lock gates. The most serious damage inflicted by the Confederates was to the Little Monocacy culvert, although George Spates estimated that with sufficient funds and labor he could complete the repairs in two to three weeks. At Harpers Ferry, the Confederates had run three B&O railcars off the bridge into the river and six into the canal.[27]

Ironically, on the Antietam Division there was only minor damage. Despite the proximity of the canal to the battlefield, a forced crossing by almost the entire Confederate army, and a skirmish in which Union soldiers used the canal as a breastwork, the division had escaped significant harm, likely because the southerners had little idle time to devote to damaging the canal. Superintendent Levin Benton reported that the soldiers had burned the planks from his stop-lock, ransacked a lock house where he kept company papers and forms, and stripped a scow. On October 6 Alfred Spates wrote that the government had also assisted the company in making some unspecified repairs to the division, probably to the canal banks where Lee had ordered Pendleton to bridge the canal or tear down its walls.[28]

FORD NEAR SHEPHERDSTOWN, ON THE POTOMAC—PICKET FIRING ACROSS THE RIVER.—SKETCHED BY MR. A. R. WARD.—[SEE PAGE 653.]

Union soldiers utilizing the canal as a breastwork opposite Shepherdstown, W. Va. *Harper's Weekly*, Oct. 11, 1862. Source: author's collection.

On the Williamsport Division the most serious damage was the burning of the lock gates at Lock Number 44 located at Williamsport. The bridge over the canal had also been torched by Federal forces under orders from General McClellan. Superintendent Masters estimated that he could complete the repairs to the canal in one week at a cost of $2,000. The lockkeeper's house at Lock Number 44 was also burned and was considered a total loss. Eleven canal boats had been set aflame by the Pennsylvania militia, one by the Confederates. Local citizens had extinguished the fires and claimed the coal in exchange for their service, which was permitted by Federal officers.[29]

In Washington County, word spread quickly that on September 19 the Pennsylvania militia had acted with unbounded disregard for the property of Unionists when it went to Williamsport to burn the bridge over the canal and to confront Stuart's cavalry. On September 24 a Hagerstown correspondent of the *Baltimore American* wrote: "The Anderson troop and a Pennsylvania cavalry company executed the order at a terrible cost to some of the best Union men of the place. They not only burnt the bridge but the lumber yards, the toll-house, a number of canal boats and two warehouses. I heard the loss estimated at forty thousand dollars. —Surely some one should be held responsible for this outrageous and senseless act, and some remuneration made to the parties for their loss." The *Hagerstown Herald of Freedom and Torch Light* was more forgiving of the militia. On October 1 it reported that only a portion of the militia was responsible for the unnecessary destruction, and that most of the men behaved in a gentlemanly fashion. The newspaper was optimistic that the government would reimburse townsmen for their losses, especially since Williamsport's citizens were among the most loyal in the county.[30]

Upon a closer inspection of the canal, company officials found that the damages were not as bad as first feared. Alfred Spates reported that except for the damage caused by the Pennsylvania militia, little or no damage would have been done to the Williamsport Division. He wrote that there was no damage west of Williamsport, and between Williamsport and Harpers Ferry the damage was not as great as expected. On September 26 the *Washington Evening Star* reported that repairs might be completed in time for the fall trade. It also noted that the closure of the canal had reversed the normal direction of trade: supplies of wheat were being delivered to millers in Georgetown from Baltimore and flour was being brought in from Philadelphia.[31]

In the aftermath of the Battle of Antietam, the Confederates maintained a threatening posture across the Potomac. In addition to their earlier destruction of the railroad bridges over the Monocacy River and the Potomac at Harpers Ferry, they began to destroy the railroad bridges from Martinsburg to Hancock as well as the B&O's roundhouse facilities in Martinsburg. On October 6 Alfred Spates wrote Ringgold that because of the suspension of railroad passenger service, he and Albert C. Greene were stranded in Cumberland and were unable to attend an upcoming meeting of the board. He advised: "We must have patience and do the best we can— things are in an awful condition in Western Maryland."[32]

Despite the damage inflicted to the waterway, the canal played a direct and important role in the Federal pursuit of the Confederates into Virginia until McClellan was relieved of command. The general wanted to use Harpers Ferry as his base of operations because it could be supplied by both railroad and canal. On September 21 his quartermaster, Rufus Ingalls, directed Quartermaster General Meigs to order the canal company to begin repairs. The next day Meigs replied: "While the right bank of the Potomac is occupied by rebels, the canal cannot be repaired or used. It is generally under artillery fire." He pointed out that the river was fordable in many of places and was not adequately defended against a raid. Instead, since the railroad bridge over the Monocacy River had been replaced recently, he recommended that McClellan protect the railroad so that company could repair its line to Harpers Ferry.[33]

Meigs's insolence angered McClellan. On September 22 he wrote directly to general-in-chief Halleck: "I urgently request that the president of the Chesapeake and Ohio Canal Company be asked to repair the canal at once. That he should do so is indispensably necessary for ulterior military operations. I also request that all the small steamers plying on the canal may be sent to Harper's Ferry as soon as the repairs shall have been completed." McClellan added that he would be responsible for the protection of the canal from Confederate raids. Halleck replied that the repair of the canal should wait until cavalry expeditions determined the position and intention of the Confederate army.[34]

While cavalry scouts were sent to locate the Confederates, McClellan continued with preparations to establish his base of operations at Harpers Ferry. He ordered a new pontoon bridge for Harpers Ferry to replace the one that the Confederates had destroyed, began repair of the telegraph, and requested heavy artillery for Maryland Heights. He also urged Halleck to send an engineer and work parties to build permanent bridges on the existing piers in the Potomac and Shenandoah rivers. On September 25 B&O work crews began removing the wrecks of the railroad bridge and trains from the river and canal.[35]

Harpers Ferry and vicinity soon became a scene of bustling activity. On September 25 a Sandy Hook correspondent of the *Washington Evening Star* wrote:

Probably at no time since the commencement of the war has this locality presented so great a scene of activity as now. Every road and lane is filled with baggage wagons and artillery. The soldiers are constantly passing and repassing. The shrill whistle of the locomotive is again heard. Supplies of all kinds are now being transported over the railroad to this point. The telegraph is being repaired, and large gangs of workmen have commenced removing the rubbish of the railroad bridge which was destroyed by the Rebels. A temporary bridge similar to the one at the Monocacy, is to be thrown over the Potomac. It will be ready for trains to pass over in about a week. The boats for the pontoon bridge have already arrived. They will immediately be placed in position. Immense numbers of soldiers have forced the Potomac; there being no means of conveyance across the river at present. . . . One long continuous train of supply and baggage wagons are crowded together on the Potomac opposite Harper's Ferry.[36]

On September 24 engineers from the Fiftieth New York Volunteer Engineers built new pontoon bridges across the Potomac and Shenandoah rivers at Harpers Ferry. These men, along with the Fifteenth New York Volunteer Engineers, originally volunteered for infantry duty. McClellan had noticed a shortage of capable engineers and, seeing that these regiments

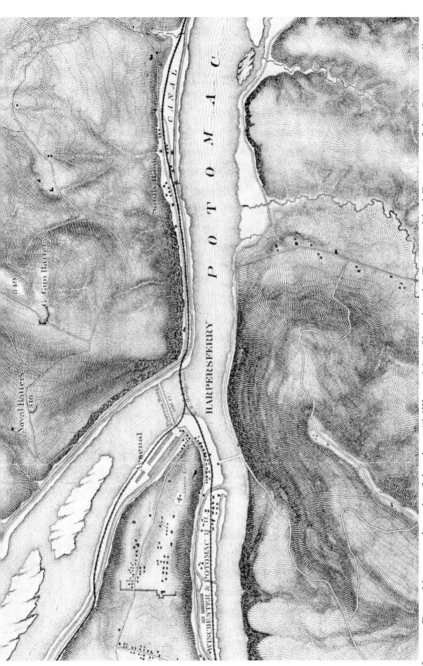

Harpers Ferry. Note canal north of the river. "Military Map Showing the Topographical Features of the Country Adjacent to Harper's Ferry, Va." (1863). Source: Library of Congress, Geography and Map Division.

were comprised of many sailors and mechanics, converted them into engineering regiments. The regiments were commanded by trained engineers who drilled the men in pontoon-duty and other engineering tasks. They subsequently built, took up, and transported their bridge material throughout the eastern theater of the war. The engineers found the canal useful to transport their pontoon material along the Potomac.[37]

On September 25 a quartermaster at Poolesville wrote that he had no means to provision the men stationed there because he could not get boats beyond Lock Number 24 near Seneca Creek. Damage to the Little Monocacy culvert, although nearly twenty miles up the canal, and breaks elsewhere had drained over forty miles of the waterway. The officer recommended that since the army also needed supplies at Sandy Hook, it should undertake repair of the canal to that point. On September 27 another quartermaster inspected the break near the Monocacy River and estimated that one hundred-fifty contrabands—liberated slaves—could make the repairs there in ten days. On October 6 George Spates informed the company office that the army had a large number of laborers at work repairing the Little Monocacy culvert and Lock Number 27. He thought that they could complete the work in eight days.[38]

McClellan was impatient to make use of the waterway because it was his only direct supply link with Washington. In the absence of the canal, his supplies were received via the Cumberland Valley and Franklin railroads, which ran between Harrisburg, Pennsylvania, and Hagerstown, and then overland by wagon. The B&O Railroad was also utilized to Sandy Hook, but supplies from Washington had to be transported north to Relay House over a single track before they began their southwesterly route toward the river. Delays and bottlenecks on the railroad supply routes angered McClellan and he urged his subordinates to push the repair of the waterway. On October 6 his quartermaster wrote to the departmental office in Washington: "General McClellan wishes to know when the canal will be in order to Harper's Ferry, and what force is at work upon it. He is anxious to make use of this canal at once. Send an officer to push forward the clothing, stationery, &c., to Hagerstown and Harper's Ferry. The delay is outrageous. Find out where the obstacles are."[39]

Union Maj. Gen. Henry W. Halleck. Source: Library of Congress, Prints and Photographs Division.

Union Brig. Gen. Montgomery C. Meigs, Quartermaster General, U.S. Army. Source: Library of Congress, Prints and Photographs Division.

The repairs to the canal went slowly. Quartermaster Sawtelle informed McClellan's quartermaster that sixty-five laborers had been at work on the damaged culvert for nearly a week. Due to McClellan's demands, the work force was increased to one hundred-fifty men. Sawtelle reported that difficulty obtaining laborers had hindered the efforts and estimated ten more days to complete the work. He noted that most contrabands had been sent to work in the supply depots or as teamsters. He also suggested that the urgency of the situation might require the presence of a party of engineers, rather than quartermasters, to oversee the work.[40]

McClellan's demands angered and frustrated his subordinates. During the first two weeks of October McClellan complained frequently to Meigs and Halleck of not receiving requested supplies and, in part, used this as an excuse to not advance against the Confederates. Meigs, on the other hand, was frustrated with McClellan's constant complaints. On October 12 he vented consternation to Halleck: "It is nearly impossible to supply such an army, having over 30,000 animals to feed, by means (limited) to two railroads. The canal will be repaired and ready for use in a few days. It was hoped that water could have been admitted to it to-day. This, if boats can be found to navigate it, will increase the power of this department to forward supplies considerably." He also noted that his department was utilizing the full capacity of both railroads and had difficulty procuring freight cars.[41]

The canal company also sought to have the army repair damages to the Williamsport Division. On October 9 the board of directors met, absent Spates and Greene who were still stranded in Cumberland, and tapped director Joseph M. Bradley to contact government officials about the repairs to the Williamsport Division. The next day Bradley informed Meigs that the company did not have the financial resources to make repairs to the Williamsport Division any time soon: "Our impression is there is no present prospect of our opening the route to the coal fields, unless we can get aid, in time for the transportation of coal sufficient even for the demand of the government, & without reference to the supply of private demand." He asked if quartermaster Rucker might make the repairs and remove obstructions west of Harpers Ferry. He also noted that during the summer the contractor had begun work on the Virginia abutment of Dam Number 5 but were forced to suspend work due to the hostilities. Bradley wrote that although carpenters would be required at some locks, mostly laborers, horsepower, and tools were needed. He estimated that the government could complete the work in five to six days.[42]

On the same day, Ringgold sent Williamsport Superintendent Masters a check for $1,000 toward the estimated $2,000 repairs needed on the Williamsport Division, but hoped to learn in a few days if the army would take on the work. Eleven days later the company still had not heard from the quartermaster's department and it eventually completed the work itself. Months later, on December 2, Greene wrote Ringgold to ask what the canal company had done to seek reimbursement for damages to its property committed by the Pennsylvania militia at Williamsport. Greene pointed out that the Borden Mining Company lost two boats and four cargoes of coal. On December 12 the secretary-treasurer replied that he expected the government to establish a commission to assess damages, and he knew of no other means by which claims could be submitted. Nevertheless, the company never received reimbursement for the damages inflicted to the division, most of which were committed by the Pennsylvania militia under orders of General McClellan.[43]

By October 13 the Union army had completed repairs to the Little Monocacy culvert and water was let in to Harpers Ferry. By October 24 the company had completed enough repairs at Williamsport to allow re-watering of the canal to Cumberland. Boats soon arrived at the western terminus and began to take on coal. The Confederates invasion had resulted in two months of inactivity on the canal during the height of the boating season, but those associated with the canal were optimistic that a brisk trade could be conducted before winter. The *Cumberland Civilian and Telegraph* wrote: "We hope for the benefit of our people, that there will be no obstruction to navigation again until cold weather shall prevent it."[44]

Once navigation had resumed, McClellan intended to prevent any interference with the movement of military supplies over the waterway. On October 24 he republished Stanton's General Orders No. 44, first issued in April. To the order McClellan added: "The provisions of this order are still in force, and the boats of the company will be allowed to pass through the lines of this army without hindrance, until otherwise directed." Alfred

Spates was given authority to issue military passes to canal boats, which he did by printing them on the back of a waybill that company officials issued to each boat.[45]

As had been the case in 1861, the B&O was still in disrepair west of Harpers Ferry and the canal was once more the only direct link with the coal fields. The railroad company resumed its practice of offloading Cumberland Coal from canal boats at Sandy Hook and transferring it to railcars. The railroad's master of the road, John L. Wilson, wrote in his report for the fiscal year that ended on September 30, 1862: "The transfer of coal from canal boats into B&O cars at Sandy Hook continued from the close of last fiscal year. Additional derricks were erected, and by this means the supply of coal for Company's use east of Harper's Ferry, and upon the Washington Branch, was fully maintained." The railroad company also transferred other material—including gas coal from Newburg (in western Virginia), lumber, and crossties—from the canal to the rails.[46]

To facilitate the passage of troops to Virginia, McClellan ordered engineers to construct another pontoon bridge across the river east of Harpers Ferry. Initially he planned to place it at Edwards Ferry, but later decided on Berlin. The engineers of the Fiftieth New York transported the material to Berlin and constructed the bridge on October 25. The engineers also placed bridges across the recently re-watered canal, which brought the bustle in the Maryland coal region to another standstill—the bridges were built too low to allow canal boats to pass. On November 7 the news reached Cumberland and the activity on the docks ceased. When the news reached the coal pits, many miners packed up and left for the Pennsylvania coal fields. On November 13 Albert C. Greene explained the sentiment of the miners: "They very naturally concluded that if the army got hold of the Canal there was an end of it for this season at least." Greene found some blame for the division superintendents. He complained that they were not promptly reporting stoppages in navigation to Cumberland. With only rumor to go on, Greene had no words of assurance to give the miners that might have prevented their departure.[47]

Greene also accused Williamsport Superintendent Masters of inefficiency for his failure to have Dam Number 5 repaired. The responsibility lay with the contractor and circumstances beyond its control, however. On

November 3 Stake and Simms wrote to the board and explained that when they first attempted the work the opposing armies occupied both sides of the river. A large freshet followed. The contractor was later able to commence the work and was within three weeks of completion when on September 6 the armies came too close to the dam for the workmen to remain. After the Confederates left Maryland, the Federal commander at Williamsport, Brig. Gen. John Kenly, had forbidden anyone to cross the river to Virginia. The contractor reported that they lost tools, machinery, provisions, and building material as a result of the military occupation of the river. Although the deadline to rebuild the abutment had expired, Stake and Simms expressed a willingness to complete the work when conditions improved.[48]

As the Army of the Potomac prepared to cross the river the canal delivered some of their supplies. In October, quartermasters established a supply depot at the mouth of Seneca Creek and sent stores up the canal to the river lock at Edwards Ferry so that canal boats could be sent across the river and unloaded onto wagons on the turnpike. Boats were also forwarded to Berlin and Sandy Hook where troops replenished supplies before they crossed the pontoon bridges. McClellan had intended to build another pontoon bridge at Edwards Ferry, which was forwarded up the canal, but subsequent events rendered the construction of the bridge moot.[49]

As the Army of the Potomac prepared to leave Maryland, many of the troops looked fondly on their time in the state. Other than the battles at South Mountain and Antietam, the soldiers' service was pleasant compared to their experience on the Virginia Peninsula where they had endured a summer in the rain, heat, and marshes of the Virginia tidewater, fighting not only the Confederates but insects and disease. David W. Judd, a correspondent of the *New York Times* who traveled with the Thirty-Third New York Infantry, wrote:

> The men very much enjoyed the time spent in Maryland. . . . Never did painter's eye rest upon more beautiful and picturesque scenery than that from Williamsport to Harper's Ferry. The wide but shallow Potomac winds gracefully among the hills and through the rich valleys, lined on either side with stately oaks, spreading elms and weeping willows, which furnished a refreshing shade during the heat of the day. Every few rods little rivulets come leaping and dashing

down from the highlands, while an occasional larger stream, like the Antietam, gives variety to the scene. The canal runs nearly parallel with the river for the whole distance, divided from it by the narrow towpath. The boatmen must have loved to reach this part of their journey, where the tall trees hide out the sun, and their overhanging branches form one continuous arbor for the drivers."[50]

Following the Battle of Antietam, President Lincoln became dissatisfied with the pace and nature of McClellan's pursuit of the Confederates and relieved the general of command. On November 5 he promoted Maj. Gen. Ambrose Burnside to command the Army of the Potomac. Burnside quickly began to plan an advance against Richmond by way of Fredericksburg, Virginia. Like McClellan before him, Burnside planned to utilize canal boats to transport supplies for his army. On November 7 Burnside wrote to a staff officer: "In connection with this movement in the direction of Fredericksburg, I would suggest that at least thirty canal-boats and barges be at once loaded with commissary stores and forage, and be towed to the neighborhood of Aquia Creek, from which place they can be brought into Belle Plain after the arrival of our force in that vicinity. . . . A great portion of this, I think, could be towed up the Rappahannock, under convoy of light draught gunboats." He wrote that two pontoon bridges should be placed across the Rappahannock. The Quartermaster's Department subsequently forwarded barges and canal boats loaded with provisions and supplies to Aquia Creek to support Burnside's advance.[51]

To cross the Rappahannock River, Burnside planned to use the pontoon bridge material that was then along the Potomac. One unutilized convoy of pontoon material—referred to as a pontoon train or bridge train—that had been intended for Edwards Ferry was moored in the canal at Berlin along with other excess bridge material. Along with those in active use as bridges, a total of two-hundred pontoons were available at Berlin. In early November Capt. Ira Spaulding of the Fiftieth New York Volunteer Engineers placed all of the excess bridge components in the canal for transportation to the quartermaster depot in Washington. His men also dismantled the bridges over the river and the canal, most of which was returned to Washington via the waterway. During the next month the bridge material was sent to the

Rappahannock River to aid Burnside's offensive against the Confederates at Fredericksburg.[52]

With the removal of the army's bridges over the waterway at Berlin in mid-November, canal traffic resumed slowly. Tolls collected in November amounted to just over $6,000, less than one-half of August's total. In December the company collected about $9,200, still over $4,000 less than the amount garnered in August. Due to the extended interruption in canal and rail traffic, coal from outside of the mid-Atlantic region had begun to fill the demand in the northeast. Gas coal was so scarce in Philadelphia and Baltimore that wholesalers were receiving supplies from Nova Scotia.[53]

The canal company's prolonged financial difficulties took a toll on its employees. On November 8 an officer in the quartermaster's department wrote Spates that a lockkeeper above Georgetown had quit his position because the company had not paid him in "some time." The quartermaster had hired a temporary lockkeeper to keep the boats moving, but asked Spates to send a replacement.[54]

In light of its financial problems, the company reconsidered an earlier decision to revoke tolls imposed on boats that were destroyed by the Confederates. In early November the company decided to assess tolls to the point that southern troops had destroyed canal boats. On November 5 Ringgold instructed the toll collector to impose tolls on the eleven boats that the southerners had burned at Williamsport.[55]

The news did not sit well with many of the boat owners. On January 14, 1863, the Georgetown toll collector, J. Hollingsworth, wrote that many boat owners had refused to pay tolls for September 1862. Two coal companies declined to remit tolls on boats that had been burned at Williamsport, while another was reluctant to pay fares on thirteen boats that had returned to their port of origination after encountering the Confederates crossing the river. Hollingsworth noted that some of the outstanding waybills were incurred by boats that had been taken into government service and the boatmen did not consider it fair that the company had imposed tolls on boats not in their charge. He added: "There has been a great confusion on the canal by the belligerent operations of the two armies, also by the seizure of canal boats by [the] Government before their tolls were settled. In some instances captains have skedaddled into Pa. with all their papers."[56]

In the spring of 1863 the company clarified the limits of its responsibility for damages to boats and cargoes resulting from invasion of 1862 and for future incursions. On March 13 the company notified one coal company that the canal company could not guarantee the safe delivery of coal and would only remit tolls when the claimant could show that company officers had been negligent. In April the company agreed to remit tolls for the thirteen boats that had turned around after learning of the 1862 invasion, but reiterated its decision to not to remit tolls on boats burned by the Confederates because the company was not responsible for their destruction.[57]

Once navigation on the canal had resumed in November 1862, Alfred Spates made a final attempt to obtain an official post with the government. Although he had previously solicited a position from Stanton, Meigs, and McClellan, on November 4 he wrote directly to President Lincoln. He pointed out that although the canal was of great importance to the government and the citizens of Washington and Maryland, the government had not paid a dollar for its use of the waterway, while the company's revenues were greatly reduced as a result of the war. Spates wrote that he used his personal resources to make some of the repairs and that for the past two years he had not received his salary as president of the company. He asked Lincoln for appointment as colonel or manager of the canal and enclosed a copy of McClellan's recently reissued General Orders No. 44 as evidence of his fidelity to the government. "It would be but justice to give me such an appointment in consideration of services rendered to government," he wrote. He also pledged to execute any "order or wish" of the government as he had done in the past. For a personal reference, he again referred Lincoln to District of Columbia Marshal Ward Hill Lamon, the president's former law partner from Illinois.[58]

Spates's claim that he had not received his salary as president for the previous two years may have been an exaggeration to garner sympathy from Lincoln. The company's annual reports show that despite financial difficulties, it continued to pay officers' salaries. It is possible that a portion of his salary and that of the other officers was deferred. In its 1865 Thirty-Seventh Annual Report, the company reported that it had liquidated several outstanding claims from prior to 1862, among them "arrears of officers' salaries." Perhaps what Spates intended to say, or perhaps deliberately avoided saying in his campaign to secure a position, was that he had not received any additional pay when the positions of engineer, general superintendent and paymaster were consolidated into the office of the president.[59]

After the Battle of Antietam, Union and Confederate pickets confronted each other across the Potomac much as they had in 1861. In the last quarter of the year, skirmishes and raids occurred with some frequency. Union cavalry patrols crossed the river to capture Confederate pickets and spies, while Confederate cavalry crossed to rout Union camps or raid civilian shops. In particular, the region near Dam Number 4 in Washington County was subject to a number of cross-border raids perpetuated by both sides. In one account, an anxious Union raiding party waited along the canal for orders to cross the river at Dam Number 4: "We were lying along the canal, with no pretense of concealment. Canal-boats were passing every few minutes. On them, and straggling along after them, were many men and boys whose sympathies were unknown to us. That some of them might be rebel scouts, on the look out for just such matters, was not a violent presumption. Under such conditions, what a death-trap could be set for us?"[60]

On November 19 a canal employee named Dunn, who lived on the Virginia side of the river, attempted to move his family to Maryland near Dam Number 4. Other refugees from Virginia helped place his family and household goods in boats when a small party of Confederate horsemen dashed out of the woods. All were captured except Dunn, who fled. Later a small party of friends volunteered to cross the river and transport the family to Maryland. As soon as they reached the Virginia shore the Confederates reappeared and called on the party to surrender. Two men did so but a third, Mortimer Cookus, attempted to return to the Maryland shore in a boat. Southern troops opened fire and struck Cookus, who sprang into the river and sunk to the bottom.[61]

Cookus was a respected Unionist from Virginia and his death outraged local citizens. It was suspected that a small band of guerrillas from Shepherdstown, led by Confederate cavalry Capt. Redmond Burke, was responsible for this attack as well as earlier raids against civilians. Brig.

Gen. George H. Gordon, who commanded the brigade guarding the Potomac from Antietam to Opequon creeks, wrote of Burke: "In harrying Union men, whether he robbed them, burned their dwellings, or shot them in cold bold, he had no equal." Gordon also suspected that Dunn was a Confederate sympathizer and had arranged the ambush with Burke. An unsuspecting "canal superintendent" had written a note asking a regimental commander to allow the Virginians to cross the river. Gordon wrote that an investigation determined that Dunn and a "canal agent and his son" were Confederate sympathizers and that Burke had been a partner of the canal agent.[62]

Gordon had spies and informants along the border as well, including the keeper of a tavern along the canal who had helped Federal officers devise a plan to capture Burke and his party at their hideout in Shepherdstown. On November 24 Col. Silas Colgrove of the Twenty-Seventh Indiana Infantry led a party of seventy-five men across the river at night and surrounded the house that Burke used as headquarters. They captured five members of the band, two of whom disputed credit for killing Cookus the week before. Burke tried to escape but was shot and killed. Other suspicious houses were searched and a Confederate scout was captured opposite Mercersville (Taylors Landing), about 3 miles above Shepherdstown. The following day Colgrove wrote: "There is general rejoicing by the loyal citizens here [Sharpsburg]. Burke and his party had become a perfect terror to all law-abiding men." Other than Dunn, the accused southern sympathizer who worked for the canal company was not identified and there is no record that Gordon asked the canal company to dismiss any of its employees.[63]

As 1862 drew to a close, winter set in early. On December 11 the Cumberland Civilian and Telegraph wrote: "Navigation on the Canal having been obstructed by ice, no boats have left for the past few days. There is an ice cutter at work breaking the ice in order to enable the boats to descend with coal for the eastern market. We understand that it is the intention of the energetic President, Col. Spates, to endeavor to keep the canal open during the present winter." The army had damaged and destroyed the company's ice breakers at the western terminus, however, which hampered Spates's efforts. To sustain navigation as long as possible, the president had one boat repaired and a new one built.[64]

§

Late in 1862 the government began to reconsider its strategy of defending the B&O Railroad and the canal in light of its failure to defend either adequately during the first two years of the war. Francis Thomas introduced a bill in the House that called for the army to establish camps of instruction for raw troops in towns south of the railroad, such as Romney and Winchester. Heretofore the army had trained green troops behind the lines, many in Washington, D.C. Thomas argued that placing troops on the frontier would speed their effectiveness and swell number of troops defending the railroad and canal, both of which the army and navy utilized to receive coal and military supplies.[65]

Thomas's bill created a stir in Brig. Gen. Benjamin Kelley's new command. On December 16 Kelley had been given responsibility for protecting the railroad from Harpers Ferry to the Ohio River in the newly created Middle Department, Eighth Army Corps, under the command of Maj. Gen. Robert C. Schenck. As early as November 6, 1861, Kelley had advocated the occupation of Romney, Martinsburg, and Harpers Ferry as a means to defend the railroad. On December 9, 1862, Kelley reiterated his views in a letter to Maj. Gen. Halleck. He also recommended that the army occupy Winchester and Leesburg with a force strong enough to resist a Confederate advance toward the Potomac. He added, "thousands of tons of coal are now ready for shipment from this point [Cumberland] to the eastern market, where it is wanted for the government vessels, as well as by manufacturers and citizens."[66]

Lt. Col. Gabriel E. Porter, who served under Kelley at Cumberland, also addressed Thomas's bill. In a December 27 letter to his commander, he wrote: "The bill of the honorable Francis Thomas, for the establishment of camps of instruction in the vicinity of the Baltimore and Ohio railroad, etc., in a somewhat modified form, ought to be adopted." He suggested, however, that the army create camps of instruction closer to the railroad, such as at New Creek (present-day Keyser, W. Va.), Cumberland, Hancock, Martinsburg, and Harpers Ferry, with light troops at Winchester, Romney, and perhaps one or two other locations in northwestern Virginia. "The vulnerable points along the Baltimore and Ohio railroad and the Chesapeake and Ohio canal, are between New Creek and Harper's Ferry. . . . By forming these encampments, as indicated, ample protection would be at once afforded." He pointed out that if one location was attacked it could be reinforced by nearby troops over the rails. Porter advised that new troops would be much more attentive and subject to discipline when trained on the frontier rather than behind the lines. He predicted that if his suggestions were adopted, the price of transportation would fall throughout the country. Kelley approved of Porter's suggestions, and on January 10, 1863 he forwarded them and his own recommendations to Thomas. Thomas in turn had the letters read before the House and referred to his Committee on Military Affairs on January 20, 1863.[67]

§

For the C&O Canal Company, 1862 was even more disastrous than 1861. In its *Thirty-Fifth Annual Report* the president and board informed the stockholders: "The causes which prostrated the business of the Canal for the preceeding [sic] year have occurred in like manner during the past; frequent interruptions from military incursions, low water in the river, and occasional breaches in the Canal; and although the latter have been comparatively inconsiderable in duration, or in cost of repairs, yet the insecurity and uncertainty of boating, from these occurrences, have reduced the general business of the canal, even lower than that of the preceeding [sic] year."[68]

Goods shipped during 1862 dropped by over 21,000 tons over 1861, a 14 percent decline. Coal shipments fell by 14,000 tons, a drop of 21 percent. Tolls decreased by just over $6,500. Only in May and August did tolls total over $10,000. Expenses exceeded revenues by over $14,000. This loss was only about half of the company's deficit in 1861, but the company was only able to complete repairs most necessary to resume navigation. Less urgent repairs and routine maintenance tasks were postponed due to insufficient resources. The army's repair of Lock Number 27, the Little Monocacy Culvert, the breaches on the Monocacy Division, and their work on the Antietam Division had also saved the company from an even greater loss.[69]

Nevertheless, as 1862 came to a close, a few bright spots loomed on the horizon. Flour shipped down the canal in 1862 increased by almost 4 percent and wheat by 55 percent, indicative of increased demand from the government to feed the army. Most agricultural products were farmed in the counties that bordered the middle and eastern portions of the canal and thus were less exposed to raids as it traveled to market. The absence of a significant Confederate invasion until after the summer growing season also permitted more flour and wheat to reach market. The canal company's relationship with the government had grown closer over the past year, culminating in publication and re-publication of General Orders No. 44, in which the government had officially taken responsibility for defending and aiding the canal, while acknowledging Spates's role as president. As additional evidence of the improved relationship, Spates learned on December 1 that, upon his recommendation, the government had appointed six company employees as revenue agents with the Treasury Department. He wrote Ringgold that the appointments were "more of a *compliment* than otherwise," suggesting that they were an acknowledgment of the loyalty and important services rendered to the government by the company.[70]

The army had also come to the realization that its strategy to defend the railroad and canal was inadequate and had begun to consider other ideas, such as those promoted by Thomas, Kelley, and Porter. These alternatives would be debated in the House of Representatives in 1863.

CHAPTER 5

THESE SHAMEFUL RAIDS: 1863

On January 6 the Baltimore and Ohio Railroad completed repairs to its main stem, which restored transportation from Wheeling to Baltimore for the first time since early September 1862. Two weeks later the *Frederick Examiner* reported: "An immense forwarding of Cumberland coal is going on, day and night, over the Baltimore and Ohio Railroad." The canal company was not unduly alarmed at a renewal of competition with its old rival. As a result of its heavy repair expenses, the B&O raised freight rates on coal and flour, which drew frequent complaints from citizens. On January 13 Albert C. Greene wrote Ringgold that the railroad company's decision to increase its rates would stimulate the building of new canal boats as shippers looked for less expensive modes of moving goods to market. The canal company attempted to keep up with the competition by using ice cutters to keep the channel clear. As a result, the January 8 *Cumberland Civilian and Telegraph* noted that canal boats were continually leaving port "ladened with the black diamonds."[1]

To insure sustained boating, however, the canal was in need of the usual winter maintenance. On January 1 George Spates reported that many lock gates, waste weirs, and flumes on the Monocacy Division needed repair. In a mid-January meeting, the president and board agreed to halt navigation on February 1 to complete the work, with boating to resume on March 1. On the appointed date the water was drawn off and repairs began. At the end of February George Spates informed the company that his repairs were delayed because the government needed the canal near Harpers Ferry and had re-watered it for three or four days. By March 5 the company had completed the maintenance work and began to re-water the canal.[2]

Those associated with the canal and coal trade were optimistic about the upcoming season. On March 5 the *Cumberland Civilian and Telegraph* wrote: "There never was a season when the prospects were as encouraging as the present bids to be for a brisk trade." Although the Confederates had won a lopsided victory in the December 1862 Battle of Fredericksburg, the contending armies still faced each other across the Rappahannock River, well removed from the Potomac. On January 26 Lincoln tapped Maj. Gen. Joseph Hooker to replace Burnside in command of the Army of the Potomac, which raised the spirits of the army. The Union army also occupied advanced positions in the Shenandoah Valley.[3]

With the resumption of navigation, the company had to overcome a few obstacles that threatened to hinder trade. In late March a strike broke out on the coal wharves in Georgetown. It had only lasted a few hours before wages were boosted twenty-five cents per day "as labor was badly wanting, and coal constantly arriving," wrote the Georgetown correspondent to the *Washington Evening Star*.[4]

Military interference and the imposition of cumbersome regulation on canal trade also threatened to suppress boating. Although in 1861 Lincoln forbade commerce with states in rebellion, in early 1863 the Union army occupied large portions of Virginia. New guidelines were needed to clarify how goods were to be delivered to Unionists and U.S. troops in Virginia, while maintaining a prohibition against trade with Confederate sympathizers. As a result, on January 12 the Treasury Department issued regulations that prohibited the shipment of trade goods to Virginia. Merchandise could be sent south in quantities sufficient for a single family if evidence of the family's loyalty to the government could be furnished to the customs officer. Two days later Maj. Gen. Robert C. Schenck issued orders to enforce the regulations in the Middle Department. Among other things, Schenck's order authorized military officers at Point of Rocks, Berlin, Harpers Ferry, Williamsport, Hancock, Cumberland, and New Creek to examine permits and itemized bills of goods before issuing passes necessary to cross the river. Goods for the use of soldiers, officers, and authorized sutlers were also allowed south if the loyalty of those who handled the goods could be affirmed. Anyone reselling goods was to be arrested. Schenck also forbade the transport south of spirits and contraband articles. The canal employees previously appointed revenue aides had authority to grant permits, although they were subject to review by military officers who alone could issue passes to cross the river.[5]

Other officers placed additional layers of regulation on trade across the river, measures that directly affected the canal. On March 11 General Kelley was relieved of command of the Defenses of the Upper Potomac by Brig. Gen. Benjamin S. Roberts. Roberts, who had little experience along the river in comparison to Kelley, almost immediately raised the ire of the canal company. The general issued General Orders No. 2 which, among other things, designated Harpers Ferry and Point of Rocks as the only ports between the Monocacy River and Sir John's Run (located about four miles southwest of Hancock in Virginia) where goods from the railroad and canal could be discharged to Virginia. In addition, railroad conductors and canal boat captains were directed to record the names and residences of passengers and where the travelers had disembarked. Roberts also ordered his subordinates to "seize and keep in their possession all the boats, scows, and skiffs and other water craft within their respective districts, and close all river crossings and ferries for either passengers, goods or merchandise of any kind." His troops subsequently scoured the Potomac for vessels and seized, among others, scows that the canal company were using to make repairs to Dam Number 5.[6]

Alfred Spates was incensed at the seizure of the company's boats. He wrote two letters to Roberts to protest the orders and enclosed a copy of McClellan's General Orders No. 44. On March 28 Roberts replied that reliable persons had informed him that a large contraband trade was taking place between Maryland and Virginia using small boats kept along the river and canal, often hidden under bridges and culverts. He had learned that many boats used in the illicit commerce belonged to the canal company and that some company agents and boat captains had participated in the trade. Roberts replied that he knew that the canal trade was important to the government, but warned Spates that the company would suffer consequences if it tolerated the illegal trade and employed persons who were engaged in it. He wrote that when the repair scows were needed at Dam Number 5, he would issue orders to have the boats released. Nothing further came of the dispute. On March 27 Kelley was assigned to the First Division of the Eighth Army Corps, Middle Department, and again given responsibility for the defense of the railroad from the Monocacy to the

Ohio River, while Roberts was given command of the Fourth Separate Brigade and assigned to western Virginia.[7]

In Congress, Francis Thomas continued the legislative fight on behalf of the canal company. Nothing emerged from Congress regarding the relocation of camps of instruction, although ironically in the spring of 1863 the Union army already occupied advanced positions in Virginia, as Kelley, Porter, and Thomas had recommended. On another front, Thomas's year-long effort to have Congress appropriate funds to raise the bridges over the canal in Georgetown came to fruition. On March 3 Congress passed legislation that appropriated $13,000 from the Federal treasury to raise the bridges and market house over the canal in Georgetown to compensate the company for the army's seizure of the Potomac Aqueduct. On March 12 the president and board decided that Alfred Spates should meet with the municipal authorities of Georgetown to facilitate raising the bridges. Although the money was appropriated for the fiscal year that ended June 30, 1864, the company would not obtain the funds until the war was over.[8]

Maintenance problems continued to hound the company. In May Captain E.S. Allen of the Quartermaster Department asked the company to repair the tidal lock in Georgetown. He reported that the mitre sills had broken away, which caused leaks and prevented the lock from being filled with water. The lock gates were also in bad condition, "so much so that for the past six months it has cost the Govt. not less than five (5) dollars for each & every boat locked through." The company was frustrated by Allen's request because the government made heavy use of the tidal lock to transport coal from the canal to the navy yard, Alexandria, and other points. The company ordered the Georgetown Superintendent Horace Benton to repair the lock, but on May 29 Ringgold replied to Allen: "In as much as it may require repairs beyond the available means of the company, and as it is and has been used for sometime past almost exclusively for the United States, and the injury has arisen in some degree from their agents, and further that the U. States have made free use of the canal, without payment of tolls, I would suggest whether it would not be proper that they should contribute to the repairs of the lock in question." The June 1863 Confederate invasion of Maryland prevented the company from making the repairs. In early July the government attempted to rebuild the lock, but two months later Benton reported that the army had abandoned the work and had left it in worse condition than before.[9]

On August 21, 1862, the company had asked Secretary Stanton for an exemption from the draft for its employees. Ringgold had written that "superintendents, boatmen and lock keepers may become subject to this draft and the result may be that its [the company's] business will be nearly if not entirely destroyed." The secretary did not grant the request, and in April 1863 the company received a claim from an individual representing two lockkeepers who had been drafted into the army. The advocate wrote that the two were very poor men with families, and that the company owed each $200. There is no record that the company responded to the lockkeepers' request, however.[10]

In April boating began in earnest. By the end of the month over 425 boats had left Cumberland, carrying over 46,000 tons of coal. The company collected over $17,000 in tolls for the month, which was about equal to its best month during the war so far. Since the railroad had already raised its freight rate on coal, the canal company saw an opportunity to recoup some of the losses incurred during the previous two years. On April 10 it raised the toll on coal to five-sixteenths of a cent per ton mile, an increase of one-sixteenth of a cent per ton mile, which was set to expire on November 30. The Maryland Commission of Public Works, which had the authority to approve or decline an increase in tolls, subsequently authorized the hike. As a result of the increase and a stretch of uninhibited boating, the company collected over $26,000 in tolls in May, by far the highest amount collected during the war to that time. The army also made heavy use of the canal shipping goods from Williamsport to Harpers Ferry to supply the Union army in Virginia.[11]

As summer approached, all seemed well along the Potomac. On June 1 the Maryland Commission of Public Works reelected Spates and the existing board of directors to another term with the canal company. On June 4 the *Civilian and Telegraph* wrote: "Great credit is due to this Board for its good and efficient management of the Canal and the industry used to keep the same in order. . . . We know of no man more worthy the position of president of the Company than Col. Alfred Spates."[12]

At Harpers Ferry, military engineers had finished several projects designed to improve its defense and upgrade supply and transportation facilities. A double-track pontoon bridge, assembled in Baltimore, was constructed upriver at Dam Number 3. Engineers also built a drawbridge over the canal at the dam, constructed roads from the bridges to Maryland Heights, and positioned artillery to protect the railroad, the pontoon bridges, and the canal. At Berlin, engineers erected a pivot bridge over the canal.[13]

Work on Dam Number 5 progressed during the late spring and early summer. On June 8 Andrew K. Stake informed Ringgold that his stonemason, William Brown, would be ready to lay stone to the Virginia abutment of the dam within a week. He noted that Brown had had to do considerable work to the dam's existing cribs before he could proceed with the masonry. With regard to his company's contract, of which the work was nine months past due, Stake wrote: "I have done all in my power to fulfill my contract and shall continue to do so even [though] ruin may stare me in the face, which I fear will be the case should anything occur to interrupt the works again." An interruption was in the offing, however.[14]

As a prelude to the subsequent invasion of Maryland, on June 10 Confederate partisan ranger Major John S. Mosby, led his first raid across the Potomac. Mosby had planned to cross the Potomac the previous night, but his guide became lost and he did not arrive at the ford below Seneca until after daylight. After his command crossed the river, they proceeded up the towpath and seized five mules from a canal boat. A Union cavalry patrol was captured, but a man escaped and alerted the Union camp. Mosby's men moved up the canal for another mile until they came upon a bridge near Seneca where they found Federal soldiers drawn up in line of battle. Mosby ordered a charge, and the Union force gave way and a running battle ensued for a mile beyond the bridge. After the Federals were dispersed, Mosby returned to Seneca and destroyed the Union camp before he and his command re-crossed the river at the same ford. Other than the mules that Mosby's men had taken, the waterway was not affected by the raid.[15]

Mortimer Moulden, provost marshal of Montgomery County, visited the site of Mosby's raid and became convinced that many local citizens and canal employees had aided Mosby. A Federal sergeant had told him that a citizen communicated with the Confederates by displaying a signal light from the upper story of his home. In a June 15 letter to Provost Marshal General Col. James B. Fry, Moulden wrote: "The Chesapeake and Ohio Canal is almost wholly officered and worked by men having little or no sympathy for our Government. I speak of the superintendents and lock-keepers on the line; two very important points on the canal (the locks at the Great Falls and the Seneca locks) are in the hands of our enemies."[16]

The allegation that a local citizen displayed signal lights to guide Mosby's men is dubious since the raid had been planned for the previous day but was delayed after the guide became lost. Mosby also used a different ford than he had intended, further undermining the sergeant's claim. However, the canal company likely had employees with Southern sympathies, especially in Montgomery County. The company had previously acknowledged its responsibility to not employ disloyal workers, but it had requested proof—witnesses or other evidence—before it would remove an employee on such grounds. It is not unlikely that some employees on the Georgetown and Monocacy divisions were sympathetic toward the South, but it is doubtful that they would have openly aided the Confederacy. Considering the canal's close relationship with the government, to have done so would not only subject them to dismissal, but arrest. A close reading of Provost Marshal Moulden's letter shows that he saw Southern sympathizers everywhere. He complained that the citizens who lived along the Potomac were disloyal as well as the superintendent of the Washington Aqueduct (which carried water from the Potomac to Washington) and all of his employees. In Maryland, where political sentiments were divided and the Federal capital was nearby, suspicions were heightened. Moulder found it convenient to blame Mosby's raid on southern sympathizers when a more obvious cause was simply inadequate defense of the river. Mosby and other Confederate raiders would repeatedly demonstrate the weakness of Federal border defenses throughout the war. Following Mosby's June 10 raid, there is no record that the government complained directly to the canal company about disloyal employees on the eastern divisions of the canal. In September the company removed Horace Benton, the superintendent of the Georgetown Division, although subsequent correspondence shows that his removal resulted from neglect of his division rather than from disloyalty.[17]

Williamsport and Falling Waters. "Map of the Vicinity of Hagerstown, Funkstown, Williamsport, and Falling Waters, Maryland," (1879). Source: Library of Congress, Geography and Map Division.

By the second week of June the Confederates were moving toward the Potomac. Union pickets along the river were put on alert and ordered to keep the canal full of water to inhibit an advance into Maryland. On June 15 a staff officer in the Department of Washington ordered the commander at Poolesville to consolidate his command and post a strong force to guard the Monocacy Aqueduct. "Your line is a long and difficult one for your numbers," he wrote, "but it is impossible to send you more troops now. Something must be risked to save the canal."[18]

Late on June 15 Confederate Lt. Gen. Richard S. Ewell's Second Corps approached the Potomac. Maj. Gen. Robert E. Rodes's division forded the river at Williamsport, where he remained for three days. During that time Confederate engineers constructed a pontoon bridge across the river at Falling Waters and a crew of pioneers under Capt. Arthur M. Chichester began to tear apart the Conococheague Aqueduct. Ewell sent cavalry and quartermasters ahead to Hagerstown, Greencastle, and Chambersburg to obtain provisions and supplies. Maj. Gen. Edward Johnson's division crossed the river at Blackfords Ford near Shepherdstown and detached a brigade to damage the canal, destroy canal boats, and seize grain and flour stored in mills along the river. On June 19 the remainder of Ewell's Corps was sent north toward Pennsylvania as other Confederate forces moved to cross the river at the fords and pontoon bridge.[19]

To disrupt Federal communications and prevent supporting units from using the rails, on June 7 Lee dispatched Brig. Gen. John Imboden's cavalry toward the Potomac in western Virginia. On June 17 Imboden's command appeared on Shriver's Hill below Cumberland. Federal cavalry went to investigate and were driven away. The Confederates fired four rounds of artillery into the town and then asked for its surrender, which was quickly granted. The southern troops occupied the town for two or three hours and obtained goods in exchange for Confederate script before they departed.[20]

Over the next three days Imboden's men set fire to six railroad bridges between North Branch and the Little Cacapon River, including the B&O bridge over the canal below Cumberland. The cavalrymen also burned railroad stations and other property between Cumberland and the Little Cacapon (twenty-five miles east), and destroyed blockhouses at South

Branch and Pattersons Creek that the U.S. army had built to fend off raids. The southern horsemen also dug out the banks of the canal near Oldtown and broke several lock gates. On June 20 Lee informed Jefferson Davis: "The Chesapeake and Ohio Canal, about 2 miles above Old Town, where the embankment is about 40 feet high, has been cut, and General Imboden reports that when he left it the entire embankment, for about 50 yards, had been swept away. A similar crevasse, with like results, was also made in the canal, about 4 miles below Old Town." On June 20 Superintendent Lloyd Lowe informed Ringgold that, in addition to the breaks in the canal, the Confederates had also damaged several lock gates. He estimated that the damages extended over a distance of twenty miles, from Lock Number 75 (nine miles below Cumberland) to the Paw Paw Tunnel.[21]

Imboden continued east and on June 22 his men entered Hancock. Diarist James Ripley Smith wrote that the Confederates took nearly all of the goods in town and let the water out of the canal. Several days earlier a small unit of Confederate cavalry commanded by Capt. John H. McNeill had occupied the town.[22]

Confederate Brig. Gen. John D. Imboden. Source: Library of Congress, Prints and Photographs Division

Union. Brig. Gen. Henry W. Benham. Source: Library of Congress, Prints and Photographs Division

In response to the Confederate move toward the Potomac, Federal units south of the Rappahannock were withdrawn and the pontoon bridges across the river were taken up and sent to Washington. On June 16 Brig. Gen. Henry W. Benham, who commanded the Engineer Brigade, received orders to have 1,200 feet of pontoon material in the canal for Nolands Ferry by daylight of June 18. In all, Benham sent nearly 600 men up the canal to protect the pontoon train and lay the bridge.[23]

Hooker had assigned Benham to command the engineer brigade in March. The previous commander, Brig. Gen. Daniel P. Woodbury, was a mild-mannered, scholarly engineer who was well-respected by his men. In temperament Benham was the opposite of Woodbury—jealous, proud, strict, and mean-tempered. Benham's men had little respect for his engineering skills and dreaded his tendency to push them beyond what they thought their duties—as engineers—should be. True to form, as the Confederate invasion of Maryland commenced, Benham drove his engineers relentlessly. On June 17 he gave instructions to Col. William H. Pettes, commander the Fiftieth New York Volunteer Engineers: "The [pontoon] boats, after getting into the canal, will be pushed forward as fast as possible to Nolands Ferry, where the bridge is ordered to be laid before noon of the 18th. Teams, if possible, will be procured from Washington, to haul the boats along the canal. . . . If the teams are not ready in Georgetown, the boats will be pushed along the canal as fast as possible by the men." The teams did not arrive until early afternoon, which required the engineers to use manpower to pull the boats along the lower canal.[24]

By June 19 the pontoon train had arrived at the Monocacy River, just below Nolands Ferry. On the same day Maj. Gen. Henry W. Slocum, Twelfth Corps commander who had been ordered to Leesburg, suggested to Hooker's chief of staff that the pontoon bridge should be built at Edwards Ferry because it was more secure from raids and because supplies could be sent up the canal and across the bridge to his command. Only two days after Lt. Col. Elijah V. White had led a Confederate raiding party across the river at nearby Point of Rocks, Hooker relented and ordered the engineers to build the pontoon bridge at Edwards Ferry.[25]

Upon his arrival at Edwards Ferry the next morning, Maj. Ira Spaulding, who commanded the detachment of engineers, discovered a problem. He had 1,200 feet of bridge material to span the river at Nolands Ferry, but the river at Edwards Ferry was 1,400 feet across. Spaulding asked Benham to forward additional bridge material and turned over the construction of the bridge to engineer Capt. Charles N. Turnbull. The additional material was pushed forward and early on June 21 Turnbull constructed the bridge over the river.[26]

To meet the Confederate invasion, most of the Army of the Potomac crossed the river over the pontoon bridge at Edwards Ferry. Cavalry patrols and additional troops were sent out from Washington. Such a large movement of men, horses, artillery, and wagon trains played havoc with the canal. On June 24 Turnbull wrote: "If heavy supply trains are to continue crossing this bridge, we shall need at once a sufficient quantity of 2-inch plank to cover the roadway, 1,580 feet in length, in order to save the chesses. The bridge over the canal also needs repairs badly, and I have no lumber to do it with." On June 19 Horace Benton, superintendent of the Georgetown Division, wrote that an officer had ordered his men to tear down the towpath crossover bridge above the Potomac Aqueduct because the large number of soldiers passing over it had "depressed it so much that it became in the way of the Gov. transports passing up the canal." He requested permission from the Quartermaster's Department to build an incline to the mouth of the aqueduct so that the mules and horses could pass over the trestlework bridge that the government had built to the aqueduct in late 1861.[27]

To facilitate the passage of the army, Hooker ordered his engineers to build another pontoon bridge at the Monocacy, although a day later Hooker ordered Turnbull to stop the material at Edwards Ferry and construct the second bridge at that point. The pontoons arrived on June 25, a day later than expected "on account of the crowded state of the canal," according to Turnbull. The engineers built the bridge in three hours. In all, military engineers constructed two bridges across the river at Edwards Ferry, two bridges over the canal and one over the mouth of Goose Creek in Virginia, opposite Edwards Ferry.[28]

The Quartermaster Department established a temporary supply depot along the canal at Edwards Ferry to service the troops crossing the Potomac. Quartermaster Sawtelle directed officers to receive surplus property and to issue clothing and forage to the troops and animals streaming back into Maryland to meet the Confederate invasion.[29]

After having crossed the pontoon bridges, many units headed up the canal towpath to the Monocacy River. Brig. Gen. Andrew A. Humphreys, who commanded the Second Division, Third Army Corps, wrote that his men reached the Monocacy after a difficult march of over twenty-five miles, much of it in the rain. The next morning the men began to cross the Monocacy Aqueduct for Point of Rocks. Edwin B. Houghton of the Seventeenth Maine wrote that "several ludicrous incidents" occurred in passing over the aqueduct. "One or two officers' horses became unmanageable, and backed into the canal," he wrote, "and several pack animals, loaded with bedding and cooking utensils, after reaching the middle of the crossing, with characteristic stubbornness decided to go no further. The soldiers, whose path they were obstructing, would belabor them with their muskets, and not unfrequently 'Mr. Mule' and his entire load would be unceremoniously hustled into the canal."[30]

By June 27 the last of the Federal troops had crossed the river at Edwards Ferry. On that day and the next the pontoon bridges were taken up. Some bridge material was loaded onto wagons for transportation back to Washington via road. The remaining material was placed in the canal for Georgetown. George Spates came to the area three days later and reported that the bridge over Lock Number 25 at Edwards Ferry was damaged and unable to turn on its pivot, explaining that the damage resulted from "the entire army of the Potomac having crossed at that lock."[31]

Several days earlier General Lee had authorized Jeb Stuart's cavalry to cross the Potomac between the Federal army and Washington. Stuart was delayed, however, by the presence of the Union troops moving toward the pontoon bridges at Edwards Ferry. Late on June 27 Stuart's men reached the river and learned from local citizens that the ford below Seneca Creek was about two feet higher than usual. After his men examined another ford and found it no better, the horsemen proceeded to cross the river at Seneca with ammunition in their hands to prevent it from getting wet. Once across the Potomac, the Confederates had difficulty crossing the canal. To solve the problem the men stopped the first boat to approach and compelled the captain to turn the boat across the canal and throw down his gangplank. Twenty men crossed the canal over the boat and established videttes on the Maryland shore. Others began to construct a bridge across Lock Number 24, located just below the aqueduct over Seneca Creek. By early morning of the next day Stuart's entire command had forded the river and crossed the canal.[32]

Stuart quickly set his sights on the waterway. He later wrote: "The canal, which was now the supplying medium of Hooker's army, soon received our attention. A lock gate was broken, and steps taken to intercept boats. At least a dozen were intercepted, and the next morning several loaded with troops, negroes, and stores were captured." After a short rest Stuart took possession of Rockville and captured a long wagon train within three to four miles of Washington. The Confederates also seized twenty-five teams of horses that the Quartermaster Department had sent toward Edwards Ferry to draw the pontoon boats down the canal. Two days after the affair George Spates examined the Seneca region and reported that the Confederates had burned nine boats, one of which had been burned in the

Confederate Maj. Gen. J. E. B. Stuart. Source: Library of Congress, Prints and Photographs Division.

chamber of the Seneca Aqueduct. Two or three other boats had grounded when Stuart's men drew the water out of the canal. The cavalrymen had broken the lock gates at Seneca as well those at the inlet lock behind Dam Number 2. On July 1 Halleck wrote: "The destruction of unguarded property on the canal along the Potomac has been terrible."[33]

Union Brig. Gen. Benjamin F. Kelley. Source: Library of Congress, Prints and Photographs Division.

On June 28 Department of Washington commander Maj. Gen. Samuel Heintzelman had warned Halleck that the withdrawal of Federal forces from the river to join the Army of the Potomac would "leave the Potomac unguarded from the fortifications of Washington to the mouth of the Monocacy," and permit "a small force of guerrillas to cross into Maryland, destroy the canal, and interrupt the railroad communication between

Washington and Baltimore." Heintzelman did not know that Stuart had already accomplished much of what he had predicted.[34]

The damage to government property could have been much worse. The Confederates missed intercepting the pontoon material from Edwards Ferry that engineers had taken up on June 28 and were returning to Georgetown on the canal. In addition, on June 25 the entire volunteer engineer corps, along with the remaining pontoon material at the depot in Washington, was ordered to join the Army of the Potomac in the field. The three mile long train was in Poolesville, about five miles from Seneca, when Stuart crossed the river. In his memoir, Maj. Wesley Brainerd noted the large plume of dust and smoke to the east on the morning of June 28.[35]

Fortunately for the Union army, Stuart's men only drained the water from the canal and did not damage its walls. The canal was quickly re-watered and military engineers, who had accompanied the pontoon train, repaired the lock gates at Seneca. Using ropes to work the locks, the men made forty-three passes to move one-hundred pontoon boats to Georgetown, along with eighteen canal boats carrying military stores. George Spates, on his June 30 visit to Seneca, informed the company: "Boats are now passing over the entire division each way in the employ of the U.S. Government."[36]

At Harpers Ferry, Federal forces were at risk of being isolated and captured by the advancing Confederates, as had happened in 1862. Consequently, the troops had abandoned the town and withdrew to Maryland Heights with as much ordnance and supplies as they could move up the mountain. On June 26 Hooker had asked Halleck for authority to abandon Maryland Heights, which the general-in-chief refused. The confrontation resulted in Hooker tendering his resignation due to interference from Washington. Lincoln accepted the resignation and promptly placed Maj. Gen. George G. Meade at the head of the Army of the Potomac. Halleck subsequently gave Meade authority to dispose of the garrison at Harpers Ferry as he wished.[37]

On June 28 Meade ordered Maryland Heights abandoned and all government property moved to Washington. The troops dismantled the forts and brought the stores, guns, and munitions from the mountain and loaded them into canal boats that soldiers had seized from the waterway. Because of the risk of raids, Meade directed Maj. Gen. William French to detail a heavy contingent of troops to escort the canal boats to Georgetown. On June 30 twenty-six canal boats loaded with the government property departed for Washington with an escort of about 3,500 troops. The supplies and munitions, delayed by the broken lock gates at Seneca, arrived safely at Georgetown on July 4. In their haste to reach safety, and perhaps because of their inexperience with canal locks, the Federal troops inadvertently damaged gates at Lock Number 13, located about five miles below Great Falls, and Lock Number 16, sited less than a mile below the head of Great Falls.[38]

As a result of the Confederate invasion, activity at the Georgetown docks quickly dwindled. On July 9 the Georgetown correspondent of the *Washington Evening Star* reported that the wharves were clear of vessels: "Business is at a stand still, and all seem awaiting the result of the grand military operations now taking place."[39]

As the Confederates moved into Pennsylvania, those along the canal enjoyed an all too brief respite from the war. At Williamsport, Jacob B. Masters reported the he had begun to make repairs to his division, but progress was slow because the invasion had scattered his laborers and the Confederates had taken all of his tools. Alfred Spates was in Baltimore when the Confederates crossed into Maryland. As the southerners proceeded to Pennsylvania, Spates decided to personally inspect the Hancock Division since he had yet to hear from its superintendent regarding any damage. He arrived in Hagerstown on the evening of July 1. After its repulse on the third day of the Battle of Gettysburg, the Confederate army retreated back toward the river fords at Williamsport. On July 6 Spates was in Hagerstown when southern horsemen took control of the city from Federal cavalry. When the Confederates reached Williamsport they found the Potomac swollen from recent rains and learned that Federal cavalry had destroyed its pontoon bridge. As the southern troops waited for the river to fall, they prepared entrenchments on the heights above Williamsport, started to ferry their wounded across the river, and began to rebuild their pontoon bridge.[40]

On July 9 the *Cumberland Civilian and Telegraph* reported that Cumberland Division superintendent Lloyd Lowe was "busily engaged with a night and day force in order to speedily put the canal in navigable order between this city and Hancock." Lowe had great incentive to begin the work promptly. On July 4 Halleck had ordered Brig. Gen. Benjamin Kelley to harass Lee's retreating army, and Kelley wanted to use the canal to transport supplies from his base at Cumberland to Hancock. Kelley subsequently agreed to pay for the repairs if the superintendent could complete them in a week. By July 10 Lowe completed temporary repairs that permitted him to re-water the canal to Hancock for boats drawing no more than three and one-half feet of water, while a crew continued to work on the largest break near Cumberland. Hancock resident James Ripley Smith recorded that the company began repairs in his town on July 11. On July 10 Company H of the Second Potomac Home Brigade escorted three canal boats carrying commissary and quartermaster stores from Cumberland. At times low water in the canal forced the men to engage in "mule duty" to bring the boats down. On July 18 the boats arrived at Hancock. Although Hancock Division Superintendent Thomas Hassett had not quite finished his repairs, Kelley forced him to water the canal so that the boats could pass. Lowe continued with repairs and on July 30 informed the company that his division was ready for boating.[41]

After Lowe had expedited the work as Kelley had requested, he had difficulty obtaining payment from the general. On July 13 he informed the company office: "Gen'l Kelly refuses to pay for the work as agreed on between him and myself (he [now] says that he promised to pay for it *if the company failed to do so*). He [originally] told me if I could repair the canal in 7 or 8 days . . . to do so & he would pay for it [emphasis added]." Several weeks later Kelley relented. On July 30 Lowe informed the company office that Kelley had offered $800 toward the repair work, which the superintendent expected to receive in a few days. Lowe wrote that he had borrowed money against the promised sum in order to pay some of the laborers. The actual cost of the repairs was $1,100.[42]

Repairs at Seneca also progressed rapidly. On July 5 Meade's chief of staff ordered Benham to send a party of engineers and pontoons for two bridges up the canal to Harpers Ferry. To facilitate their passage, on July 6 Quartermaster General Meigs sent a team of quartermasters up the canal to complete the repairs of the lock gates at Seneca. The next day, less then twenty-four hours after receiving the order and before the quartermasters had completed work on the Seneca locks, Benham wrote: "Major Brainerd, with about 200 men and one full bridge, started at 8 a.m., and are on the way to the canal above Georgetown." He put the second bridge train on the rails, which departed the next morning. He sent a third bridge by land the same day. On July 8 the bridges sent by canal and railroad arrived opposite Harpers Ferry. A week later, after Federal forces crossed the river and drove a small contingent of Confederates from the town, the engineers built the bridges.[43]

At Williamsport the Confederates constructed a new pontoon bridge to replace the one that Federal cavalry had destroyed. John Harman, the Confederate's resourceful and energetic quartermaster, appropriated boards from several nearby sawmills and supplemented his supply with lumber torn from warehouses and disabled canal boats. He built new pontoons and floated them down river to Falling Waters where a new bridge was built. The Confederates quickly began to take their wagons and artillery across the bridge. The water in the ford at Williamsport soon dropped to four and a half feet, which allowed the infantry and cavalry to cross. On July 14 the last of the southern troops, under heavy pressure from Union cavalry, crossed the pontoon bridge to Virginia.[44]

While at Williamsport the Confederates had days to inflict damage to the canal on their crossing and re-crossing of the ford. On July 19 Superintendent Jacob B. Masters informed the company office: "I find the damage on this division by the Rebels together with the late heavy rains to be very serious." The Confederates had torn apart the stonework on the Conococheague Aqueduct at the four corners down to the bottom of the canal and removed enough stone from one of the arches to create a ten-foot gap. They had also torn away the coping and railing around the aqueduct and thrown it into the creek. At Lock Number 44, the Confederates had burned the gates and removed two rows of stone from the lock and tossed them into the canal. Lee's men had also dug out the banks of the canal in four places to allow passage of their wagons and artillery and had ransacked the toll collector's office.[45]

On July 14 Brig. Gen. Gouverneur K. Warren, chief engineer of the Army of the Potomac, ordered Spaulding to construct another pontoon bridge at Berlin. A break in the canal one-quarter mile below Berlin complicated matters, however. The break occurred about July 10 and was probably caused by high water after a week of rain. On July 13 Warren authorized Spaulding to send one-hundred men to help repair the canal if it did not interfere with laying the pontoon bridge at Harpers Ferry. Spaulding, still at work on the first bridge, replied: "After receiving your order to build the bridge here, I could not spare men to work on the canal. The canal superintendent [George Spates] has gone down to do the work, but I don't think he has fairly commenced the work yet. It will take him two days to repair the break, with plenty of wheelbarrows, which he has not on hand."[46]

On July 15 Benham put two bridge trains in the canal for Berlin. Surplus bridge components were forwarded from Harpers Ferry, and engineers began to repair defective bridge material in order to have enough pontoons to span the river at Berlin. After Spaulding had completed the bridge at Harpers Ferry on July 14, he sent a party of engineers to help the canal company repair the break below Berlin. With the assistance of the engineers—and fifty wheelbarrows provided by the army—the break was repaired on July 16. The pontoon bridge was laid the next day. On July 17 the final complement of bridge material arrived via canal and engineers began work on a second pontoon bridge at Berlin, which was completed the following day.[47]

On the morning of July 15 Meade set his army in motion for the river crossings in pursuit of Lee's army. He directed four corps to the as-yet un-built bridge at Berlin and three corps to the pontoon bridge at Harpers Ferry. Brig. Gen. Rufus Ingalls, chief quartermaster of the Army of the Potomac, established supply depots at Berlin, Sandy Hook, and Harpers Ferry, all of which were linked with both the railroad and canal. Stores sent up the canal were slow to arrive, however, because a portion of the canal had to be re-watered following the repair of the break.[48]

Over the next ten days Meade's army crossed the Potomac over the pontoon bridges at Berlin and Harpers Ferry. On July 26–27 the engineers took up the two bridges at Berlin. The Potomac was full of bridge debris, however. Two pontoon bridges had been cut loose in the river since the commencement of the Gettysburg Campaign: the new Federal bridge built at Dam Number 3 near Harpers Ferry that Union soldiers had destroyed when they evacuated the town, and the first Confederate pontoon bridge at

RUINS OF THE AQUEDUCT ON THE OHIO AND CHESAPEAKE CANAL, AT WILLIAMSPORT.—SKETCHED BY C. E. H. BONWILL.

Conococheague Aqueduct at Williamsport. Note damage to corners of aqueduct. *Frank Leslie's Illustrated Newspaper*, Aug. 1, 1863. Source: author's collection.

Falling Waters, which Federal cavalry had burnt and hacked apart. In addition, a quantity of damaged and unutilized bridge components had been abandoned at Berlin the previous autumn. A company of engineers was detailed to remove stray bridge material from the river. An engineer estimated that $12,000 was saved by removing bridge components from the river. The original bridges and the salvaged material was placed in the canal and returned to the engineer depot in Washington.[49]

Canal boatmen faced a period of relative inactivity until the company completed repairs to the waterway. Those whose boats had been seized by the government went to Georgetown to claim their property. On July 15 the *Washington Evening Star* wrote that many boat captains were taking their boats as far up the canal as possible, explaining: "This will enable them to pasture their mules until the canal is repaired at a much less expense than feeding them in town."[50]

Soon limited boating resumed at the eastern end of the canal. Boats that had been stranded in the waterway east of Harpers Ferry began to arrive at port. On July 30 the Georgetown correspondent of the *Washington Evening Star* reported that the first load of coal since the Confederate invasion had arrived, and that seven more boats were expected. In anticipation of full navigation, the prices of grain, coal, and other commodities had begun to fall.[51]

At Williamsport, where the canal suffered the most extensive damage, the company had no assistance from the government and the work progressed slowly. Superintendent Masters estimated that repairs would cost $3,000, nearly three times the amount required on the Cumberland division. He initially thought he could complete the work in three weeks, but as August approached the work lagged. Until the company completed repairs, the waterway was essentially cut in two, with local boating getting underway on the eastern and western ends of the canal.[52]

In late July Albert C. Greene traveled to Williamsport to check the status of the repair work. On July 25 he informed the company that Masters had work crews removing sand bars in the canal bed and mending the breaks in the towpath. Work on the aqueduct had not yet begun, although the superintendent was making the necessary preparations. Greene was surprised that the damage to the canal at Williamsport was not greater: "Its

Union pontoon bridges at Berlin. Note the canal just below the river. Source: Library of Congress, Prints and Photographs Division.

[sic] really wonderful that a month's hostile occupancy of the canal should have resulted in so little damage."[53]

Masters expedited repairs to the aqueduct so that boating could resume. On August 1 he informed Greene that he was permanently replacing the stonework on the towpath side of the aqueduct, but was only making temporary repairs on the berm side. A few days later he told the company office that he would only make repairs to the water mark because his supply of stone was limited. On August 8 he completed enough repairs at Williamsport to re-water the canal.[54]

Despite the opening of the canal for through navigation, boats were slow getting started from Cumberland. The boatmen demanded twenty-five cents per ton more to transport coal, which would have raised their rate to $2.00 per ton. The coal companies refused, however, and, after enduring about two months of inactivity due to the late invasion, the boatmen relented and went back to work at the old rate. By late August, 121 boats had left Cumberland carrying over 13,000 tons of coal.[55]

Once boating began, Confederate cavalry conducted numerous small-scale raids across the Potomac that inhibited commerce on the canal. From August through September, Confederate horsemen made at least a dozen raids into Maryland. Particularly hard hit was that portion of the canal east of the Monocacy River, especially between Whites Ford and Edwards Ferry. On August 27 the *Cumberland Civilian and Telegraph* wrote: "Since the completion of repairs and resumption of navigation on the canal, several boatmen have been plundered of their stock by predatory bands, which has very seriously interfered with the shipments of coal, by giving rise to so great a sense of insecurity among the boatmen as to induce many of them to decline boating." Citizens and newspapers along the Potomac called for stronger defense of the river. The *Frederick Examiner* was particularly critical of the head of the Department of Washington, Heintzelman, in whose jurisdiction most of the raids were committed. After two raids on the Monocacy Division occurred on August 28, the newspaper opined: "Our cavalry forces about Washington are either insufficient for the work or badly managed. It is time that these raids were brought to a summary ending."[56]

Additionally, west of the Monocacy the company again experienced interference with its operations by Union forces. After the Confederates retreated to Virginia, Pennsylvania Governor Curtin quickly mobilized state militia in response to an emergency call from the president. Although technically a component of Maj. Gen. Darius Couch's Department of the Susquehanna, the militia was sent forward to serve on the Potomac while the Army of the Potomac pursued the retreating Confederates. On August 11 Alfred Spates wrote nearly identical letters to Lincoln and Stanton announcing that the company had resumed navigation and asking for military protection of the canal. He added: "We have at present, much trouble & difficulty made by the Penn Militia now occupying a considerable portion of the Canal from Hancock to Harpers Ferry in Washington and Frederick Counties." Spates also wrote that other Federal units hampered navigation, including Capt. Samuel C. Means of the Loudoun Virginia Independent Rangers whose horsemen were stationed at Point of Rocks. Spates related that Means's men had seized horses and mules used by canal boatmen and company officials.[57]

On August 19 a Union staff officer assured Spates that McClellan's General Orders No. 44 was still in force, and that the War Department had directed Generals Couch, Kelley—the last named now heading the Department of West Virginia which included all of Maryland west of Monocacy—and Brig. Gen. William H. Morris—temporarily head of the Middle Department—to protect the canal within their commands. On August 31 Kelley informed Spates that Means had denied seizing canal company horses and mules, but that he had ordered him and commanding officers at Harpers Ferry and Hagerstown to correct the problems of which Spates had complained. On August 24 the commander at Hagerstown, Brig Gen. William F. Smith, informed Spates that he had sent copies of General Orders No. 44 to all his officers stationed along the river and asked the canal president to let him know what damage his men had caused and to identify the troops under suspicion.[58]

In August Spates wrote to Heintzelman to complain about the raids across the river in the Department of Washington. On August 22 Heintzelman replied that he had assigned cavalry to guard the canal from Georgetown to the Monocacy, which he thought sufficient. The raids continued, however, encouraged by a late summer drought that allowed easy fording of the river. On September 19 George Spates wrote that Lock numbers 26 and 27, located below the Monocacy River, needed repairs, but he feared that if he drew off the water Confederate horsemen would cross and capture additional teams of mules and horses.[59]

Albert C. Greene, in a September 2 letter to Ringgold, expressed the continuing frustration of those associated with the canal trade:

You cannot have failed to learn that the canal is again practically closed by the neglect of the Government to afford the Boatmen protection against robbery of their teams by the Virginia guerrillas. The few boats which arrive at Cumberland decline to load and tie up their boats being unwilling and, in fact, unable to risk the loss of, in many cases, everything they have. We all understand that the military authorities promised to secure the navigation, but a large number of boats have since been disabled by the loss of their teams, and have stopped. I think it would meet the unanimous approbation of this whole community if Moseby [sic] or White or whoever leads these incursions should ride into Washington some fine night and carry off with them, to parts unknown, Gen. Halleck, Sec. Stanton, and everybody else whose duty it was to prevent these shameful raids.

Greene added that a heavy rain would help correct the problem by raising the river and making it un-fordable, "but our old fashioned drought is upon us with no prospect of a let up until winter."[60]

In response to public criticism and its need for Cumberland Coal, the army began to bolster river defenses. It strengthened cavalry patrols and constructed blockhouses to defend vulnerable fords. On September 30 George Spates wrote that he had difficulty obtaining good lumber to build and repair lock gates because the government had cut the best trees to build blockhouses and forts. He also noted that strong cavalry forces patrolled the most exposed portions of his division.[61]

Federal cavalry also had some success capturing border raiders in late 1863. On September 20, just a few weeks after a band of Confederate cavalry had captured three sutlers' wagons near Hyattstown, Marylander Maj. Henry Cole led three Union cavalry battalions that captured eleven members of the band west of Leesburg, all Marylanders from Company B of the Thirty-fifth Virginia Cavalry, commanded Lt. Col. Elijah V. White. On December 9 notorious raider Evan Dorsey was captured attempting to cross Federal lines at Monrovia. On December 16 the *Frederick Examiner* suggested that the bushwackers "should at least be placed beyond the reach of doing harm until their probation be satisfactory [served], instead of being strewed along the banks of the Potomac, where they can readily concoct schemes of mischief and combine with a reasonable chance of successful execution. Such a fellow as Dorsey would be a fit instrument to carry out some reckless Rebel plot."[62]

Political troubles struck the canal in August. In late July Alfred Spates was in Baltimore where he met a number of friends and acquaintants. Their conversation turned to the recent Confederate invasion. Spates—in what he later said was a case of playful boasting to a group of "old personal friends"—related that while the southern troops were in Hagerstown he had met with Lt. Gen. Ewell regarding the damages to the canal, and that he had obtained a pass to cross Confederate lines directly from General Lee. One party to the conversation, Henry W. Hoffman, informed the provost marshal of Spates's claims. Hoffman, the customs collector for the Port of Baltimore, was a former Congressman and former canal company treasurer whom Spates believed desired the presidency of the canal company. As a result of Hoffman's information, the provost marshal of the Middle Department arrested Spates and questioned him. He was released, wrote a letter to explain his conduct [see Appendix C], but was rearrested about September 1 and confined to Fort McHenry in Baltimore. Although in mid-September Spates posted bond and was released, it was apparent that the government was taking the allegations against the canal company president very seriously. In the absence of Spates, on September 10 the canal's board of directors appointed director and former company president Lawrence J. Brengle of Frederick County president ad interim.[63]

The government put Spates on trial by military commission (only members of the army are subject to courts martial), which began in Baltimore on September 16, 1863. In his defense, Spates explained that on July 6 he had been trapped in Hagerstown by the Confederate army as it retreated from Gettysburg. Two days later he had run into General Lee's aide, Col.

Charles Marshall, whom he had known in Baltimore before the war. The next day he had gone to the Confederate camp to seek Marshall's help in obtaining recompense for a local farmer whose cattle had been taken. While in Marshall's presence he asked for and received a pass to cross Confederate lines—signed by Marshall—which he claimed he sought so that he could attend to the canal. While leaving, Marshall spied General Lee surrounded by a small crowd of local citizens. Marshall introduced Spates, pleasantries were explained, and after a few moments the canal president departed the camp.[64]

After a three week trial, on October 6 the case was sent to the commission of eight army officers for deliberation. On December 4 the commission announced that it had found Spates guilty of crossing Confederate lines and communicating with the enemy, which included obtaining a pass from the Confederates; but not guilty of giving aid and intelligence to the enemy. Spates was subsequently taken into custody and sentenced to spend the remainder of the war confined in Fort Warren in Boston's harbor. After previously writing two letters to Secretary Stanton in an attempt to escape the charges against him, on December 13 he wrote a letter to Assistant Secretary of War Peter H. Watson, proclaiming his innocence and asking Watson to urge Stanton to arrange for his release. He explained, "the whole case against me grew out of the malice of Charles M. Thruston and Henry W. Hoffman . . . and is no case. I went to Washington County to put the Chesapeake and Ohio Canal in order—and did—for the use of the Government and Genl. Kelly [sic] now here will state I did and he used it." While he waited for his case to be reviewed, Spates was sent to Fort Warren.[65]

Additional political problems arose from the Confederate occupation of Hagerstown. William Brown, stonemason for Stake and Simms, was also arrested and confined to Fort McHenry. Brown's home, located on Franklin Street in Hagerstown, was used as a temporary headquarters during the Confederate retreat from Gettysburg. It was rumored that a dinner for Confederate cavalry leader Jeb Stuart was given in Brown's home. As a result of the stonemason's arrest, work on Dam Number 5 was suspended. Andrew K. Stake wrote Brengle that Brown was "our main dependence in stone work." Stake was unsure of the charges against Brown, but did not think that he was disloyal. With low water in the river and the Confederates now south of the Potomac, it was an ideal time for work on the dam. Stake wrote: "This arrest as well as that of Alfred Spates, esq., has had the effect to cause a suspension of the work on the construction of the Virginia abutement [sic] of Dam No. 5, and at a time too when the work can ill afford to stand idle."[66]

Brengle informed Stake and Simms that if the work at Dam Number 5 was not commenced by October 1, the canal company would consider the work abandoned. William Simms, the other partner in the company, replied that only Brown possessed the skills necessary to complete the work. He reported that after the stonemason had posted bond, he went north to see his ill son. Simms said that Brown had always wanted to finish the work and that he would try to convince him to take the loyalty oath. The next day, October 1, Simms telegraphed Brengle that Brown had arrived in Baltimore and would be at Dam Number 5 two days later.[67]

In October Brown began to work on the dam again. He placed temporary coffer dams in the river to divert water from the work site. Unfortunately, heavy rains washed away portions of the coffer dams. The river remained high throughout October. When it dropped, Brown commenced the stonework to the abutment until December when cold weather and the formation of ice stopped him.[68]

With the decline of border raids due to high water and strengthened defenses, business on the canal flourished. During October the company shipped nearly 38,000 tons of coal from Cumberland and collected about $26,000 in tolls, a sum virtually equal to the amount collected in May. In November, despite the expiration of the higher freight rate adopted earlier in the year, tolls dropped to just over $19,000, which was still the third greatest monthly total collected during the first three years of the war.[69]

In late November Alfred Spates, free on bond while his case was being deliberated, was back at work in Cumberland. On November 26 the *Civilian and Telegraph* wrote: "He is here and is putting forth his usual energies in aid of the Chesapeake and Ohio Canal to profit the interests of Allegany County. We have been informed that it is his intention to keep the Canal open as long as possible during the winter. He has contracted with our boat-builders for additional boats to be used as ice-breakers in order to accomplish this important task. Should he be so fortunate as to keep the canal open so as to extend the season of navigation there will be a very large coal business done." A cold snap struck the eastern United States late in the year, however. On January 1 James Ripley Smith recorded that the ice had closed the canal at Hancock.[70]

§

The year was an important one for the canal company. During the Gettysburg Campaign it played its most important role in any single campaign of the war as it facilitated the Army of the Potomac's confrontation with Confederates north of the Potomac and its pursuit of the southern army south of the river. The year was also a profitable one for the company, its first during the war. In its annual report, the directors noted: "The business of the Canal for the past year has been much better than that of the preceeding [sic] years; there was less interruption to the trade from military movements and other casualties to which it had been subjected, and but for the invasion of June last, which in a great measure suspended business for two months of the most active period of the year, the revenues of the company would have exceeded those of any former year." Revenue for the year totaled over $160,000, more than twice that of the preceding year, and exceeded expenses by over $60,000. The company shipped nearly 230,000 tons of coal in 1863, almost two and one-half times the amount shipped in 1862. Flour descending the canal increased by 17 percent while shipments of wheat rose by 36 percent, despite a suspension of navigation for 2 months during the middle of the summer.[71]

The company's success in 1863 was not as great as it first appeared. Neither revenue nor total tons shipped came close to equaling that of 1860. In addition, the company still owed nearly $50,000 in interest on currents debts and $10,000 in interest on outstanding toll certificates, exclusive of unpaid interest on its construction and repair bonds. In addition, $37,308 in toll certificates was outstanding. Although in the past two years the company had paid all current expenses and over $91,000 toward its floating debt, it still owed about $380,000 to contractors, merchants, employees, banks, and other debt holders. Additionally, the board estimated that it had lost about $50,000 in revenue as a result of the Confederate invasion.[72]

§

In 1863 political turmoil in Maryland would indirectly affect the state's relationship to the canal. In November statewide elections were held for comptroller and to fill seats in the General Assembly and U.S. Congress. A political division had been growing in the state's Union Party, mostly over slavery. By 1863 both wings generally agreed that the institution was dying politically, if not economically, but differed on the solution to the problem. One branch, which became known as the Unconditional Unionists, led by flamboyant Maryland politician Henry Winter Davis, favored the immediate emancipation of Maryland's slaves and encouraged their enlistment in the Union army. The other group, the Conservative Unionists, led by Montgomery Blair, initially favored a gradual and compensated emancipation of slaves. This group feared the equality of the races and competition for laboring jobs, and urged the colonization of ex-slaves to Haiti, Africa, or other countries. It was also opposed to the enlistment of ex-slaves into the army.

The election results were a victory to the Unconditional Unionists. The party won four of the five House congressional seats, although in three of the districts the Unconditional Unionist candidate ran unopposed, including the fourth congressional district where Francis Thomas was reelected. In the House of Delegates, the Unconditionals garnered fifty-two of seventy-four seats, and in the state Senate at least twelve of twenty-one seats. In addition, in the only race for a statewide office, the Unconditional Unionists candidate, Henry Goldsborough, won the comptroller post with sixty-nine percent of the vote.

Following the success of the Unconditional Union Party, there was much momentum to address the existence of slavery in Maryland. With Lincoln's issuance of the Emancipation Proclamation and the success of Union arms, the future of human bondage in the state was in doubt. The 1851 state constitution, however, forbade the legislature from interfering with the institution. A constitutional convention was the only legal way to reopen the slavery issue, and the Unconditional Unionists, not without support from some Conservative Unionists including Governor Bradford, began to make plans for a convention in the next year. The convention would open the state's entire constitution for revision. In addition to addressing slavery, in the coming year the state's relationship to its public works, particularly the canal, would be debated in convention.[73]

CHAPTER 6

WE PREDICT AN INCREASED AND PROFITABLE BUSINESS
JANUARY–AUGUST 1864

The C&O Canal Company anticipated a successful boating season in 1864. The Army of the Potomac went into winter quarters around Culpeper, Virginia, while the Army of Northern Virginia took positions south of the Rapidan River, both far from the Potomac. Economic conditions also signaled a rosy forecast for the coal business. The directors of the Hampshire and Baltimore Coal Company, whose mines were located near Westernport, Maryland, informed its stockholders:

> The price of anthracite coal being so high will induce an increased consumption of our [bituminous] coal, which now costs considerably less than anthracite in New York and Boston. And the great activity of the engine-shops, shipyards and rolling mills, supplying the government with iron gunboats, &c., and for whose purpose our coal is the most suitable, also causes an increased demand. In addition, the high rate of exchange excludes, in a great measure, foreign coal from the market. On the other hand, the limited supply, arising from scarcity of labor and transportation facilities, combines with the former in enabling us to sell our produce readily at good prices.[1]

Over the winter the Union army continued to bolster the defense of the river. On February 29 Monocacy Division Superintendent George Spates reassured the company board that a vulnerable stretch of the canal from Muddy Branch, about three miles below Seneca Creek, to Point of Rocks was strongly guarded by infantry and cavalry. After the army had seized and inadvertently sunk his ice breaker in January, it must have been with some apprehension that Spates wrote on March 31: "The Government has been using my scow some two weeks moving and building block houses at the different fords on the river in order that the canal may be strongly guarded this coming season."[2]

Early in 1864 the company also received good news concerning Alfred Spates's detention. As a matter of routine, Judge Advocate General Joseph Holt reviewed the outcomes of courts martial and trials by military commission. He found problems with Spates's trial. He wrote that the conviction for crossing enemy lines was not justified because at the time in question the Confederate army had advanced into Pennsylvania, leaving no guard in Hagerstown. Additionally, when Spates had gone from Hagerstown to Dam Number 5 and back he was only performing his "ordinary avocation." Holt also found that the commission improperly excluded testimony that may have benefited the accused, such as why Spates had gone to Dam Number 5 and what he did there. Holt also wrote that it was not evidence of disloyalty for a citizen to obtain a pass from an occupying army when one is caught inadvertently within enemy lines.[3]

The judge advocate general did not completely exonerate Spates, however. He pointed out that Spates had initially told his friends that he had conversed with Confederate officers, denied doing so in a letter to the provost marshal, and then again admitted to doing so in his written defense. Regarding Spates's multiple accounts of his actions, Holt wrote: "It may be observed that it is a suspicious circumstance in the case and one tending to destroy confidence in the prisoner." Holt also found it suspicious that Spates seemed to move at ease amongst the Confederates: "The testimony respecting the movements of the accused during this period of time and his conduct as regard the rebel leaders shows a degree of fraternizing on his part with the military commanders of the insurgent forces and an immunity and even conscious security enjoyed by him, quite at variance with all our ideas of what *should be* the conduct of, or treatment to be expected by, a prominent, loyal citizen, in the confidence of his government, thrown accidentally among public enemies." Although most witnesses testified that they knew Spates as a loyal man, the judge advocate general noted, one witness—Spates's old nemesis Charles M. Thruston—told the commission that Spates's loyalties were with the secession party, even though he could not name a specific word or act of disloyalty on Spates's part. In his recommendation to Stanton, Holt concluded that, "it may be doubted whether a citizen whose loyalty seems to hang so loosely upon him should escape the consequences of suspicious conduct in the past without some very satisfactory security for the future."[4]

In early January 1864 Stanton issued orders, approved by President Lincoln, that would grant Spates's release "upon his giving a written bond of parole." On February 2, 1864 the War Department issued Special Orders No. 51, paragraph 40, which allowed for the release of Alfred Spates after he had posted bond. Upon his release he almost immediately resumed his duties as president of the canal and served throughout the remainder of the war without prejudice from the government.[5]

The bright prospects for the year might have been reconsidered had the canal company been privy to Confederate plans. In late January, Maj. Gen. Jubal A. Early, who now commanded Jackson's old Valley District, began to move toward the Potomac. On January 30 Brig. Gen. Thomas Rosser's brigade intercepted a train leaving New Creek (present-day Keyser, W.Va.), about eighteen miles southwest of Cumberland. He moved east and proceeded down Pattersons Creek to collect cattle and damage the B&O Railroad. On February 2 he burned the railroad bridges over the creek and over the North Branch of the Potomac. Rosser then crossed the Potomac and destroyed a bridge over the canal and damaged Lock Number 72, located just above Pattersons Creek. Superintendent Lloyd Lowe estimated that it would cost $1,200–$1,800 to repair the damage.[6]

A week later Confederate Maj. Harry Gilmor created an uproar when he stopped a train about sixteen miles west of Harpers Ferry. His men robbed the passengers of their money and personal possessions. Canal director Albert C. Greene, a passenger on the train, was robbed of a watch and cash totaling $300. Gilmor later claimed that he had not known his men were stealing from private citizens. There was such an outcry after the event that Confederate authorities arrested Gilmor and tried him before a court martial, although after a week-long trial he was acquitted.[7]

The company kept the canal open through January, but closed it the next month to complete maintenance tasks. On March 10 the *Cumberland Civilian and Telegraph* noted: "The season for boating on the Chesapeake and Ohio canal has again returned, and already we begin to notice the busy signs of preparation. . . . Should the canal be kept free from rebel raids, we predict an increased and profitable business on the canal the coming season."[8]

By 1864 wartime inflation had begun to seriously undermine the wages of workers, including those who worked for the canal and coal companies. Several hundred-thousand men served in the Union army and navy, no longer producing goods and services, but still consuming them. The government was also a large buyer of food, fuel, and other goods to supply to its army and navy, which increased demand for limited resources. Additionally, the opposing armies destroyed crops and goods and damaged transportation facilities, all of which caused shortages and scarcities. By 1864 the purchasing power of a worker's wages had fallen dramatically. In the mines and on the docks and boats, workers began to demand an increase in wages.

On March 14 Lloyd Lowe reported that the canal had been open for ten days, but only two or three boats, all of which had been loaded the previous season, had started down the canal. He wrote: "The boatmen are holding back for an increase on freight [from the coal companies], they are having trouble to get hands. I found it necessary last month to advance the pay of laborers, and will have to continue it to obtain old hands." He also wrote that a reliable lockkeeper had threatened to quit if the company did not increase his wages. On the Monocacy Division George Spates also reported that his workers were demanding higher wages.[9]

Effective March 1, the canal company raised the toll on coal, which had lapsed to one-quarter cent per ton mile in November of the preceding year, back to five-sixteenths of a cent per ton mile. Director Greene, also superintendent of the Borden Mining Company, urged the board not to raise tolls further because transportation costs had risen throughout the east and threatened to undermine the profits of the coal companies. On March 23 he advised: "Encourage the development of the Canal trade by inspiring confidence that the Canal Co. will *not interpose* to take away *all* the profits, as the B&O RR does." Nevertheless, on May 1 another increase went into effect, which raised the toll on coal to three-eights of a cent per ton mile, or sixty-nine cents to transport a ton of coal from Cumberland to Georgetown. On the same day the company raised the wages of its superintendents, collectors, lockkeepers, and work crew bosses.[10]

The boatmen, who were paid by the ton to take coal to the wharves at Georgetown and other points, initially received a quick advance from the coal companies, which stimulated the building of new canal boats. Greene, however, was concerned that the boatmen would demand further increases. On March 18 he wrote: "We shall have a season of great trouble, I fear, in our business. The Boatmen have gone to work at two doll[ar]s freight 'for the present.' I do not doubt they will make a demand for more, later in the season." Greene also reported trouble in the mines: "The miners are concocting a strike for 25¢ a ton additional! So we go. These demands cannot be granted and I have hardly a hope of avoiding serious suspension of business." Five days later Greene reported that the miners were "uneasy and restless." He continued: "I have no doubt they are fixing for a strike. How it will end I cannot now tell. The prospect is not flattering for the season's business." In early April boatmen who arrived in Georgetown reported that the miners had indeed struck for higher wages.[11]

Greene's fears also came to fruition on the Borden Mining Company docks in Georgetown. In late March the men ceased work and demanded an increase of fifty cents a day. After the coal companies refused to concede, many of the men, "principally colored laborers," went back to work, wrote the March 29 *Washington Evening Star.* The dockworkers remained dissatisfied. On April 18 the *Star* reported that the laborers had struck for wages of $2.00 per day. On the following day the *Star* wrote: "The strike appeared among the Borden Company, but soon extended to all the docks. The agents succeeded in persuading them to resume their labors, by promising that they shall be satisfied next Saturday night." It seems that the canal company's decision to increase the wages of its employees had given impetus to the strikes in the mines and on the docks.[12]

While the labor situation was in flux, heavy spring rains caused the Potomac to rise and further slowed the resumption of navigation. After an early April freshet, rumors circulated that the water had swept away both the Chain Bridge and Dam Number 5. When the river receded the company found only minor damage. Within two weeks the company completed repairs and resumed navigation.[13]

Yet another freshet raced down the river valley in mid-May. This time the high water swept away the pontoon bridge at Harpers Ferry and a new one that military engineers had built across the Potomac at Falling Waters a month earlier. The Engineer Depot in Washington only had pontoons enough to replace the bridge at the Ferry, and the engineers quickly placed a bridge train in the canal. William P. Smith, the B&O's master of transportation, had an engine and cars standing by in Washington to transport the same material. On May 18 Smith wrote Stanton and urged him to place the bridge on his trains, which he said he could deliver to the Ferry in only eight hours, while the same material required twenty-four hours via canal. Stanton concurred, but the pontoon train had already begun its voyage up the waterway. The pontoons did not reach the Ferry until May 20, after having spent nearly three days on the canal, likely delayed by flood-related damages. The pontoon bridge was placed in position the next day.[14]

The spring flooding caused only minor damage to the canal. Once repaired, boating was heavy. Buoyed by two toll increases, the canal company collected its highest tolls during the war. In April the company took in nearly $23,000, in May nearly $39,000, and in June over $40,000. In the last-mentioned month the coal companies shipped an average of about 11,000 tons of coal per week via canal.[15]

As the boating season began, the company had several improvements in mind that would expand the capacity of the canal in the future. To relieve congestion at Georgetown, the company considered the construction of an incline plane or outlet locks above the town. In April a group of canal company directors and members of the Maryland Commission of Public Works visited the Morris Canal in New Jersey. The 102-mile Morris Canal was completed in 1836 between Phillipsburg on the Delaware River and Jersey City on the Hudson River, and connected the anthracite coal fields of Pennsylvania's Lehigh Valley to markets in New Jersey and New York. To overcome a change in elevation of 1,674 feet, engineers on the Morris Canal had built 23 lift locks and 23 incline planes. Incline planes operated by floating canal boats onto a railcar which was then drawn up or lowered down the incline using scotch turbines powered by water from the canal. The largest plane transported boats 100 feet. The C&O Canal directors also considered expanding the length of the locks, which would permit one boat to tow another over the length of the waterway without having to disconnect the second boat to utilize the locks.[16]

Following the visit to the Morris Canal, the Maryland Commission of Public Works sought to influence Congress on behalf of the canal company. In a June 13 memorial [see Appendix B], commission President Frederick Fickey, Jr., asked Congress to appropriate $100,000 to the company for the construction of outlet locks, rather than an incline plane, at or near Georgetown. Fickey explained that when the army took possession of the Potomac Aqueduct, it had "confined its [the canal's] business within the narrow limits of its wharves in Georgetown, which are inadequate for the delivery of the large amount of coal transported over the said Canal. The Boats are therefore detained an unnecessary length of time in the delivery of their cargoes, the coal is materially damaged by handling and . . . the purchaser must pay thirty cents per ton for the handling of coal at Georgetown and wait until his turn comes to get up to the wharves." After extensive handling bituminous coal, being relatively soft and friable, suffered considerable breakage and a portion was lost as coal dust. With outlet locks, Fickey noted that canal boats could pass into the river, relieving congestion in Georgetown, and be towed to the Navy Yard, or discharge coal directly to government steamships "with a single handling and with a great saving of time and money to the government." Francis Thomas agreed to take charge of the memorial in the House on behalf of the Canal Company, but ultimately no further aid was granted by Congress. Although the company offered no reason for preferring outlet locks over an incline plane, perhaps it considered the technology too daunting or deemed it unlikely that the government would appropriate funds for the project. The company would eventually undertake construction of an incline plane about a mile above the Potomac Aqueduct, but not until a decade after the war.[17]

In addition to the resolution concerning outlet locks, on May 30 Thomas introduced another to deepen the channel of the Potomac from the wharves in Georgetown to the Long Bridge in Washington. With a deeper channel, vessels drawing a large draft of water could proceed to and from Georgetown and eliminate an additional handling of coal. The canal company, on the other hand, was not warm to Thomas's proposal. It feared that the dredging machinery and barges would obstruct the river and interfere with existing trade. The Committee on Commerce agreed to consider the matter, but, after already appropriating money to raise the bridges over the canal through Georgetown, it was unwilling to appropriate an additional sum that would benefit the canal company.[18]

In mid-June Confederate General Lee directed Early to enter the Shenandoah Valley to thwart the advance of Maj. Gen. David Hunter and threaten Washington. Early united with Maj. Gen. John C. Breckinridge's command and subsequently caused Hunter, near Lynchburg, to retreat into the mountains of West Virginia with scarcely a fight. Early gave up the pursuit of Hunter and moved down the Valley without resistance. On July 2 he reached Winchester and received a dispatch from Lee to prepare to strike the B&O Railroad and the C&O Canal. Early subsequently sent Imboden's cavalry to the South Branch of the Potomac to destroy the railroad bridges from that point to Martinsburg. Additional cavalry was ordered to burn the railroad bridge over Back Creek, a tributary of the Potomac in Virginia located five miles west of Dam Number 5, and assist Breckinridge in an attack on the Union force that was guarding the railroad at Martinsburg. Early was aided by Mosby's and McNeill's ranger units to the east and west of his line of advance.[19]

On July 4 Federal authorities began to receive reports of Confederate raids from Pattersons Creek to Point of Rocks, a stretch of the border that extended over one hundred and twenty-five miles. In the west Imboden's command attacked the railroad bridge over the South Branch of the Potomac defended by a small Federal force in a blockhouse with an artillery piece mounted on an iron-reinforced railcar, called an "iron-clad car." By late morning Confederate artillery had disabled the ironclad car and Federal forces had abandoned the blockhouse. Southern troops set fire to the bridge and a number crossed the Potomac and set fire to canal boats. On the same day Capt. John H. McNeill's partisan rangers set fire to the Pattersons Creek railroad bridge, but a reinforced Union post repulsed the southern horsemen at the North Branch railroad bridge just east of Cumberland. Kelley at Cumberland was besieged to the east and fearful that the Confederates might continue to move up the line of the railroad toward his headquarters and farther west. He ordered troops at Altamont and Clarksburg, West Virginia, to reinforce the railroad depot at New Creek.[20]

Kelley also feared that Imboden, who had moved down the Potomac after his attack at South Branch, might next strike the bridges over the Cacapon River or Sir John's Run, located about eight miles and five miles southwest of Hancock respectively. On July 5 he informed Hunter: "I have sent 200 infantry with one gun by canal-boats to-day to re-enforce those points and supply them with rations." He also directed an engine and three ironclad cars to patrol the railroad between South Branch and Sir John's Run. Affirming Kelley's instincts, on July 6 Imboden attacked both bridges. The ironclad cars and reinforced posts successfully prevented the destruction of the bridges. The Confederates did, however, destroy the railroad water station and track at Sir John's Run on the Virginia side of the river.[21]

Further east, on July 4 Mosby crossed the river above Point of Rocks to sever communication with Washington, thereby screening Early's advance. While the cavalryman's artillery on the Virginia side lobbed shells into the Federal camp, the Rangers rode up the towpath toward Point of Rocks and chased away Federal cavalry. The Confederates came upon the steam packet *Flying Cloud* in the canal that seventeen clerks from the Treasury Department had used to travel to Harpers Ferry for the national holiday. When they learned of the invasion, the clerks had turned the boat around and had nearly reached Point of Rocks when they came under artillery fire. The passengers abandoned the boat at Lock Number 28, located just above the Point, and fled into the hills. The horsemen raided the boat and took cigars, liquor, and other delicacies before they set it afire. The raiders also fired artillery rounds at an advancing train, but the engineer had been alerted to the presence of the Confederates by the burning canal boat and reversed the engine toward Sandy Hook while many passengers jumped the train and fled into the mountains.[22]

The main body of Mosby's horsemen proceeded down the towpath toward Point of Rocks. Although Federal troops had removed the planking of the bridge that crossed the canal, Mosby's men tore the planks from a nearby building and re-laid the flooring. The horsemen crossed the canal and drove the Federal forces from Point of Rocks. The Confederates plundered the Union camp and local stores in what they later called the Great Calico Raid, so named for the bolts of cloth that they had carried away from the shops. The July 6 *Baltimore American and Commercial*

Confederate Maj. Gen. Jubal Early. Source: Library of Congress, Prints and Photographs Division.

Advertiser reported: "They [Mosby's men] robbed the loyal storekeepers as well as the Rebel sympathizers, leaving nothing but crockery ware and such articles as were not easily carried off."[23]

Later that evening Mosby sent Walter "Wat" Bowie back into Maryland to cut telegraph wires and create havoc for the Federals. Bowie and his small force crossed the river at Nolands Ferry, cut the wires, and advanced up the towpath. The men arrived at the mouth of the Monocacy River and charged onto the aqueduct to disperse Federal soldiers. One of

Confederate Col. John S. Mosby. Source: Library of Congress, Prints and Photographs Division.

the raiders wrote that his fellow rangers "went over the flag-stones at a dead run, the enemy on the other side of the canal firing at them. If a man or a horse had been wounded there it would have been death to him, with the river on the right, twenty feet below, and the canal on their left." Other horsemen left the towpath and took the road that passed under the aqueduct to a store, which they subsequently robbed. The Confederates also set fire to four canal boats before fleeing back to Virginia as Federal cavalry closed on them. A few days later Mosby crossed the Potomac again at Seneca.

He found the Union camp at Poolesville abandoned and took camp stores and thirty head of cattle back to Virginia.[24]

Meanwhile, Breckinridge had captured Martinsburg and Harpers Ferry, chasing the Federals at each post across the river and atop Maryland Heights. The Confederates proceeded to Shepherdstown and on July 4 began to cross the Potomac where they seized supplies and began to burn canal boats. On July 5, as the Confederate invasion was progressing, Alfred Spates wrote to the company office from Cumberland: "The canal is badly damaged, a large number of boats burned & teams captured. The boatsmen [sic] discouraged & leaving the canal." He noted that the river was very low, but the company would begin repairs as soon as it was safe to approach the waterway.[25]

The Confederates advanced to Hagerstown and on July 6 ransomed the town, under the threat of the torch, for $20,000, shoes, and clothing. They then moved east and ransomed the small village of Middletown for $1,500. Thereafter, they proceeded to Frederick and skirmished with Federal troops for two days before the Union troops evacuated the town and took positions behind the Monocacy River. The Confederates entered Frederick and on July 9 ransomed that town for $200,000. Afterward, canal director and Frederick resident Lawrence J. Brengle wrote to Ringgold: "We've had the Rebels on us in full force & made us pay $200,000 to prevent them from plundering and robbing our institutions, stores & private houses. The whole country through which they passed were stripped of horses & cattle & every thing else they could lay their hands on."[26]

At Georgetown, activity on the docks dwindled. On July 9 the *Washington Evening Star* reported: "There is nothing doing in the canal, although the panic created by the rebel raid has subsided. The water [in the canal] continues to be very low, which would hinder the passage of laden boats, even if no other hinderance [sic] of trade existed."[27]

Once the Confederates had moved on, Kelley assessed the condition of the railroad under his charge. The Pattersons Creek railroad bridge was badly burned, but most of the trestles were in good condition. The South Branch bridge was in an even better state. An ironclad car had dispersed the Confederates before they could damage the bridge over the Cacapon River. At Sir John's Run, the bridge was undamaged but some track was

THE REBELS DESTROYING THE CHESAPEAKE AND OHIO CANAL.—[See First Page.]

Confederates breaking the canal. *Harper's Weekly*, July 30, 1864. Source: author's collection.

torn up and the depot burned. The small bridge over Back Creek was burned, however. Kelley's decision to reinforce threatened portions of his command from more secure sections had helped prevent more serious damage. In a July 7 letter to B&O President Garrett, Kelley wrote that the railroad "has been saved by the pluck of my small and scattered command." Repairs to the railroad began almost immediately so that Hunter, who on July 2 Halleck had ordered to the line of the B&O, could be brought quickly back to the region.[28]

Early's invasion created great anxiety in Washington. Although Halleck, now the Union army's chief of staff, thought the number of Early's troops exaggerated, he realized that the defenses of Baltimore and Washington would be unable to repel them. Those who manned the capital's defenses were mostly militia or invalids. On July 5 Halleck sent a telegraph to Lt. Gen. Ulysses Grant, who Lincoln had designated commander-in-chief of all Union armies on March 12, requesting that he forward troops to defend Washington. Grant, in the midst of his assault on Petersburg, subsequently ordered the Sixth and Nineteenth corps to Washington. Halleck originally intended for a portion of Grant's troops to advance to the Monocacy River via the canal. The Sixth Corps troops, commanded by Brig. Gen. James B. Ricketts, were sent by steamers to Baltimore, however, and the first arrivals took B&O railcars to the Monocacy.[29]

In the meantime, Maj. Gen. Lew Wallace, who commanded the Middle Department, Eighth Army Corps, took steps to slow the advance of the Confederates. He advanced his small force of less than 3,000 men from Baltimore to Monocacy Junction where on July 7 they were joined by an additional 3,000 troops under Ricketts. Early's force, estimated from 15,000 to 20,000 men, approached the river on July 9, precipitating the Battle of Monocacy, which delayed Early's advance on Washington by one day. The battle is generally credited with saving Washington from capture because it provided time for two additional Sixth Corps divisions to arrive and file into the fortifications ringing Washington.[30]

As the Confederate army advanced against Washington, its officers dispatched work parties to blow up culverts under the canal and cut trees so that they fell into the waterway. Union troops who picketed the Potomac withdrew toward the capital and tried to impede the Confederate advance.

Maj. D.W.C. Thompson of the Second Massachusetts Cavalry, whose men picketed the Potomac east of the Monocacy, had been ordered to withdraw but to remain in position to observe the position of the Early's army. Thompson organized fatigue parties to obstruct the roads and placed surplus camp supplies on a canal boat. On July 10 the Confederates appeared on the towpath near Muddy Branch. Thompson's men began to retreat down the canal with their boat, harassed by the fire of Confederate skirmishers. At one point the southern troops managed to put an artillery round through the canal boat. The men quickly commandeered another boat and transferred their camp equipment to the new vessel. They pushed down the canal and arrived safely at Georgetown the next morning.[31]

Early reached Washington on July 11, but the heat and fatigue of the summer march had caused much straggling and foraging by his weary troops. With the aid of the telescope, Early observed additional Federal reinforcements filling the forts and he abandoned his proposed attack on the Federal capital. A further plan to send a cavalry expedition to free Confederate prisoners from Point Lookout in southern Maryland was also abandoned. A cavalry force under Marylanders Bradley T. Johnson and Harry Gilmor did proceed to the outskirts of Baltimore, destroyed railroad property, and torched the home of Maryland governor Augustus W. Bradford, purportedly in retaliation for Hunter's burning of former Virginia Governor Letcher's home in Lynchburg, Virginia. At dusk on July 12, Early began to withdraw up the Potomac. On July 14 his command forded the river back into Virginia at Whites and other nearby fords.[32]

Once the Confederates returned to Virginia, it was obvious to all that the southern soldiers had significantly damaged the canal. The July 27 *Frederick Examiner* wrote:

> The Rebel raiders and thieves seem to have made the Chesapeake and Ohio Canal, the special object of their fury and wantonness in their late plundering excursion. To such an extent has it been damaged that it is impossible to tell when navigation will be resumed. The acqueduct [sic] at the mouth of the Antietam, a work of considerable magnitude, is very materially injured, and will require the expenditure of a large sum of money before the Canal can again be put in navigable order. A great many of the locks and culverts

have also been blown up and otherwise destroyed. In fact, the work destruction marking the route of the free-booters over the line of this public highway, has been so thoroughly effected, that no definite period can be assigned for the completion of necessary repairs. In addition to the damages to the Canal itself, over one hundred boats have been burnt, so that when navigation is once more resumed, the trade hitherto carried on will be diminished at least one-fourth, for years to come, much to the inconvenience of hundreds of loyal citizens who gain their livelihood solely by means of boating.[33]

The canal company began to assess the damage to the waterway. Cumberland Division Superintendent Lloyd Lowe informed the company office that Imboden's men had burned the bridge over Lock Number 68 near South Branch and had damaged the lock. They had also burned eight canal boats below the lock. Although there was no damage to the Hancock Division, the Williamsport Division suffered considerably. On July 18 Superintendent Masters informed the company that southern troops had burned one loaded and eight empty boats, damaged six lock gates, burned the lock shanty, and tore the railing off of the Conococheague Aqueduct. Down river at Big Slackwater, the bridge over the inlet lock was damaged. On the same day Williamsport toll collector Henry Miller wrote that the Confederates had burned twenty-five canal boats near the town and that Dam Number 5 was leaking so badly that boats could not pass even if the canal were undamaged. "Every branch of business is at a perfect halt at present," he added.[34]

On the Antietam Division, where most of Early's command had crossed the Potomac, the Confederates inflicted the most serious damage. On July 20 Levin Benton reported that the southern troops had "torn the acqueduct [sic] at Antietam very badly." The next day Benton described the destruction in detail: "The bermside of the acqueduct [sic] over the Antietam is torn entirely down into the arches, the ring stone being torn out[,] it will require a frame under the arches to build them up again. The towpath side is about two thirds down and the stone thrown into the creek and a great many of [them] broken." The Confederates had also burned four lock gates on the division, along with thirty-eight canal boats, a bridge over the canal, and the planks from the stop lock. Benton estimated that it would take six to eight weeks to make the repairs, at a cost of at least $6,000. He asked the company for several good masons to oversee the stonework, and added that he had not yet begun repairs because the river was so low that the Confederates could cross at will and destroy any repairs he began.[35]

The Monocacy Division suffered damage when Early's army crossed back into Virginia after threatening Washington. George Spates reported damage to locks 24, 25, 26, and 29 that extended over a distance of over twenty-eight miles, from just below Seneca Creek to just below Catoctin Creek. At Lock Number 26 near Whites Ford, where most of Early's command had passed, the Confederates had removed the stone from one lock wall down two or three feet over a distance of thirty feet in length. At Edwards Ferry they damaged the river lock and burned the bridge over the canal. In addition to the destruction of the packet boat *Flying Cloud*, the Confederates had burned an ice breaking scow and took a quantity of tools. Ironically, the southerners had also attempted to burn a company house boat, but, according to the superintendent, were chased away by a female cook in charge of the boat. The superintendent estimated that he could restore his division by August 1 for about $300 if the Confederates stayed away from the river.[36]

At Georgetown, stocks of coal were being depleted rapidly with no means of replenishment. The July 16 *Washington Evening Star* reported that "the suspension of active business is felt by all Georgetown merchants, but falls most heavily upon the coal companies, whose reliance for supplies is upon the Chesapeake and Ohio canal." In addition to the suspension of the coal trade, the interruption of navigation cut off trade in most agricultural products, especially goods supplied from Washington County, Maryland, "that region of the canal from which comes the chief flour, grain and produce trade."[37]

Although back on Virginia soil, Early continued to threaten the line of the Potomac. After he had crossed the river, the general rested briefly at Leesburg before he moved back into the Shenandoah Valley. Most of Hunter's command, meanwhile, had advanced by rail to the vicinity of Harpers Ferry. Early attacked and defeated a portion of Hunter's command, under Brig. Gen. George Crook, at the Second Battle of Kernstown on

July 24. He then proceeded to Martinsburg and tore up the recently repaired railroad. Kelley, at Cumberland, was vexed when he learned that Early was again between him and Hunter. On July 25 he wrote Halleck and asked for reinforcements from Ohio or Indiana, fearing that Early would send another force west to destroy the railroad and canal. He reminded Halleck that he had only four regiments, three of which were one-hundred days men, to protect the railroad between Sleepy Creek and the Ohio River. Kelley also wrote B&O President John W. Garrett and asked if any troops had been sent over the railroad to strengthen Hunter. Kelley, who knew that Garrett had influence with the Lincoln administration, appealed to him for assistance: "Unless he [Hunter] is reenforced promptly . . . I fear the railroad west of Martinsburg will be destroyed as well as the canal. My force is so small and scattered I cannot protect these great works if the enemy are permitted to occupy the country in the vicinity of Harper's Ferry, Martinsburg, and Winchester without being pushed by our troops. I know of no force that can be sent me from the West. Please do all in your power to enable me to prevent the destruction of railroad and canal."[38]

Early, meanwhile, had received information that Hunter's forces had burned the homes of prominent Virginians in Jefferson County, and on July 29 he sent a cavalry expedition back across the river west of Williamsport, under the command of Brig. Gen. John McCausland. To screen the advance, Early sent cavalry and a portion of Maj. Gen. Robert E. Rodes's division across the Potomac at Williamsport and cavalry toward Harpers Ferry. On July 30 McCausland's force advanced into Pennsylvania and took possession of Chambersburg. The general levied a ransom on the town of $500,000 or $100,000 in gold. When the citizens, whose chief officials had fled, failed to produce the money, the town was set afire. The Confederates left Chambersburg in mid-day and spent the night at McConnellsburg, Pennsylvania.[39]

The following day the Confederates reentered Maryland and proceeded to Hancock. McCausland ordered a ransom of $30,000 applied to the town. The Marylanders in the expedition, especially Gilmor and Johnson, remonstrated with McCausland against the imposition of a levy against the small town, especially since many of its citizens were sympathetic to the South. McCausland refused to relent, but before the Confederates could collect any money, Federal cavalry under Brig. Gen. William W. Averell arrived and chased the southern horsemen out of town. Local diarist James Ripley Smith wrote that while in possession of Hancock, the Confederates had plundered the town's stores, all of which faced the canal, and burned canal boats, one of which they torched in front of his shop. He wrote that the gray-clad troops had taken about $2,000 in goods and cash from his store and the hat from his head. After Averell's cavalry had chased the southern horsemen out of town, the Confederates burned bridges and felled trees to slow their pursuers.[40]

The raiders continued west and arrived near Cumberland on August 1. General Kelley, who had advance warning of the Confederate approach, had posted his men and a section of artillery on the National Road several miles outside of town. About two-hundred citizens from Cumberland, who had enrolled in volunteer militia companies under the command of former Brig. Gen. Charles M. Thruston, formed on Kelley's right. Some skirmishing ensued, but McCausland realized that he could not afford to get bogged down in a fight while Averell's cavalry was approaching from the rear. The Confederate general demanded the surrender of Cumberland, but at the same time sent Gilmor to find a ford across the Potomac below Cumberland.[41]

Gilmor seized a local citizen as guide and proceeded toward the river. At daylight on August 2 scouts that he had sent ahead to examine the ford returned with the news that 800 infantry, an battery mounted in an ironclad car, and a blockhouse defended the ford at Green Spring station on the Virginia side. The Federal post was on high alert, not only because southern cavalry was north of the Potomac, but because a few days earlier about 100 of McNeill's Rangers had crossed the river and robbed the stores in Oldtown. Gilmore, soon joined by Johnson's men, rebuilt a bridge over the canal and took positions between the waterway and the river where some Union forces had taken position on a ridge. A heavy skirmish ensued before the Federals retreated to Virginia and the protection of their blockhouse and ironclad car. The Confederates attempted to storm across the ford, but encountered difficulty ascending the steep bank under heavy fire. They placed two artillery pieces in position on the ridge and subsequently disabled the ironclad car. Rather than undertake another attempt to storm the ford, someone suggested that they demand surrender of the blockhouse. The request was delivered promptly, and the Federal commander agreed to do so if his men and officers were paroled rather than made prisoner. The Confederates, apprehensive of Averell's cavalry, quickly agreed to the conditions and all of McCausland's command escaped to Virginia. On August 7 Averell finally caught up with the exhausted southern cavalry at Moorefield and took them by surprise, capturing 300. While along the canal near Oldtown, McCausland's men burned a canal boat and damaged Cresap's Mill.[42]

In order to cover the escape of McCausland's force, Early moved toward the Potomac on August 4. Imboden demonstrated near Harpers Ferry, while on August 5 Rodes's and Ramseur's divisions crossed the Potomac at Williamsport and Breckinridge crossed at Shepherdstown. On August 6 the entire Confederate force withdrew across the river at Williamsport. The canal at Williamsport suffered additional damage during the Confederate screening operations in late July and early August. The southern troops had damaged the Conococheague Aqueduct, made a small breach in the towpath near the aqueduct, burned a canal boat, and took provisions and tools intended for canal company workers.[43]

To also divert attention away from McCausland, on July 30 Mosby sent three companies across Cheeks and Nolands fords. He just missed intercepting a train, but instead routed picket posts, tore down telegraph wires, and captured horses. Three days later George Spates reported that it was dangerous to travel on the towpath of the Monocacy Division "as the whole line is infested in the guerrillas."[44]

§

For the canal company, what had begun as an optimistic season turned into a gloomy one. The Confederates had crippled the canal at the height of the boating season and had committed more significant damage to the waterway than during any previous military campaign. They had materially damaged the Antietam Aqueduct and burned about eighty boats, which reduced the number of boats navigating the canal by about one-third. Additionally, following the raids Early remained within striking distance of

Canal from Dam Number 6 to Dam Number 8 (Numbers added to indicate location of dams). Note the Paw Paw Bends between Little Orleans and Paw Paw. "Map of the Shenandoah Valley, to Illustrate the Valley Campaign of 'Stonewall' Jackson, 1862," (1880). Source: Library of Congress, Geography and Map Division.

the Potomac, which served to hamper efforts to repair the waterway. It was feared that the coal trade, both by rail and canal, would likely be suspended for the remainder of the year.

Soon, however, General Grant would devise a strategy to better protect the right flank of his army and the transportation lines behind it. The officer he would select to implement it would quickly raise the spirits those associated with the canal trade.

CHAPTER 7

AFFAIRS ABOUT THE BASIN BEGIN TO
LOOK QUITE LIVELY:
AUGUST–DECEMBER 1864

With the Confederates back in Virginia, the Union army began to make repairs to the B&O Railroad bridge and the pontoon bridge at Harpers Ferry, the last of which Federal forces had destroyed to inhibit the invasion. Another pontoon train was placed in the canal for Harpers Ferry where on August 18 engineers built a bridge above Dam Number 3. The railroad bridge at Harpers Ferry was repaired on August 14.[1]

On August 10 Alfred Spates ordered the division superintendents to begin repairs. The work went slowly, however. The repairs to the Antietam Division required significant stone work and an experienced engineer to superintend. In addition, the water level in the river remained low, which provided the Confederates with many places to ford the Potomac. The superintendents were also hesitant to begin work when southern soldiers— who in some cases could be seen across the river—could easily cross and destroy recent repairs. The invasion had also scattered the company's laborers and craftsmen. When the workers reported for duty, the company found that many of them were skittish. On August 20 Williamsport Division Superintendent Masters wrote: "On this day our hands all quit work on account of a report that the Rebels were near, as also they did, on yesterday."[2]

The continuing work on Dam Number 5 was once more delayed. In the spring Masters had discovered that the Virginia end of the dam had given way to high water. He made temporary repairs when the river fell. Due to Early's invasion, William Brown had suspended his work on the Virginia abutment of the dam. When he was ready to resume his labor Union officers would not allow him to cross to the Virginia side. A tightening of the dam was also desperately needed as the summer drought, coupled with the leaking dam, made navigation unreliable.[3]

At the Georgetown wharves, a speedy resumption of boating was thought unlikely. On August 22 the *Washington Evening Star* wrote:

Business upon the canal amounts to nothing comparatively. All that was received since the 1st of August by the canal was wood from farms within 20 miles of town. Ice from Middleton's ice-houses, 12 miles distant, and a few hundred bushels of grain from points on the canal, the most distant of which is Berlin, 55 miles. The total number of arrivals was 20, an average of one daily up to last Saturday. The prospect of a reopening of the coal trade this season is regarded by the agents of the companies as very unpromising.[4]

In late August heavy rains began to fall in the mountains of western Maryland, which raised the water in the Potomac and inhibited Confederate raids. Although high water did not create good conditions for work on Dam Number 5, it did give the superintendents the opportunity to expedite repairs to their divisions without the threat of Confederate raids.[5]

After enduring a major raid into Maryland in each of the previous three years, in addition to numerous cavalry incursions, Maryland Governor Augustus Bradford devised a plan to defend the fords of the Potomac with a new home guard force composed of citizens from Maryland and Pennsylvania. Governor Andrew G. Curtin of Pennsylvania agreed to endorse the plan, and on July 21 Bradford wrote to Lincoln to obtain approval. Although the plan was ultimately denied, Bradford's actions highlighted the inadequacy of the Union army's border defenses. Seemingly any determined Confederate force could cross the river and commit depredations against military and civilian targets with impunity. The Union army ultimately fell back on the plans developed two years before but never successfully carried out—to occupy a line of positions in advance of the river with force sufficient to repel assaults. Numerous Federal commanders had attempted to occupy the lower Shenandoah Valley permanently—Banks, Franz Sigel, Hunter, for example—only to be driven away in the face of aggressive Confederate offensives. The Federal army needed a commander equally as aggressive; someone who could drive the Confederates from the Valley, thereby securing the Army of the Potomac's right flank, inhibiting raids, and permitting the successful operation of the railroad and canal.[6]

On August 2 Grant ordered Maj. Gen. Philip H. Sheridan to Washington. Sheridan had graduated from West Point in 1853, one year behind his class after serving a one-year suspension that resulted from a dispute with a fellow-cadet. He began the war as a lieutenant and initially served in administrative and support positions in the West. On May 25, 1862 he became colonel of the Second Michigan Cavalry in the Army of the Mississippi and subsequently began a meteoric rise through the ranks of the Union army. Shortly thereafter he was promoted to brigadier general and given command of a cavalry brigade. Later in 1862 he was given divisional command in the Army of the Ohio and then also in the Army of the Cumberland, earning promotion to major general on December 31, 1862. On November 25, 1863, during the Chattanooga Campaign, Sheridan's division was one of two that broke Confederate lines on Missionary Ridge and the only division to maintain enough discipline to pursue the retreating enemy. On April 4, 1864, Grant gave Sheridan command of the Cavalry Corps in the Army of the Potomac.

On August 6 Grant ordered Sheridan to Monocacy Junction to assume command from Hunter. The next day Grant assigned him to command of a new military district, the Middle Military Division. Within this division Sheridan was responsible for the Middle Department and the departments of Washington, Susquehanna, and West Virginia. The general-in-chief thought that a unified command would result in a more coordinated and effective response to future raids. Sheridan was also permitted to retain the Sixth Corps and the Nineteenth Corps that Grant had sent to defend Washington.[7]

Sheridan immediately put his army in motion to drive the Confederates from the lower Shenandoah Valley. On August 6 he assumed command at Harpers Ferry and four days later his army was underway for Berryville, Virginia. Early withdrew from positions at Bunker Hill and headed for Winchester. By August 12 Early halted in front of Strasburg. In a matter of days Sheridan had maneuvered Early from the Potomac. By the end of August Early made his way north to Bunker Hill again, but subsequently withdrew to Winchester in early September.

Union Lt. Gen. Ulysses S. Grant. Source: Library of Congress, Prints and Photographs Division.

Union Maj. Gen. Philip H. Sheridan. Source: Library of Congress, Prints and Photographs Division.

As August lapsed into September, the nation's capital began to feel the effects of the break in the canal. Although Sheridan had pushed Early away from the Potomac, he had not defeated him in battle and the Confederate general remained within striking distance of the border. On September 14 Halleck wrote Grant that if Sheridan was not strong enough to defeat Early, reinforcements should be sent to him:

It is represented to me by reliable business men that the long and continued interruption of the Ohio and Chesapeake Canal and

Baltimore and Ohio Railroad is very seriously affecting the supply of provisions and fuel for public and private use in Baltimore, Washington, Georgetown, and Alexandria. Unless the canal can be opened very soon a sufficient supply of winter's coal cannot be procured before the close of navigation. The gas companies are already thinking to stop their work for want of coal. The canal and railroad have been several times repaired, and as often destroyed. They, therefore, urge the great importance of driving Early far enough south to secure these lines of communication from rebel raids.[8]

Sheridan subsequently undertook an offensive in the Shenandoah Valley that gave the railroad and canal companies opportunity to complete repairs. Following a visit from Grant, on September 19 Sheridan defeated Early in the Third Battle of Winchester. He followed it with a September 22 victory at Fishers Hill, southwest of Strasburg. Grant was pleased at Sheridan's progress and on the date of the latter battle wrote his subordinate: "It [the victory] has been most opportune in point of time and effect. It will open again to the Government and to the public the very important line of road from Baltimore to the Ohio, and also the Chesapeake Canal." In order to supply Sheridan's Army of the Shenandoah, the Union army helped repair the canal to Harpers Ferry. Once navigation to the Ferry was restored, grain, forage, and other stores were sent over the canal to the mouth of the Monocacy and Harpers Ferry for Sheridan's army.[9]

Sheridan's victories created optimism along the Potomac and allowed the canal company to expedite repairs. On September 13 the *Washington Evening Star* began to anticipate the resumption of navigation: "The news from the western divisions of the canal is cheering. The repairs are progressing rapidly, and it is hoped that the empty boats which are lying at Georgetown, about fifty in number, will be able to go through to Cumberland before the close of this week, and that next week the coal trade will be reopened, and all the docks be as noisy as ever, with the busy heavers employed in receiving the cargoes for shipment at the wharves." The September 22 *Cumberland Civilian and Telegraph* was hopeful that the start of navigation would cause the price of goods to fall.[10]

Work on the seriously damaged Antietam Division held up the resumption of boating to Cumberland, however. In September,

Superintendent Levin Benton removed twenty-four burned boats and their cargoes from the canal and built four new lock gates. Enough of the masonry work on the aqueduct was completed to allow the passage of boats by late September, although additional stonework on the exterior remained to be completed. At the end of September, boats began to arrive at Cumberland and soon departed with coal for eastern ports. On September 29 the *Cumberland Civilian and Telegraph* observed: "Affairs about the Basin begin to look quite lively again."[11]

The September 21 *Cumberland Alleganian* predicted that as a result of Confederate raids, navigation would not return to normal levels for some time:

> The boatmen . . . seem determined to run only in the day-time, laying up during the night, in order to avoid interruption from the predatory bands that infest the border. Trips, therefore, will require about double the length of time as heretofore; still, the resumption of navigation will give an impetus to business in this locality, the want of which has for so long been badly felt. It is to be regretted that a season which opened so auspiciously, has had so many and such serious drawbacks.[12]

On October 3 Grant proposed to recall a large portion of Sheridan's troops. In an October 4 letter to Grant, chief-of-staff Halleck expressed concern that weakening Sheridan's force would undermine the protection of the railroad and canal. He suggested that if Grant withdrew the troops, he should also establish a line of defense to protect both carriers from Confederate raids. He recommended a strong garrison at Manassas Gap, which could operate on both sides of the Blue Ridge Mountains, supported by garrisons at Thoroughfare Gap and Manassas Junction. He also recommended that all Virginia residents behind Federal lines be sent South and that Sheridan "clean out" Mosby's Rangers. He wrote: "If these dispositions are approved and carried out, it will not be necessary to keep so large a force at Harper's Ferry and guarding the canal and Baltimore and Ohio Railroad."[13]

§

Following the victory of the Unconditional Union Party in the 1863 Maryland state elections, a constitutional convention was widely expected to address the future of slavery in the state. Many believed that the institution would have died a natural death had the war never erupted. From 1850 to 1860 Maryland's total slave population had fallen three and one-half percent, while the total free black population had risen twelve percent. In fact, in 1860 the number of free blacks was only 3,247 less than the total slave population, and more free blacks lived in Maryland than any other state in the Union. During the war other factors undermined the institution. When northern troops came to Maryland, some slaves fled into the army's lines. While the troops harbored some of them, officers returned many others to their owners for fear of inciting opposition to the war among slave-holding Unionists. On April 16, 1862, Congress passed a measure that freed slaves in the District of Columbia. As a result, many of Maryland's slaves living near the District slipped across the border to the nation's capital, which further subverted the institution. Lastly, Lincoln's Emancipation Proclamation, which took effect January 1, 1863, freed the slaves in those states that had rebelled against Federal authority. If indeed the Union army prevailed in the war, Maryland was faced with the prospect of being surrounded by free states that would serve as magnets to its slaves.

On February 3 the General Assembly passed a bill that authorized Marylanders to decide if a constitutional convention should be called and, at the same time, to elect delegates. At the April 6 canvas, the voters approved the measure by a two-to-one margin. Several delegates elected were familiar to the canal company, including Albert C. Greene and attorney George A. Thruston of Allegany County (son of Charles Mynn Thruston), and canal company director Henry W. Dellinger of Washington County. The delegates began meeting in Annapolis on April 27.[14]

Over the summer, the Convention debated the state's relationship with its internal improvement projects. It replaced the elected Commission of Public Works with a three-member Board of Public Works, composed of the governor, treasurer, and comptroller of the treasury. The delegates agreed that the old elected commission was too narrowly focused on the region they represented rather than the welfare of the entire state. The Convention expected the three new officials, as the chief financial officers of the state, to pay closer attention to the economic condition of Maryland and be less subject to persuasion from outside influences.[15]

For at least twenty years there had been consensus across Maryland to halt the state's involvement with public works projects due to high indebtedness and taxation. An 1843 act of the General Assembly—passed before the canal had even reached Cumberland—had authorized the sale of the state's investments in a number of internal improvement projects, among them the Chesapeake and Ohio Canal. The legislation had authorized the canal's sale for not less than five-million dollars. Additionally, the Constitution of 1851 had expressly forbidden the state from further sponsorship of internal improvement projects. The delegates to the 1864 constitutional convention continued the trend toward divestiture.[16]

The convention's Committee on the Legislative Department initially drafted a proposal that would have directed the General Assembly to lease or dispose of the state's interest in internal improvement projects with proceeds to be applied to the state debt and thereafter to a fund supporting public education. The provision to permit the lease of the state's public works, supported by canal advocates, was later dropped. The convention also later granted the officers of the new Board of Public Works, instead of the General Assembly, the discretion to sell public works rather than a mandatory obligation to dispose of the state's interests in railroads and canals.[17]

Lengthy debate ensued concerning the value of the state's various public works and whether any should be exempted from sale. The value of the Chesapeake and Ohio Canal, to both the state and potential buyers, figured prominently in the discussions. Proponents of its sale argued that the canal was an unproductive investment, never having returned one dollar on Maryland's investment of two million dollars in bonds and five million dollars in stock. According to a report from Maryland's treasurer, the canal company also owed the state just over nine million dollars in interest.[18]

On July 23 Peter Negley of Washington County proclaimed his support for the sale of all the state's investments in public works. He was one of a handful of delegates who subscribed to the popular notion that all the canal's problems resulted from the political appointment of its officers. He told the convention:

The Chesapeake and Ohio Canal is nothing but an instrumentality of corruption. . . . They do not pay their debts; they make no provision for their debts. Nobody knows exactly how the tolls are used. In our county they have contracted for repairs; men have had faith in them, and have gone largely into debt upon the promises of the Chesapeake and Ohio Canal Company to pay; have built their dams, repaired their canal, but have never been paid for it. The officers and men who control it seem to absorb all the money, and the outside world gets none of it; it is a miserable instrumentality of corruption and fraud, and the sooner the State gets rid of its interest in it the better.

Negley later moderated his hyperbole and, after viewing a financial statement from the canal company, admitted that the cost of keeping the canal in repair and paying salaries absorbed nearly all of the tolls collected.[19]

Oliver Miller of Anne Arundel County described the canal company as a "vast political machine." He believed that the company only paid the salaries of its officers and employees to perpetuate them in their positions, but ultimately "producing revenue for nobody, not even for the bondholders."[20]

Other delegates argued that public works were not originally built to return revenue, but to develop the state, particularly the mineral resources of western Maryland, which benefit the whole state. On August 3 Joseph B. Pugh of Worcester County said of the canal:

The Chesapeake and Ohio Canal is a highway, an avenue to market . . . . It is a benefit to all the people who live alongside the canal, for they can go upon that canal all upon an equal footing, without paying one dollar but the tolls, and so with other canals, and so it would be with a turnpike road, or with a State railroad. These internal improvements benefit the whole people of a State, and the State receives its remuneration through the increased taxes it receives from the people who are thus benefitted [sic].[21]

As a result of Early's invasion, on July 9 the convention had passed a preamble and resolution which affirmed its loyalty to the Union and castigated disloyal Marylanders as "unworthy citizens." The delegates then adjourned and until July 19 were unable to obtain a quorum. When the convention resumed debate, it was with full knowledge of the damage inflicted by the Confederates to the canal, railroad, and private property across the state.[22]

Delegate Archibald Stirling, Jr., of Baltimore argued that the value of the canal, estimated at two and one-half million dollars, was at its lowest point as a result of the war. On August 3, with Early's invasion fresh in his mind and Confederate horsemen still riding in western Maryland, he posed a question: "Is a time of civil war a proper time in which to sell that internal improvement, when its locks are being continually blown up by the public enemy, and its whole condition is affected by the civil war?" Later he added: "It is perfectly possible that ten years hence the canal will be worth three times what it is worth now. Now is the very worst time to sell it, because its whole condition is paralyzed by the existence of the present civil war."[23]

Opponents of selling the canal also argued that a buyer might purchase it and use it against the public interest. Although Negley strongly favored the sale of the canal, he was concerned that the waterway might fall into the hands of the B&O Railroad and that that company would then raise tolls to the maximum allowed in the canal's charter and divert the entire canal trade onto the rails. Another delegate feared that a rival railroad might buy the waterway and then divert much of the coal trade through Pennsylvania. Others argued that the canal should not be sold at all for these reasons.[24]

Those opposed to the sale of the canal also pointed out that the company owed $2.2 million to creditors other than the state of Maryland, debt which did not have a lien on canal property. This amount included the company's floating debt of about $380,000 due to contractors and merchants. Additionally, the company owed $565,108 to script holders and those who had been issued post notes and bonds for script. Furthermore, interest on these non-state debts totaled $1,253,564. Legislation passed in 1842 required that if sold, the company was to pay these creditors within twenty years after ownership was transferred, which made the sale of the canal unlikely. Some suggested that the legislature pass a law to pay these claims from public funds. Others countered that since the estimated value of the canal was only $2.5 million dollars, nearly equal to its non-state debt, the effect would be to give away the canal for nothing while materially injuring that portion of the state that depended on the waterway.[25]

Delegate John L. Thomas, Jr., of Baltimore predicted that western Maryland would not support a new constitution if it provided for the sale of the canal. On July 26 Thomas, an Allegany County native, addressed the convention:

> I know that every man in Allegany, rich and poor, has his hopes and affection fixed upon the development and progress of the Chesapeake and Ohio Canal company. . . . Close up the Chesapeake and Ohio Canal, and you close up your mines. Close up your mines, and you close up your rolling mills. Close up your mines and rolling mills, and you throw thousands and thousands of poor men out of employment. Bring this thing up in the canvass, and tell the people of Allegany that this convention has gone to work to part with the State's interest and therefore its protection and guardianship of the Chesapeake and Ohio Canal; and you will not get 600 votes in that county for your constitution.[26]

Delegate Stirling argued that private owners would invariably raise tolls and that only public ownership would ensure that tolls were kept at reasonable levels. Like Thomas, he believed that if the new constitution allowed for the sale of the canal, the document would lose the support of all of western Maryland.[27]

Eventually, the convention decided to permit the sale of the canal subject to a major check. An amendment by Frederick Schley of Frederick County and Daniel Clarke of Prince George's County was adopted that subjected the sale of any of the state's ownership in canals to ratification by the next General Assembly, thereby allowing the voters to elect assemblymen who were for or against a proposed sale and permitting the next legislature to review the purchaser's intentions before approving the transaction. To address the concern that a rival transportation line might purchase the canal and close it, Negley discovered that the canal company's charter provided for its forfeiture if the waterway was not kept open and in repair. In addition, a late amendment by Hopewell Hebb of Allegany County was approved that allowed any combination of Montgomery, Frederick, Washington, and Allegany counties to issue a bond to purchase the canal from the state.[28]

The new constitution was submitted to the voters for approval on September 18, 1864. The outcome turned on the issue of slavery, which the constitution outlawed without compensation to slave owners. Most of southern Maryland and the eastern shore, where slavery was most strongly ensconced, voted against it, led by Charles County where only one percent of the voters supported the constitution. The document had strong support in Baltimore city (83%), and western Maryland, led by Washington County (71%), Allegany County (66%) and Frederick County (60%). The polling of Maryland soldiers in the field was conducted and their support (91%) assured passage of the constitution by a mere 375 votes out of 59,973 cast.[29]

§

Once the canal was ready for navigation in the late summer, labor difficulties threatened the resumption of trade. The miners and boatmen demanded another advance in wages from the coal companies. After a meeting, the companies agreed to meet the workers' demands. The rate for the miners was set at $1.00 per ton and for the boatmen at $3.00 per ton.[30]

The long period of inactivity on the canal, coupled with the hot and dry summer, resulted in a short delay in the resumption of boating, however. On 1 Oct. the *Washington Evening Star* reported: "The water was let in on the 17th instant [September], the banks being exceedingly dry the absorption was so great as to keep the water below the levels several days, and to this cause may be added the numerous leaks of minor importance at various points. The boats having been laid up drying for so long a time, the seams of many opened and starting west empty, a number sunk, and these had to be raised and it delayed the arrival of laden boats three or four days." On September 30 Alfred Spates was at Georgetown to welcome the arrival of the first fleet of thirty canal boats, and he planned to travel to Cumberland to urge reluctant boatmen to resume navigation.[31]

Following Early's raid, the company had to deal with the usual claims resulting from the destruction of boats and cargoes. The company restated its position that tolls were due on boats to the point where they had been destroyed. The company permitted owners to claim any unburned coal that the superintendents had recovered from the canal, such as at Dam Number 4 where nineteen boats had been burned and a significant amount of coal had been removed from the waterway. In late October its owners claimed the coal but did not want to pay tolls to transport it to Williamsport since they had paid the toll before the boats had been burned. The company instructed its collector to not assess tolls unless the coal was transported further than the distance for which the tolls were originally paid.[32]

The resumption of canal trade brought Confederate raiders out of hiding. Their partisan activities, conducted behind Union lines, were largely immune from Sheridan's offensive. In late September the southern horsemen robbed two canal boats of their horses near Cumberland, and on September 27 McNeill's Rangers raided several coal mines in western Maryland and collected about fifty horses. On September 29 Albert C. Greene complained to Alfred Spates: "In the meantime Gen Kelly [sic] sits in Cumb surrounded by thousands of men, but takes no steps to prevent or punish these maraudings [sic]. I wish you could impress upon Stanton the facts and Consequences resulting from them—the Canal trade is paralyzed by reason of them."[33]

On October 13 Mosby struck the recently repaired railroad near Kearneysville, west of Harpers Ferry. In what became known as the Greenback Raid, his men tore up the track and waited for a train to approach. When a locomotive derailed, the cavalrymen captured two Federal paymasters who had over $100,000 in Federal currency in their possession. The raiders also took money, jewelry, and other valuables from the passengers and then set the train afire.[34]

On October 14 Mosby sent a detachment of several hundred men, under the command of Capt. William H. Chapman, across the Potomac at Whites Ford. The Greenback Raid had caused a suspension in rail traffic, however, and Chapman was unable to intercept a train as he had intended. Instead, he stole horses, tore down telegraph wires, plundered stores, and burned canal boats. When the rangers approached the river at Point of Rocks, the horsemen discovered Federal soldiers removing the planks of the bridge over the canal. He chased them away, rebuilt the bridge, and re-crossed the river at Cheeks Ford. George Spates later reported that the Confederates had burned four boats and had taken about fifteen mules from the canal. On October 17 another body of southern cavalry crossed the river below Edwards Ferry and stole a dozen mules. Concerning the raids, the October 19 *Cumberland Alleganian* noted: "The misfortune has somewhat discouraged the boatmen generally, but as yet there is no perceptible falling off in shipments of coal by canal."[35]

Before long the repeated Confederate raids began to suppress canal traffic and disrupt picket routines. After the mid-October raids on the Monocacy Division, George Spates reported that a twenty-five mile stretch of the river, from Nolands Ferry to Muddy Branch, was unprotected by Federal pickets and that many boats had stopped at Nolands Ferry and would not resume navigation unless accompanied by a military escort. On October 15 the *Washington Evening Star* noted that "the stealing of a team or two, or the destruction of a boat, is sufficient to alarm the boatmen, who before lost heavily by the raids of Mosby and the invasion of Early, and induce them to refuse freight and stay at home."[36]

In response to the raids along the border, General Kelley resorted to subterfuge to ensure the safety of canal boats through his jurisdiction. On October 18 Kelley's adjutant issued the following instructions to an officer from the Sixth West Virginia Infantry: "You will proceed with your detachment, supplied with ten days' rations, on board the canal-boat in waiting, and patrol the canal from Oldtown to a point opposite Paw Paw. You will keep your men under cover as much as possible, in order to prevent the thieves and robbers from knowing that there are armed men on board the boat. You will frequently move at night, and especially if there are large numbers of boats moving, in order to convoy them safely past that portion of the country you are expected to protect."[37]

The hole in the Federal picket line on the Monocacy Division was corrected promptly and during November canal traffic was heavy. For the month, an average of over one hundred coal-laden boats left Cumberland each week, transporting a total of just over 43,000 tons of coal. Buoyed by an August 1 increase in tolls on coal, from three-eighths to one-half cent per ton mile, fares collected in November reached record highs for the war period. Nearly $44,000 was collected by the company's agents during the month, by far the largest monthly total collected during the first four years of the war.[38]

Despite a few raids along the border during the autumn—most of which did not affect the canal—Alfred Spates was optimistic about the future of the waterway. The December 1 *Washington Chronicle* published an account of an interview with the canal company president:

He reports that the canal has never been in so good order as at this time, and, therefore, boats run night and day. About twenty-three hundred tons of coal are shipped daily to Georgetown from the mines. Very little of this coal stops here, but it goes on to the Northern cities upon return voyages of vessels that bring cargoes from those points to General Grant's army, to Point Lookout, and to Washington, Alexandria and Georgetown. Mr. Spates says that one thousand boats may be as easily run on the canal as the two hundred and fifty that are now engaged in the transportation of coal, flour, &c. When, therefore, its capacity for navigation is fully tested, some nine thousand tons would reach us daily, which would employ in the transport to Northern cities a very large number of vessels, and make this point a busy mart of commerce.[39]

Despite Spates's rosy outlook, behind the scenes the company was again struggling with its financial resources. Three months of inactivity and high repair bills associated with Early's raid had put the company in difficult financial straits. With all their previous efforts to obtain compensation from the government having come to naught, the company retained attorney Stephen W. Downey. A July 4, 1864, Act of Congress had established procedures by which loyal citizens could seek reimbursement for supplies and subsistence provided to the army. On September 5 Downey wrote to Stanton and presented an account of $5,151.60 to the government for outstanding tolls on quartermaster's and subsistence stores shipped on the canal. Downey erroneously said that this was "the only account which the Canal Company has presented during the entire war." He continued: "It is hoped immediate action will be had on it as the money is greatly needed at this time to defray some of the expenses attending the repairing of the canal." A month went by with no response from the government. The company sought aid from Representative Thomas, who personally placed a copy of the account in the hands of Assistant Secretary of War Charles A. Dana and followed it with a letter.[40]

The War Department had referred the company's claim to the Quartermaster General's Office, where it was under review by Col. Lewis B. Parsons, Chief of River and Railroad Transportation. Until August, Parsons had served almost exclusively in the west and had no direct knowledge of the use of the canal by the government. On November 18 he asked Downey to supply the names of the quartermasters who had used the canal. On November 25 Downey replied that shipments made from Georgetown were "principally" made by quartermasters Rucker and Flagg at Williamsport and from Cumberland by special order of General McClellan to Lt. Col. G. Ellis Porter of the Second Regiment, Potomac Home Brigade. The quartermaster's office was scoured for records and then compared with the canal company's records. After discrepancies and overcharges were deducted from the claim, the quartermasters found records of additional shipments via the canal that the company's records did not reflect, charges that approximately equaled the amount previously deducted. On December 14 Rucker forwarded the report to Quartermaster General Meigs, but added an account of his own against the canal company for expenses incurred by the army when it had made repairs to the waterway. The army's account totaled $8,765.49 for expenses incurred on July 1 and September 19, 1863. On the first date, the Quartermaster Department had spent $6,757.04 to repair broken lock gates and restore navigation at Seneca so that it could remove its pontoon bridges, munitions, and stores to safety during the Gettysburg Campaign. On the latter date, quartermasters had expended $2,008.45 in an attempt to repair the tidal lock at Georgetown. Meigs did not immediately reply to the company's claim.[41]

Following Sheridan's defeat of the Confederates in the October 19 Battle of Cedar Creek, which effectively ended Early's threat to the border, the Union general prepared to disperse his army. The Sixth Corps was returned to Grant in early December. Maj. Gen. George Crook's division was sent back to West Virginia to defend the railroad. Two divisions of the Nineteenth Corps remained. In a December 28 letter to Grant, Sheridan considered sending another division to the Army of the Potomac but acknowledged that some would protest: "The only argument against this is the insecurity which it might create along the extended and sensitive line from Alexandria to the Ohio, and where there are so many troublesome interests—some loyal and some disloyal—some interested in coal-oil speculations, some in the Baltimore and Ohio Railroad, and some in the canal." On February 9, 1865, Sheridan received the "Thanks of Congress" for his successful Shenandoah Valley Campaign of 1864.[42]

Some Union efforts to prevent raids across the river put the canal at risk. On December 8 Capt. B. Spence, provost marshal and picket commander at Point of Rocks, informed the commander of the Military District of Harpers Ferry that he was blockading all culverts under the canal and digging rifle pits at prominent fords so that Confederate raiders could not get across the waterway. Military officials prevented Superintendent George Spates from removing the obstructions, and presumably Alfred Spates was unable to talk them out of the tactic. On December 20 he wrote directly to Secretary Stanton and informed him that the obstructions would prevent the drainage of small creeks, streams, and storm run-off. With no outlet, during heavy rain the water would eventually wash out the canal. "Without your interposition the canal must be destroyed beyond all hope of the Canal Company being able to repair," he wrote. The War Department recognized the danger and ordered commanders to remove the obstructions, which was accomplished by early January 1865.[43]

A cold snap struck the region in early December. The December 15 *Cumberland Civilian and Telegraph* reported that the canal was closed by ice. On December 21 James Ripley Smith recorded that about thirty boats had tied up at Hancock for the winter.[44]

§

In is annual report for 1864 the president and board informed its stockholders: "We have the satisfaction to state that the business of the Company for the past year has heen [sic] more prosperous than any preceeding [sic] year since its organization; that the condition of the Canal has been better than for many years previously; and that the transportation upon it was more regular and less interrupted, until the invasion of the enemy in July last, when material damages were sustained, and navigation was suspended for three months of the most active and profitable portion of the year." The effects of Early's raid, noted the company's president and board, had a significant financial impact on the canal: "The cost of repairs from the destruction of the works did not exceed $12,000, but it is estimated that the revenues of the Company were diminished by this casualty to the extent of $200,000, and about eighty boats were destroyed, thus reducing the means of transportation after the resumption of navigation."[45]

Even so, nearly 260,000 tons of coal went to market over the canal, an increase of more than 30,000 tons over 1863, and only about 40,000 tons shy of the best year on record. Tolls collected during 1864 totaled almost $226,000, an increase of about $71,000 over the prior year. The company noted that maintenance expenses were greater than usual, however, and prices for labor and materials had also increased. It also pointed out that some necessary repairs and improvements were not made. Instead the company used over $171,000 of its resources to pay outstanding debts it had incurred prior to 1862, including legal expenses, balances due to contractors, money owed to superintendents for labor and materials, toll certificates and acceptances on bonds, arrears of officers' salaries, and interests due. The company noted that about $300,000 in floating debt remained, which it hoped could be liquidated in 1865 with a prosperous year of business and further development of the Maryland coal fields.[46]

On the other hand, shipments of both flour and wheat sent down the canal declined in 1864, the former by percent thirty percent and the latter by thirty-two percent. Although both products descending the canal had increased significantly in the preceding year, as a percentage of total tonnage each had fallen sharply. These developments would foreshadow the canal's near-total loss of the trade in flour during the remaining years of the waterway's existence as shippers moved the product to market over other carriers.[47]

The state of Maryland had moved politically closer to the Union in 1864. The new state constitution, which took effect November 1, not only outlawed slavery but required elected or appointed state officials to take an oath of loyalty to the state, the new state constitution, the United States

Constitution, and to affirm that they had never provided aid or encouragement to the Confederacy. Director Albert C. Greene was unsure if the state constitution required canal officials to take the oath. On November 29 he wrote the company office: "I presume we can all take the oath with a good conscience. I enclose mine herein for your files."[48]

Other provisions of the constitution affected state voting rights. Anyone who had served in the Confederate army, who had aided or advocated the Confederate cause, or who had committed any other disloyal act or uttered a disloyal statement was subject to disqualification from voting or holding state office. Election officials were authorized to administer a loyalty oath to suspicious would-be voters, although taking the oath alone was not sufficient in itself to gain one the right to vote. One's voting rights could only be restored by a two-thirds vote of the General Assembly or subsequent service in the United States military. This provision would play a significant part in Alfred Spates's post-war career.[49]

CHAPTER 8

THE WHARFS ARE CONSTANTLY CROWDED
WITH BOATS:
1865 AND POSTWAR

As 1865 opened, the Confederacy was in a shambles. In the Shenandoah Valley, in the deep South, and in the entrenchments around Petersburg, the Confederate army was on the defensive. For the C&O Canal Company, the prospects for the year's business were very promising.

On January 12 the company drew the water from the canal to commence maintenance work. The canal was re-watered in early February, but the weather turned very cold and remained so into the early spring. Thick sheets of ice formed on the upper Potomac, which engendered fears that a sudden freshet might bring the ice raging down the river valley and cause material damage to the canal. As a result, the water was drawn off again on February 22. While awaiting the resumption of navigation, large quantities of goods accumulated on the wharves and in the warehouses in Cumberland.[1]

Early in the year Confederate raiders continued to harass Union picket posts along the Potomac. In January the *Washington Star* noted: "The guerillas who infest the banks of the river have become very troublesome of late, and that hardly a night passes without their firing upon our pickets or making an attempt to cross the river at some point." Federal soldiers captured small numbers of guerrillas engaged in plundering expeditions on Maryland soil in late December and early January. In the last days of January a handful of Confederates crossed the river near Monocacy and robbed a store at the foot of Sugar Loaf Mountain. In February two raids were conducted near Edwards Ferry by Marylanders from Elijah White's Thirty-fifth Virginia Cavalry Battalion. During the first incursion seven members were captured after they had crossed over the frozen Potomac. During the second raid the squad attacked a Federal camp and robbed a neighborhood store.[2]

On January 19 a number of Mosby's men derailed another train near Harpers Ferry. The band had intelligence that a Federal paymaster was aboard the next train and hoped to duplicate the Greenback Raid. Actually, the train was a special freight transporting delicacies to Federal officers. Instead of cash, Mosby's men carried off wine, beer, cakes, candy, oysters, and other luxury items. The Rangers also robbed the passengers and unsuccessfully attempted to set the cars afire. The raiders named this excursion the Coffee Raid.[3]

The winter raids were highlighted by one of the most daring exploits of the war when McNeill's Rangers captured generals Kelley and Crook from their beds in Cumberland. Lt. Jesse McNeill held a grudge against Kelley because in 1862 the general had arrested his mother, sister, and younger brother after they had requested a pass to visit Jesse's father, the leader of the Rangers. On February 21 McNeill's men, dressed in Federal uniforms, crossed into Maryland west of Cumberland near Brady's Mill. They captured the first picket they encountered, forced the countersign from him, and proceeded past other picket posts to Cumberland. The band then quietly entered the hotels where the generals slept and apprehended them. The Rangers left town by the most direct route to West Virginia via the canal towpath, overpowered the first Federal guard they encountered, and outfoxed the second picket when they claimed to be Crook's personal bodyguard going to intercept the raiders. The cavalrymen crossed the Potomac at Wileys Ford below Cumberland and conveyed the prisoners to Richmond and Libby prison until they were exchanged the next month.[4]

Navigation on the canal was slow to resume in 1865. A wet winter caused the Potomac and its tributaries to swell. In mid-March Hancock diarist James Ripley Smith recorded that the river was as high as it had been during the two previous years. Structures on the canal that the company had not properly maintained during the war began to fail. On March 6 Williamsport Division Superintendent Masters informed the company office that the north side of the Conococheague Aqueduct had fallen into the creek. He wrote: "There has been a crack in it for the last 6 or 8 years, and I suppose the blasting by the rebels, and the severe freezing weather this winter, caused it to give way." The gap in the aqueduct was nearly one-hundred feet in length. In order to expedite the resumption of navigation,

Masters installed a wooden trunk rather than undertake costly and time-consuming masonry work.[5]

High water and ice in late February caused additional damage, including to the troublesome Virginia abutment of Dam Number 5. On April 3 Masters wrote that it would take considerable work to repair the cribs due to "the shattered condition they are in." The flooding had also swept away the temporary crib inserted into the end of the dam near the Virginia shore. Masters advised: "The whole dam except the stone work is in bad order and needs to be rebuilt with stone, or in some other substantial manner, as all our experience proves that no reliance can be placed in cribs." The freshet also caused two breaks on the Georgetown Division, one at Great Falls, the other five miles above Georgetown."[6]

By the end of March the company was completing repairs. The coal companies, boatmen, and dockworkers anxiously awaited the resumption of navigation. On March 29 the *Alleganian* noted:

The work of repair along the line of the Chesapeake & Ohio Canal is now about completed, and this important avenue to market of the wealth of our mineral region is now ready for navigation. —No coal had yet been loaded at our wharves, but the busy note of preparation is everywhere heard, and in the course of a day or two we may expect active operations to begin. Large numbers of boats are daily arriving, and the canal basin presents quite an animated aspect.[7]

Navigation languished, however, as the boatmen demanded an increase in their wages. On March 29 the *Alleganian* wrote that the boatmen had demanded $4.00 per ton of coal, while the coal companies had offered $3.00. By early April the two sides were still at loggerheads. A week later the *Alleganian* reported that the boatmen had lowered their demand to $3.50 per ton, but the coal operators were insisting on $3.00 ton because they had already contracted to ship coal based on the old rate. The newspaper also noted that consensus was growing amongst the boatmen to return to work at $3.00 a ton, which indeed occurred.[8]

Following the cessation of hostilities after Lee's surrender to Grant at Appomattox on April 9, followed by Gen. Joseph E. Johnston's surrender to Maj. Gen. William T. Sherman on April 26, a slump almost immediately developed in the coal market. Without the prospect of large armies in the field and an expanding steam fleet patrolling the waters, it quickly became apparent that the demand for coal would slacken. Accordingly, the price of coal on the open market dropped sharply. On April 26 Alfred Spates wrote to Ringgold: "About all the Coal Cos. have stopped Shipping Coale [sic]— on account of the high rates of freight, mining, tools, &c &c. The Canal is doing nothing now. No Boats loading all stopped or will in a day or so— Everything must come down [in price] to enable the Coal Cos to make further shipments of Coal from here and compete with other coales [sic] now in the northern market. So says the Coal men here." The boatmen continued to ship coal that had already been mined, but by mid-May shipments slowed to a trickle.[9]

Another surge of high water struck the canal in May. In particular, the wharves at Georgetown were damaged by the freshet. Two weeks were required to make the repairs. With the canal damaged and the miners on strike, traffic on the waterway came to a virtual standstill.[10]

The coal companies sought to reduce expenses by offering the miners sixty cents per ton, a reduction of forty percent, which miners would not accept. The June 1 the *Cumberland Civilian and Telegraph* wrote: "It is evident that the price of mining has come down, and we hope the operators and the miners may come to some agreement soon, and not mutually injure each other by remaining idle." In Pennsylvania the mine operators and laborers were in a similar state, with the miners refusing to accept a sharp reduction in wages. In early June Maryland's miners agreed to return to work at seventy-five cents per ton. On June 8 the *Civilian and Telegraph* wrote: "We are happy to say that work in the Mining Region has been resumed, and, that although but little has been done so far this week, yet the sight of trains of cars, loaded with coal on their way to market, is again to be seen."[11]

As a result of the weak demand for coal, six western Maryland mining companies asked the canal company to reduce tolls. In a June 12 joint letter, the coal companies advised: "The coal trade is almost prostrate by the suspension of all industries, consequent upon the sudden transition from War to Peace." The operators wrote that they had recently reduced the price of coal by $3.00 a ton, but had only achieved a reduction of $1.50 in production and freight costs, which left them in an uncompetitive position against other coals. They acknowledged that the C&O Canal's tolls on coal were less than those on Pennsylvania and New Jersey canals, but pointed out that Cumberland coal had a much greater distance to travel to market, including additional freight costs to ship their product to northern markets on coastal vessels. Lastly, the companies noted that Pennsylvania and New Jersey canals had recently reduced tolls on coal from twenty-five to thirty-three percent. The canal company board considered the matter in July, but ultimately decided not to reduce tolls, likely because of the extensive backlog of maintenance work that had been neglected during the war and the damages that had resulted from the spring freshets.[12]

Meanwhile, the company's claim for $5,161.30 for tolls continued to work its way through the military bureaucracy. Early in the year the company attorney Downey met with an officer from the Quartermaster Department. He was informed that the quartermasters had expended a considerable sum to repair the canal, which would be applied against the company's claim. Downey consulted with the canal company and decided to present another claim for damages and property confiscated by the government from May 1862 through 1864, in addition to its previously submitted claims of $5,190 for April through September 1861, and $75,391.96 for September 1861 through April 1862, neither of which had been acted upon. On March 1 both Spates and Downey wrote to Secretary Stanton and informed him of the new claim, which totaled $292,330. Downey pointed out that much of the claim was for company property seized by the government and was thus subject to reimbursement under the July 4, 1864 Act of Congress. He asked that while the government considered the larger figure, it immediately reimburse the claim for tolls so that the company could make necessary repairs to the canal. The company asked Representative Francis Thomas to call upon the War Department on its behalf.[13]

Six weeks later the government finally came to a decision regarding the canal company's claims. On April 14 Quartermaster General Meigs informed Stanton that when his assistant had submitted the "set-off claim" of $8,765.49 against the canal company's claim, the company had responded with additional claims totaling over $367,000. Meigs opined: "I cannot from any evidence in this office recommend the allowance of any part of these last claims, and am of opinion that nothing should be paid the

Canal Company on the claim of $5161.60, as the amount expended by the Government on account of said Canal is considerably greater than the amount of said tolls." Without further explanation the government denied all of the company's claims for tolls, property confiscated by the government, and war related damages. Meigs's letter to Stanton suggested that the canal company had only submitted the second claim because the government had rejected the one for tolls; however, the company's claims for $5,190 and $75,391.96 had been submitted three years earlier, but the government had not acted on them.[14]

Even when both sides agreed the amounts were valid, the company still had trouble collecting tolls from the government. In November 1864 an assistant quartermaster had shipped three lots of forage from near Dam Number 4 to Harpers Ferry. The officer was relieved from duty before toll collector Henry Miller could get the money due the company. In December Miller swore an affidavit before a judge of the Washington County Circuit Court that the amount of $84.91 was "true and just" in favor of the canal company. A voucher was submitted to the quartermasters' department, and the officer who shipped the grain certified that it was valid. Yet a year later the government had taken no action against the company's claim. On August 8, 1866, the company resubmitted the claim to Meigs, but there is no record that it was ever paid.[15]

With the passage of a new constitution in 1864, the four-member elected Commission of Public Works was replaced by the three-member Board of Public Works, consisting of the governor, treasurer, and comptroller of the treasury. On July 6 the Board met in Annapolis and chose to return only three existing canal company directors, Lawrence J. Brengle of Frederick County, Charles Abert of Montgomery County, and Albert C. Greene of Allegany County. The new directors were Henry D. Cook of Georgetown, Lawrence A. Dawson of Montgomery County, and E.F. Anderson of Washington County. Anderson subsequently chose not to serve and on October 4 the Board returned Lewis Watson of Washington County to fill the vacancy. Although no dissatisfaction with Alfred Spates was recorded, he was not selected to return to the board.[16]

Prior to the meeting of the Board of Public Works, several parties were engaged in behind-the-scenes campaigning for the office of president of the C&O Canal. Edward Watts, former engineer with the company, actively campaigned for the post. He sought the support of Judge Daniel Weisel of Hagerstown who told him that he supported Jacob Snively, a merchant from Hancock, but that he particularly desired to see a resident of Washington County get the position. Washington County had more miles of the canal within its boundaries—about forty percent of the total mileage—than any other county. Watts left his meeting with Weisel under the impression that the judge was favorable to him and would use his influence with Governor Bradford, who was a member of the Board. The judge had agreed that an engineer at the post would be beneficial since the war had left many structures on the canal in dilapidated condition, and the offices of engineer and president could be combined under one salary. In addition, Watts, who lived in Hagerstown, was a Washington County resident. Watts also sought the influence of other state officials with the governor.[17]

To the chagrin of Watts, the Board elected Jacob Snively president. Snively was a miller from Hancock who had once run for Congress as a Whig in the 1840s. With the opening of the canal to Cumberland in 1850, he rose to prominence as a miller and merchant, utilizing the waterway to ship grain and other agricultural products from the Cumberland Valley to port cities. He had been voted to the board of directors with the B&O Railroad as late as March 23, 1864.[18]

Despite a break in the canal in late June, the summer of 1865 was one of thriving navigation. On July 13 the *Cumberland Civilian and Telegraph* wrote: "The Canal is now in excellent condition, and is doing a more thriving business than at any time in its previous history, and the prospects are flattering for a steady increase. A large number of new boats are on the stocks in the various yards and the demand still continues good." In July more coal was shipped over the canal than during any previous month in the history of the canal, including the pre-war years. On July 27 the newspaper observed: "The Canal Trade still continues in the most thriving condition, and the wharfs are constantly crowded with boats." During the month 552 boats departed Cumberland for Georgetown, carrying about 60,000 tons of coal. Tolls collected during the month totaled just over $54,000.[19]

Breaks in the canal, however, continued to interrupt navigation. At the end of July one occurred on the Monocacy Division. It was quickly repaired, but another occurred in mid-August just below Evitts Creek on the Cumberland Division. The *Civilian and Telegraph* wrote: "The fates are still averse to the successful operation of this thoroughfare, and we have to record another break of rather serious nature. A few days since some forty of fifty feet of the towpath was washed away to the depth of ten feet below the bed of the canal." Officials estimated five days to mend the break.[20]

Throughout the remainder of the year the canal company board continued to deal with issues resulting from the war. In June citizens in the Pattersons Creek and South Branch regions began clamoring for the company to replace bridges over the canal that the Confederates had destroyed during the war. Superintendent Lowe had not rebuilt the bridges due to the high price of lumber in the aftermath of the raids. In July 1865 the board instructed Lowe to make the requisite repairs.[21]

In August the owner of the Pioneer Cotton Factory in Georgetown again wrote to the board and asked it to waive four years of unpaid water rents. He explained that in 1861 a steamship bringing cotton from Baltimore to his mill was turned back in consequence of the war. The ship was eventually taken into government service and the entire freight line disbanded. He noted that the railroads were under government control, transportation uncertain, and freight rates were too high to utilize the rails. He continued: "I was thus by the consequence of the war compelled to suspend operations and the factory has in consequence remained entirely idle for over four years—not a pound of cotton spun, not a dollar of rent, or income of any kind received, on the contrary quite a large expenditure in insurance, watching and other expenses incurred." The canal company was unwilling to forgive the debt, explaining that it has suffered "similar circumstances," but offered to waive interest on amount owed and permit the owner to forfeit his water rights.[22]

On August 7 P.C. Savin, a former supervisor on the Antietam Division, requested that company pay him wages he had not received. He reminded the board that some who worked under him were also due back wages, many of whom went into the army and were in great need of the money. Savin held a grievance against Alfred Spates and the previous canal board and believed that his treatment was born of politics: "I know that you will frankly admit that such a state of things is hard for poor &, I may add, loyal & true men to endure, whilest . . . *Rebels* against their country & govt. have been paid every cent due them by the late administration of the canal."[23]

Other claims were received by the company, including one from a merchant who had supplied the company with beef totaling $248, likely used to feed company laborers. He continued: "Having had my house broken into & robbed by the rebels during Lee's invasion all my books & papers were destroyed and it will be impossible for me to give the items, but I can be qualified as to the amt. due me. Please inform me what to do."[24]

In mid-December navigation ceased for the season, which ended a profitable year for the canal company. In four of the last six months of the year the company collected over $50,000 in tolls, including over $56,000 in August, a record up to that time. Gross tolls collected for the year were over $346,000, about $120,000 more than in 1864. Although revenue exceeded expenses by nearly $154,000, this was exclusive of the debt owed for construction bonds, repair bonds, outstanding script and toll certificates, and unpaid interest. The company had, however, made progress toward reducing its floating debt to merchants, contractors, and former employees. During 1865 the company paid $146,026 toward these obligations and hoped to pay the approximately $155,000 remaining in 1866. Over 80,000 more tons of coal was shipped in 1865 than in 1864, over 57,000 more tons than that shipped in 1860. Total tonnage shipped over the waterway exceeded that of 1864 by about 81,500 tons, over 1860 by about 28,000 tons.[25]

In the canal company's annual report, president Snively summarized the good news to the stockholders:

> Although the resumption of business was late in the season, commencing in April, and during the two following months of May and June, reduced more than one-half by the partial suspension of coal shipments, caused by disagreements with miners and transporters, the following months of the year till the close of navigation by ice early in December, were comparatively active, with occasional interruptions during the months of September and October, by inconsiderable breaches in the Canal. With these exceptions the navigation was well maintained during the season.[26]

Table A

Total Tonnage and Coal Tonnage Shipped on the C&O Canal, 1860-1865

Year	Total Tonnage	% of 1860	Coal Tonnage	% of 1860	% of Total Tonnage
1860	344,532	100%	283,249	100%	82%
1861	148,064	43%	119,893	42%	81%
1862	126,793	37%	94,819	33%	75%
1863	265,847	77%	229,416	81%	86%
1864	290,772	84%	260,368	92%	90%

Source: C&O Canal Co., *Thirty-Third Annual Report*, 13; ibid, *Thirty-Fourth Annual Report*, 8; ibid, *Thirty-Fifth Annual Report*, 7; ibid, *Thirty-Sixth Annual Report*, 8-9; ibid, *Thirty-Seventh Annual Report*, 9-10; and ibid, *Thirty-Eighth Annual Report*, 10-12.

Table B

Flour Tonnage Shipped on the C&O Canal, 1860-1865*

Year	Flour Tonnage	% of 1860	% of Total Tonnage
1860	11,087	100%	3%
1861	7,067	64%	5%
1862	7,340	66%	6%
1863	8,566	77%	3%
1864	5,962	54%	2%

Source: C&O Canal Co., *Thirty-Third Annual Report*, 13; ibid, *Thirty-Fourth Annual Report*, 8; ibid, *Thirty-Fifth Annual Report*, 7; ibid, *Thirty-Sixth Annual Report*, 8-9; ibid, *Thirty-Seventh Annual Report*, 9-10; and ibid, *Thirty-Eighth Annual Report*, 10-12.

* Totals are for flour sent down the canal.

Despite the rosy picture for 1865, the outlook for the canal's future was uncertain. Charles P. Manning, the company's new engineer and general superintendent, reminded the stockholders that only the most pressing repairs were made in 1865. The Conococheague Aqueduct continued to function with the wooden trunk that had been installed following the collapse of the masonry berm wall in March 1865. Manning wrote that Dams number 1 and 2, at Little Falls and Seneca respectively, were "dilapidated & ineffective for a full supply of water when the river is low." In addition to their repair, Manning recommended that the company build a second larger feeder canal to bring water into the canal behind Dam Number 1. The government had maintained Dam Number 3 at Harpers Ferry during the war, but the company expected the structure to need additional work once the army pulled out. Dam Number 4, Manning noted, was in better condition and needed only a little back filling of loose stone or gravel, but Dam Number 5 needed repairs "without delay."[27]

In addition, many of the lockkeepers' houses needed repairs. Manning estimated that ordinary maintenance costs would amount to $1,000 per mile, or a total of $184,500; he expected the completion of Dam Number 5, repair of Dams Number 1 and 2, and the restoration of the lockkeepers' houses to cost $100,000; and he anticipated the construction of a new feeder canal at Dam Number 1 to cost $40,000. Of the $324,500 total repair estimate, he expected that $250,000 would be required in 1866 and the remainder during the following year.[28]

During the summer of 1865 the company continued the work on Dam Number 5. Spring freshets had caused numerous leaks and Superintendent Masters put crews to work tightening the cribs. On August 9 the board declared Stake and Simms' contract to complete the Virginia abutment of the dam abandoned. The work was three years past due and a spring freshet had nearly ruined all of work that the contractors had completed. Accordingly, on August 15 the canal company ordered Masters to take possession of the work and materials on behalf of the company. Throughout the later summer and fall, Masters oversaw a crew that repaired the foundation of the dam, the cribs, and began the masonry work on the abutment. On October 13, aided by two months of good weather, he completed the masonry to the abutment on the Virginia side of the dam.[29]

To reach final completion, Dam Number 5 only needed three-hundred feet of stonework across the breadth of the dam to the Maryland shore. In the spring the canal company had advertised for proposals from contractors to finish the dam. Only three proposals were received—including one from Andrew K. Stake—but none proved satisfactory to the directors. The work was undertaken by the company the following year, but flooding washed out the new stonework before it could be secured. The work at Dam Number 5 remained an ongoing problem for the company; it was not completed until 1869.[30]

The repercussions of the Civil War continued to impact the canal during the postwar years. Early in 1865 the canal company regained possession of four lots along the Rock Creek basin when a court decision dispossessed three tenants. The tenants had been renting the property to the Quartermaster Department for use as a coal yard. The company offered to continue to rent the property to the army at the same rate as the previous tenants had rented it. A year after the offer was made, a quartermaster officer replied that the army would continue to rent the wharf property at the rates paid by renters of adjoining lots, but that twenty feet of the property was never intended to be rented and was "reserved for the convenience of passing boats through the locks." Thus, the army decided to deduct rents for the twenty-foot lot previously paid to the late tenants from the rent due to the canal company.[31]

The quartermaster's decision incensed the canal company directors. On May 29, 1866, Ringgold wrote Quartermaster Rucker:

The canal was used for transportation during the entire period of the war by the United States without restriction and without the payment of the usual tolls, many restrictions on its trade were imposed by the military authorities, and great losses sustained by the destruction of its property for which no compensation has been made. I cannot therefore but deem the course now proposed arbitrary and unjust and ask your reconsideration of the subject.

He pointed out that the twenty foot lot in question had been and was still occupied by the army. Two months later Ringgold sent another letter that asked the army to continue the terms of the lease made with the former tenants and again requested that the government begin paying rent for the twenty foot lot. No documented resolution of the matter exists in the company's files, although the army continued to occupy one hundred-fifty feet of wharf property along the basin until January 31, 1868.[32]

The government also continued to hold the Potomac Aqueduct well after the war. On September 5, 1866, the company board resolved to ask President Andrew Johnson to intervene on their behalf and secure release of the aqueduct from the army. When the government finally relinquished the aqueduct in 1867, the Alexandria Canal Company was left with a canal that had deteriorated after five years of neglect. The canal was leased to the Alexandria Railroad and Bridge Company who restored the canal and in 1868 built a highway toll bridge above the trough of the aqueduct so that the bridge could serve both ground and canal traffic. Eventually the aqueduct became obsolete and was sold to the government in 1886. Two years later it built a new highway bridge on the original piers.[33]

Efforts to raise the bridges of Georgetown continued to lag during the postwar period. Although on April 10, 1865 the city of Georgetown had approved rising the bridges and market house to the height of eleven feet above the canal, the canal company could not determine what had become of the funds appropriated by Congress. In July 1866 Walter S. Ringgold learned from the Treasury Department that Alfred Spates had claimed the money on behalf of the company, presumably before he had left office. The company asked him to return the money to the Treasury Department or make it available to the company. Perhaps as a result of bitterness over his dismissal or animosity with the current board, Spates delayed his response and only grudgingly turned over the money. In early autumn of 1866 the company let a contract to raise the bridges over the canal to sufficient height for the passage of the largest class of boats. The work was expected to be completed by November 15 of that year. The company also wrote the mayor of Washington, D.C., and urged him to raise the bridge over the canal at K Street to facilitate the passage of boats.[34]

The immediate postwar period saw a general deflationary trend in prices throughout the United States. In order to better compete with the railroads, in the spring of 1866 the company voted to reduce the toll on coal, but on May 2 the Maryland Board of Public Works disapproved the decrease as "inexpedient." In the autumn the canal company again voted to reduce tolls from one-half to two-fifths of a cent per ton mile, which the Board of the Public Works subsequently approved. The change reduced the cost to transport a ton of coal from Cumberland to Georgetown from 92 cents to 74 cents.[35]

A year after his removal as president of the canal, Alfred Spates sought the office of state senator from Allegany County as a Democrat. The results of the election were close, with initial counts giving the incumbent, Dr. Charles H. Ohr, a majority of twelve votes. Spates contested the election in the legislature, however, and the Senate established a Committee on Elections to review Spates's contention. Spates and Ohr deposed witnesses, gathered evidence, and submitted it to the Senate. In the end, the committee awarded the seat to Spates. Although the Maryland Constitution of 1864 disenfranchised citizens who were suspected of disloyalty during the war, the committee determined that the election judges in Allegany County District 10 had disqualified thirty-one voters for no legitimate reason or assigned no reason for rejecting their ballots, all of whom had intended to vote for Spates. The committee also determined that the election judges had allowed others to act as judges who had not been appointed and had not taken the requisite oath. A recount of all the votes, conducted by Spates and his supporters before two deputy clerks, showed that miscounts were made and that the challenger had actually accumulated thirty-five more votes than the incumbent. Testimony also established that a small group of Republicans had heard rumors that Democrats were coming to the polls to demand their right to vote notwithstanding the provisions of the state constitution, threatening violence, and that several former members of McNeill's Rangers would lead them. The Republicans had organized a small militia company to defend the polls with arms, contrary to state law, which, according to the committee, served to intimidate and discourage Democrats from voting. Lastly, election officials had apparently inadvertently not reported returns from District 5 as required by law, where Ohr had a majority of over one-hundred votes, which disallowed those votes. As a result, a majority of the committee determined that Spates had won the election in Allegany County by 149 votes.[36]

Perhaps hoping to benefit from Spates's new political influence, and remembering the energy he exerted in behalf of the company during the difficult war years, the Board of Public Works reappointed him president of the canal company on August 27, 1867. He would hold the position until June 1869.[37]

Canal historian Walter S. Sanderlin identified the period from 1870 to 1875 as the "Golden Age" of the canal. Sanderlin wrote that during this time the canal experienced its most stable, successful, and profitable period of operation. The immediate postwar years set the stage for subsequent success, however. Tonnage shipped over the canal increased steadily from 1865 through 1869, reaching 723,938 tons in the latter year, almost double the tonnage shipped in 1865. During this period the company made significant repairs and improvements to restore the canal to prewar condition, and made significant efforts to reduce its debt. These actions reduced the profitability of the canal immediately following the war, but laid the groundwork for its later success.[38]

Alfred Spates played a prominent role in setting the stage for the future recovery of the waterway. During his second term as president he placed special emphasis on completing maintenance chores that had been neglected during the war and generally restoring the canal to prewar condition. The company made extensive repairs to lock houses, bridges, culverts, aqueducts, locks and lock gates, and waste weirs, and completed the work to Dam Number 5. The company's bottom line suffered in the short term. Despite transporting just over 500,000 tons of coal in 1868, the company's revenue exceeded expenses by only about $12,000. The company's annual report of June 1869, the last report Spates issued as president, noted: "While the above-mentioned expenditures may be considered heavy, yet the condition of the canal was such after the close of the war, from the fact of its being continually damaged by the contending armies, as to make it absolutely necessary to employ a large force to enable the Board to place its condition beyond any ordinary contingency. This the Board, with judgment and discreetness, have done; and they now have the pleasure of reporting to the Stockholders the canal fully recovered from all damages growing out of the war. The whole line is now in thorough, complete, and safe condition."[39]

The period from 1871 through 1875, as described by Sanderlin, were indeed profitable. The company averaged over $245,000 in profits per year during this time. An annual average of 931,360 tons of goods were transported, about ninety percent of this consisting of coal. In 1875 the canal transported 973,805 tons; the company never exceeded this figure during the remaining years of its operation.

The company used its profits during the early 1870s to begin repaying its long-suffering creditors. In 1871 it repaid the last of the interest and principal on the repair bonds of 1849 and began paying the interest due on the construction bonds of 1844. The profitability of the canal during this period rekindled interest in extending the canal to the Ohio River, although all such efforts came to naught.

In 1871 the company made a final push to receive compensation from the government for war damages. On February 2 company President James C. Clarke wrote Meigs, still the army's quartermaster general, and asked if the company should present its claims to his office, to the War Department, or to Congress. Clarke acknowledged that a portion of the claim was not likely to be approved, but noted that a part totaling $35,030 "for the use, occupation, and destruction of the Houses, Boats & Scows which were the property of the Canal Company, and were destroyed by the United States troops" ought to be paid. On February 8 Meigs's subordinate, M.S. Sudington, informed Clarke that the original decision of the Quartermaster Department was still valid. On February 24 Meigs responded to Clarke directly and defended his decision: "This office has done what seemed right in the matter and cannot now change its action." This ended the company's efforts to obtain reimbursement from the government for its use of the canal during the war and damages resulting from the conflict.[40]

Heavy postwar use of the canal was not without negative consequences. Long backlogs formed at Georgetown as boats lined up awaiting an opportunity to unload their cargo. In 1871 President Clarke reported that often sixty to eighty boats, forming a queue up to a mile long, awaited opportunity to discharge cargo. The shortage of coastal vessels caused coal to pile up on the wharves. In light of the bottleneck at Georgetown, the canal company again considered building an outlet lock to the river above the town, an idea first contemplated during the war. The company selected a location for the lock about two miles above the Rock Creek basin and approximately a mile above the Potomac Aqueduct. In 1872 the company contracted with a group of private investors who financed the construction of an incline plane for the right to charge a usage fee, although the canal company reserved the right to purchase the plane and lock at a later date. The plane was completed in 1876. To pass into the river, a laden canal boat was floated onto a water-filled caisson which, utilizing steel cables, pulleys, and counterweights, was lowered down the embankment and released into the Potomac. The incline plane was considered an engineering marvel in Europe and was upheld as an example of America's engineering prowess at the Paris Exposition in 1878.[41]

Alfred Spates maintained his courtship with controversy in the postwar years. After he completed his second term as president of the canal, the company made an accounting of its finances and lodged charges of impropriety against him. Spates was reluctant to answer the charges before a committee appointed by the company because he believed that most of its membership was hostile to him. He wrote that nearly all canal employees who had supported his re-nomination as president had been replaced with those opposed to him. As a sitting state senator, in 1870 the Maryland Senate's Committee on Investigation heard the charges against him. The canal company made nine specific charges against Spates, accusing him of appropriating company funds for his personal use. It is likely that some of the charges were politically motivated and grew out of his contested election for state senate. J.J. Bruce, a political opponent in a state Senate race, was the sole witness against Spates for three of the charges. Defense witnesses, many of whom had worked under Spates during his administration of the canal, offered explanations for most of the charges. Only one charge raised significant suspicions of impropriety against Spates. The company had appropriated $10,000 to condemn and purchase land and claimed that Spates had submitted a $739.00 voucher for a land purchase that had previously been paid. In addition, the company presented altered condemnation records and vouchers into evidence, implying that Spates had made the alterations. Spates pointed out that the condemnation records in question had been filled out during Jacob Snively's administration of the canal, and that the alterations were likely done by J. Phillip Roman, the company's attorney who had charge of the fund. The company also noted that Spates had met with the new company president, Arthur Pue Gorman, and when presented with the discrepancy had refunded $739.00 to the canal company on September 16, 1869. The committee exonerated Spates by pointing out that there was no evidence to show who had altered the records and that Spates had settled the matter by reimbursing the company for the amount in question. It even admonished the canal company for bringing the charge against Spates after he had returned the money and was no longer in office.[42]

In addition to serving as a delegate to the 1867 Maryland Constitutional Convention, Spates continued to serve in the state senate until he was defeated in 1873. In 1876 he was again the Democratic nominee for the seat but lost the election. He contested the results of this election as well, charging that Maryland Delegate Arthur Pue Gorman, the leader of the state Democratic machine and incumbent canal company president, had used company employees and funds to defeat his nomination, including the payment of citizens to vote again him. Both Democrats, Gorman and Spates had been close before a split in the party in Allegany County. According to Spates, in gratitude for political support, Gorman had appointed him shipping agent at Cumberland in 1873, and two years later had given him control of patronage appointments on the canal in Allegany County. Spates also claimed that Gorman had appealed to him, because of his popularity among the boatmen, to obtain resolutions of support from the men following a change in how tolls were applied on one-way trips over the canal. A House committee, however, found no substance in Spates's claims against the popular and influential Gorman.[43]

Although Spates next worked as a purchasing agent for the West Virginia Central Railroad, he worked intermittently for the canal company over the decades that followed. At the time of this death in 1892 at age eighty, he was again employed by the canal company as wharf master and inspector at Cumberland. In noting his death, the *Sentinel*, from his native Montgomery County, wrote that since Spates had moved to Cumberland "he was employed in the business of the Chesapeake and Ohio Canal, and from that time to the present, except at short intervals, he has been directly or indirectly connected with it, and probably knew its history as well as any man in the State." The November 19, 1892, *Cumberland Daily News* observed: "Many people believe his administration of canal affairs to have been the best that greatly abused public work ever had."[44]

§

During the Civil War the Chesapeake and Ohio Canal played a significant role as a supply line for the Union army, especially as a coal carrier. The U. S. Navy's fleet, which had grown from 90 vessels in 1861 to over 600 vessels by the end of the war—most of them steam propelled or using a combination of steam and sail—consumed large amounts of coal to enforce the blockade of the Confederacy, to interdict smugglers in the lower Potomac and Chesapeake Bay, and to fight the Union's battles on water. Western Maryland's coal was ideally suited for steamship use and was in great demand from the government. Coal was also in demand to heat home and factories, generate steam to run machinery, and to produce iron. The demand for coal was such that, despite the uncertainty caused by war, the number of western Maryland mining companies increased from seventeen in 1861 to twenty-one in 1865. One newcomer, the Consolidation Coal Company, had acquired the assets of three other coal companies and would grow to become one of the largest bituminous coal companies in the nation. Despite repeated interruptions as a result of the war and weather, from April 1861 through April 1865 the canal transported over 700,000 tons of coal.[45]

By virtue of its position on the north-south border, the canal played a direct or indirect role in many of the battles and campaigns in the east. One of the objectives of Patterson's 1861 campaign, for example, was to reestablish communication and trade on the canal and the railroad, while one of Lee's secondary objectives during the Antietam Campaign was to disrupt both the railroad and canal. As McClellan prepared to pursue Lee following Antietam, the canal was utilized to forward supplies to his army. When Burnside replaced McClellan the canal was used to transport supplies back to Georgetown for further transport to Aquia Creek, Virginia. In 1863, as Lee's army again crossed into Maryland, the Union Army of the Potomac passed over the river to intercept him on pontoon bridges that had been sent up the canal and received supplies from temporary depots established along the waterway. It served a similar function during Meade's pursuit of Lee after Gettysburg. In 1864 the canal was utilized to supply Sheridan's army as he finally rid the Shenandoah Valley of a significant Confederate presence. Canal boats, although privately owned, were utilized to transport supplies to McClellan's army on the Peninsula, were seized to build bridges, and kept in readiness to blockade the Potomac against the ascent of the Confederate ironclad *Virginia*.

In addition to its role in various campaigns and battles, the canal played a daily role in the life of Federal pickets on the Potomac. Records show that pickets along the canal routinely used canal boats to move their camps or entire commands to different points on the border, and that they were often supplied and provisioned via the waterway. East of Point of Rocks there was no quicker means to move material from supply depots in Washington to picket posts and supply depots along the river. Pickets and cavalry patrols routinely utilized the towpath as a patrol route throughout the war. The towpath itself was of great value as a military road and was used to move columns of troops along the river, such during Stone's expedition in June 1861 and by Union troops at the beginning of the Gettysburg Campaign. To a limited extent the canal was used to evacuate wounded and ill soldiers to hospitals.

During portions of the first two years of the war, the canal was the only transportation and supply link along the north–south border, a fact often overlooked by historians. When the Confederates disabled the B&O Railroad in early June 1861 it remained out of commission until March 1862. The canal, although damaged at the same time, was fully repaired in late August 1861 and for most of the remaining year reestablished the critical Union supply route to the coal fields. The early restoration of navigation led directly to Jackson's assaults against Dam numbers 4 and 5 in December 1861, by which he hoped to sever the remaining connection with the coal mines. A similar situation occurred the next year following the Battle of Antietam when the canal was repaired two and one-half months earlier than the railroad and thus reconnected Washington to the mines.

Perhaps no greater testament to the canal's significance was that made by the political and military leaders of the Confederacy. Nearly every significant Confederate military figure in the east advocated or executed attacks against the canal, including Jefferson Davis, Robert E. Lee, "Stonewall" Jackson, Joseph E. Johnston, Jubal Early and Jeb Stuart. Similarly, some of the most significant political and military leaders for the Union made efforts to protect, defend, and repair the canal, including Abraham Lincoln, Edwin M. Stanton, Robert Patterson, Montgomery C. Meigs, George B. McClellan, George G. Meade, Phillip Sheridan, Benjamin Kelley, and Charles P. Stone. Even Ulysses S. Grant, a westerner who likely had little foreknowledge of the canal, quickly learned of its value to the government and directed his subordinates to protect it.

However much the Confederates desired to disable the canal, they never devoted enough resources and time to its destruction. During the Antietam Campaign, for example, generals Daniel H. Hill and John G. Walker found tools and resources insufficient to damage the Monocacy Aqueduct in the allotted time. If it had been severely damaged, the aqueduct, which consisted of seven arches and was over 500 feet long, would have been difficult, expensive, and slow to repair in wartime. If its destruction had been accomplished, the canal likely would have remained cut in two throughout the war and may have ceased to operate altogether. In retrospect, Lee would have accomplished more during the invasion of Maryland had he simply crossed his army in force to defend the complete destruction of the aqueduct as well as the bridges and culverts on the B&O, thereby severing both links with the coal fields, inhibiting the blockade of Southern ports, and permitting more trade between the South and Europe.

Historians have largely overlooked the role of the canal in the Civil War, perhaps because of the part played by the Baltimore and Ohio Railroad. The B&O was the most significant supply and transportation line during the war. Its single-track connection with Washington, the Washington Branch, double-tracked in 1863, was the only railroad link with the Federal capital. All goods that moved by train entered Washington over the tracks of the B&O. This branch line was largely unmolested during the war and served as a secure and reliable supply route. Other northern railroads connected with the B&O north of Baltimore, which provided the government with access to supplies from the northeast and mid-west. The main stem of the B&O was much more exposed to Confederate raids. Consequently, it was disabled by the southern troops more frequently than the canal. When in repair, however, the main stem provided a connection with the west as far as St. Louis—a feat the canal could not match. In 1863 and 1864 the main stem was in operation as frequently as the canal. In November 1863 it played a significant role in moving troops to Maj. Gen. William S. Rosecrans to help lift the siege of Chattanooga, Tennessee. Such significant contributions to the war effort by the Washington Branch throughout the war, and by the main stem later in the war, may have overshadowed the role of the canal and caused it to be largely overlooked.

Another reason why the canal's role in the war has been discounted may have resulted from suspicion that the canal company was ridden with disloyal employees. Alfred Spates's well-publicized arrest, trial, and conviction may have helped create the impression that the company was replete with southern sympathizers. Complaints against various employees, especially those who worked on the eastern divisions, were made periodically throughout the war, and while the company professed its intention not to harbor disloyal workers, it demanded evidence of disloyalty before it considered removing suspicious employees. Records show that very few employees were removed during the war, aside from personnel changes made when the company reorganized in 1862.

Historians share some of the responsibility for neglecting the role of the canal in the war. In one case an otherwise fine historian of some renown wrote that just prior to Early's 1864 raid, Lee had directed Early to remain in the lower Shenandoah Valley to destroy the B&O Railroad. The source cited, however, states that Lee had ordered Early to remain in the lower Valley to destroy *both* the B&O Railroad and the C&O Canal. In addition, many of the published narratives of Jackson's Shenandoah Valley Campaign and biographies of the general fail to place his expeditions to destroy Dam numbers 4 and 5 into the context of the canal being the last remaining link to western Maryland's coal fields.[46]

The C&O and B&O received different treatment by the Federal government during and after the war. The railroad received freight payments throughout the war while the canal company often did not receive tolls on goods transported by the army. Although the canal company claimed that the government never paid a penny toward tolls, existing quartermasters' records show that in some cases it contracted directly with boat captains to transport supplies and provisions over the canal. In these cases the government paid tolls indirectly by paying the boatmen, who in turn paid the fares to the company. In the same way, the government indirectly paid tolls on the coal it purchased from the coal companies throughout the war. In several cases, however, the government arranged to forward goods on the canal, but the officer who made the agreement left the area before the tolls could be collected from him. Additionally, there is no evidence that the army paid tolls when it seized canal boats and piloted them rather than contracting with boatmen. Although the B&O received postwar reimbursement for much of their property that was damaged and destroyed by the Union army, the canal company's claims for damaged and confiscated property were dismissed outright.[47]

Some reason for the discrepancy in postwar treatment of the canal may be explained by the various claims the company submitted to the government. The company initially submitted a claim for $5,190 for toll and confiscated, and damaged property to September 1861, followed by another for $75,391.96 covering the period from September 1861 through April 1862. In September 1864 the company submitted an additional claim of $5,151.60 for tolls on goods transported under the provisions of the July 4, 1864 Act, which attorney Stephen W. Downey erroneously referred to as the only claim submitted to the government. When the Quartermasters' Department pointed out that it had a counterclaim of $8,765.49, the company submitted an additional claim for damages of $292,330 encompassing the period from May 1862 through 1864, for a total war claim of $378,063.56. When the company resumed efforts for reimbursement in 1871, President Clarke asked for $35,030 from the government. The multiple submission of claims and partial claims, accompanied by Downey's inaccurate statement that no other claim had been submitted, may have helped to create the impression in the Quartermasters' Department that the company was constantly adjusting its claims to extort money from the government. The fact that the company was in heavy debt prior to the war and that delegates to the state Constitutional Convention of 1864 openly advocated its sale, also likely contributed to the impression that the company was fishing for money to overcome its financial woes.

The nature of canal and railroad technologies may have contributed to the disparity in treatment at the hands of the government. Canals were an old technology, dating to at least the thirteenth century. The first American canals were in operation in the late eighteenth century, which, by the time of the Civil War, gave citizens over sixty years to see canals in operation, to ride canal boats, and/or to work on canals. During the Civil War the Union army showed no disinclination to appropriate canal boats, load them with stores, and, perhaps clumsily and haphazardly, operate the locks, causing damage in a few cases. Railroads, on the other hand, were a relatively new technology. The B&O, for example, broke ground in 1828 and reached Cumberland in 1842, nineteen years before the war. To operate a steam powered locomotive required skills that could not easily be inferred. Additionally, it required training and experience to manage the complexities of the rail line. Most of the B&O line was single-tracked and required a skilled operator to manage the passage of trains in both directions over a single line. A natural respect for rail transportation grew out of the complexity of skills needed to operate a railroad as opposed to a canal.

The different personalities and political skills of the leaders of the two carriers may also have played a role in determining how the government dealt with each. John W. Garrett was a prominent banker from a family of bankers before ascending to the head of the B&O. He had natural leadership abilities and political influence. Despite Garrett's pre-war speeches in which he described his railroad as a "Southern line," due to his foresight and political skills he was able to overcome initial government suspicions of him and gain the complete confidence of President Lincoln and the Union army. An example of the trust that developed between the B&O president and the government occurred when Lincoln allowed Garrett to accompany him to Antietam Battlefield in October 1862. Lincoln's confidence in Garrett was further displayed when the government gave him responsibility for managing the relief and reinforcement by rail of Maj. Gen. William S. Rosecrans at Chattanooga in late 1863.[48]

Alfred Spates, on the other hand, clearly had less political skill than Garrett. Although he displayed great energy during the war, as he moved up and down the canal to oversee repairs and pressed the needs of the company to Federal officials, controversy seemed to follow him. He had a large group of friends and supporters, but an equally vehement group of enemies and detractors. While some of his unpopularity and the resultant conflict was no doubt due to the political nature of his position, at inopportune times he displayed poor judgment. His flirtation with the Confederates after their retreat from Gettysburg in 1863 resulted in his arrest, conviction and imprisonment, which subjected him and the canal company to embarrassment and may have contributed to a negative postwar impression of the canal's contribution to the war. His personal dispute with Charles Mynn Thruston and his appeals to the War Department to have the general dismissed may have removed an adversary, but it also created animosity that contributed to his conviction in 1863. Spates's involvement in numerous postwar disputes further displayed his tendency to become embroiled in controversy.

Despite the canal company's contentious relationship with the Union army during the war, the association became symbiotic, with each party needing what the other provided. The army needed the canal for the transportation facilities it provided, which brought coal, flour, and other supplies to the depots in Washington and various commands in the field. On the other hand, it is difficult to imagine the canal company surviving the war without military assistance. Although the army made repairs to the canal to serve its own transportation and supply needs, it did not keep tabs of its expenses in most cases, and its assistance helped to ensure the survival of the company at a time when its resources were scant. Additionally, the huge amounts of coal purchased by the government, and the tolls paid by the boatmen, provided the company with just enough revenue to make the most necessary repairs to keep the canal operational, which was especially important since the company could not obtain credit during the war. Lastly, the defense of the canal provided by the army, although generally inadequate, prevented the Confederates from committing more serious damages to the waterway. Had not the Federal troops put up such as stiff resistance at Dam Number 5 in December 1861, for example, Jackson's men may have ripped a large hole in the dam that subsequent high water would likely have enlarged, which may have caused the entire dam to wash away and threatened the very existence of the waterway. The canal company had to endure the army's interference in its operations, the imposition of cumbersome regulation, and bureaucratic inefficiency in the various branches of the government, but in doing so its survival was linked to the success of Union arms. As a result of the Union military victory, the canal company was assured of a share in the nation's post-war economic recovery.

Indeed, in the decade that followed the war the canal experienced its most profitable period. The war helped to establish the canal as a significant coal carrier at a time when steam power was growing in tandem with the industrial expansion of the country. Coal helped to power the development of the country by fueling steam engines, providing heat to homes and factories, and by being used to smelt and forge iron. The canal company simply had to emerge from the war intact to share in the prosperity that followed. By providing direct competition to the B&O Railroad and other transportation lines in the mid-Atlantic region, the C&O Canal helped keep transportation costs low, which provided momentum to the industrial revolution.

EPILOGUE
TAKE TIME OFF AND COME WITH ME

After the mid-1870s, the canal began a gradual decline. Hyper-competition with the railroads, outmoded facilities, economic downturns, and continual problems with floods and droughts all played a part in the ultimate failure of the canal within the fifty-eight years that followed the Civil War.

During the mid-1870s the canal faced increased competition from railroads. President Gorman, who was appointed in 1872, proposed a number of improvements to enhance the competitiveness of the waterway, such as constantly dredging those areas that filled with silt, buying or leasing wharf facilities, and lengthening the locks so as to permit longer boats. A nationwide economic depression slowed implementation of the improvements, however, and few were actually completed. In addition, rate wars between the canal and the railroads ensued over the declining coal trade, which further suppressed the profitability of the canal.

A major flood caused extensive damage to the canal in 1877. The state of Maryland, which held a preferred mortgage on canal property, bailed the company out of its woes by waiving its lien on canal property to strengthen the market for new repair bonds, and by restricting the competitive actions of the B&O Railroad.

Late in the decade and in the beginning of the next, the company dealt with additional problems. Strikes by the miners and boatmen and significant droughts and floods in the Potomac hindered navigation. In addition, the canal required continuing repairs and improvements to keep pace with the enhancements in rail transportation. The company incurred additional debt to make the most necessary repairs. In 1886 three successive floods raged down the Potomac River. Additional repair bonds were authorized by Maryland, and were sold at eighty percent of face value. Those who anticipated the ultimate failure of the canal, particularly the B&O

Railroad, bought the bonds in hopes of acquiring a controlling interest in the canal.

Several disasters struck the canal in 1889. In early spring a major break in the canal occurred near Shepherdstown, followed by a rock slide below the Paw Paw Tunnel. From May 30–June 1 a major flood roared down the Potomac, setting another record for high water. Initial estimates to restore the canal ranged from $500,000 to $1,000,000. Unable to raise the necessary funds, the canal company entered bankruptcy. Its old rival, the B&O Railroad, gained control of the receivership as holders of preferred mortgages on the property and revenues of the canal. The B&O, concerned that a rival enterprise might build a rail line on the canal bed, offered to restore and operate the canal at its own expense rather than see the court sell it, in which case it would have had to buy the canal outright. The state of Maryland, the secondary mortgage holder, requested sale of the company in 1890, but subsequent court decisions permitted the B&O to operate the canal under the receivership if it could do so profitably.

The B&O completed repairs to the canal in 1891 and created a subsidiary, the Chesapeake and Ohio Transportation Company, to operate the canal. The railroad pumped enough money into its subsidiary to show a profit and stave off a forced sale. In 1905 the court agreed to permit the transportation company to guarantee no annual loss rather than show a profit. By such means the B&O put off the sale of the canal and prevented a competitor from assuming control of the waterway.

In 1902 the B&O Railroad organized the Canal Towage Company to operate the canal more efficiently. The company provided the boats and teams, cut freight rates, and designated where cargoes could be offloaded. The establishment of this company is generally considered to have ended the romantic era of the canal. The boats were now assigned a number rather than given a unique name by their owners. Independent boatmen could not compete with the new company and were forced off the canal. The new boatmen were employees of the Towage Company and had to adhere to its schedule and rules. Lost was the era when a man could earn his livelihood as an independent boatman, piloting his own boat when and for whom he chose.

During the early twentieth century, the canal was nearing the end of its usefulness. In 1904 the state disposed of its canal stock and the receivers began selling some company lands to power companies and the Federal government. During World War I, however, the canal had aided the American war effort by carrying coal to the United States Proving Ground at Indianhead, Maryland, utilizing tugs to transport the boats in the Potomac.

In 1924 another major flood struck the canal. Although the water did not reach the heights of 1889, significant damage to the canal occurred near Cumberland. The receivers avoided the expense of restoring the entire canal and only repaired the Georgetown Division. Although water rents from mill operators in Georgetown financed an office staff, active boating ended. The B&O convinced the courts that it had not abandoned the canal, but had only temporarily suspended navigation.

In 1934 the United States government showed interest in purchasing that portion of the canal east of Point of Rocks. The railroad, struggling under the effects of the Great Depression, offered to sell the entire canal. The parties agreed to the price of $2,000,000, and in 1938 the Federal government assumed control of the Chesapeake and Ohio Canal. The Dam Number 2 inlet at Violetts Lock was restored by the Civilian Conservation Corps, a Depression-era agency designed to alleviate national unemployment. The work was intended to provide recreational opportunities to area residents.

The government initially proposed constructing a scenic parkway over the canal from Great Falls to Cumberland, similar to the Shenandoah National Park's Skyline Drive. However, a small but committed cadre of nature enthusiasts advocated the preservation of the canal as a national park. The position of the preservationists was strengthened when Supreme Court Justice William O. Douglas joined their cause. In early 1954 he issued a challenge to the editors of the *Washington Post* who had come out in favor of the parkway: "I wish the man who wrote your editorial of January 3, 1954, approving the parkway would take time off and come with me. We would go with packs on our backs and walk the 185 miles to Cumberland. I feel that if your editor did, he would return a new man and use the power of your great editorial page to help keep this sanctuary untouched."[1]

The *Post's* editors accepted the challenge. The walk took place during a week in March 1954 amidst much media attention, and the *Post's* editors subsequently advocated changes to the parkway plan that would lessen its impact on the canal. At the end of the hike Douglas and other canal preservationists established the Chesapeake and Ohio Canal Committee to help save the old waterway. In 1961 President Eisenhower designated the canal a national monument. Preservationists were not successful in halting the construction of the George Washington Memorial Parkway (in 1989 designated the Clara Barton Parkway), which when completed in 1970 encroached upon the old canal for seven miles from the Chain Bridge to MacArthur Boulevard at Carderock, Maryland. Disputes between those who wished to build water reservoirs along the river or dams in the Potomac—which would have flooded canal land—slowed plans to preserve the canal as a park. Public opinion in favor of saving the waterway mounted over time, however, aided by support from the Secretary of the Interior in the Nixon administration, Walter J. Hickel. On January 8, 1971 President Nixon signed legislation that indeed preserved the canal as a National Historical Park.

§

Today the canal is enjoyed by thousands of hikers, bikers, joggers, horseback riders, boaters, fishermen, bird-watchers, and history enthusiasts. The National Park Service has restored small sections of the canal, but much of the line is barely discernible amidst the trees and brush that have grown up in the former canal channel. Nature has overrun much of the canal on both sides of the towpath and obstructed the line of sight that existed at the time the waterway was in operation. Some of the locks have been filled in to prevent them from collapsing and most other structures in various stages of disrepair or collapse. The canal largely sits in quiet isolation from the modern world.

One-hundred and fifty years ago, however, the canal played a major role in sustaining the Union war effort. Officials at the highest level of the Confederate government and army planned operations to disable it, while Union political and military officials devised strategies to protect it. The brave and unheralded boatmen often risked their lives to pilot their boats between the opposing armies in order to provide for their families. The agents of the canal company worked with much vigor and few means to keep the waterway in operation, despite great and unprecedented obstacles. The beauty and peacefulness of the present-day Chesapeake and Ohio Canal National Historical Park is a fitting tribute to those who expended so much sweat and blood over the "Old Ditch" during the country's fratricidal struggle.

APPENDIX A

Report of the Maryland Commission of Public Works, March 8, 1864

To the General Assembly of Maryland, the Commissioners of Public Works respectfully represent that owing to the disturbed condition of the country, they have found it impossible to obtain such information of the condition of the various works of Internal Improvement in which the State is interested as to enable them to report as required by article 7th, section 1st, of the Constitution of the State.

But in obedience to an order of the Senate of the 7th inst., they submit the following containing all the information they could obtain to the present time. . . .

The civil war during the past three years has borne heavily upon the business of the Chesapeake and Ohio Canal.

In 1861 the usual spring freshet caused some damage to the work and the hostile occupation of the line of the Potomac prevented the company from making repairs until late in the spring.

The General Government besides in that year made large requisitions upon the canal for the boats employed in the transportation of coal and produce, withdrawing them from the line and using them at distant points on the lower Potomac and on the Virginia Peninsula.[1] The transportation of coal in that year (and this is the main source of revenue) was reduced to 105,000 tons. In 1862 from the same causes of interruption, the coal tonnage sank still lower and did not exceed 98,000 tons, a smaller amount than had been reached since the year 1852.

The work of the Canal too, in that year suffered severely from the enemy during their invasion of the State. The boats taken by the Government in the previous year were mainly lost and destroyed, and of course could not be restored that season; but the increasing confidence of the people in the ultimate and probably near suppression of the rebellion manifested itself in the vigor and energy with which the parties engaged in the coal trade addressed themselves to the repair of the losses and damages to their means of transportation, and the steady determination with which the canal company again and again promptly repaired the damages to the works, and through great discouragements succeeded in maintaining navigation.

Accordingly, we find that in 1863 the coal tonnage amounted to nearly 217,000 tons, notwithstanding more than two months in the height of the season were totally lost by Lee's invasion of Maryland, and the damage to the works caused thereby. The season closed with the fairest prospects of a trade for the ensuing season that has ever been known in the history of the canal; a large number of new boats have been built this winter, and many more are now in process of construction.

Should we have uninterrupted navigation, which so far as regards dangers from natural causes, we consider next to certain, we believe the trade for the present year will be very large, though the outlet to Alexandria by way of the aqueduct, which is for the present appropriated by the Government for a viaduct, will necessarily restrict the tonnage to the facilities supplied by the city of Georgetown.

The condition of the canal at this time is better than for several years, if not since its completion; the dams on the upper Potomac are now considered safe from all ordinary dangers, and it is in contemplation by the company to finish during the ensuing summer, if possible, the stone work at Dam No. 5, which will remove the last cause of uneasiness.

[1]The canal boats in question were actually seized in February and March, 1862.

Source: Minutes, Md. Commission of Public Works, 149, 151-153.

APPENDIX B

Commissioners of Public Works of the State of Maryland to the Senate and House of Representatives of the United States, June 13, 1864

To the Honorable, the Senate and House of Representatives of the United States, The Commissioners of Public Works of the State of Maryland respectfully beg leave to represent,

That in the year 1861 the Government of the United States did for military purposes take possession of the aqueduct connecting the Chesapeake & Ohio Canal with the Alexandria Canal and did convert the said acqueduct [sic] into a wagon road, and did thereby deprived [sic] the Chesapeake & Ohio Canal of its outlet to tide water and thereby confined its business within the narrow limits of its wharves in Georgetown, which are inadequate for the delivery of the large amount of Coal transported over the said Canal, the boats are therefore detained an unnecessary length of time in the delivery of their cargoes, the coal is materially damaged by handling and besides that the purchaser must pay thirty cents per ton for the handling of the Coal at Georgetown and wait until his turn comes to get up to the wharves.

We have heretofore remained silent notwithstanding the fact that the depriving of the Canal Company of the aqueduct deteriorated the quality of the coal transported over it, and increased the expenses by the handling thereby made necessary, because we believed and still believe that possession of the aqueduct by the Government of the United States is a military neccessity [sic]. The Canal Company has also suffered a large amount of damage and loss, by the incursions of the Rebels, as well as by the Federal soldiers who have destroyed Lock Houses and other buildings; but these losses have been the results of War and we make no complaint concerning them, we only ask the Government to place us where they found us (with an outlet to tide water).

Outlet locks can be erected above Georgetown, through which the canal boats, can be taken to the navy yard, or wherever else they may be required and their cargoes discharged upon Government Steamers with a single handling and with a great savings of time and money to the Government.

The cost of such Outlet Locks will most probably exceed the sum of one hundred thousand dollars.

Now therefore we do respectfully ask the Government to appropriate the sum of one hundred thousand dolls., or so much as may be needed to enable the Chesapeake & Ohio Canal Company to erect Outlet Locks at or above Georgetown.

Firmly believing that the first one hundred thousand tons of coal which the Government will draw from the said Canal will fully reimburse them for the appropriation which we ask, and hoping that you will recognize in this appeal the justice of the claim we make

We are Yours Truly
Fred Fickey Jr. Secy.

By order of the Board of Commissioners of Public Works of the State of Maryland
Baltimore, June 13, 1864

Source: Minutes, Md. Commission of Public Works, 161-163.

APPENDIX C

Exhibit 1
Alfred Spates to Col. Fish, August 25, 1863

Baltimore, Aug. 25th, 1863
Col Fish, Provost Marshal &c

Dear Sir

It is an old adage that "politics makes us acquainted with strange bed fellows," and I find that a little gasconade or indiscretion on my part has placed me in rather a strange position with the military authorities of the department; and the matter having assumed so serious a forum, I deem it a duty to which I owe to myself as well as to my country that I should make a brief statement of the facts which has led to this unpleasant and unwarrantable state of things.

During the latter part of July I met at the Fountain Hotel of this city, several personal friends, among whom were Messrs. Clabaugh, Harris, Herbert and Hoffman, and by a casual conversation I made use of remarks (as far as my memory serves me) to the following effect, which was a mere piece of gasconade or badinage, and so supposed it to be understood by the company present: "That I had had a conversation with the rebel General Ewell respecting the damage done to the Acqueduct [sic] on the Canal. That I had seen General Lee, and received from him a pass." All of which is untrue and without foundation in fact. Supposing that I was in company with sound Union men and old personal friends, (some of whom being under the greatest obligation to me) I felt free to indulge in some foolish remarks as before stated.

I would also remark that at this time all that I am worth in the world is invested in the canal and subject entirely to the control of the U.S. Government, and my own pecuniary interest, even if I had no more patriotic motive, would preclude the possibility of my doing any thing against the government, especially when that government has placed such confidence in me and conferred upon me such favors as are stated in General Orders No. 44, dated April 21st, 1862, and renewed on August 19th, 1863, a copy of which is herewith enclosed.

By this Order the canal is relieved of all military control and placed under the exclusive management of myself. I am responsible to the War Department and report in and receive all orders directly from that Department concerning the canal, and at this date my relations with that Department are of the most friendly character, and I may add that the Secretary of War is fully acquainted with the report above referred to.

Trusting that this explanation may be satisfactory, and sincerely regretting my indiscretion,

I am yours, very respectfully,
Alfred Spates

Source: Spates to Fish, August 25, 1863, U.S. vs. Spates.

Notes and Bibliography

ABBREVIATIONS

OR . . . . . .United States, War Department. *War of the Rebellion: A Compilation of the Official Records of the Union and Confederate Armies.*
ORN . . . . United States, Navy. Naval War Records Office and United State Office of Naval Records and Library. *Official Records of the Union and Confederate Navies in the War of the Rebellion.*
OR Suppl. . Janet Hewett, at al, ed., *Supplement to the Official Records of the Union and Confederate Armies.*
SHSP . . . *Southern Historical Society Papers.*

NOTES

PROLOGUE

1. Gutheim, *Potomac*, 28.
2. John Quincy Adams quoted in Ward, *The Early Development*, 89.
3. Ward, *The Early Development*, 44-45.
4. Snyder, "The Chesapeake & Ohio Canal and the Underground Railroad," *Along the Towpath*, 42, no. 1 (March 2010): 13-14; Curry, "Narrative of James Curry, A Fugitive Slave," *The Liberator*, Jan. 10, 1840.
5. Morris, "Andrew Jackson, Strikebreaker," *American Historical Review*, 55, no. 1 (Oct. 1949): 54-68.
6. Sanderlin, *The Great National Project*, 285; Unrau, *Historic Resource Study*, 105.
7. Maryland, *Laws Made and Passed by the General Assembly of the State of Maryland* [1842-1843], chapt. 301; Md. Constitution of 1851, art. 3, sec. 22, in Md. Constitutional Convention of 1851, *Debates and Proceedings of the Maryland Reform Convention to Revise the State Constitution*, 2: 9-10.
8. Unrau, *Historic Resource Study*, 63; Sanderlin, *The Great National Project*, 162.
9. Horatio Nelson Taft, "Diary," 3: June 28, 1864; Owen, *"Dear Friends at Home,"* 13.

10. *Hagerstown Herald of Freedom and Torch Light* [hereinafter *Hagerstown Herald*], April 11, 1860 and June 6, 1860.

11. "Map of the Cumberland Coal Basin Showing the Proportions of the Great Coal Seam Owned by the Various Coal Companies, 1880," in Scharf, *History of Western Maryland*, 2: [between pages 1446 and 1447]; Thruston, Semmes & Humbird to Commissioners of Public Works & Pres. & Dirs. of C&O Canal Co., n.d., in *Cumberland Civilian and Telegraph* [hereinafter *Cumberland Civilian*], Aug. 16, 1860. Cumberland Coal has been classified as semibitumious, "an unfortunate misnomer. It is applied to a kind of coal that is really a super-bitumimous, ranking higher than bituminous. . . . Semibituminious coal – of which the entire production of the Maryland mines consists – is outstanding among all other coals. The best grade of this coal has no superior in heating value, and for this reason it is unexcelled for steaming and other purposes that require a high degree of heat;" see Fairbanks & Hamill, *Coal-Mining Industry of Maryland*, 6.

12. "The Cumberland Coal Trade for 1862," in *Cumberland Civilian*, Feb. 19, 1863.

13. Statement of Articles Transported, C&O Canal Papers.

14. The capacity of the company's steam pump is from C&O Canal Co., *Thirtieth Annual Report*, 6.

15. C&O Canal Co., *Thirty-Second Annual Report*, 6; Ligon to Gentleman of the Senate and House of Delegates, Jan. 6, 1858, in Md. Governor (Proceedings), MSA SM 172-4, MdHR M3162-3.

16. C&O Canal Co., *Thirty-Second Annual Report*, 6-8.

17. Ibid, 10-11.

18. The company's "floating debt" was defined by the secretary-treasurer in Ringold to Watkins, 6 March 1865, Ltrs. Sent, M, 174, C&O Canal Papers; C&O Canal Co., *Thirty-Second Annual Report*, 12; *Annual Report of the Comptroller of the Treasury Department, for the Fiscal Year Ended 30th September, 1860, to the Governor of Maryland*, 13.

19. Hicks to Gentlemen of the Senate and House of Delegates, Jan. 4, 1860, in Md. Governor (Proceedings), MSA SM 172-4, MdHR M3162-3.

20. *Frederick Republican Citizen*, Jan. 27, 1860; *Message of the Governor of Virginia*, xxxi.

21. *Hagerstown Herald*, March 21, 1860.

22. C&O Canal Co., *Thirty-Second Annual Report*, 12-13, 14-15.

23. *Cumberland Civilian*, July 19, 1860.

24. Thruston, Semmes & Humbird to Commissioners of Public Works & Pres. & Dirs. of C&O Canal Co., n.d., in *Cumberland Civilian*, Aug. 16, 1860.

25. Ibid.

26. Ibid.

27. Ibid.

28. Ibid.

29. C&O Canal Co., *Thirty-Third Annual Report*, 8-9.

30. Shriver to Coale, Oct. 22, 1859, in Stiverson, ed., *"In Readiness to Do Every Duty Assigned,"* 5-6.

CHAPTER 1

1. C&O Canal Co., *Thirty-Third Annual Report*, 3-4, 8-9; *Williamsport Ledger*, n.d., in *Hagerstown Herald*, Feb. 20, 1861; *Cumberland Civilian*, Feb. 21, 1861.

2. Proceedings of Pres. & Dirs, Feb. 6, 1861, K, 240-241, C&O Canal Papers; *Cumberland Civilian*, March 14, 1861; Sanger, ed., *Statutes at Large*, 182.

3. C&O Canal Co., *Thirty-Third Annual Report*, 7, 10; *Cumberland Civilian*, April 11, 1861; *Hagerstown Herald*, April 17 & 24, 1861; *Baltimore American and Commercial Advertiser* [hereinafter *Baltimore American*], April 19, 1861; *Washington Eve. Star*, April 17, 1861.

4. For a look at Maryland–Virginia relations during the opening days of the Civil War, see Snyder, "Border Strife on the Upper Potomac." For an examination of why Maryland did not secede, especially the role played by Governor Hicks, see Snyder, "Making No Child's Play of the Question."

5. Wenner to Governor, April 30, 1861, in Md. House of Delegates, *Journal, 1861*, 179-181.

6. Wenner to Sheriff of Frederick Co., April 24, 1861, Document B, in Md. Gen. Assembly, *Documents, 1861*; Wenner to Sheriff of Frederick Co., April 25, 1861, ibid.; Haller to Governor, April 27, 1861, ibid.

7. Md. House of Delegates, *Journal, 1861*, 53-55, 63; Maryland, *Supplement to the Maryland Code, 1861-1862*, 1: 110.

8. Md. House of Delegates, *Journal, 1861*, 176-177; Crump to Letcher, May 5, 1861, McCue Papers; *Message of the Governor of Virginia*, v-vi; *OR* (all references are to series 1, unless indicated otherwise), 2: 849; Hicks to Letcher, May 1, 1861, Md. Governor (Letterbook), 213; Letcher to Hicks, May 3, 1861, Ibid, 213-214; Jackson to Letcher, May 6, 1861, in Md. Governor (Letterbook), 221; Hicks to Lincoln, May 8, 1861, Md. Governor (Letterbook), 216.

9. Md. House of Delegates, *Journal, 1861*, 142-143, 145, 177, 178-179; *Hagerstown Herald*, May 15, 1861.

10. Md. House of Delegates, *Journal, 1861*, 181; *OR*, 51, part 2: 71-72, 78; Virginia Advisory Council, *Proceedings*, 62-63; [aide of John Letcher] to Hicks, May 10, 1861, Md. Governor (Letterbook), 220. The Virginians seized at least one other canal boat in April. A year after the incident, the boat's owner asked the canal company to release him from the tolls he owed on a boatload of salt that the Confederates had seized, to which the company agreed. There is no record that the

owner ever sought reimbursement for the cargo from Virginia; see Proceedings of Pres. & Dirs., May 5, 1862, K, 290, C&O Canal Papers.

11. Proceedings of Stockholders, May 2, 1861, E, 101-102, C&O Canal Papers; *Cumberland Civilian*, May 9, 1861; *Frederick Examiner*, May 8, 1861; *Baltimore Sun*, Jan. 11, 1861; OR, series 2, 1: 601.

12. *Montgomery County Sentinel*, Nov. 25, 1892; "Alfred Spates Qualification as Deputy Clerk," March 11, 1853, Spates Papers; Proceedings of Military Commission, 20-21, U.S. vs. Spates; Md. Adjutant General (Militia Appointments), 51.

13. Spates to Ringgold, May 6 & 13, 1861, Ltrs. Rcd., C&O Canal Papers. Also see Ringgold to Spates, May 15, 1861, Ltrs. Sent, L, 474, C&O Canal Papers.

14. *OR*, 2: 806.

15. Ibid, 809-810, 822, 825.

16. Douglas, *I Rode with Stonewall,* 5; *Baltimore American*, May 21 & 23, 1861; *Montgomery County Sentinel*, May 31, 1861; C&O Canal Co., *Thirty-Fourth Annual Report*, 9.

17. Spates to Stake, May 27, 1861, *Williamsport Ledger*, n.d., in *Hagerstown Herald*, June 5, 1861; B&O Railroad Co., *Thirty-Fifth Annual Report*, 46; *OR*, 2: 881. For a description of Bollman's Rock from an adventurer who climbed to the pinnacle before the war, see Clark and Hahn, Eds., *Life on the Chesapeake & Ohio*, 35-36.

18. *OR*, 2: 652.

19. *Hagerstown Herald*, May 29 & June 5, 1861.

20. *Baltimore American*, June 8 & 10, 1861; *Philadelphia Public Ledger*, June 12, 1861; *Frederick Examiner*, June 12, 1861; *Baltimore Exchange*, n.d., in *Philadelphia Public Ledger*, June 14, 1861; Johnston, *Narrative*, 23.

21. *Philadelphia Public Ledger*, June 14, 1861.

22. Ibid; *Baltimore American*, June 10, 11 & 12, 1861.

23. *Frederick Examiner*, June 12, 1861.

24. *OR*, 2: 863; *Philadelphia Public Ledger*, June 4, 1861; *Hagerstown Herald*, May 22, 1861; *Williamsport Ledger*, n.d., in *Hagerstown Herald*, June 12, 1861; Douglas, *I Rode With Stonewall*, 7; *Baltimore American*, May 22, 1861, June 11, 12 & 14, 1861.

25. *OR*, 2: 471-472; Johnston, *Narrative*, 22-23; *Baltimore American*, June 14, 1861.

26. *New York Times*, June 14, 1861; Spates to Ringgold, June 13, 1861, Ltrs. Rcd., C&O Canal Papers.

27. *Baltimore American*, June 14, 1861; *Hagerstown Herald*, June 12, 1861.

28. Md. House of Delegates, *Journal, 1861*, 276-277; Md. Senate, *Journal, 1861*, 197-198, 215; Maryland, *Supplement to the Maryland Code*, 113.

29. *OR*, 2: 472, 686; Johnston, *Narrative*, 22-23; *Baltimore American*, June 15, 1861; Barry, *Strange Story*, 105; *Frederick Examiner*, June 19, 1861; *Cumberland Civilian*, June 20, 1861.

30. *OR*, 2: 668.

31. Ibid, 104-105, 106-107, 108.

32. Ibid, 107, 915, 917; ibid, 51, part 1: 400.

33. Ibid, 51, part 1: 400, 401; ibid, 2: 109, 110, 112.

34. Ibid, 2: 113.

35. Ibid, 115-116, 118-119.

36. Ibid, 119; ibid, 51, part 1: 407.

37. Ibid, 2: 686, 691, 692, 693; *Baltimore American*, June 15, 1861.

38. *OR*, 2: 691, 695, 696, 698, 701, 707, 725, 730; Johnston, *Narrative*, 25-26.

39. C&O Canal Co., *Thirty-Fourth Annual Report*, 9; Ibid, *Thirty-Third Annual Report,* 4.

40. *Cumberland Civilian*, May 23, 1861; *Pottsville Miners' Journal*, June 1, 1861, in Harvery, *Best Dressed Miners*, 149; also see *Baltimore American*, Jan. 1, 1862.

41. *Middletown Valley Reg.*, May 31, 1861; *Hagerstown Herald*, May 29, 1861.

42. Williamson to Pres. & Directors, June 20, 1861, Ltrs. Rcd., C&O Canal Papers.

43. Stake to Spates, June 26, 1861, Ltrs. Rcd., C&O Canal Papers; *Baltimore American*, June 11, 1861.

CHAPTER 2

1. *OR*, 2: 157-158, 160, 161, 162, 179-180, 738.

2. Ibid, 164-165, 165, 166, 170.

3. Ibid, 175, 763.

4. Stake to Spates, July 6, 1861, Ltrs. Rcd., C&O Canal Papers.

5. *Frederick Examiner*, July 10, 1861; Ringgold to Stake, July 10, 1861 & Ringgold to Watts, July 10, 1861, Ltrs. Sent, M, 3, C&O Canal Papers; *Cumberland Civilian*, July 18, 1861.

6. *Frederick Examiner*, July 10, 1861; *Cumberland Civilian*, July 18, 1861; *OR*, 2:172; Spates to Ringgold, July 24, 1861, Ltrs. Rcd., C&O Canal Papers; *OR*, series 3, 1: 338-339. On Oct. 9 Thomas was authorized to raise two companies of artillery, although there is no evidence that an effort was made to recruit them; see Scott to F. Thomas, Oct. 9, 1861, Ltrs. Sent by the Secretary of War, m6, roll 46, Secretary of War's Records. Only three of the four infantry regiments and the cavalry battalion were raised.

7. Biographical information on Thomas is from Proud, *Biographical Memoirs*, 13-19 [quotation page 14]; U.S. Congress, *Biographical Directory*, 1927; *Lamb's Biographical Dictionary*, 7: 314; Page Andrews, *Tercentenary History of Maryland*, 4: 883-884; Thomas & Williams, *History of Allegany County*, 1: 277-287;

Scharf, *History of Western Maryland*, 1: 403-404; Eisenberg, *Marylanders Who Served the Nations*, 216.

8. Lowdermilk, *History of Cumberland*, 395-396.

9. *Frederick Examiner*, July 10, 1861. The July 18, 1861 *Cumberland Civilian* reported that Spates, not Thomas, had obtained military protection for the canal from Scott.

10. *OR*, 2: 175, 763, 770; ibid, 5: 554, 560.

11. *OR*, 5: 557-558, 559, 567.

12. *Hagerstown Mail*, Aug. 2, 1861; *Cumberland Civilian*, Aug. 15, 1861; Spates to Ringgold, Aug. 13, 1861, Ltrs. Rcd., C&O Canal Papers.

13. Fairbanks and Hamill wrote of Cumberland Coal: "Inasmuch as it is nearly smokeless and requires less bunker space per unit of heat than other coals, it is regarded as the best coal for steamship use, and particularly for naval vessels;" see Fairbanks & Hamill, *Coal-Mining Industry of Maryland*, 6.

14. *Cumberland Civilian*, Aug. 29 & Sept. 5, 1861; *Frederick Examiner*, Sept. 4, 1861.

15. *OR*, 5: 127-128, 197-199, 569, 593-594, 600; ibid, 51, part 1: 39-40; *Pottsville Miners' Journal*, Aug. 24, 1861, in Harvey, *Best-Dressed Miners*, 150; Leo W. Faller to sister, Sept. 31, 1861, in Faller & Faller, *Dear Folks at Home*, 28-32; Owen, *In Camp and Battle*, 56; Geary to Williams, Aug. 26, 1861, box 15, Banks Papers; Kenly to Williams, Aug. 22, 1861, box 15 & Gould to Geary, Sept. 11, 1861, box 16, Banks Papers; *Cumberland Civilian*, Sept. 26, 1861.

16. Gilmor, *Four Years*, 18.

17. *OR*, 5: 858-859. On Oct. 10 Confederate President Jefferson Davis wrote Maj. Gen. Gustavus W. Smith that although the southern army was not strong enough to expel Federal troops from Maryland, the army's morale could be maintained by raids across the Potomac, such as one against Banks to destroy the canal; see ibid, 5: 894.

18. *OR Supp.*, serial no. 84: 481-482; *Boston Advertizer*, Oct. 10, 1861, in *Cumberland Civilian*, Oct. 24, 1861; *Hagerstown Herald*, Oct. 2, 1861; *OR*, 5: 946.

19. Froth to Pres. of C&O Canal, Sept. 5, 1861, Spates Papers; Sanger, ed., *Statutes at Large*, 12: 257; McPherson, *Political History*, 149.

20. Kenly to Williams, Sept. 2, 1861, box 16, Banks Papers.

21. Barry, *Strange Story*, 114-115; *OR*, 5: 239-248; *Hagerstown Herald*, Oct. 23, 1861; Stearns, *Three Years*, 34-36; Bryant, *History of the Third Regiment*, 28-35; U.S. Congress, *Report of the Joint Committee*, 2: 351-352.

22. *OR*, 5: 290-291, 293-295, 299-300, 304, 308-309; ibid, 51, part 1: 499.

23. Ibid, 5: 295-299, 309-312. The estimate of Federal casualties is from Farwell, *Ball's Bluff*, 134-135.

24. *OR*, 5: 294, 296, 298; ibid, 51, part 1: 500; *OR Supp.*, serial no. 38: 296; "Journal of the First Maryland," 87; *History of the First Regiment*, 78; Wright, *No More Gallant a Deed*, 84; *Minnesota*, 15; Abbott to his mother, Oct. 24, 1861, in

Abbott, *Fallen Leaves*, 67; Gorman to Smith, Oct. 26, 1861, in Moore, ed., *Rebellion Record*, 3: 248-250. The Nov. 16, 1861 *Frank Leslie's Illustrated Newspaper* depicts the crossing of Federal troops on a bridge of boats from Edwards Ferry to Virginia. Although such a bridge was seriously contemplated, it was never built. An existing sketch of the proposed bridge shows seven canal boats, linked by ladders, extending across the river from Virginia to Maryland; see Collis illustration, box 16, Banks Papers.

25. *Washington Eve. Star*, Oct. 28, 1861; Holmes, Jr., *Touched With Fire*, 23-29, 32; Shaw to mother, Oct. 22, 1861, in Shaw, *Blue-Eyed Child*, 155. Canal boats were also used to evacuate wounded Union soldiers in Dec. 1861. When General Banks moved his headquarters from Darnestown to Frederick, about 200 sick and wounded soldiers were moved to the mouth of Seneca Creek to await canal boats that would move them to new hospital facilities. Due to delays, some were left exposed to the element for a day, but all were eventually moved by canal boat to Point of Rocks, then overland to hospitals in Frederick; Quint, *Potomac and Rapidan*, 62-65; Quint, *Record of the Second Massachusetts*, 53; Comey, ed., *A Legacy of Valor*, 27-28; *Baltimore American*, Dec. 9, 1861.

26. In Feb. 1862 the Joint Committee deposed Alfred Spates and former general superintendent Andrew K. Stake about the strength of Confederate forces opposite Williamsport during Patterson's campaign; see U.S. Congress, *Report of the Joint Committee*, 2: 224-226.

27. Ringgold to Spates, Oct. 12, 1861, Ltrs. Sent, M, 10, C&O Canal Papers; Proceedings of Pres. & Dirs., Oct. 1, 1861, K, 258, C&O Canal Papers; Spates to Ringgold, Nov. 3, 1861, Ltrs. Rcd., C&O Canal Papers.

28. *Cumberland Civilian*, Oct. 10, 1861 & Jan. 2, 1862; Carleton to Ringgold, Oct. 21, 1861, Ltrs. Rcd., C&O Canal Papers; C&O Canal Co., *Thirty-Fourth Annual Report*, 9; B&O Railroad Co., *Thirty-Fifth Annual Report*, 49.

29. Hemphill, Journal, Nov. 2, 1861. For an account of the flooding in the vicinity of Point of Rocks, see Geary to Copeland, Nov. 4, 1861, box 16, Banks Papers. For a description of the flooding above Edwards Ferry, see Lyon, *"Desolating This Fair Country,"* 50.

30. *Middletown Valley Reg.*, Nov. 15, 1861; *OR*, 5: 936, 949; *Winchester Republican*, Nov. 15, 1861.

31. Stone to Banks, Nov. 5, 1861, box 16, Banks Papers; Stone to Spates, Nov. 10, 1861 & pass issued by Stone to Spates, Nov. 10, 1861, Spates Papers.

32. Spates to Ringgold, Nov. 3, 1861, Ltrs. Rcd., C&O Canal Papers; Proceedings of Pres. & Dirs., Nov. 12, 1861, K, 262, C&O Canal Papers; Read to Ringgold, Nov. 26, 1861, Ltrs. Rcd., C&O Canal Papers.

33. Thruston to McLaughlin, Nov. 18, 1861; Thruston to Keesekamp, Nov. 18, 1861; Thruston to L. Thomas, Nov. 20, 1861; all in Ltrs Rcd. by the Secretary of War, main series, m221, roll 202, Secretary of War's Records. Biographical information on Thruston is from *Lamb's Biographical Dictionary*, 7: 339; *Appleton's Cyclopaedia*,

6: 107-108; Heitman, *Historical Register*, 1: 960; Warner, *Generals*, 504-505; Baird, "Violence," *Maryland Historical Magazine,* 66, no. 2 (Summer 1971): 121-133; *Hagerstown Mail*, Jan. 12, 1843.

Thruston had intended to offer his services to the government in March 1861. He traveled to Washington but found General Scott too busy and decided to make the offer by letter. On his return to Cumberland he was struck by an ailment in his feet and ankles that disabled him for some time. On July 10 he was asked to raise a regiment of three-year volunteers but declined due to his health problems. On Sept. 5, after his condition had improved, he went to Washington and met with Scott, with whom he was friendly from their mutual service in the army. Scott sent Thruston to the secretary of war with a message: "This note will be handed to you by my friend, Col. C.M. Thruston, of Cumberland, Md., one of the finest men in the country, a West Pointer, a capital soldier & a thoro Union man. I beg for him the commission of a brigadier general of volunteers connected with the Maryland regiments. He will be of the greatest value to us." Thruston's letter was passed on to Lincoln who added an endorsement ordering the appointment as Scott had requested; see Thruston to Townsend, July 22, 1861; Scott to Cameron, Sept. 5, 1861; and Thruston to L. Thomas, Sept. 9, 1861; all in Ltrs. Rcd. by the Adjutant General, m619, roll 63, Adjutant General's Records; U.S. Congress, Senate, *Journal of Executive Proceedings*, Thirty-Seventh Congress, Second Session, Dec. 24, 1861, 57.

Thruston's grandfather of the same name was a minister in the Episcopal Church and served as an officer in the Revolutionary War, where he was known as the "warrior parson." After the war he became a judge and legislator. His son, Buckner Thruston, father of the latter Charles Mynn Thruston, emigrated to Kentucky, became a lawyer, a U.S. Senator, and the U.S. judge for the District of Columbia; see *Lamb's Biographical Dictionary*, 7: 339; *Appleton's Cyclopaedia*, 6: 107-108.

34. *Hagerstown Mail*, Feb. 21, 1840; Thruston to L. Thomas, Nov. 20, 1861, Ltrs. Rcd. by the Secretary of War, main series, mm221, roll 202, Secretary of War's Records.

35. Blocher to Dennis, Sept. 24, 1861, in Gary, *Answering the Call*, 133-134; Thomas to Lincoln, Sept. 2, 1861, Lincoln Papers.

36. Jones to Pres. C&O Canal Co., Oct. 5 & Nov. 11, 1861, Ltrs. Rcd., C&O Canal Papers.

37. Ringgold to Soper, Nov. 14, 1861, Ltrs. Sent, M, 13, C&O Canal Papers; Account to the United States from the C&O Canal Co., 20 Nov. 1861, box 305, Consolidated Correspondence File, Quartermaster General's Records.

38. *Thirty-Second Annual Report*, 6.

39. Van Vliet to Meigs, Nov. 30, 1861, box 305, Consolidated Correspondence File, Quartermaster General's Records.

40. Haley, *Rebel Yell*, 40-43; Mowris, *History*, 43-44; Morse, *Letters*, 101-102; Bowen to [Guild], Jan. 15, 1862, in Bowen, *From Ball's Bluff*, 64; Williams to Lew, Nov. 5, 1861, in Williams, *From the Cannon's Mouth*, 26-27. For other solders' accounts

of picket duty on the canal, see Black to Jennie, July 20, 1863, in Coles & Engle, eds, "'Powder, Lead, and Cold Steel,'" 59-60; Bowen to Davis, Fannie, Myron & Minnie, Sept. 13, 1861, in Bowen, *From Ball's Bluff*, 19-24; Haynes, *History*, 19-31; Bickell to Editor, Oct. 1, 1861 in *Chelsea* (Mass.) *Telegraph and Pioneer*, Oct. 12, 1861 ; Bicknell to Editor, Nov. 11, 1861, in *Chelsea* (Mass.) *Telegraph and Pioneer*, Nov. 23, 1861; L. Faller to sister, Sept. 31, 1861, Faller & Faller, *Dear Folks*, 29-31.

41. *Frederick Examiner*, Nov. 20, 1861; *Cumberland Civilian*, Nov. 21, 1861; Carleton to Ringgold, Dec. 9, 1861, Ltrs. Rcd., C&O Canal Papers; *OR*, 5: 677.

42. *OR*, series 3, 1: 463; ibid, 5: 193, 194-195.

43. Hicks, *Message of the Governor of Maryland*, 9; Md. Comptroller of the Treasury Dept., *Annual Report . . . Fiscal Year Ended 30th September, 1861*, 14.

44. Spates to McClellan, Nov. 24, 1861, Ltrs. Sent, M, 14-15, C&O Canal Papers; Spates to Meigs, Nov. 25, 1861, Ltrs. Sent, M, 15-16, C&O Canal Papers.

45. Special Order No. 322, Dec. 6, 1861, Spates Papers; *Cumberland Civilian*, Dec. 12, 1861; *Frederick Examiner*, Dec. 11, 1861.

46. *OR*, 5: 685; Stone to Spates, Dec. 11, 1861, Spates Papers; Ringgold to Spates, Dec. 17, 1861, Ltrs. Sent, M, 18, C&O Canal Papers; Stone to Spates, Dec. 12, 1861, Spates Papers.

47. *OR*, 5: 668-669.

48. Moore to wife, Dec. 7 & 9, 1861, Moore Papers; Paxton to wife, Dec. 9, 1861, in Paxton, *Civil War Letters*, 28; Robinson to Leonard, Dec. 9, 1861, in *New York Times*, Dec. 15, 1861; Stevens to Editors, Dec. 11, 1861, in *Baltimore American*, Dec. 14, 1861.

49. Robinson to Leonard, Dec. 9, 1861, in *New York Times*, Dec. 15, 1861; Nesbitt, "Nesbitt's Civil War Memoirs," 187; Moore to wife, Dec. 9, 1861, Moore Papers; *New York Times*, Dec. 13, 1861.

50. Robinson to Leonard, Dec. 9, 1861, in *New York Times*, Dec. 15, 1861; *New York Times*, Dec. 13, 1861; *Hagerstown Herald*, Dec. 11, 1861; Banks to McClellan, Dec. 8, 1861, reel 14, McClellan Papers; A.W. to father, Dec. 12, 1861, in *Boston Daily Courier*, Dec. 31, 1861; Percussion to Editor, Dec. 10, 1861, in *Boston Saturday Evening Gazette*, Dec. 14, 1861; *Baltimore American*, Dec. 10, 1861; Moore to wife, Dec. 9 & 16, 1861, Moore Papers; Paxton to wife, Dec. 9, 1861, Paxton, *Civil War Letters*, 28.

51. Brown to Holt, Jan. 17, 1862, in Bowman-Howard-Domingos Family Collection. For an identical conclusion about Union marksmanship at the dam, see Moore to wife, Dec. 9, 1861, Moore Papers.

52. *OR*, 5: 989; Leonard to Banks, Dec. 12, 1861, box 17, Banks Papers; Hemphill, Journal, Dec. 11, 1861; B. to Editors, Dec. 11 & 13, 1861, in *Baltimore American*, Dec. 14 & 17, 1861.

53. C. Trueheart to mother, Dec. 12, 1861, in Trueheart & Trueheart, *Rebel Brothers*, 35; Hemphill, Journal, Dec. 11 & 13, 1861; B. to Editors, Dec. 13, 1861, in

Baltimore American, Dec. 17, 1861. For Williams' account of his capture, see the *Warsaw Northern Indianian*, Dec. 31, 1874.

54. *OR*, 5: 395.

55. Ibid, 390, 398; C. Trueheart to Cally, Dec. 26, 1861, in Trueheart & Trueheart, *Rebel Brothers*, 38-40; Langhorne to mother, Dec. 23, 1861, Langhorne Family Papers; Apperson, *Repairing*, 169; Rice to Viola, Dec. 18 & 19, 1861, in Rice, *Civil War Letters*, 18-20; *Baltimore American*, Dec. 19, 1861; *New York Times*, Dec. 19 & 23, 1861; Liscom to Parents & Sister, Dec. 21, 1861, Liscom Letters; Viles to Frank, Dec. 18, 1861, Viles Letters.

56. Langhorne to mother, Dec. 23, 1861, Langhorne Family Papers; C. Trueheart to Cally, Dec. 26, 1861, in Trueheart & Trueheart, *Rebel Brothers*, 38-39; unidentified Boston newspaper, n.d., in *Frank Leslie's Illustrated Newspaper*, Jan. 18, 1862.

57. Poague, *Gunner*, 13-14; Kinzer Dairy; Apperson, *Repairing*, 170; *OR*, 5: 398.

58. Unidentified Boston newspaper, n.d., in *Frank Leslie's Illustrated Newspaper*, Jan. 18, 1862; *OR*, 5: 398; Clark, *History of Hampton Battery*, 12; Kearns Diary; Apperson, *Repairing*, 170; Langhorne to mother, Dec. 23, 1861, Langhorne Family Papers; *Baltimore American*, Dec. 21, 23 & 24, 1861; *Hagerstown Herald*, Dec. 25, 1861.

59. Unidentified Boston newspaper, n.d., in *Frank Leslie's Illustrated Newspaper*, Jan. 18, 1862; C. Trueheart to Cally, Dec. 26, 1861, in Trueheart & Trueheart, *Rebel Brothers*, 39-40; Casler, *Four Years*, 61; Moore to wife, Dec. 24, 1861, Moore Papers.

60. *OR*, 5: 399, 1005, 1007.

61. Ibid, 392; Moore to wife, Jan. 3, 1862, Moore Papers; Langhorne to mother, Dec. 31, 1861, Langhorne Family Papers; *OR Supp.*, serial no. 84: 72.

62. Leonard to Banks, Dec. 23 & 30, 1861, box 17, Banks Papers.

63. Barnard, *Report on the Defenses*, 79-80.

64. Ibid, 80n. Barnard did not specify which canal company was strongly opposed to the seizure of the aqueduct, but certainly both the C&O and the Alexandria Canal Company were affected adversely and would have objected.

65. *Washington Eve. Star*, Dec. 5, 16 & 23, 1861; Barnard, *Report on the Defenses*, 80.

66. C&O Canal Co., *Thirty-Fourth Annual Report*, 4, 8; *Baltimore American*, Jan. 1, 1862.

67. C&O Canal Co., *Thirty-Fourth Annual Report*, 3-5.

68. Davis, Jr., *Three Years in the Army*, 17.

CHAPTER 3

1. *OR*, 5: 390-392, 396; Smith, "Diary," 22-23.

2. Flagg to Banks, Jan. 4, 1862, box 18, Banks Papers; Gorman to Banks, Jan. 5, 1862 [two letters], box 18, Banks Papers; Tyndale to Banks, Jan. 4, 1862, box 18, Banks Papers; Tyndale to Copeland, Jan. 5, 1862 [two letters], box 18, Banks Papers; Tyndale to Banks, Jan. 5, 1862 [two letters], box 18, Banks Papers; Banks to Williams, Jan. 4, 1862, reel 15, McClellan Papers; [Gorman] to Williams, Jan. 5, 1862, reel 15, McClellan Papers.

3. Jackson to Officer Commanding, Jan. 5, 1862, vol. 3, Lander Papers; Clark, *History of the Thirty-Ninth Regiment*, 46-47; Lander to Banks, Jan. 5, 1862, box 18, Banks Papers; Smith, "Diary," 22-23.

4. Lander to Marcy, Feb. 20, 1862, reel 47, McClellan Papers.

5. Williams to Lew, Feb. 3, 1862, in Williams, *Cannon's Mouth*, 54-55; Testimony of Ellen Barton, in St. Thomas' Protestant Episcopal Church vs. U.S., 18.

6. Geary to wife, Feb. 15, 1862, in Geary, *Politician Goes to War*, 32; *Middletown Valley Reg.*, March 7, 1862; Dana to Williams, March 10, 1862, George Brinton McClellan, Sr., Papers; *OR*, 5: 732.

7. Minutes, Md. Commission of Public Works, 113; Wilner, *The Maryland Board of Public Works*, 47, 48.

8. Minutes, Md. Commission of Public Works, 117-118; Proceedings of Stockholders, Jan. 30, 1862, E, 105-107, C&O Canal Papers; Proceedings of Pres. & Dirs., Feb. 12, 1862, K, 272-274, C&O Canal Papers; *Cumberland Civilian*, Feb. 6, 1862.

9. Proceedings of Pres. & Dirs., Feb. 12, 1862, K, 272-273, C&O Canal Papers; C&O Canal Co., *Thirty-Fourth Annual Report*, 5; *Cumberland Civilian*, Feb. 20, 1862.

10. Proceedings of Pres. & Dirs., May 16, 1860, K, 183-185, C&O Canal Papers; *Hagerstown Herald*, Dec. 7, 1859, Feb. 8, 1860; C&O Canal Co., *Thirty-Second Annual Report*, 18. Of those whose political sympathies can be determined, Masters had been an officer in the Williamsport Union Home Guard during the climactic opening weeks of the war when Guard skirmished with the Confederates opposite the town. In April 1861 both Levin Benton and Thomas Hassett had been appointed to the Washington County Union Central Committee. The Cumberland *Civilian and Telegraph* noted that Lloyd Lowe was a "staunch Union man;" see Masters to Hewett, April 26, 1861, in *Hagerstown Herald*, May 15, 1861; *Hagerstown Herald*, May 1, 1861; *Cumberland Civilian*, July 4, 1861.

11. Leonard to Banks, Dec. 23, 1861, box 17, Banks Papers; Charlton to Spates, Jan. 8, 1862, Ltrs. Rcd., C&O Canal Papers.

12. *Middletown Valley Reg.*, Jan. 31, 1862. After the war, William Allan and Jed Hotchkiss, both of whom served under Jackson, wrote that the January freshet

had widened the breach in the dam and later drained a long section of the canal. See Allan, *Stonewall Jackson's Valley Campaign*, 11-12; Hotchkiss, *Virginia*, 199.

13. Leonard to Link, Feb. 6, 1862, Spates Papers; Hemphill, Journal [not dated, but follows Jan. 29, 1862 entry].

14. *Washington Eve. Star*, March 4, 1862.

15. Rittenhouse, Fant & Co. to Governor, March 6, 1862, Governor, (Miscellaneous Papers), box 75, folder 5, MSA S1274-75, MdHR 6636, MSA.

16. Spates to Cameron, Jan. 8, 1862, Ltrs. Rcd. by Secretary of War, main series, m221, roll 202, Secretary of War's Records.

17. Spates to Blair, Jan. 8, 1862 (two letters), Ltrs. Rcd. by Secretary of War, main series, m221, roll 202, Secretary of War's Records.

18. Stone to [L. Thomas], Feb. 3, 1862, Ltrs. Rcd. by the Secretary of War, main series, m221, roll 547, Secretary of War's Records.

19. Thruston to Secretary of War, Feb. 26, 1862 & Thruston to L. Thomas, April 21, 1862, Ltrs. Rcd. by the Adjutant General's Office, 1861-70, m619, roll 145, Adjutant General's Records; U.S. Congress, Senate, *Journal of Executive Proceedings*, Thirty-Seventh Congress, Second Session, March 3, 1862, 138; Thruston to Stanton, June 25, 1862, Ltrs. Rcd. by the Secretary of War, Main Series, m221, roll 208, Secretary of War's Records; *Middletown Valley Reg.*, May 23, 1862.

20. *OR*, 5: 341, 342; U.S. Congress, *Report of the Joint Committee*, 2: 297-301, 302-303, 334-338, 356-357, 373, 388-390, 428-429, 430-431, 442, 494-495.

21. Stone to McClellan, Dec. 23, 1861, reel 14, document 7254, McClellan Papers; *OR*, 5: 1035; U.S. Congress, *Report of the Joint Committee*, 2: 430-431.

22. *OR*, 5: 1035. After the war, Col. Eppa Hunton, who served opposite Stone in 1861, wrote: "General Stone was a very superior man – a man of fine intelligence and military attainments. He was a gentleman, and conducted the war in the most gentlemanly manner;" see Hunton, *Autobiography*, 26. Stone spent just over six months in prison and the army never charged him with an offense. For nearly the first two months he was confined at Fort Lafayette in New York harbor; then, when doctors expressed concern for his health, the army transferred him to Fort Hamilton, also at New York harbor where he was allowed exercise. Friends and politicians lobbied for a trial and eventually Congress passed a bill that, among other things, prohibited the army from arresting and holding officers for more than thirty days without bringing charges. From the date the legislation passed, July 17, 1862, the army waited an additional thirty days before they released Stone. Authorities brought no charges against him and provided no reason for his arrest. He reported for duty but was given no orders. In the winter of 1863 he appeared before the Joint Committee again, was allowed to see the testimony of the refugee, and calmly refuted the accusations. Banks, well acquainted with Stone from their service on the Potomac, requested his service in the Department of the Gulf. In the spring Stone was assigned to Banks's command and served with him for about a year before he was recalled to Washington for unknown reasons. He resigned from the volunteer army in April

1863. For about a month he was assigned to the Army of the Potomac as an officer in the regular army, but resigned from the military altogether in Sept. 1864, still under a cloud of rumor and suspicion. The best work on the impact of the Battle of Ball's Bluff on Stone's career is Farwell, *Ball's Bluff*.

23. Thomas to Stanton, Feb. 17, 1862, Frost to Meigs, March 8, 1862, Meigs to Stanton, March 11, 1862, & Frost to Meigs, March 12, 1862, all in "Alteration of Bridges Across the Chesapeake and Ohio Canal," U.S. Congress, House of Reps., Executive Documents, Thirty-Seventh Congress, Second Session, Exe. Doc. No. 102, 8: 2, 3, 5.

24. U.S. Congress, House of Reps., *Journal of the House of Representatives,* Thirty-Seventh Congress, Second Session, April 10, 1862, 528-529; Ringgold to Greene, April 16, 1862, Ltrs. Sent, M, 36, C&O Canal Papers; Meigs to Stanton, April 19, 1862; Waters to General, April 19, 1862; Stanton to Grow, April 21, 1862, all in "Alteration of Bridges Across the Chesapeake and Ohio Canal," U.S. Congress, House of Reps., Executive Documents, Thirty-Seventh Congress, Second Session, Exe. Doc. No. 102, 8: 1, 6, 10-11; Sibley to Rucker, April 16, 1862 & Rucker to Meigs, April 25, 1862, both in box 305, Consolidated Correspondence File, Quartermaster General's Records.

25. *Cumberland Civilian*, June 5, 1862.

26. Spates to Stanton, Feb. 20, 1862, in "Alteration of Bridges Across the Chesapeake and Ohio Canal," U.S. Congress, House of Reps., Executive Documents, Thirty-Seventh Congress, Second Session, Exe. Doc No. 102, 8: 4.

27. Spates to Banks, Feb. 21, 1862, box 18, Banks Papers; A. McClellan to Spates, March 3, 1862, Spates Papers; Marcy to Van Vleit, March 7, 1862, "Alteration of Bridges Across the Chesapeake and Ohio Canal," U.S. Congress, House of Reps., Executive Documents, Thirty-Seventh Congress, Second Session, Exe. Doc. No. 102, 8: 6; Spates to Marcy, March 8, 1862, Spates Papers; Spates to Meigs, March 15, 1862, box 305, Consolidated Correspondence File, Quartermaster General's Records.

28. Rucker to Meigs, March 22, 1862, box 305, Consolidated Correspondence File, Quartermaster General's Records.

29. Spates to Stanton, March 27, 1862, "Alteration of Bridges Across the Chesapeake and Ohio Canal," U.S. Congress, House of Reps., Executive Documents, Thirty-Seventh Congress, Second Session, Exe. Doc. No. 102: 8: 6-8; Lamon to Stanton, March 27, 1862, "Alteration of Bridges Across the Chesapeake and Ohio Canal," U.S. Congress, House of Reps., Executive Documents, Thirty-Seventh Congress, Second Session, Exe. Doc. No. 102, 8: 8.

30. *OR*, 5: 677-678, 692-693.

31. Ibid, 725. In military engineering parlance of the period, "pontoons" were made of inflatable rubber, often covered with canvas. Wooden bateau boats were adapted from those developed by the French army. In this manuscript, references to pontoon bridges and boats will refer to the bateau variety that the U.S. Army

predominantly used on the Potomac. McClellan, who was trained and excelled as an engineer, had a decided preference for bateau boats over the rubber variety; ibid, 24.

32. Masters to Spates, Feb. 5 [sic; March], 1862, Ltrs. Rcd., C&O Canal Papers; Miller to Christian and Amelia, Feb. 17, 1862, in Wetterer, trans., *Letters of the Jacob Miller Family*, 26.

33. *OR*, 5: 48, 727; ibid, 51, part 1: 541; *Frederick Examiner*, March 5, 1862. For a period description of military engineers building a pontoon bridge, see Goss, *Recollections*, 19-20.

34. *OR*, 5: 49, 728, 730; *Middletown Valley Reg.*, March 7, 1862; B&O Railroad, *Thirty-Sixth Annual Report*, 52-53; Banks to Spates, March 6, 1862, Spates Papers; Banks to Marcy, March 1, 1862, reel 17, McClellan Papers; List of Quartermaster's Stores Forwarded by Flagg to Holeberd, March 18, 1862, reel 66, Flagg Papers; Salmon Portland Chase, "Notes on the Union of the Armies of the Potomac and the Army of Virginia," in Schuckers, *Life and Public Services*, 446.

35. Welles, *Diary*, 1: 61-65; Browning, *Diary*, 532-533; Dahlgren, *Memoir*, 358-360; Nicolay & Hay, *Abraham Lincoln*, 5: 226-227, 232; *ORN*, (all references to series 1*)*, 7: 75. As Stanton feared, on Feb. 28, 1862, a Confederate naval officer wrote to Jefferson Davis and suggested that he send the *Virginia* up the Potomac. He wrote that southern Maryland, a strong slaveholding region, would be liberated from Federal control and would rise up and attack Washington. The *Virginia* could ascend to near the U.S. arsenal and threaten the Long Bridge, which would cause the Federal army in northern Virginia to be withdrawn. At the very least, the officer suggested, the arsenal, the navy yard and the "president's house" should be destroyed as well as shipping on the Potomac. See Forrest to [Davis], Feb. 28, 1862, *ORN*, 7: 737-739.

36. Boats & Names of Owners Held by the U.S. Govt., April 17, 1861 [sic; 1862], Spates Papers; *ORN*, 7: 76; Wolfe to Ringgold, March 10, 1862, Ltrs. Rcd., C&O Canal Papers; C&O Canal Co., *Thirty-Fourth Annual Report*, 5-6.

37. *ORN*, 7: 24, 76, 77, 78, 80, 101-102, 120; ibid, 5: 24; Dahlgren to McClellan, March 9, 1862, Dahlgren Papers; [Dahlgren] to Wyman, March 8 [sic; 9], 1862, Dahlgren Papers; Welles, *Diary*, 1: 66-67; Dahlgren, *Memoir*, 360; Boats & Names of Owners Held by the U.S. Govt., April 17, 1861[sic; 1862], Spates Papers.

38. Welles, *Diary*, 1: 67.

39. Ringold to Greene, March 24, 1862, Ltrs. Sent, M, 31, C&O Canal Papers; Minutes, Md. Commission of Public Works, 151-152; *OR*, 5: 743, 747; ibid, 11, part 1: 134-139, 142, 158-160, 165, 175, 343, 344, 614, 618; ibid, part 2: 483; ibid, part 3: 353.

40. Oath, Henry Artz, April 17, 1862, Flagg Papers; Flagg to Loyd, April 18, 1862, Flagg Papers; White to Flagg, May 5, 1862, Flagg Papers.

41. Greene to Ringgold, March 20 & April 1, 1862, Ltrs. Rcd., C&O Canal Papers; Ringold to Greene, March 24, 1862, Ltrs. Sent, M, 31, C&O Canal Papers.

42. Lowe to Ringgold, March 8, 1862, Ltrs. Rcd., C&O Canal Papers; Lowe to Spates, March 12, 1862, Ltrs. Rcd., C&O Canal Papers; G. Spates to A. Spates,

March 8, 1862, Ltrs. Rcd., C&O Canal Papers.

43. Claim number 228, box 772, Claims and Related Papers for Damage to Property by Troops in the Service of the United States, Record Group 92, Quartermaster General's Records. Williams's Feb. 3 order appointing the board of survey, Special Orders No. 33, is included the above box.

44. Spates to Stanton, April 16, 1862, "Alteration of Bridges Across the Chesapeake and Ohio Canal," U.S. Congress, House of Reps., Executive Documents, Thirty-Seventh Congress, Second Session, Exe. Doc. No. 102, 8: 9-10.

45. Greene to Ringgold, April 7 & 11, 1862, Ltrs. Rcd., C&O Canal Papers.

46. C&O Canal Co., *Thirty-Fourth Annual Report*, 5-6; Greene to Ringgold, April 11, 1862, Ltrs. Rcd., C&O Canal Papers.

47. Ringgold to F. Thomas, April 17, 1862, Ltrs. Sent, M, 36, C&O Canal Papers; Boats & Names of Owners Held by the U.S. Govt., April 17, 1861 [sic; 1862], Spates Papers.

48. Meigs to Lincoln, April 15, 1862, Henry Horner Lincoln Collection [Lincoln's endorsement of this letter, which he forwarded to Stanton on the same day, is in Lincoln, *Collected Works*, 4: 191, minus the full text of the original note from Meigs to the President. Stanton's decision is on the back of April 15, 1862 Meigs to Lincoln letter in the Henry Horner Lincoln Collection]; Ringgold to Greene, April 16, 1862, Ltrs. Sent, M, 36, C&O Canal Papers.

49. Greene to Ringgold, April 19 & 21, 1862, in Ltrs. Rcd., C&O Canal Papers.

50. *OR*, 12, part 3: 94, 97-98, 105, 114-115, 121, 124, 429; ibid, 51, part 1: 584.

51. *OR*, 12, part 3: 97.

52. *Cumberland Civilian*, May 1, 1862.

53. Masters to Pres. & Dirs., April 8, 1862, Ltrs. Rcd., C&O Canal Papers; Masters to Ringgold, May 22, 1862, Ltrs. Rcd., C&O Canal Papers; Proceedings of Pres. & Dirs., May 5 & 29, 1862, K, 292, 295-296, C&O Canal Papers.

54. Stake & Simms to Pres. & Dirs, May 29, 1862, Ltrs. Rcd., C&O Canal Papers; Proceedings of Pres. & Dirs., May 29, 1862, K, 296-297, C&O Canal Papers; Ringgold to Stake, May 30, 1862, Ltrs. Sent, M, 43, C&O Canal Papers.

55. Greene to Ringgold, April 21 & 29, 1862, Ltrs. Rcd., C&O Canal Papers.

56. *OR*, 11, part 3: 194.

57. C&O Canal Co., *Thirty-Fourth Annual Report*, 5-6.

58. Ibid.

CHAPTER 4

1. Smith, Diary, 24; *Cumberland Civilian*, June 12, 1862; L. Benton to Ringgold, June 3, 1862; Spates to Ringgold, June 4, 1862; & Masters to Ringgold, June 5, 1862; Greene to Ringgold, June 12, 1862, all in Ltrs. Rcd., C&O Canal Papers.

2. Greene to Ringgold, June 12, 1862, Ltrs. Rcd., C&O Canal Papers.

3. Greene to Ringgold, June 21, 1862, Ltrs. Rcd., C&O Canal Papers; Proceedings of Pres. & Dirs., June 26, 1862, C&O Canal Papers; *Cumberland Civilian*, July 10, 1862.

4. Hassett to Ringgold, July 19, 1862; Greene to Ringgold, Aug. 4, 1862; & Greene to Ringgold, Aug. 11, 1862, all in Ltrs. Rcd., C&O Canal Papers.

5. C&O Canal Co., *Thirty-Fifth Annual Report*, 8; *Cumberland Civilian*, June 12, 1862.

6. *Cumberland Civilian*, Aug. 14, 1862; Greene to Ringold, Aug. 4, 1862, Greene to Ringold, Aug. 6, 1862; & Greene to Ringold, Aug. 11, 1862, all in Ltrs. Rcd., C&O Canal Papers.

7. Proceedings of Pres. & Dirs., May 5, 1862, K, 293-294, C&O Canal Papers; Greene to Ringgold, Aug. 11 & 12, 1862, Ltrs. Rcd., C&O Canal Papers. On Dec. 11, 1862 the board passed a resolution that again required the superintendents to report any suspension of navigation. It also mandated that the superintendents inspect their entire divisions at least once a week and issue monthly reports to the board. Any negligence was considered grounds for dismissal; see Proceedings of Pres. & Dirs., Dec. 11, 1862, K, 315, C&O Canal Papers.

8. Bamford to Dirs. of C&O Canal, Aug. 28, 1862, Ltrs. Rcd., C&O Canal Papers.

9. Ibid.

10. *Frederick Examiner*, April 16, 1862; Bootman to Dirs., April 4, 1862, Ltrs. Rcd., C&O Canal Papers; Proceedings of Pres. & Dirs., Sept. 4, 1862, K, 309, C&O Canal Papers; Ringgold to Bamford, Sept. 4, 1862, Ltrs. Sent, M, 57, C&O Canal Papers.

11. *Congressional Globe*, June 23, 1862, 2879, & July 12, 1862, 3292; U.S. Congress, House of Reps., *Journal of the House of Representatives,* Thirty-Seventh Congress, Second Session, June 23, 1862, 912.

12. See, for example, Lee to Davis, Sept. 6, 1862, in Lee, *Wartime Papers*, 296.

13. *OR,* 19, part 1: 532-533; ibid, part 2, 174-175, 184-185.

14. Early, *Memoirs*, 134; Hotchkiss to wife, Sept. 8, 1862, reel 4, Hotchkiss Papers; *OR*, 19, part 1: 533, 1019; ibid, part 2: 185, 187, 188-189; Petition, Oct. 14, 1862, Ltrs. Rcd., C&O Canal Papers; Smith, Reminiscences, 4; Hotchkiss, *Make Me a Map*, 78. Regarding lockkeeper Walter, after the invasion the company dismissed him from his post under suspicion of disloyalty. His friends submitted a petition that claimed he had tried to dissuade the Confederates from doing greater harm to the canal, but the company refused to reinstate him; see Proceedings of Pres. & Dirs., Oct. 9 & Nov. 6, 1862, K, 311, 312, C&O Canal Papers.

15. *OR*, 51, part 1: 795.

16. *New York Tribune*, Sept. 15, 1862; Lee to Davis, Sept. 6, 1862, in Lee, *Wartime Papers*, 296.

17. *Washington Eve. Star*, Sept. 12, 1862.

18. Walker, "Jackson's Capture of Harpers Ferry," 604, 606; *OR*, 19, part 1: 912-913; Burgwyn, *Captain's War*, 17, 48-49.

19. *OR*, 19, part 1: 42-43.

20. Ibid, 120, 852-856; ibid, part 2: 285. Interestingly, Maj. John F. Edwards, McLaws's chief commissary officer, later wrote that he was unable to grind seized grain into flour because the mills in the region operated by water power supplied by the canal. However, Maryland law prohibited the canal company from renting water power to grist mills as a result of legislative efforts to protect Baltimore millers. Karen Gray has suggested that likely the Confederates had previously disabled the mills, which were certainly powered by small creeks and streams that drained under the canal. Edwards, searching for a viable mill, was unable to find one in the region and likely made the mistaken assumption that the mills utilized canal water, especially since the canal has also been disabled. Certificate of Maj. John F. Edwards, Oct. 10, 1885, McLaws Papers; Sanderlin, *The Great National Project*, 199-200; Karen Gray, e-mail message to author, May 31, 2009.

21. *OR*, 19, part 2: 320, 321; Phelps, "Reminiscences of Antietam," in Kirk, ed., *History of the Fifteenth Pennsylvania Cavalry,* 52-53; Spates to Ringgold, Oct. 6, 1862, Ltrs. Rcd., C&O Canal Papers; Miller to Ringgold, Nov. 3, 1862, Ltrs. Rcd., C&O Canal Papers. Governor Curtin also wrote that Williamsport resident Capt. Charles Russell, First Maryland Cavalry, had been ordered to the town to destroy the bridge and aqueduct. Perhaps he served as a guide for the militia. For another account of a scouting expedition sent up the canal to burn bridges at Williamsport, see Anspach, "Antietam," in Kirk, ed., *History of the Fifteenth Pennsylvania Cavalry,* 38-39.

22. Chilton to Pendleton, Sept. 16, 1862, in Pendleton, *Memoirs*, 224; Hotchkiss, *Make Me a Map*, 83.

23. *OR*, 19, part 1: 142, 339-340, 345, 367-368, 832-835, 957, 986, 1004-1005; Gerrish, *Army Life*, 40-44; Donaldson, *Inside the Army*, 127-138.

24. Chamberlain to Fanny, Sept. 21, 1862, Chamberlain Papers.

25. Parker & Carter, *Henry Wilson's Regiment*, 199-200.

26. *OR*, 19, part 1: 142, 820-821; ibid, part 2: 248, 248-249, 267-268, 333, 357; Blackford, *War Years*, 152-154; von Borcke, *Memoirs*, 242-256; McClellan, *I Rode With Jeb Stuart*, 134; Masters to Pres. & Dirs., Dec. 31, 1862, Feb. 2 & March 2, 1863, Ltrs. Rcd., C&O Canal Papers.; Masters to Ringgold, March 17, 1863, Ltrs. Rcd., C&O Canal Papers.

27. G. Spates to Ringgold, Sept. 13, 1862, Ltrs. Rcd., C&O Canal Papers; Bates to Col., Sept. 27, 1862, box 305, Consolidated Correspondence File, Quartermaster General's Records; B&O Railroad Co., *Thirty-Sixth Annual Report*, 56.

28. L. Benton to Ringgold, Oct. 15, Nov. 25 & Dec. 18, 1862; Spates to Ringgold, Oct. 6, 1862; all in Ltrs. Rcd., C&O Canal Papers.

29. Masters to Ringold, Sept. 22, 1862; Miller to Ringold, Nov. 3, 1862; Spates to Ringgold, Oct. 6, 1862; Masters to Pres. & Dirs., Feb. 8, 1864; all in Ltrs. Rcd., C&O Canal Papers.

30. *Baltimore American*, Sept. 27, 1862; *Hagerstown Herald*, Oct. 1, 1862. Local newspapers roundly criticized the conduct of the Pennsylvania militia during the Antietam Campaign. The Oct. 8, 1862 *Chambersburg Valley Spirit* wrote that farmers along the road between Chambersburg and Hagerstown "dread, but little more, the advent of a Rebel army . . . than another advance of the Pennsylvania Militia. Fences burned for fuel, young timber wantonly destroyed, whole fields of growing corn cut down and carried away, and numberless other vandalisms [sic] attest to the kind of 'protection' their property received." The *American* correspondent wrote that the militiamen almost mutinied when they learned they would have to fight outside of their home state, but after "they were finally shamed out of their cowardice," they seized horses and wagon from citizens at the point of a gun so that would not have to march to battle on foot. It was reported that every field they camped in was stripped of livestock, fruit, vegetables, and grain. The correspondent continued: "Our people were rejoiced when they came among us to assist in driving out our enemies as well as to protect their own State, but never were people more rejoiced than when they left us;" also see *OR*, 19, part 2: 329, 332.

It is unclear if the Pennsylvania militia or the Confederates committed most of the damage at Williamsport. The Confederates had several opportunities. Jackson passed through the town on his way to command the investment of Harpers Ferry. He was in a great hurry, however, and likely did not pause to commit damages. If the southerners did inflict damage, it was likely after the Battle of Antietam when Stuart's and Hampton's cavalry crossed back into Maryland at Williamsport for two days in order to create a diversion to allow the remainder of Lee's army to escape.

31. Spates to Ringgold, Oct. 6, 1862, Ltrs. Rcd., C&O Canal Papers; *Washington Eve. Star*, Sept. 26, 1862.

32. *OR*, 19, part 2: 24, 345, 363, 382-383; *Frederick Examiner*, Oct. 29, 1862; B&O Railroad Co., *Thirty-Sixth Annual Report*, 56; ibid, *Thirty-Seventh Annual Report*, 41-42; Spates to Ringgold, Oct. 6, 1862, Ltrs. Rcd., C&O Canal Papers.

33. *OR*, 19, part 2: 339-340, 342.

34. Ibid, 343, 347.

35. Ibid, part 1: 10; ibid, part 2: 343, 353, 355, 356, 360-361; B&O Railroad Co., *Thirty-Sixth Annual Report*, 57; B&O Railroad Co., *Thirty-Seventh Annual Report*, 42; *Washington Eve. Star*, Sept. 26, 1862.

36. *Washington Eve. Star*, Sept. 26, 1862.

37. *OR*, 19, part 2: 358; *OR Supp.*, serial no. 56: 89-90, 96, 122, 148, 158; *OR*, 5: 24;

38. Beckwith to Rucker, Sept. 25, 1862 & Bates to Rucker, Sept. 27, 1862, box 305, Consolidated Correspondence File, Quartermaster General's Records; G. Spates

to Ringgold, Sept. 30, 1862, Ltrs. Rcd., C&O Canal Papers; G. Spates to Ringgold, Oct. 6, 1862, Ltrs. Rcd., C&O Canal Papers.

39. *OR*, 19, part 2: 388.

40. Ibid, 388-389.

41. Ibid, part 1: 7-13, 20-22.

42. Proceedings of Pres. & Dirs., Oct. 9, 1862, K, 310-311, C&O Canal Papers; Bradley to Meigs, Oct. 10, 1862, box 305, Consolidated Correspondence File, Quartermaster General's Records.

43. Ringgold to Masters, Oct. 10, 1862, Ltrs Sent, M, 59, C&O Canal Papers; Ringgold to Spates, Oct. 21, 1862, Ltrs. Sent, M, 58, C&O Canal Papers; Greene to Ringgold, Dec. 2, 1862, Ltrs. Rcd., C&O Canal Papers; Ringgold to Greene, Dec. 12, 1862, Ltrs. Sent, M, 63, C&O Canal Papers.

44. *OR*, 19, part 2: 43, 426; *Cumberland Civilian*, Oct. 30, 1862; *Cumberland Civilian*, Nov. 13, 1862.

45. Circular, Oct. 24, 1862, Spates Papers; *Cumberland Civilian*, Nov. 13, 1862; Spates to Ringgold, Nov. 23, 1862, Ltrs. Rcd., C&O Canal Papers.

46. B&O Railroad Co., *Thirty-Sixth Annual Report*, 57.

47. *OR*, 19, part 1: 75, 86; ibid, part 2: 386; *OR Supp.*, serial no. 56: 96, 122, 177, 187; Greene to Ringgold, Nov. 13, 1862, Ltrs. Rcd., C&O Canal Papers.

48. Greene to Ringgold, Nov. 13, 1862, Ltrs. Rcd., C&O Canal Papers; Stake & Simms to Pres. & Directors, Nov. 3, 1862, Ltrs. Rcd., C&O Canal Papers; Proceedings of Pres. & Dirs., Nov. 6, 1862, K, 313, C&O Canal Papers.

49. *OR*, 19, part 1: 87; ibid, part 2: 75, 137, 495, 496, 499; ibid, 21: 146; ibid, 51, part 1: 905.

50. Judd, *Story of the Thirty-Third N.Y.S. Vols.*, 203-204. For another soldier's account of the beauty of Maryland compared to the Peninsula, see Evans, "Enemy Sullenly Held," *Civil War Times Illustrated*, 7, no. 1 (April 1968): 33-34.

51. *OR*, 19, part 2: 553; ibid, 51, part 1: 1097.

52. OR, 19, part 2: 572, 580, 581; ibid, 21: 85-87, 148-149, 793-795, 840-841; *OR Supp.*, serial no. 56: 148, 159.

53. C&O Canal Co., *Thirty-Fifth Annual Report*, 8; *Frederick Examiner*, Nov. 26, 1862.

54. Rucker to Spates, Nov. 8, 1862, Ltrs. Rcd., C&O Canal Papers.

55. Ringgold to Miller, Nov. 5, 1862, Ltrs. Sent, M, 60, C&O Canal Papers.

56. Hollingsworth to Pres. & Dirs., Jan. 14, 1863, Ltrs. Rcd., C&O Canal Papers. Also see Hollingsworth to Pres. & Dirs., April 9, 1863, Ltrs. Rcd., C&O Canal Papers; and Detmold to Ringgold, March 14, 1863, Ltrs. Rcd., C&O Canal Papers.

57. Ringgold to Detmold, March 13 & April 13, 1863, Ltrs. Sent, M, 77 & 83, C&O Canal Papers; Proceedings of Pres. & Dirs, April 9, 1863, K, 328, C&O Canal Papers. For record of the interesting claim of Jacob Miller, who owned a sawmill near Sharpsburg, see J. Miller to Pres. & Dirs., May 1, 1863, Ltrs. Rcd., C&O Canal Papers; Proceedings of Pres. & Dirs., March 12 & May 28, 1863, K, 324-325, 340, C&O Canal

Papers. Also see J. Miller to C. & A. Hauser, Dec. 7 1862, in Wetterer, trans., *Letters of the Jacob Miller Family*, 31.

58. Spates to Lincoln, Nov. 4, 1862, Ltrs. Rcd. by the Secretary of War, Irregular Series, m221, Secretary of War Records.

59. C&O Canal Co., *Thirty-Seventh Annual Report*, 5.

60. During this period records document two Confederate raids against Union camps at Poolesville and another at Urbana; see *OR*, 21: 12, 692 ; G. Spates to Ringgold, Nov. 26, 1862, Ltrs. Rcd., C&O Canal Papers; *Middletown Valley Reg.*, Nov. 28, 1862; *Frederick Examiner*, Dec. 3, 1862; *Frederick Examiner*, Dec. 17, 1862; Myers, *Comanches*, 146-148; McDonald, *History of the Laurel Brigade*, 108. Union forays across the Potomac in the vicinity of Dam Number 4 include one opposite the dam and others at Williamsport, Mercersville (Taylor's Landing), and Shepherdstown; see *OR*, 19, part 2: 148-153; *Hagerstown Herald*, n.d., in *Middletown Valley Reg.*, Nov. 7, 1862; Morse, *Letters*, 109-110; Brown, *Twenty-Seventh Indiana*, 273-277.

61. *Hagerstown Herald*, n.d., in *Middletown Valley Reg.*, Nov. 28, 1862; Gordon, *War Diary*, 14-15.

62. Gordon, *War Diary*, 14-17. It is unlikely that Antietam Division Superintendent Levin Benton was the suspected Confederate sympathizer since in April 1861 he was appointed a member of the Union Central Committee for Washington County; see *Hagerstown Herald*, May 1, 1861. The "canal agent" may not have been an employee of the company. Many people, including contractors, warehousemen, grain dealers and even boatmen, were affiliated with the canal, but not directly employed by the company.

63. *OR*, 21: 7-8; Gordon, *War Diary*, 16-23; Morse, *Letters*, 108.

64. *Cumberland Civilian*, Dec. 11, 1862; Spates to Ringgold, Dec. 12, 1862, Ltrs. Rcd., C&O Canal Papers.

65. U.S. Congress, House of Reps., *Journal of the House of Representatives*, Thirty-Seventh Congress, Third Session, Jan. 12, 1863, 184.

66. Kelley to McClellan, Nov. 6, 1861 & Kelley to Halleck, Dec. 9, 1862, both in "Protection to Baltimore and Ohio Railroad and Chesapeake Canal," U.S. Congress, House of Reps., Miscellaneous Documents, Thirty-Seventh Congress, Third Session, Misc. Doc. No.15, 1: 2-3.

67. Porter to Kelley, Dec. 27, 1862 & Kelley to [F. Thomas], Jan. 10, 1862, both in "Protection to Baltimore and Ohio Railroad and Chesapeake Canal," U.S. Congress, House of Reps., Miscellaneous Documents, Thirty-Seventh Congress, Third Session, Misc. Doc. No. 15, 1: 1-2, 3-5; U.S. Congress, House of Reps., *Journal of the House of Representatives*, Thirty-Seventh Congress, Third Session, Jan. 20, 1863, 210.

68. C&O Canal Co., *Thirty-Fifth Annual Report*, 3.

69. Ibid, 3-4, 7-8; *Cumberland Civilian*, Feb. 19, 1863.

70. C&O Canal Co., *Thirty-Fifth Annual Report*, 7; Spates to Ringgold, Dec. 1, 1862, Ltrs. Rcd., C&O Canal Papers; Proceedings of Pres. & Dirs., Dec. 11, 1862, K, 315, C&O Canal Papers.

CHAPTER 5

1. B&O Railroad Co., *Thirty-Seventh Annual Report*, 43; *Frederick Examiner*, Jan. 21, 1863; Greene to Ringgold, Jan. 13, 1863, Ltrs. Rcd., C&O Canal Papers; *Cumberland Civilian*, Jan. 8 & Jan. 15, 1863.

2. G. Spates to Pres. & Dirs., Jan. 1, 1863, Ltrs. Rcd., C&O Canal Papers; Proceedings of Pres. & Dirs, Jan. 15, 1863, K, 318, C&O Canal Papers; G. Spates to Ringgold, Feb. 25, 1863, Ltrs. Rcd., C&O Canal Papers; *Cumberland Civilian*, March 5, 1863; Smith, "Diary," 25.

3. *Cumberland Civilian*, March 5 & 19, 1863.

4. *Washington Eve. Star*, April 1, 1863.

5. *OR*, 21: 972-973; Circular, March 16, 1863, in Shaw, *Guarding the River*, [not paginated].

6. *OR*, 25, part 2: 184; *Cumberland Union*, March 21, 1863; *Middletown Valley Reg.*, March 20, 1863; *OR Supp.*, 38: 211.

7. Roberts to Spates, March 28, 1863, Spates Papers; *OR*, 51, part 1: 997, 997-998.

8. Sanger, ed., *Statutes At Large*, 12: 753-754; Proceedings of Pres. & Dirs., March 12, 1863, K, 325, C&O Canal Papers.

9. Allen to Ringgold, May 20, 1863, Ltrs. Rcd., C&O Canal Papers; Proceedings of Pres. & Dirs., May 28, 1863, K, 338, C&O Canal Papers; Ringgold to Allen, May 29, 1863, Ltrs. Sent, M, 91, C&O Canal Papers; H. Benton to Pres. & Dirs., July 8, 1863 & Sept. 1, 1863, Ltrs. Rcd., C&O Canal Papers.

10. Ringgold to Stanton, Aug. 21, 1862, Ltrs. Sent, M, 56, C&O Canal Papers; White to Pres. & Dirs., April 10, 1863, Ltrs. Rcd., C&O Canal Papers.

11. *Cumberland Civilian*, April 30, 1863; C&O Canal Co., *Thirty-Sixth Annual Report*, 10; Proceeding Pres. & Dirs., April 10, 1863, K, 329-330, C&O Canal Papers; C&O Canal Co., *Thirty-Sixth Annual Report*, 10; *Cumberland Civilian*, June 4, 1863; H. Miller to Ringgold, June 11, 1863, Ltrs. Rcd., C&O Canal Papers.

12. *Cumberland Civilian*, June 4, 1863.

13. *OR*, 25, part 2: 67-68, 69, 76; ibid, 27, part 2: 13-16; ibid, part 3: 148; *OR Supp.*, serial no. 56: 160-161.

14. Stake to Ringgold, June 8, 1863, Ltrs. Rcd., C&O Canal Papers.

15. *OR*, 27, part 2: 786-787; Williamson, *Mosby's Rangers*, 69-71; Scott, *Partisan Life*, 98-100; Mosby, *Mosby's War Reminiscences*, 159-161; G. Spates to Ringgold, June 12, 1863, Ltrs. Rcd., C&O Canal Papers.

16. *OR*, series 3, 3: 363.

17. Ibid; Proceedings of Pres. & Dirs., Sept. 10, 1863, K, 348-349, C&O Canal Papers; Ringgold to H. Benton, Sept. 11, 1863, Ltrs. Sent, M, 103, C&O Canal Papers; Abert to Ringgold, Oct. 24, 1863, Ltrs. Rcd., C&O Canal Papers. Of Horace Benton, Alfred Spates wrote: "There is no doubt of the fact that he give[s] his division little or no attention"; see Spates to Ringgold, Dec. 1, 1862, Ltrs. Rcd. C&O Canal Papers.

18. *OR*, 27, part 2: 295-296; ibid, part 3: 115, 121.

19. *OR*, 51, part 1: 1060; ibid, 27, part 2: 442-443, 550; Hotchkiss, *Make Me A Map*, 153; E. Johnson to Major, Sept. 30, 1863, in *SHSP* 6, 255.

20. *OR*, 27, part 3: 221-222, 865, 866; ibid, 51, part 1: 1060; *Cumberland Civilian*, June 18, 1863.

21. *OR*, 27, part 2: 296-297, 307, 316; ibid, part 3: 221-222; Lowe to Ringgold, June 20, 1863, Ltrs. Rcd., C&O Canal Papers; *Cumberland Civilian*, June 25, 1863.

22. Smith, "Diary," 26; Verbum Sat. to Editors, in *Harrisonburg Rockingham Register*, July 31, 1863; *Cumberland Civilian*, June 25, 1863.

23. *OR*, 27, part 1: 226-228; ibid, part 3: 73; Brainerd, *Bridge Building*, 156-157.

24. *OR*, 25, part 2: 150; ibid, 27, part 3: 179; Brainerd, *Bridge Building*, 134-135; *OR*, 25, part 1: 227

25. *OR*, 27, part 3: 208-209, 228; Brainerd, *Bridge Building*, 158.

26. *OR*, 27, part 3: 224, 228-229, 246.

27. Ibid, 283; H. Benton to Rucker, June 19, 1863, box 305, Consolidated Correspondence File, Quartermaster General's Records.

28. *OR*, 27, part 3: 272, 279, 282, 287, 310-311, 316; *OR Supp.*, serial no. 56: 92, 110-111, 124, 170.

29. *OR*, 27, part 3: 339.

30. *OR*, 27, part 1: 530; Houghton, *Campaigns of the Seventeenth Maine*, 77-78; Haley, *Rebel Yell*, 96-97; Mattocks, *"Unspoiled Heart,"* 42-43; Collins, *Memoirs*, 127-129.

31. *OR*, 27, part 3: 353, 354; G. Spates to Pres. & Dirs., June 30, 1863, Ltrs. Rcd., C&O Canal Papers.

32. *OR*, 27, part 2: 693; ibid, part 3: 913, 923; Blackford, *War Years*, 223; H. McClellan, *I Rode With Jeb Stuart*, 323-324; Weller, "Last Orders," *Confederate Veteran*, 23, no. 4 (April 1915): 174-175.

33. *OR*, 27, part 2: 694; H. McClellan, *I Rode With Jeb Stuart*, 323-324; Reade, *In the Saddle*, 74; *Washington Eve. Star*, June 29, 1863; *OR*, 27, part 3: 380, 527; G. Spates to Pres. & Dirs., June 30, 1863 Ltrs. Rcd., C&O Canal Papers; H. Benton to Pres. & Dirs., July 8 & Aug. 4, 1863, Ltrs. Rcd., C&O Canal Papers; *OR*, 27, part 1: 71. Captain Weller of the First Virginia Cavalry, later a staff officer under Stuart, wrote that forty-two canal boats had backed up in both directions as Stuart crossed at Seneca. He said that Stuart had ordered him to burn the boats, but he was concerned that many were owned by families who had all their possessions on board. Weller wrote that Stuart allowed him to turn all the boats across the canal and

then destroy the feeder gate to the river which, he said, would tear a large hole in the canal and disable it for sixty to ninety days; see Weller, "Last Orders," *Confederate Veteran*, 23, no. 4 (April 1915): 174-175.

34. *OR*, 27, part 3: 380.

35. Brainerd, *Bridge Building*, 159-161; Owen, *"Dear Friends,"* 12; *OR Supp.*, serial no. 56: 111, 124, 170, 189.

36. *OR*, 27, part 3: 527; *OR Supp.*, serial no. 56: 170; G. Spates to Pres. & Dirs., June 30, 1863, Ltrs. Rcd., C&O Canal Papers.

37. *OR*, 27, part 1: 60, 61, 62-63, ibid, part 3: 369.

38. *OR*, 27, part 1: 21, 67, 68, 71, 144, 488, 580; ibid, part 3: 401-402, 473; Haynes, *A History*, 33-34; Gilson, *History of the 126th Ohio*, 11; *OR Supp.*, serial no. 5: 37; ibid, serial no. 38: 660, 664, 668, 677, 691; ibid, serial no. 58: 43, 51, 90; ibid, serial no. 67: 233, 255, 642, 655, 669; ibid, serial no. 72: 745, 755, 775; ibid, serial no. 86: 160; H. Benton to Pres. & Dirs., July 8, 1863, Ltrs. Rcd., C&O Canal Papers.

39. *Washington Eve. Star*, July 9, 1863.

40. Masters to Ringgold, June 25, 1863, Ltrs. Rcd., C&O Canal Papers; Defence, 5-6, 9-10, 11-12, U.S. vs. Spates.

41. *Cumberland Civilian*, July 9, 1863; *OR*, 27, part 3: 528; Lowe to Ringgold, July 13 & 18, 1863, Ltrs. Rcd., C&O Canal Papers; Smith, "Diary," 26; *OR*, 27, part 2: 281; *OR Supp.*, 38: 444; Hassett to Ringgold, July 17 & Aug. 2, 1863, Ltrs. Rcd., C&O Canal Papers; Lowe to Ringgold, July 30, 1863, Ltrs. Rcd., C&O Canal Papers.

42. Lowe to Ringgold, July 13 & 30, 1863, Ltrs. Rcd., C&O Canal Papers.

43. *OR*, 27, part 3: 547, 564, 565, 566, 569, 574, 590-591, 603, 618, 688, 690, 691; Brainerd, *Bridge Building*, 165, 167-168; *OR Supp.*, serial no. 41: 91, 139; ibid, serial no. 56: 111, 125, 151, 181, 189. Brainerd and the volunteer engineers had been ordered back to Washington on July 1; see Brainerd, *Bridge Building*, 162;

44. *OR*, 27, part 1: 17; Ibid, part 2: 275; Ibid, part 3: 619, 693; *OR Supp.*, serial no. 60: 449, 631, 643; Imboden, "Confederate Retreat," in *Battles and Leaders of the Civil War*, 3: 428; Casler, *Four Years*, 182; Scheibert, *Seven Months*, 120.

45. Masters to Pres. & Dirs., July 19 & Aug. 4, 1863, Ltrs. Rcd., C&O Canal Papers; H. Miller to Ringgold, July 22, 1863, Ltrs. Rcd., C&O Canal Papers.

46. *OR*, 27, part 3: 672, 690, 691, 692, 697.

47. Ibid, 692, 701, 715; Brainerd, *Bridge Building*, 168; *OR Supp.*, serial no. 56: 111, 125, 162, 181, 189.

48. *OR*, 27, part 1: 94, 223; Ibid, part 3: 703, 716, 718.

49. Owen, *"Dear Friends,"* 13; Brainerd, *Bridge Building*, 169-170; Geary to wife, July 17, 1863, in Geary, *Politician*, 101; *OR Supp.*, serial no. 56: 111, 125, 162, 181, 189.

50. *Washington Eve. Star*, July 15, 1863.

51. Ibid, July 30, 1863. The conclusion that prices of commodities began to fall at Georgetown was obtained by comparing the prices at market printed in the *Washington Eve. Star* of July 9 & July 30, 1863.

52. Masters to Ringgold, July 19 & Aug. 4, 1863, Ltrs. Rcd., C&O Canal Papers.

53. Greene to Ringgold, July 25, 1863, Ltrs. Rcd., C&O Canal Papers.

54. Greene to Ringgold, Aug. 1, 1863, Ltrs. Rcd., C&O Canal Papers; Masters to Pres. & Dirs,, Aug. 4 & Sept. 2, 1863, Ltrs. Rcd., C&O Canal Papers; *Frederick Examiner*, Aug. 12, 1863.

55. *Cumberland Civilian*, Aug. 13 & 27, 1863.

56. Ibid.; *Middletown Valley Reg.*, Aug. 21, Sept. 18 & 25, 1863; *Frederick Examiner*, Sept. 2, 16 & 23, 1863; *OR*, 29, part 1: 92-93; Myers, *Commanches*, 217-218; *OR Supp.*, serial no. 5: 538-540.

57. Spates to Stanton, Aug. 11, 1863 & Spates to Lincoln, Aug. 11, 1863, in Ltrs. Rcd. by the Secretary of War, Main Series, m221, roll 231, Secretary of War's Records.

58. Hardie to Spates, Aug. 19, 1863, Ltrs. Sent by the Secretary of War, m6, roll 52, Secretary of War's Records; Kelly to Spates, Aug. 31, 1863, Spates Papers; Smith to Spates, Aug. 24, 1863, Spates Papers.

59. Heintzelman to Spates, Aug. 22, 1863, Spates Papers; G. Spates to Brengle, Sept. 19, 1863, Ltrs. Rcd., C&O Canal Papers.

60. Greene to Ringgold, Sept. 2, 1863, Ltrs. Rcd., C&O Canal Papers. Confederate cavalrymen John D. Imboden twice sought permission to lead raids across the upper Potomac, including one in which he offered to burned every bridge between Martinsburg and New Creek, damage the canal, and burn the coal mines. On Nov. 2, however, Lee informed Imboden that he was unable to reinforce him for the proposed operation because he had received reports that the Federal army was moving in force toward the Rappahannock. Instead, he recommended quick cavalry raids against the railroad and other Federal supply lines; see *OR*, 29, part 1: 107, 491; ibid, part 2: 814-815.

61. G. Spates to Pres. & Dirs., Sept. 30, 1863, Ltrs. Rcd., C&O Canal Papers.

62. *Frederick Examiner*, Sept. 16 & 23, Dec. 16, 1863; Myers, *Comanches*, 220-223; Goodhart, *History*, 104-106.

63. *Baltimore American*, Sept. 3, 1863; Spates to Fish, Aug. 25, 1863 [Exhibit 1], U.S. vs. Spates; Fickey, to Ringgold, Sept. 1 & 3, 1863, Ltrs. Rcd., C&O Canal Papers; Proceedings of Pres. & Dirs., Sept. 10, 1863, K, 349, C&O Canal Papers; Ringgold to Fickey, Sept. 11, 1863, Ltrs. Sent, M, 104, C&O Canal Papers. For biographical information on Hoffman, see Eisenberg, *Marylanders Who Served the Nations*, 100-101.

64. Proceedings of Military Commission, 1-2, U.S. vs. Spates; Defence, 9-10, 11-12, 13-14, 16 U.S. vs. Spates.

65. Proceedings of Military Commission, 162, [163-164], U.S. vs. Spates; Spates to Stanton, Sept. 6, 1863, Ltrs. Rcd. by the Secretary of War, Main Series, m221, roll 231, Secretary of War's Records; Spates to Stanton, Nov. 18, 1863, Ltrs.

Rcd. by the Secretary of War, Main Series, m221, roll 240, Secretary of War's Records; Spates to Watson, Dec. 13, 1863, U.S. vs. Spates.

66. Proceedings of Military Commission, 105-109, U.S. vs. Spates; Stake to Brengle, Sept. 17, 1863, Ltrs. Rcd., C&O Canal Papers.

67. Simms to Brengle, Sept. 30 & Oct. 1, 1863, Ltrs. Rcd., C&O Canal Papers.

68. Masters to Brengle, Oct. 23 & 27, 1863; Brengle to Ringgold, Oct. 14, 1863; Masters to Ringgold, Nov. 13, 1863; & Masters to Pres. & Dirs., Jan. 1, 1864; all in Ltrs. Rcd., C&O Canal Papers.

69. C&O Canal Co., *Thirty-Sixth Annual Report*, 10; *Cumberland Civilian*, Nov. 12, 1863.

70. *Cumberland Civilian*, Nov. 26, 1863; Smith, "Diary", 27-28.

71. C&O Canal Co., *Thirty-Sixth Annual Report*, 3, 4, 7-8.

72. Ibid, 3-5. A floating debt balance of $380,807 was obtained from taking the $301,024 outstanding floating debt existing in 1865, adding $171,367 that had been paid toward in since 1862, which equals a total floating debt of $472,391 at the beginning of 1862. Through 1863 the company made payments of $91,584 toward this debt, which leaves a balance of $380,807 at the beginning of 1865; see C&O Canal Co., *Thirty-Seventh Annual Report*, 5 & *Thirty-Sixth Annual Report*, 4.

73. For a discussion of Maryland's political parties during this time see Baker, *Politics of Continuity*, and Clark, *Politics in Maryland*.

CHAPTER 6

1. Quote from 1864 Hampshire & Baltimore Coal Company report to its Stockholders in Harvey, *Best Dressed Miners*, 159.

2. G. Spates to Pres. & Dirs., Feb. 29 & March 31, 1864, Ltrs. Rcd., C&O Canal Papers.

3. Holt to Stanton, Dec. 29, 1863, U.S. vs. Spates.

4. Ibid. Thurston's testimony is in Proceedings of Military Commission, 85-90, U.S. vs. Spates.

5. Canby to Willett, Jan. 10, 1864, U.S. vs. Spates; Special Orders No. 51, Feb. 2, 1864, U.S. vs. Spates.

6. *OR*, 33: 29-31, 37-38, 42-46, 504, 1142; Rosser, *Riding with Rosser*, 16-18; McDonald, *History*, 218-220; Lowe to Ringgold, Feb. 3, 1864, Ltrs. Rcd., C&O Canal Papers.

7. *Middletown Valley Reg.*, Feb. 19, 1864; Gilmor, *Four Years*, 143-146; *Cumberland Civilian*, Feb. 18, 1864; *OR*, 33: 151-154.

8. Proceedings of Pres. & Dirs, Jan. 23, 1864, K, 365-366, C&O Canal Papers; *Cumberland Civilian*, March 10, 1864. During the closure, Monocacy Division Superintendent George Spates removed the bottoms of the boats that Jeb Stuart's

men had burned when they crossed the river near Seneca in June 1863; see G. Spates to Pres & Dirs., Feb. 29, 1864, Ltrs. Rcd., C&O Canal Papers.

9. Lowe to Ringgold, March 14, 1864, Ltrs. Rcd., C&O Canal Papers; G. Spates to Pres. & Dirs., March 31, 1864, Ltrs. Rcd., C&O Canal Papers.

10. C&O Canal Co., *Thirty-Sixth Annual Report*, 5; Greene to Ringgold, March 23, 1864, Ltrs. Rcd., C&O Canal Papers; Proceedings of Pres. & Dirs., April 15, 1864, K, 382-383, C&O Canal Papers.

11. Greene to Ringgold, March 18 & 23, 1864, Ltrs. Rcd., C&O Canal Papers; *Washington Eve. Star*, April 9, 1864.

12. *Washington Eve. Star*, March 29, April 18 & 19, 1864.

13. *Washington Eve. Star*, April 11, 1864; *Cumberland Civilian*, April 21, 1864.

14. Smith, "Diary," 28-29; *OR*, 37, part 1: 468-469, 470, 477, 481, 486-487, 504, 513; B&O Railroad Co., *Thirty-Eighth Annual Report*, 4, 53-54, 55-56. For information on the construction of the Falling Waters pontoon bridge, including a proposed access bridge over the canal, see *OR*, 33: 894-895; J. Meigs to C. Thomas, April 16, 1864, reel 12, Meigs Papers.

15. *Cumberland Civilian*, June 9, 16, 23 & 30, 1864; C&O Canal Co., *Thirty-Seventh Annual Report*, 9.

16. Proceedings of Pres. & Dirs., Feb. 18 & April 14, 1864, K, 370, 379, C&O Canal Papers. Information on the Morris Canal is from the Morris Canal Fact Sheet.

17. Minutes, Md. Commission of Public Works, 159, 161-163; Ringgold to Fickey, June 11, 1864, Ltrs. Sent, M, 146, C&O Canal Papers.

18. U.S. Congress, House of Reps., *Journal of the House of Representatives, Thirty-Eighth Congress, First Session*, May 30, 1864, 715.

19. Early, *Memoirs*, 371, 373-379, 382-383.

20. *OR*, 37, part 1: 186; ibid, part 2: 42, 51, 52; *OR Supp.*, serial no. 38: 452. During the 4 July attacks an officer stationed at Green Spring Station, along the railroad south of the Potomac, informed Kelley that the Confederates had boarded a canal boat with an artillery piece and were advancing toward his position; see *OR*, 37, part 2: 48.

21. *OR*, 37, part 1: 187; ibid, part 2: 69, 120; Smith, "Diary," 29; *OR Supp.*, serial no. 38: 452.

22. *OR*, 37, part 1: 3-4; ibid, part 2: 37-38, 64, 65; Alexander, *Mosby's Men*, 77-80; Scott, *Partisan Life*, 238-241; Goodhart, *History*, 132-133; Mantz to Smith, July 5, 1864, in Smith, *B&O in the Civil War*, 99-100; Wiley to Smith, July 6, 1864, in Smith, *B&O in the Civil War*, 102; *Philadelphia Inquirer*, July 7, 1864.

23. *OR*, 37, part 1: 4; Munson, *Reminiscences*, 94; Goodhart, *History*, 132-133; Williamson, *Mosby's Rangers*, 185-186; Alexander, *Mosby's Men*, 81-82; Scott, *Partisan Life*, 240-242; *OR*, 37, part 2: 72; *Baltimore American*, July 6, 1864.

24. Munson, *Reminiscences*, 99-101; Scott, *Partisan Life*, 250; *OR*, 37, part 1: 4.

25. *OR*, 37, part 1: 176; ibid, part 2, 76, 592; Hotchkiss, *Make Me a Map*, 214; Spates to Ringgold, July 5, & July 6, 1864, Ltrs. Rcd., C&O Canal Papers. Confederate soldiers remained near the Potomac guarding provisions they had seized. On July 9 a Federal artillery officer on Maryland Heights reported to his commander's adjutant that "the captain of the canal-boat which lies near here states that he went to his house in Sharpsburg this a.m., where he learned that about 1,000 or 1,500 rebels were guarding a large lot of stores they had collected in the vicinity at or near Shepherdstown, on the Maryland side of the Potomac;" see *OR*, 37, part 2: 144.

26. *OR*, 37, part 2: 144; Brengle to Ringgold, July 20, 1864, Ltrs. Rcd., C&O Canal Papers. For a period account of the July 7-8 skirmishing in front of Frederick and subsequent evacuation of Union troops, see *Philadelphia Inquirer*, July 12, 1864.

27. *Washington Eve. Star*, July 9, 1864.

28. *OR*, 37, part 1: 187; ibid, part 2: 8-9, 68, 107, 120; B&O Railroad, *Thirty-Eighth Annual Report*, 56-57.

29. *OR*, 37, part 2: 59, 60, 100, 100-101.

30. *OR*, 37, part 1: 347-348; ibid, part 2: 191-192; Grant, *Personal Memoirs*, 356.

31. *OR*, 37, part 2: 142, 142-143; *Washington Eve. Star*, July 11, 1864.

32. *OR*, 37, part 1: 348-349; Early, *Memoirs*, 392-395.

33. *Frederick Examiner*, July 27, 1864.

34. Lowe to Ringgold, July 25, 1864, Ltrs. Rcd., C&O Canal Papers; Hassett to Spates, July 21, 1864, Ltrs. Rcd., C&O Canal Papers; Masters to Ringgold, July 18, 1864, Ltrs. Rcd., C&O Canal Papers; H. Miller to Ringold, July 18, 1864, Ltrs. Rcd., C&O Canal Papers; Masters to Spates, July 21, 1864, Ltrs. Rcd., C&O Canal Papers.

35. L Benton to Ringgold, July 20, 1864, Ltrs. Rcd., C&O Canal Papers; L. Benton to Spates, July 21, 1864, Ltrs. Rcd., C&O Canal Papers; also see *Frederick Examiner*, July 27, 1864.

36. G. Spates to Ringgold, July 16, 1864, Ltrs. Rcd., C&O Canal Papers; G. Spates to Pres. & Dirs., July 25, 1864, Ltrs. Rcd., C&O Canal Papers.

37. *Washington Eve. Star*, July 16 & 21, 1864.

38. *OR*, 37, part 2: 439, 440.

39. Early, *Memoirs*, 401-402, 404; Gilmor, *Four Years*, 205-206, 209-213; Booth, *Personal Reminiscences*, 128-130; *OR*, 37, part 1: 354-355; ibid, part 2: 508.

40. Gilmor, *Four Years*, 213; Booth, *Personal Reminiscences*, 130-131; *OR*, 37, part 1: 355; Smith, "Diary," 30; *OR*, 37, part 2: 568.

41. Gilmor, *Four Years*, 215; Booth, *Personal Reminiscences*, 131; *OR*, 37, part 1: 355; ibid, part 2: 576, 578; *Cumberland Civilian*, Aug. 4, 1864. Documentation that Thruston was placed in command of the local militia companies is from Lowdermilk, *History of Cumberland*, 416-417.

42. Gilmor, *Four Years*, 215-221; Booth, *Personal Reminiscences*, 131-134; *OR*, 37, part 1: 355-356; ibid, part 2: 517, 533, 535, 578, 579, 588; ibid, 43, part 1: 4-8;

Early, *Memoirs*, 405; Lowe to Ringgold, Aug. 25, 1864, Ltrs. Rcd., C&O Canal Papers.

43. *OR*, 43, part 1: 719, 720; Early, *Memoirs*, 402-403; *Middletown Valley Reg.*, Aug. 12, 1864; H. Miller to Ringgold, Aug. 1, 1864; Masters to Ringgold, Aug. 20, 1864; & Watson to Ringgold, Aug. 4, 1864; all in Ltrs. Rcd., C&O Canal Papers.

44. *OR*, 37, part 1: 5; Williamson, *Mosby's Rangers*, 197-202; Crawford, *Mosby*, 234-235; Alexander, *Mosby's Men*, 98-103; Hard, *History*, 307-311; Brengle to Ringgold, Aug. 1, 1864, Ltrs. Rcd., C&O Canal Papers; G. Spates to Ringgold, Aug. 2, 1864, Ltrs. Rcd., C&O Canal Papers.

CHAPTER 7

1. *OR*, 43, part 1: 795, 805; *OR Supp.*, serial no. 75: 514. At Sheridan's request, in Dec. 1864 military engineers sent another pontoon bridge up the canal to span the Shenandoah River at Harpers Ferry, which engineers installed by the end of the month; see *OR*, 43, part 2: 783, 798, 835.

2. Spates to Ringgold, Aug. 10, 1864; L. Benton to Spates, July 21, 1864; & Masters to Ringgold, Aug. 20, 1864; all in Ltrs. Rcd., C&O Canal Papers.

3. Masters to Pres. & Dirs., July 1, 1864; Masters to Spates, July 21, 1864; Masters to Ringgold, Aug. 20, 1864, all in Ltrs. Recieved, C&O Canal Papers.

4. *Washington Eve. Star*, Aug. 22, 1864.

5. *OR*, 43, part 1: 887.

6. Bradford to Curtin, July 19, 1864; Curtin to Bradford, July 20, 1864; & Vincent to Gov. of Md., Aug. 1, 1864; all in Md. Governor (Letterbook), 566-567 ,567-568, 569, MSA SM 170-3, MdHR M3169; *OR*, series 3, 4: 533-534, 534-535. Bradford's plan was denied in part because a Feb. 13, 1862, Act of Congress had prohibited troops from being mustered into the army for service exclusively within a specific state or territory, except for those previously authorized [such as the Potomac Home Brigade, Maryland Volunteers].

7. *OR*, 43, part 1: 719; ibid, part 2: 131.

8. Ibid, part 2: 83-84.

9. Ibid, part 1: 61-62; ibid, series 3, 5: 388.

10. *Washington Eve. Star*, Sept. 13, 1864; *Cumberland Civilian*, Sept. 22, 1864.

11. L. Benton to Pres. & Dirs., Sept. 19 & Oct. 1, 1864, Ltrs. Rcd., C&O Canal Papers; *Cumberland Civilian*, Sept. 29, 1864.

12. *Cumberland Alleganian*, Sept. 21, 1864.

13. *OR*, 43, part 2: 272-273.

14. Maryland, *Laws of the State of Maryland* [1864], 7; Md. Constitutional Convention of 1864, *Debates of the Constitutional Convention*, 3.

15. Md. Constitutional Convention of 1864, *Debates of the Constitutional Convention*, 1083-1088.

16. Maryland, *Laws Made and Passed by the General Assembly of the State of Maryland* [1842-1843], chapt. 301; Md. Constitution of 1851, art. 3, sec. 22, in Md. Constitutional Convention of 1851, *Debates and Proceedings of the Maryland Reform Convention to Revise the State Constitution*, 2: 9-10

17. Md. Constitutional Convention of 1864, *Debates of the Constitutional Convention*, 814-815, 899-900, 904, 906, 911-912, 1111, 1139, 1153.

18. Ibid, 904-905, 909-910, 966-967, 971. Also see Md. Comptroller of the Treasury Dept., *Annual Report . . . Fiscal Year Ended 30ᵗʰ September, 1863*, 13-14.

19. Md. Constitutional Convention of 1864, *Debates of the Constitutional Convention*, 904-905, 970.

20. Ibid, 1149.

21. Ibid, 909, 965, 968, 1124.

22. Ibid, 787-788, 800.

23. Ibid, 1115.

24. Ibid, 908-910, 968, 1117-1118, 1123-1124, 1149.

25. Ibid, 1116-1117, 1119, 1120, 1123-1124, 1155-1157.

26. Ibid, 969.

27. Ibid, 1115-1116.

28. Ibid, 970, 1112, 1143, 1159-1160.

29. Ibid, 1926. The provision of the constitution that outlawed slavery was article 24 of the Declaration of Rights. Incidentally, the other county that bordered the canal, Montgomery – which had a 30% slave population in 1860 – voted three-to-one against the constitution (24%).

30. *Cumberland Alleganian*, Sept. 21, 1864.

31. *Washington Evening Star*, Oct. 1, 1864.

32. Proceedings of Pres. & Dirs., Sept. 9, 1864, K, 398, C&O Canal Papers; Miller to Ringold, Oct. 20, 1864, Ltrs. Rcd., C&O Canal Papers; Ringgold to Miller, Oct. 24, 1864, Ltrs. Sent, M, 159, C&O Canal Papers.

33. Greene to Spates, Sept. 29, 1864, Ltrs. Rcd., C&O Canal Papers; *Middletown Valley Reg.*, Oct. 7, 1864.

34. *OR*, 43, part 1: 633; ibid, part 2: 368-369; Munson, *Reminiscences*, 221-227; Scott, *Partisan Life*, 335-339; *Frederick Examiner*, Oct. 19, 1864.

35. *OR*, 43, part 2: 369, 370, 371, 413; Goodhart, *History*, 170-171; Williamson, *Mosby's Rangers*, 264; Munson, *Reminiscences*, 227; Scott, *Partisan Life*, 340-341; G. Spates to Pres. & Dirs., Oct. 16 & 17, 1864, Ltrs. Rcd., C&O Canal Papers; *Cumberland Alleganian*, Oct. 19, 1864. For a personal account of the robbery of a store in Adamstown during Chapman's raid, see *Frederick Examiner*, Oct. 26, 1864.

36. G. Spates to Pres. & Dirs., Oct. 16 & 17, 1864, Ltrs. Rcd., C&O Canal Papers; *Washington Eve. Star*, Oct. 15, 1864.

37. *OR*, 43, part 2: 408-409.

38. *Cumberland Civilian*, Dec. 1, 1864; C&O Canal Co., *Thirty-Seventh Annual Report*, 6, 9.

39. *Washington Chronicle*, Dec. 1, 1864, in *Cumberland Alleganian*, Dec. 7, 1864.

40. Sanger, ed., *Statutes at Large*, 13: 381-382; Downey to Stanton, Sept. 5, 1864, box 305, Consolidated Correspondence File, Quartermaster General's Records; F. Thomas to Dana, Oct. 3, 1864, box 305, Consolidated Correspondence File, Quartermaster General's Records.

41. Downey to Quartermaster General, Nov. 2, 1864; Parons to Downey, Nov. 18, 1864; Downey to Quartermaster General, Nov. 25, 1864; Lacey to Rucker, Dec. 13, 1864; Rucker to Meigs, Dec. 14, 1864; & "Statement Showing Expenses Incurred in Repairing the Chesapeake and Ohio Canal in the Years of 1862 and 1863; Statement of Differences in the Account Marked _____ of the Chesapeake and Ohio Canal Company,"; all in box 305, Consolidated Correspondence File, Quartermaster General's Records.

42. *OR,* 43, part 2: 833.

43. Ibid, 764; G. Spates to Pres. & Dirs., Nov. 30, 1864, Ltrs. Rcd., C&O Canal Papers; Spates to Stanton, Dec. 20, 1864, Ltrs. Rcd. by the Adjutant General, m619, roll 310, Adjutant General's Records; E. Tyler to Spates, Dec. 21, 1864, Spates Papers; Cook to Adams, Jan. 8, 1865, Ltrs. Rcd. by the Adjutant General, m619, roll 310, Adjutant General's Records.

44. *Cumberland Civilian*, Dec. 15, 1864; Smith, "Diary," 31.

45. C&O Canal Co., *Thirty-Seventh Annual Report*, 3.

46. Ibid, 4-7.

47. Ibid, 9.

48. Md. Constitution of 1864, art. 1, sec. 7 & 8, in Md. Constitutional Convention of 1864, *Proceedings of the State Convention*, 729-730; Greene to Ringgold, Nov. 29, 1864, Ltrs. Rcd., C&O Canal Papers.

49. Md. Constitution of 1864, art. 1, sec. 4, in Md. Constitutional Convention of 1864, *Proceedings of the State Convention*, 727-728.

CHAPTER 8

1. "Chesapeake and Ohio Canal Notice," Jan. 5, 1865, in *Cumberland Civilian*, Jan. 5, 1865; *Washington Star*, [n.d.], in *Hagerstown Mail*, Feb. 24, 1865.

2. *Washington Star* [n.d.], in *Frederick Examiner*, Jan. 11, 1865; *Middletown Valley Reg.*, Jan. 6, 1865; *New York Times*, Feb. 26, 1865; *Frederick Maryland Union*, Feb. 2, 1865; Myers, *Comanches*, 357.

3. *OR*, 46, part 2: 182-183, 188-189; *Wheeling Intelligencer* [n.d.], in *Middletown Valley Reg.*, Jan. 27, 1865; Crawford, *Mosby*, 328-329; Baylor, *Bull Run*, 296. Baylor's postwar memoir of the raid states that it occurred on Feb. 3, but local newspapers and *OR* accounts indicate it occurred late on Jan. 18 or early the next day.

4. Crook, *General George Crook*, 135-136; *Cumberland Civilian*, Feb. 23, 1865; *Frederick Examiner*, March 8, 1865; McNeill, "Capture of Generals Kelly and Crook," in *Confederate Veteran*, 14, no. 9 (Sept. 1906): 410-413; Fay, "Daring Invasion," in Thomas and Williams, *History of Allegany County*, 1: 389-398; Duffey, "Capture of Generals Crook and Kelly," in *Confederate Veteran*, 33, no. 11 (Nov. 1925): 420-423, 437.

5. Smith, "Diary," 32; Masters to Ringgold, March 6, 1865, Ltrs. Rcd., C&O Canal Papers.

6. Masters to Pres. & Dirs., March 2, 1865; Masters to Ringgold, March 3, 1865; Masters to Ringgold, March 20, 1865; Masters to Pres. & Dirs., April 3, 1865; all in Ltrs. Rcd., C&O Canal Papers; *Cumberland Alleganian*, March 15, 1865.

7. *Cumberland Alleganian*, March 29, 1865; *Middletown Valley Reg.*, March 31, 1865.

8. *Cumberland Alleganian*, April 6, 1865; *Cumberland Civilian*, April 27, 1865.

9. Spates to Ringgold, April 26, 1865, Ltrs. Rcd., C&O Canal Papers.

10. *Cumberland Civilian*, May 25, 1865.

11. *Cumberland Civilian*, May 25 & June 1, 1865; *Pottsville Miners' Journal* [n.d.], in *Cumberland Civilian*, June 1, 1865; *Cumberland Civilian*, June 8, 1865.

12. Detmold, Bramholt, Culter, Borden, Potts, and Campbell to Pres. & Dirs., June 12, 1865, Ltrs. Rcd., C&O Canal Papers.

13. Downey to Stanton, March 1, 1865, box 305, Consolidated Correspondence File, Quartermaster General's Records; Spates to Stanton, March 1, 1865, Ltrs. Sent, M, 173, C&O Canal Papers; F. Thomas to Dana, March 6, 1865, box 305, Consolidated Correspondence File, Quartermaster General's Records; [Dana] to F. Thomas, March 7, 1865, box 305, Consolidated Correspondence File, Quartermaster General's Records; Parsons to Meigs, March 11, 1865, box 305, Consolidated Correspondence File, Quartermaster General's Records.

14. Meigs to Stanton, April 14, 1865, box 305, Consolidated Correspondence File, Quartermaster General's Records; [Dana] to F. Thomas, April 21, 1865, box 305, Consolidated Correspondence File, Quartermaster General's Records.

15. H. Miller to Ringgold, Dec. 1, 1864, April 3, May 8 & Nov. 1, 1865; all in Ltrs. Rcd., C&O Canal Papers; Bradly to Meigs, Dec. 1864; Affidavit of Henry S. Miller, Dec. 14, 1864; & Tarr to Meigs, Dec. 17, 1866; all in box 305, Consolidated Correspondence File, Quartermaster General's Records.

16. Minutes, Md. Board of Public Works, July 5, 1865, 174; Proceedings of Stockholders, July 6, 1865, E, 118-119, 122, C&O Canal Papers.

17. Watts to Findlay, July 1, 1865, Md. Governor (Miscellaneous Papers) box 85, folder 22, MSA S1274-85, MdHR 6636.

18. Minutes, Md. Board of Public Works, March 23, 1864 & July 5, 1865, 156, 174; Proceedings of Stockholders, July 6, 1865, E, 118-119, C&O Canal Papers;

Hagerstown Mail, Feb. 4, 1881; U.S. Census, 1860, Washington County, Md., Hancock District, roll 483, 1047.

19. *Cumberland Civilian*, June 29, July 6, 13, 20, 27 & Aug. 3, 1865; C&O Canal Co., *Thirty-Eighth Annual Report*, 14.

20. *Cumberland Civilian*, Aug. 3, 10 & 17, 1865.

21. Lowe to Ringgold, June 26, 1865, Ltrs. Rcd., C&O Canal Papers; Proceedings of Pres. & Dirs., July 13, 1865, K, 434, C&O Canal Papers; Ringgold to Lowe, July 14, 1865, Ltrs. Sent, M, 186, C&O Canal Papers.

22. Wilson to Pres. & Dirs., Aug. 4, 1865, Ltrs. Rcd., C&O Canal Papers; Ringgold to Wilson, Aug. 12, 1865, Ltrs. Sent, M, 190, C&O Canal Papers.

23. Savin to Snively, Aug. 7, 1865, Ltrs. Rcd., C&O Canal Papers.

24. Angle to Ringgold, Aug. 27, 1856[65], Ltrs. Rcd., C&O Canal Papers.

25. *Cumberland Civilian*, Dec. 14, 1865; C&O Canal Co., *Thirty-Eighth Annual Report*, 3-5, 14.

26. C&O Canal Co., *Thirty-Eighth Annual Report*, 3.

27. Ibid, 4-9.

28. Ibid, 9-10.

29. Masters to Pres. & Dirs., July 1[two letters; one reporting the condition of the Williamsport Division during July should have been dated 1 Aug. 1865] & July 31, 1865; Masters to Ringgold, July 18, Aug. 10, Sept. 9 & Oct. 13, 1865; & Masters to Pres. & Dirs., Nov. 1, 1865; all in Ltrs. Rcd., C&O Canal Papers; Proceedings of Pres. & Dirs., Aug. 9, 1865, K, 439, C&O Canal Papers; Ringgold to Stake & Simms, Aug. 12, 1865, Ltrs. Sent, M, 190, C&O Canal Papers; Ringgold to Masters, Aug. 15, 1865, Ltrs. Sent, M, 192, C&O Canal Papers.

30. C&O Canal Co., *Thirty-Eighth Annual Report*, 4-5; Preeceedings of Pres. & Dirs., April 12, May 10 & Aug. 9, 1865, K, 423, 427, 439, C&O Canal Papers; Shaffer, *"We Are Again in the Midst of Trouble,"* 39. For accounts of the Oct. 1866 freshet that disrupted the work to complete Dam Number 5, see Master to Ringgold, Oct. 16, 1866 & Masters to Pres. & Dirs., Nov. 2, 1866, both in Ltrs. Rcd., C&O Canal Papers.

31. Ringgold to Moore, March 9, 1865, Ltrs. Sent, M, 175, C&O Canal Papers; Moore to Ringgold, May 28, 1866, Ltrs. Rcd., C&O Canal Papers.

32. Ringgold to Rucker, May 29, 1866 & Ringgold to Moore, July 24, 1866, Ltrs. Sent, M, 243-244, 250, C&O Canal Papers; Proceedings of Pres. & Dirs., Oct. 23, 1867, L, 56, C&O Canal Papers; Godey to Ringgold, Jan. 10, 1868, Ltrs. Rcd., C&O Canal Papers.

33. Proceedings of Pres. & Dirs., Sept. 5, 1866, K, 511, C&O Canal Papers. Information on the postwar fate of the Alexandria Canal is from Hahn, *Towpath Guide*, 17, and Hahn & Kemp, *Alexandria Canal*, 33-34.

34. Proceedings of Pres. & Dirs., April 12, 1865, July 12 & Aug. 9, 1866, K, 422, 501-502, 508, C&O Canal Papers; H. Smith to Spates, April 10, 1865, Ltrs. Rcd., C&O Canal Papers; Ringgold to Spates, Aug 6 & 10, 1866, Ltrs. Sent, M, 253, 254, C&O Canal Papers; Ringgold to J.P. Roman, Aug. 28, 1866, Ltrs. Sent, M, 255, C&O

Canal Papers; Ringgold to Snively, Sept. 19, 1866, Ltrs. Sent, M, 259, C&O Canal Papers; Ringgold to Wallack, Oct. 20, 1866, Ltrs. Sent, M, 264, C&O Canal Papers.

35. Ringgold to Md. Board of Public Works, April 28 & Sept. 8, 1866, Ltrs. Sent, M, 240, 257, C&O Canal Papers; Minutes, Md. Board of Public Works, May, 2, 1866, 186.

36. Md. Senate, *Journal, 1867*, 50-52; *Hagerstown Mail*, Jan. 25, 1867. The testimony and evidence presented by both sides in the contested election is contained in Document D in the above Senate *Proceedings.* The minority report of the committee, 70-73 of the Senate *Journal*, claimed that parties on both sides were armed and no evidence of intimidation was presented. The minority opined that the thirty-one Spates voters who were not allowed to vote had been disqualified by evidence of disloyalty and refused to take the loyalty oath as prescribed in the constitution. In addition, the minority report dismissed the recounted votes since those who performed the recount were not sworn and the incumbent had no notice of it and had no representative to observe the proceeding.

37. Proceedings of Stockholders, Aug. 27, 1867, June 8, 1868 & June 17, 1869, E, 141-142, 144-146, 147-148, C&O Canal Papers.

38. Sanderlin, *Great National Project*, 226.

39. C&O Canal Co., *Forty-First Annual Report*, 4.

40. Clarke to Meigs, Feb. 2 & Dec. 4, 1871; Sudington to Clarke Feb. 8 & Oct. 12, 1871; Meigs to Clarke, Feb. 24, 1871; Sudington to [Meigs], July 8, 1871; all in box 305, Consolidated Correspondence File, Quartermaster General's Records; Proceedings of Pres. & Dirs., April 12, 1871, L, 403, C&O Canal Papers.

41. Clarke to Stockholders, Dec. 27, 1871, in Proceedings of Stockholders, Dec. 29, 1871, E, 187-188, C&O Canal Papers.

42. Spates to Poe, Nov. 15, 1869, Spates Papers; Md. Senate, *Report and Testimony*, 187-197.

43. Spates to Editor, March 8, 1878, in *Baltimore American*, March 9, 1878, Spates Papers; *Cumberland Daily News*, Nov. 19, 1892.

44. *Montgomery County Sentinel*, Nov. 25, 1892; *Cumberland Daily News*, Nov. 19, 1892.

45. The increase in the number of western Maryland mining companies was determined by comparing the number of coal companies in 1862 listed in the Statistics of the Cumberland Coal Trade in the *Cumberland Civilian*, Feb. 19, 1863 with the number of active companies in 1864 published in the Jan. 5, 1865 edition of the same newspaper. Lists of active coal companies in 1861 and 1865 were not found. For information on the Consolidation Coal Company, see Beachley, *History of the Consolidation Coal Company*.

46. Franklin Cooling, *Jubal Early's Raid*, 24-25; Early, *Memoirs*, 382-383.

47. From March 1, 1861 to Jan. 1, 1862, between Baltimore and Washington the government paid the B&O Railroad three cents to transport soldiers twenty-two miles or less; two and three-quarter cents for greater distances. From Jan. 1, 1862, to

March 1, 1865, the government again paid the B&O Railroad three cents to carry soldiers twenty-two miles or less; but two and one-half cents for distances over twenty-two miles. From March 1, 1861 to March 1, 1865, the government paid the B&O $2.50 per ton for first class freight; $2.00 per ton for second class freight. It paid the B&O rates that were higher than other railroads because the B&O was situated so close to the "seat of war." See "Report of the Secretary of War," March 3, 1865.

48. Statement of Garrett is from Summers, *Baltimore and Ohio in the Civil War*, 46. A Bendann painting of Lincoln, McClellan and Garrett together at Antietam is included as one of the front pages in the Summers book.

EPILOGUE

1. *Washington Post*, January 19, 1954.

BIBLIOGRAPHY

PRIMARY SOURCES

Manuscripts

Adjutant General, Records of the Office of. Record Group 94. National Archives and
    Records Administration. Washington, D.C.

Andis, Earl Carson. The War Correspondence of Earl Carson Andis, 1861-1865
    [typescript]. Manassas National Battlefield Park. Manassas, Va.

Banks, Nathaniel Prentiss. Papers. Manuscripts Division. Library of Congress.
    Washington, D.C.

Beard, James E. Diary [typescript]. Fredericksburg and Spotsylvania National
    Memorial Military Park. Fredericksburg, Virginia.

Brand, William Francis. Papers [accession #11332]. Albert and Shirley Small Special
    Collections Library. University of Virginia. Charlottesville, Va.

Brown, W. Morton to Dr. Lee Holt [probably], 17 Jan. 1862. Bowman-Howard-
    Domingos Family Collection. Middle Georgia Archives. Washington
    Memorial Library. Macon, Ga.

Chamberlain, Joshua Lawrence to Fanny Chamberlain, 21 Sept. 1862. Joshua Lawrence
    Chamberlain Papers, 1862-1863. Pearce Civil War Collection. Navarro College.
    Corsicana, Tex.

Chesapeake and Ohio Canal Company. Papers. Record Group 79. Records of the
    National Park Service. National Archives and Records Administration II.
    College Park, Md.

Crump, William W., to John Letcher, 5 May 1861. Papers of J .Marshall McCue. Old
    Catalog Collection. Virginia Historical Society. Richmond, Va.

Dahlgren, John Adolphus Bernard. Papers, 1824-1889. Manuscripts Division. Library
    of Congress. Washington, D.C.

Edwards, John F. Certificate, 10 October 1885. McLaws Papers. Southern Historical
    Collection. University of North Carolina. Chapel Hill, N.C.

Flagg, George A. Papers [microfilm, six reels]. Harpers Ferry National Historical Park.
    Harpers Ferry, W. Va.

Garibaldi, John. Letters. Virginia Military Institute Archives. Lexington, Va.

Grabill, John H. Diary of a Soldier of the Stonewall Brigade [typescript]. Stewart Bell Jr. Archives Room. Handley Regional Library. Winchester, Va.

Hemphill, William S. Journal of the Kosciusko Guards, Company E, 12th Regiment, Indiana Volunteers. Transcribed by Marjorie Priser. Indiana Room. Warsaw Community Public Library. Warsaw, Indiana.

Hotchkiss, Jedediah. Papers [microfilm, sixty-one reels]. Manuscripts Division. Library of Congress. Washington, D.C.

Hite, John. Diary. Steward Bell Jr. Archives Room. Handley Regional Library. Winchester, Va.

Kinzer, William T. Diary [typescript]. West Virginia and Regional Collection. West Virginia University. Morgantown, W. Va.

Kearns, Watkins. Diary. Virginia Historical Society. Richmond, Va.

Lander, Frederick West. Papers. Manuscripts Division. Library of Congress. Washington, D.C.

Langhorne Family Papers. Virginia Historical Society. Richmond, Va.

Lincoln, Abraham. Papers. Manuscripts Division. Library of Congress. Washington, D.C.

Liscom, Albert M. Letters. Civil War Miscellaneous Collection. U.S. Military History Institute. Carlisle, Pa.

Maryland. Adjutant General (Militia Appointments), 1822-1862. Accession Number 5590, MSA S 348-7. Maryland State Archives. Annapolis, Md.

Maryland, Commission of Public Works/Board of Public Works. Minutes. Maryland State Archives. Annapolis, Md.

Maryland. Governor. (Miscellaneous Papers), 1848-1918. MSA S 1274. Maryland State Archives. Annapolis, Md.

_____. (Letterbook), 1838-1896. MSA SM 170. Maryland State Archives. Annapolis, Md.

_____. (Proceedings), 1838-1924. MSA SM 172. Maryland State Archives. Annapolis, Md.

McClellan, Sr., George Brinton. Papers [microfilm]. Manuscripts Division. Library of Congress. Washington, D.C.

Meigs, Montgomery C. Papers [microfilm]. Manuscripts Division. Library of Congress. Washington, D.C.

Meigs, Montgomery C., to Abraham Lincoln, 15 April 1862. Henry Horner Lincoln Collection. Illinois State Historical Library. Springfield, Ill.

Moore, Samuel J. C. Papers, 1847-1937. Southern Historical Collection. University of North Carolina. Chapel Hill, N.C.

Quartermaster General, Records of the Office of. Record Group 92. National Archives and Records Administration. Washington, D.C.

St. Thomas' Protestant Episcopal Church of Hancock, Maryland, Vestry of, vs. the United States. Box 1497. Case File 13,041. Congressional Jurisdiction Case

Files. Record Group 123. Records of the U.S. Court of Claims. National Archives and Records Administration. Washington, D.C.

Secretary of War, Records of the Office of. Record Group 107. National Archives and Records Administration. Washington, D.C.

Smiley Family Papers, 1750-1959 [accession #1807-1807a]. Albert and Shirley Small Special Collections Library. University of Virginia. Charlottesville, Va.

Smith, Otis D. Reminiscences [typescript]. Thach Family Papers. Southern Historical Collection. University of North Carolina. Chapel Hill, N.C.

Spates, Alfred. Alfred Spates Papers Concerning the Chesapeake and Ohio Canal [accession #554]. Albert and Shirley Small Special Collections Library. University of Virginia. Charlottesville, Va.

Taft, Horatio Nelson. Diary. 3 vols. Manuscript Division. Library of Congress. Washington, D.C.

United States vs. Alfred Spates. Court Martial File mm1220. Record Group 153. Records of the Office of the Judge Advocate General. National Archives and Records Administration. Washington, D.C.

Viles, John. Letters. Civil War Miscellaneous Collection. U.S. Military History Institute. Carlisle, Pa.

Virginia Executive Papers. Library of Virginia. Richmond, Va.

Newspapers

Baltimore American and Commercial Advertiser
Boston Advertizer
Boston Daily Currier
Boston Saturday Evening Gazette
Chambersburg (Pa.) *Valley Spirit*
Chelsea (Mass.) *Telegraph and Pioneer*
Cumberland Alleganian
Cumberland Civilian and Telegraph
Cumberland Daily Times
Cumberland Daily News
Cumberland Union
Frank Leslie's Illustrated Newspaper
Frederick Examiner
Frederick Maryland Union
Frederick Republican Citizen
Hagerstown Herald of Freedom and Torch Light
Hagerstown Mail
Harper's Weekly: A Journal of Civilization
Harrisonburg (Va.) *Rockingham Register*

Middletown (Md.) *Valley Register*
New York Daily Tribune
New York Times
Philadelphia Inquirer
Philadelphia Public Ledger
Rockingham (Va.) *Register*
Rockville Montgomery County Sentinel
Roxbury (Mass.) *City Gazette*
Warsaw Northern Indianian
Washington Evening Star
Washington Post
Winchester (Va.) *Republican*

Books

Abbott, Henry Livermore. *Fallen Leaves: The Civil War Letters of Major Henry Livermore Abbott*. Edited by Robert Garth Scott. Kent, Ohio: Kent State University Press, 1991.

Alexander, John H. *Mosby's Men*. 1907. Reprint, Gaithersburg, Md.: Butternut Press, n.d.

Allan, Elizabeth Preston. *The Life and Letters of Margaret Junkin Preston*. Boston and New York: Houghton, Mifflin, 1906.

Allan, William. *Stonewall Jackson's Valley Campaign, From November 4, 1861, to June 17, 1862*. 1912. Reprint, New York: Konecky & Konecky, 1995.

"Alteration of Bridges Across the Chesapeake and Ohio Canal." U.S. Congress. House of Representatives. Executive Documents. Vol. 8. Thirty-Seventh Congress, Second Session. Executive Document No. 102. Washington, D.C.: Government Printing Office, 1862.

Apperson, John Samuel. *Repairing the "March of Mars": The Civil War Diaries of John Samuel Apperson, Hospital Steward in the Stonewall Brigade, 1861-1865*. Edited by John Herbert Roper. Macon, Ga.: Mercer University Press, 2001.

Armour Newcomer, C. *Cole's Cavlary; Or Three Years in the Saddle in the Shenandoah Valley*. 1895. Reprint, Freeport, N. Y.: Books for Libraries Press, 1970.

Avirett, James B. *The Memoirs of General Turner Ashby and his Compeers*. 1867. Reprint, Gaithersburg, Md.: Old Soldier Books, 1987.

Barclay, Ted. *Ted Barclay, Liberty Hall Volunteers: Letters from the Stonewall Brigade*. Edited by Charles W. Turner. Berryville, Va.: Rockbridge, 1992

Baltimore and Ohio Railroad Company. *Thirty-Fifth Annual Report of the President and Directors to the Stockholders of the Baltimore and Ohio Railroad*

Company, for the Year Ending September 30, 1861. Baltimore: William M.
Innes, 1863.

_____. *Thirty-Sixth Annual Report of the President and Directors to the
Stockholders of the Baltimore and Ohio Railroad Company, for the Year
Ending September 30, 1862.* Baltimore: J. B. Rose, 1864.

_____. *Thirty-Seventh Annual Report of the President and Directors to the
Stockholders of the Baltimore and Ohio Railroad Company, for the Year
Ending September 30, 1863.* Baltimore: J. B. Rose, 1865.

_____. *Thirty-Eighth Annual Report of the President and Directors to the
Stockholders of the Baltimore and Ohio Railroad Company, for the Year
Ending September 30, 1864.* Baltimore: The Printing Office, 1866.

Barnard, J. G. *A Report on the Defenses of Washington to the Chief of Engineers, U.S.
Army.* Professional Papers of the Corps of Engineers U.S. Army, No. 20.
Washington: Government Printing Office, 1871.

Barry, Jospeh. *The Strange Story of Harper's Ferry, with Legends of the Surrounding
Country.* 1903. Reprint, Shepherdstown, W. Va.: Women's Club of Harpers
Ferry District, 1994.

*Battle-fields of the South, From Bull Run to Fredericksburgh; With Sketches of
Confederate Commanders, and Gossip of the Camps, by an English
Combatant.* 1864. Reprint, New York: Time-Life Books, 1984.

Baylor, George. *Bull Run to Bull Run; or, Four Years in the Army of Northern
Virginia.* Richmond: B. F. Johnson, 1900.

Beale, R. L .T. *History of the Ninth Virginia Cavalry in the War Between the States.*
Richmond: B. F. Johnson, 1899.

Blackford, W. W. *War Years with Jeb Stuart.* Reprint, Baton Rogue: Louisiana State
University Press, 1993.

Booth, George Wilson. *Personal Reminiscences of a Maryland Soldier in the War
Between the States 1861-1865.* 1898. Reprint, Gaithersburg, Md.: Butternut
Press, 1986.

Bowen, Roland E. *From Ball's Bluff to Gettysburg . . . And Beyond: The Civil War
Letters of Private Roland E. Bowen, 15th Massachusetts Infanty, 1861-
1864.* Edited by Gregory A. Coco. Gettysburg, Pa.: Thomas Publications,
1994.

Brainerd, Wesley. *Bridge Building in Wartime: Colonel Wesley Brainerd's Memoir
of the 50th New York Volunteer Engineers.* Edited by Ed Malles. Voices of
the Civil War. Knoxville: University of Tennessee Press, 1997.

Brown, Edmund Randolph. *The Twenty-Seventh Indiana Volunteer Infantry in the
War of the Rebellion, 1861-1865, First Division, 12th and 20th Corps.* c1899.
Reprint, Gaithersburg, Md.: Butternut Press, c1984.

Brown, George William. *Baltimore and the Nineteenth of April, 1861: A Study of the
War.* Johns Hopkins University Studies in Historical and Political Science,
ed. Herbert B. Adams. Baltimore: Johns Hopkins University, 1887.

Browning, Orville Hickman. *The Diary of Orville Hickman Browning*. 2 vols. Lincoln Series. Springfield, Ill.: Illinois State Historical Library, 1925.

Bryant, Edwin E. *History of the Third Regiment of Wisconsin Veteran Volunteer Infantry, 1861-1865*. Madison: Veteran Association of the Regiment, 1891.

Burgwyn, William H. S. *A Captain's War: The Letters and Diaries of William H. S. Burgwyn*. Edited by Herbert M. Schiller. Shippensburg, Pa.: White Mane, 1994.

Butler, Benjamin F. *Private and Official Correspondence of Gen. Benjamin F. Butler During the Period of the Civil War*. 5 vols. Norwood, Mass.: Plimpton Press, 1917.

Camper, Chas., and J. W. Kirkley. *Historical Record of the First Regiment Maryland Infantry*. Reprint, Baltimore: Butternut and Blue, 1990.

Casler, John O. *Four Years in the Stonewall Brigade*. Edited by James I. Robertson, Jr. Reprint, Dayton: Morningside Bookshop, 1971.

Chesapeake and Ohio Canal Company. President and Directors. *Thirtieth Annual Report of the President and Directors of the Chesapeake and Ohio Canal Company, to the Stockholders, June 7, 1858*. Frederick: Schley & Haller, 1858.

_____. *Thirty-second Annual Report of the President and Directors of the Chesapeake and Ohio Canal Company, to the Stockholders, June 4, 1860*. Frederick: Schley, Haller, 1860.

_____. *Thirty-third Annual Report of the President and Directors of the Chesapeake and Ohio Canal Company, to the Stockholders, June 4, 1861*. Frederick: Schley, Haller, 1861.

_____. *Thirty-fourth Annual Report of the President and Directors of the Chesapeake and Ohio Canal Company, to the Stockholders, June 2, 1862*. Washington: R.A. Waters, 1862.

_____. *Thirty-fifth Annual Report of the President and Directors of the Chesapeake and Ohio Canal Company, to the Stockholders, June 1, 1863*. Washington: R.A. Waters, 1863.

_____. *Thirty-sixth Annual Report of the President and Directors of the Chesapeake and Ohio Canal Company, to the Stockholders, June 6, 1864*. Washington: R.A. Waters, 1864.

_____. *Thirty-seventh Annual Report of the President and Directors of the Chesapeake and Ohio Canal Company, to the Stockholders, June 5, 1865*. Washington: R.A. Waters, 1865.

_____. *Thirty-eighth Annual Report of the President and Directors of the Chesapeake and Ohio Canal Company, to the Stockholders, June 4, 1866*. Washington: R.A. Waters, 1866.

_____. *Forty-first Annual Report of the President and Directors of the Chesapeake and Ohio Canal Company, to the Stockholders, June 7, 1869*. Georgetown: Courier Print, 1869.

Clark, Charles M. *The History of the Thirty-Ninth Regiment Illinois Volunteer Veteran Infantry (Yates Phalanx) In the War of the Rebellion, 1861-1865*. Chicago: Veteran Association of the Thirty-Ninth Regiment Illinois Volunteers, 1889.

Clark, Ella E., and Thomas F. Hahn, eds. *Life on the Chesapeake & Ohio Canal, 1859*. York, Pa.: American Canal and Transportation Center, 1975.

Clark, Walter, ed. *Histories of the Several Regiments and Battalions from North Carolina in the Great War, 1861-65; Written by Members of the Respective Commands*. 5 vols. Raleigh: E.M. Uzzell, 1901 [vol. 1]; Goldsboro, N.C.: Nash Brothers, 1901 [vol. 2-5].

Clark, William. *History of Hampton Battery F, Independent Pennsylvania Light Artillery, Organized at Pittsburgh, Pa., October 8, 1861, Mustered Out in Pittsburgh, June 26, 1865*. Pittsburgh: Werner Company, 1909.

Collins, George K. *Memoirs of the 149th Regt. N. Y. Vol. Inft. 3d Brig., 2d Div., 12th and 20th A. C.* 1891. Reprint, Hamilton, N. Y.: Edmonston Publishing, 1995.

Comey, Lyman Richard, ed. *A Legacy of Valor: The Memoirs and Letters of Captain Henry Newton Comey, 2nd Massachusetss Infantry.* Voices of the Civil War. Knoxville, Tenn.: University of Tennessee Press, 2004.

Confederate Veteran. 1893-1932. Reprint, Wilmington, N.C.: Broadfoot, n.d.

Cowden, William Firth. *Poems: Patriotic, Descriptive, Miscellaneous.* Baltimore: Printed by W. K. Boyle, 1888.

Crawford, J. Marshall. *Mosby and His Men: A Record of the Adventures of the Renowned Partisan Ranger, John S. Mosby (Colonel C. S. A.), Including the Exploits of Smith, Chapman, Richards, Montjoy, Turner, Russell, Glassock, and the Men Under Them.* 1867. Reprint, Gaithersburg, Md.: Olde Soldier Books, 1987.

Croffut, W. A., and John M. Morris. *The Military and Civil History of Connecticut During the War of 1861-65.* New York: Ledyard Bill, 1868.

Crook, George. *General George Crook: His Autobiography.* Edited by Martin F. Schmitt. 1946. Reprint, Norman, Okla.: University of Oklahoma Press, 1986.

De Peyster, J. Watts. *Gettysburg and After: Battle of Oak Ridge, at Williamsport and Falling Waters.* 1867. Reprint, Gaithersburg, Md.: Olde Soldier Books, 1987.

Dabney, R. L. *Life and Campaigns of Lieut. Gen. Thomas J. (Stonewall) Jackson.* 1866. Reprint, Harrisonburg, Va.: Sprinkle Publications, 1983.

Dahlgren, Madeleine Vinton. *Memoir of John A. Dahlgren.* Boston: James R. Osgood, 1882.

Davis, Charles E. *Three Years in the Army: The Story of the Thirteenth Massachusetts Volunteers From July 16, 1861, to August 1, 1864.* Boston: Estes & Lauriat, 1894.

Donaldson, Francis Adams. *Inside the Army of the Potomac: The Civil War Experiences of Captain Francis Adams Donaldson.* Edited by J. Gregory

Acken. Mechanicsburg, Pa.: Stackpole Books, 1998.

Douglas, Henry Kyd. *I Rode With Stonewall; Being Chiefly the War Experiences of the Youngest Member of Jackson's Staff From the John Brown Raid to the Hanging of Mrs. Surratt.* 1940. Reprint, Chapel Hill: University of North Carolina Press, n.d.

Early, Jubal A. *The Memoirs of Jubal A. Early; Autobiographical Sketch and Narrative of the War Between the States.* 1912. Reprint, New York: Smithmark Publications, 1994.

Faller, Leo W. and John I. Faller. *Dear Folks at Home: The Civil War Letters of Leo W. and John I. Faller, with an Account of Andersonville.* Edited by Milton E. Flower. Carlisle, Pa.: Cumberland County Historical Society and Hamilton Library Association, 1963.

Farrar, Samuel Clarke. *The Twenty-Second Pennsylvania Cavalry and the Ringgold Battalion, 1861-1865.* Akron, Oh. and Pittsburgh: New Werner Company, 1911.

Geary, John White. *A Politician Goes to War: The Civil War Letters of John White Geary.* Edited by William Alan Blair. University Park, Pa.: Pennsylvania State University Press, 1995.

Gerrish, Theodore. *Army Life; a Private's Reminiscences of the Civil War.* 1882. Reprint, Baltimore and Gettysburg: Butternut & Blue and Stan Clark Military Books, 1995.

Gill, John. *Courier for Lee & Jackson, 1861-1865; Memoirs.* Edited by Walbrook D. Swank. Civil War Heritage Series 3. Shippensburg, Pa.: Burd Street Press, 1993.

Gilmor, Harry. *Four Years in the Saddle.* New York: Harper & Brothers, 1866.

Gilson, John H. *History of the 126th Ohio Volunteers.* 1883. Reprint, Huntington, W.Va.: Blue Acorn Press, 2000.

Goodhart, Briscoe. *History of the Independent Loudoun Virginia Rangers, U.S. Vol. Cav. (Scouts), 1862-65.* 1896. Reprint, Gaithersburg, Md.: Butternut Press, 1985.

Gordon, George H. *War Diary of Events in the War of the Great Rebellion, 1863-1865.* Boston: James R. Osgood, 1882.

Goss, Warren Lee. *Recollections of a Private: A Story of the Army of the Potomac.* New York: Thomas Y. Crowell, 1890.

Grant, Ulysses Simpson. *Personal Memoirs of U.S. Grant.* 1885-1886. Reprint, Dover Publications, 1995.

Haley, John W. *Rebel Yell and Yankee Hurrah: The Civil War Journal of a Maine Volunteer.* Edited by Ruth L. Silliker. Camden, Maine: Down East Books, 1985.

Hard, Abner. *History of the Eighth Cavalry Regiment Illinois Volunteers, During the Great Rebellion.* 1868. Reprint, Dayton, Ohio: Morningside Bookshop, 1984.

Haynes, E. M. *A History of the Tenth Regiment, Vt. Vols., With Biographical Sketches of Nearly Every Officer Who Ever Belonged to the Regiment, and Many of the Non-Commissioned Officers and Men, and a Complete Roster of all the Men Connected with it–Showing All Changes by Promotion, Death or Resignation, During the Military Existence of the Regiment.* 1870. Second Edition, Rutland, Vt.: Tuttle Company, 1894.

Hewett, Janet B., at al, ed. *Supplement to the Official Records of the Union and Confederate Armies.* 100 vols. Wilmington, N.C.: Broadfoot, 1994-2001.

Hicks, Thomas Holliday. *Message of the Governor of Maryland to the General Assembly, Special Session, December, 1861.* Annapolis: Thomas J. Wilson, 1861.

History of the First Regiment Minnesota Volunteer Infantry, 1861-1864. 1916. Reprint, Gaithersburg, Md.: Ron R. Van Sickle Military Books, 1987.

Holmes, Oliver Wendell. *Touches With Fire: Civil War Letters and Diary of Oliver Wendell Holmes, Jr., 1861-1864.* Edited by Mark De Wolfe Howe. Cambridge: Harvard University Press, 1946.

Hotchkiss, Jedediah. *Make Me a Map of the Valley: The Civil War Journal of Stonewall Jackson's Topographer.* Edited by Archie P. McDonald. 1973. Reprint, Dallas: Southern Methodist University Press, 1989.

_____. *Virginia.* Vol. 2, *Confederate Military History In Twelve Volumes, Written by Distinguished Men of the South.* Edited by Clement A. Evans. Atlanta: Confederate Publishing, 1899.

Houghton, Edwin B. *The Campaigns of the Seventeenth Maine.* Portland: Short & Loring, 1866.

Hunton, Eppa. *Autobiography of Eppa Hunton.* Richmond: William Byrd Press, 1933.

Hussey, George A. *History of the Ninth Regiment N. Y. S. M.–N. G. S. N. Y. (Eighty-Third N. Y. Volunteers).* New York: Veterans of the Regiment, 1889.

Indiana. Adjutant General's Office. *Report of the Adjutant General of the State of Indiana.* Vol. 2. Indianapolis, Ind.: W.R. Holloway, 1865.

Jackson, Mary Anna. *Life and Letters of General Thomas J. Jackson (Stonewall Jackson).* New York: Harper & Brothers, 1892.

Jaques, John W. *Three Years' Campaign of the Ninth, N. Y. S. M., During the Southern Rebellion.* New York: Hilton & Co., 1865.

Jessup, Harlan R., ed. *The Painful News I Have to Write: Letters and Diaries of Four Hite Brothers of Page County in the Service of the Confederacy.* Baltimore: Butternut & Blue, 1998.

Johnson, Clifton. *Battleground Adventures; the Stories of Dwellers on the Scenes of Conflict in Some of the Most Notable Battles of the Civil War.* Boston and New York: Houghton Mifflin, 1915.

Johnston, Joseph E. *Narrative of Military Operations During the Civil War.* 1874. Reprint, New York: Da Capo Press, 1990.

Judd, David W. *The Story of the Thirty-third N. Y. S. Vols.: Or Two Years Campaigning in Virginia and Maryland.* Rochester, N. Y.: Benton & Andrews, 1864.

Keller, S. Roger, comp. *Crossroads of War: Washington County, Maryland in the Civil War.* Shippensburg, Pa.: Burd Street Press, 1997.

Kirk, Charles H., ed. & comp. *History of the Fifteenth Pennsylvania Volunteer Cavalry, Which Was Recruited and Known as the Anderson Cavalry in the Rebellion of 1861-1865.* Philadelphia: Society of the Fifteenth Pennsylvania Cavalry, 1906.

Lee, Robert E. *The Wartime Papers of Robert E. Lee.* Edited by Clifford Dowdey. 1961. Reprint, New York: Da Capo Press, 1987.

Leon, L. *Diary of a Tar Heel Confederate Soldier.* Charlotte, N.C.: Stone Publishing, 1913.

Letters from Two Brothers Serving in the War for the Union to their Family at Home in West Cambridge, Mass. Cambridge: H. O. Houghton, printer, 1871

Lincoln, Abraham. *The Collected Works of Abraham Lincoln.* 11 vols. Edited by Roy P. Basler. New Brunswick, N. J.: Rutgers University Press, 1953.

Lyon, Henry C. *"Desolating this Fair Country": The Civil War Diary and Letters of Lt. Henry C. Lyon, 34th New York.* Edited by Emily N. Radigan. Jefferson, N.C.: McFarland & Co., 1999.

McClellan, George G. *McClellan's Own Story: The War for the Union, the Soldiers Who fought It, the Civilians Who Directed It and his Relations to it and to them.* New York: C.L. Webster, 1887.

_____. *Report on the Organization and Campaigns of the Army of the Potomac; to which is Added an Account of the Campaign in Western Virginia, With Plans of Battle-fields.* New York: Sheldon & Co., 1864.

McClellan, H. B. *I Rode With Jeb Stuart: The Life and Campaigns of Major General J. E. B. Stuart.* Civil War Centennial Series. Bloomington: Indiana University Press, 1958.

McDonald, William N. *A History of the Laurel Brigade; Originally the Ashby Cavalry of the Army of Northern Virginia and Chew's Battery.* Edited by Bushrod C. Washington. 1907. Reprint, Baltimore: The Johns Hopkins University Press, 2002.

McPherson, Edward. *The Political History of the United States during the Great Rebellion, From November 6, 1860, to July 4, 1864.* Washington, D.C.: Philip & Solomons, 1864.

Marvin, Edwin E. *The Fifth Regiment Connecticut Volunteers; A History Compiled From Diaries and Official Reports.* Hartford, Conn.: Wiley, Waterman & Eaton, 1889.

Maryland. *Laws Made and Passed by the General Assembly of the State of Maryland, at a Session Begun and Held at Annapolis, on Monday, the 26th Day of*

December 1842, and Ended on Friday, the 10ᵗʰ Day of March 1843. Annapolis: William M'Neir, 1843.

_____. *Laws of the State of Maryland, Made and Passed at a Session of the General Assembly Begun and Held at the City of Annapolis on the Sixth Day of January, 1864, and ended on the Tenth Day of March, 1864.* Annapolis: Richard P. Bayly, printer, 1864.

_____. *Supplement to the Maryland Code, Containing the Acts of the General Assembly Passed at the Extra Sessions of 1861, and the Regular Session of 1862, Divided into Public General and Public Local Laws, and Arranged in Articles and Sections to Correspond with the Code.* Baltimore: John Murphy, 1862.

_____. *Supplement to the Maryland Code, Containing the Acts of the General Assembly Passed at the Session of 1864, Divided into Public General and Public Local Laws, and Arranged in Articles and Sections to Correspond with the Code.* Baltimore: John Murphy, 1865.

Maryland. Comptroller of the Treasury Department. *Annual Report of the Comptroller of the Treasury Department, for the Fiscal Year Ended 30ᵗʰ September, 1860, to the Governor of Maryland.* Annapolis: Thomas J. Wilson, 1861.

_____. *Annual Report of the Comptroller of the Treasury Department for the Fiscal Year Ended 30ᵗʰ September, 1861, to the General Assembly of Maryland.* Bel Air, Md.: John Cox, 1862.

_____. *Annual Report of the Comptroller of the Treasury, for the Fiscal Year Ended 30ᵗʰ September, 1863, to the General Assembly of Maryland.* Baltimore: John D. Toy, n.d.

Maryland. Constitutional Convention of 1851. *Debates and Proceedings of the Maryland Reform Convention to Revise the State Constitution.* 2 vols. Annapolis: William M'Neir, printer, 1851.

Maryland. Constitutional Convention of 1864. *The Debates of the Constitutional Convention of the State of Maryland, Assembled at the City of Annapolis, Wednesday, April 27, 1864; Being a Full and Complete Report of the Debates and Proceedings of the Convention, Together With the Old Constitution, the Law Under Which the Convention Assembled, and the New Constitution.* Annapolis: Richard P. Bayly, printer, 1864.

_____. *Proceedings of the State Convention of Maryland to Frame a New Constitution. Commenced at Annapolis, April 27, 1864.* Annapolis: Richard P. Bayly, printer, 1864.

Maryland. House of Delegates. *Journal of the Proceedings of the House of Delegates, In Extra Session.* Frederick, Md.: Elihus S. Riley, 1861.

Maryland. General Assembly. *Documents of the Maryland General Assembly in Extra Session, 1861.* Frederick, Md.: E.S. Riley, 1861.

Maryland. Senate. *Journal of Proceedings of the Senate of Maryland, in Extra Session, April, 1861*. Frederick, Md.: Beale H. Richardson, 1861.

_____. *Journal of the Proceedings of the Senate of Maryland, January Session, 1867*. Annapolis: Henry A. Lucas, 1867.

_____. *Report and Testimony of the Committee on Investigation, in the Case of the Hon. Alfred Spates*. Annapolis: W. Thompson, 1870.

Mattocks, Charles. *"Unspoiled Heart": The Journal of Charles Mattocks of the 17ᵗʰ Maine*. Edited by Philip N. Racine. Knoxville: University of Tennessee Press, 1994.

Message of the Governor of Virginia, and Accompanying Documents. Document No. 1. Richmond: William F. Ritchie, Public Printer, 1861.

Minnesota in the Civil and Indian Wars; Narrative of the First Regiment. 1890-1893. Reprint, St. Paul: Printed for the State by Pioneer Press, n.d.

Monteiro, Aristides. *War Reminiscences of the Surgeon of Mosby's Command*. 1890. Reprint, Gaithersburg, Md.: Butternut Press, n.d.

Moore, Frank, ed. *Rebellion Record: A Diary of American Events*. 12 vols. New York: G.P. Putnam, 1861-1868.

Morse, Charles F. *Letters Written During the Civil War, 1861-1865*. Privately printed, 1898.

Mosby, John S. *The Memoirs of Colonel John S. Mosby*. Edited by Charles Wells Russell. Civil War Centennial Series. 1959. Reprint, Millwood, N. Y.: Kraus Reprint, 1990.

Mosby, John S. *Mosby's War Reminiscences and Stuart's Cavalry Campaigns*. New York: Pageant Book Co., 1958.

Mowris, J. A. *A History of the One Hundred and Seventeenth Regiment, N. Y. Volunteers, (Fourth Oneida,) From the Date of its Organization, August, 1862, till that of its Muster Out, June, 1865*. 1866. Reprint, Hamilton, N. Y.: Edmonston Publishing, 1996.

Myers, Frank M. *The Comanches: A History of White's Battalion, Virginia Cavalry, Laurel Brig., Hampton Div., A. N. V., C. S. A.* 1871. Reprint, Marietta, Ga.: Continental Book Co., 1956.

Munson, John W. *Reminiscences of a Mosby Guerrilla*. New York: Moffat, Yard., 1906.

Neese, George M. *Three Years in the Confederate Horse Artillery*. 1911 Reprint, Dayton, Ohio: Morningside Bookshop, 1983.

Nicolay, John G., and John Hay. *Abraham Lincoln, A History*. 10 vols. New York: The Century Co., 1909.

Opie, John N. *A Rebel Cavalryman with Lee, Stuart and Jackson*. Chicago: W.B. Conkey, 1899.

Owen, Thomas James. *"Dear Friends at Home . . . :" The Letters and Diary of Thomas James Owen, Fiftieth New York Volunteer Engineer Regiment, During the Civil War*. Edited by Dale E. Floyd. Washington, D.C.: Historical

Division, Office of Administrative Services, Office of the Chief of Engineers, [1985].

Owen, William Miller. *In Camp and Battle with the Washington Artillery of New Orleans*. 1885. Reprint, Baton Rouge: Louisiana State University Press, 1999.

Parker, John L., and Robert G. Carter. *Henry Wilson's Regiment. History of the Twenty-Second Massachusetts Infantry, the Second Company Sharpshooters, and the Third Light Battery, in the War of the Rebellion*. Boston: Regimental Association, 1887.

Patterson, Robert. *A Narrative of the Campaign in the Valley of the Shenandoah in 1861*. Philadelphia: Sherman & Co., 1865.

Paxton, Frank. *The Civil War Letters of General Frank "Bull" Paxton, C. S. A., A Lieutenant of Lee & Jackson*. Edited by John Gallatin Paxton. Hillsboro, Tex.: Hill Jr. College Press, 1978.

_____. *Memoir and Memorials: Elisha Franklin Paxton, Brigadier-General, C. S. A., Composed of his Letters From Camp and Field While an Officer in the Confederate Army, With an Introductory and Connecting Narrative Collected and Arranged by his Son, John Gallatin Paxton*. New York and Washington, D.C.: Neale Publishing, 1907.

Pendleton, William Nelson. *Memoirs of William Nelson Pendleton*. Edited by Susan P. Lee. 1893. Reprint, Baltimore and Gettysburg: Butternut & Blue and Stan Clark Military Books, 1995.

Poague, William Thomas. *Gunner With Stonewall: Reminiscences of William Thomas Poague*. Edited by Monroe F. Cockrell. 1957. Reprint, Wilmington, N.C.: Broadfoot, 1987.

"Protection to Baltimore and Ohio Railroad and Chesapeake Canal." U.S. Congress. House of Representatives. Thirty-Seventh Congress, Third Session. Vol. 1. Miscellaneous Document No. 15. Washington, D.C.: Government Printing Office, 1863.

Quint, Alonzo H. *The Potomac and the Rapidan*. Boston: Crosby and Nichols, 1864.

_____. *The Record of the Second Massachusetts Infantry, 1861-65*. Boston: James P. Walker, 1867.

Reade, Frank Robertson. *In the Saddle with Stuart: The Story of Frank Smith Robertson of Jeb Stuart's Staff*. Edited by Robert J. Trout. Gettysburg, Pa.: Thomas Publications, 1998.

"Report of the Secretary of War communicating, in compliance with a resolution of the Senate of this date, information in relation to the amount of money paid by the War Department from the 1st day of March, 1861, to the 1st day of March, 1865, to the Baltimore and Ohio Railroad Company for the transportation of troops and munitions of war between the city of Baltimore and the city of Washington, or for any other purpose. Read March 3, 1865."

U.S. Congress. Senate. Executive Documents. Thirty-Eighth Congress, Second Session, 1864-1865. Executive Document No. 34. Washington, D.C.: Government Printing Office, 1865.

Rice, Edwin. *Civil War Letters of Edwin Rice.* Edited by Ted Perry. Neenah, Wisc.: Quality Printing, 1975.

Roe, Alfred Seelye. *The Ninth New York Heavy Artillery: A History of its Organization, Services in the Defenses of Washington, Marches, Camps, Battles, and Muster-out, With Accounts of Life in a Rebel Prison, Personal Experiences, Names and Addresses of Surviving Members, Personal Sketches, and a Complete Roster of the Regiment.* Worester, Mass.: The author, 1899.

Rosser, Thomas L. *Riding With Rosser.* Edited by S. Roger Keller. Shippensburg, Pa.: Burd Street Press, 1997.

Sanger, George P., ed. *The Statutes at Large, Treaties, and Proclamations, of the United States of America from December 5, 1859, to March 3, 1863.* Boston: Little, Brown & Co., 1863.

Scheibert, Justus. *Seven Months in the Rebel States During the North American War, 1863.* Translated by Joseph C. Hayes and edited by William Stanley Hoole. Confederate Centennial Studies 9. Tuscaloosa, Ala.: Confederate Publishing Co., 1958.

Scott, John. *Partisan Life With Col. John S. Mosby.* New York: Harper & Brothers, 1867.

Shaw, Benjamin Burbridge. *Guarding the River, the Canal, and the Railroad: Papers of Captain Benjamin Burbridge Shaw, Commanding Officer Company D, 2nd Regiment, Potomac Home Brigade, Maryland Volunteers.* Compiled by Jack Sanders. Parsons, W. Va.: McClain Printing, 1998.

Shaw, Robert Gould. *Blue-eyed Child of Fortune: The Civil War Letters of Colonel Robert Gould Shaw.* Edited by Russell Duncan. Athens, Ga.: University of Georgia Press, 1992.

Smith, William Prescott. *B & O in the Civil War, From the Papers of Wm. Prescott Smith.* Edited by William E. Bain. Denver: Sage Books, 1966.

Southern Historical Society Papers. 52 vols. 1876-1959. Reprint, Millwood, N. Y.: Kraus Reprint, 1977.

Stearns, Austin C. *Three Years With Company K: Sergt. Austin C. Stearns, Company K, 13th Mass. Infantry.* Edited by Arthur A. Kent. Cranbury, N. J.: Associated University Press, 1976.

Styple, William B., ed. *Writing and Fighting the Civil War: Soldier Correspondence to the New York Sunday Mercury.* Kearney, N. J.: Belle Grove, 2000.

Stiverson, Gregory, ed. *"In Readiness to Do Every Duty Assigned": The Frederick Militia and John Brown's Raid on Harper's Ferry, October 17-18, 1859.* Jacobsen Conference on Maryland History Document No. 1. Annapolis: Maryland State Archives, 1991.

Thompson, Gilbert. *The Engineer Battalion in the Civil War: A Contribution to the History of the United State Engineers.* Washington Barracks, D.C.: Press of the Engineer School, 1910.

Trueheart, Charles William, and Henry Martyn Trueheart. *Rebel Brothers: The Civil War Letters of the Truehearts.* Edited by Edward B. Williams. College Station, Tex.: Texas A & M University Press, 1995.

U.S. Congress. House of Representatives. *Journal of the House of Representatives.* Thirty-Seventh Congress, Second Session, April 10, 1862 and June 23, 1862.

_____. *Journal of the House of Representatives.* Thirty-Seventh Congress, Third Session, January, 12, 1863.

_____. *Journal of the House of Representatives.* Thirty-Eighth Congress, First Session, May 30, 1864.

U.S. Congress. Joint Committee on the Conduct of the War. *Report of the Joint Committee on the Conduct of the War.* 3 vols. Washington, D.C.: Government Printing Office, 1865.

U.S. Congress. Senate. *Journal of the Executive Proceedings of the Senate.* Thirty-Seventh Congress, Second Session, December 24, 1861 and March 3, 1862.

U.S. Navy. Naval War Records Office and United State Office of Naval Records and Library. *Official Records of the Union and Confederate Navies in the War of the Rebellion.* 30 vols. Washington, D.C.: Government Printing Office, 1894-1922.

U.S. War Department. *The Official Atlas of the Civil War.* 1892. Reprint, New York: Thomas Yoseloff, 1958.

_____. *The War of the Rebellion: A Compilation of the Official Records of the Union and Confederate Armies.* 128 vols. Washington, D.C.: Government Printing Office, 1880-1901.

Virginia. Advisory Council. *Proceedings of the Advisory Council of the State of Virginia, April 21-June 19, 1861.* Edited by James I. Robertson, Jr. Richmond: Virginia State Library, 1977.

Virginia. *Calendar of Virginia State Papers and Other Manuscripts From January 1, 1836, to April 15, 1869; Preserved in the Capitol at Richmond.* Vol. 11. Richmond: State of Virginia, 1893.

Von Borcke, Heros. *Memoirs of the Confederate War for Independence.* 2 vols. 1866. Reprint, N. Y.: Peter Smith, 1938.

Wahll, Andrew J., comp. *Braddock Road Chronicles, 1755.* Bowie, Md.: Heritage Books, 1999.

Wallace, Lew. *Lew Wallace: An Autobiography.* 2 vols. New York: Harper & Brothers, 1906.

Welles, Gideon. *Diary of Gideon Welles, Secretary of the Navy Under Lincoln and Johnson.* 3 vols. New York: W. W. Norton, 1960.

Wetterer, Jan, trans. *The Letters of the Jacob Miller Family of Sharpsburg, Washington County, Maryland.* Hagerstown, Md.: J. Wetterer, 1994.

Williams, Alpheus. *From the Cannon's Mouth: The Civil War Letters of General Alpheus S. Williams.* Edited by Milo M. Quaife. Detroit: Wayne State University Press and the Detroit Historical Society, 1959.

Williamson, James J. *Mosby's Rangers: A Record of the Operations of the Forty-third Battalion Virginia Cavalry, From its Organization to the Surrender, From the Diary of a Private, Supplemented and Verified With Official Reports of Federal Officers and Also of Mosby; With Personal Reminiscences, Sketches of Skirmishes, Battles and Bivouacs, Dashing Raids and Daring Adventures, Scenes and Incidents in the History of Mosby's Command.* Collector's Library of the Civil War. 1896. Reprint, New York: Time-Life Books, 1982.

Woodbury, Augustus. *A Narrative of the Campaign of the First Rhode Island Regiment in the Spring and Summer of 1861.* Providence: Sidney S. Rider, 1862.

Worsham, John H. *One of Jackson's Foot Cavalry; his Experience and What he Saw During the War 1861-1865; Including a History of "F Company," Richmond, Va., 21ˢᵗ Regiment Virginia Infantry, Second Brigade, Jackson's Division, Second Corp., A. N. Va.* 1912. Reprint, New York: Time-Life Books, 1982.

Wren, James. *Captain James Wren's Diary From New Bern to Fredericksburg; B Company, 48ᵗʰ Pennsylvania Volunteers, February 20, 1862-December 17, 1862.* Edited by John Michael Priest. Shippensburg, Pa.: White Mane, 1990.

Wright, James A. *No More Gallant A Deed: A Civil War Memoir of the First Minnesota Volunteers.* Edited by Steven J. Keillor. St. Paul: Minnesota Historical Society Press, 2001.

Articles

Anspach, Fred. J. "Antietam." In *History of the Fifteenth Pennsylvania Cavalry, which was Recruited and Known as the Anderson Cavalry in the Rebellion of 1861-1865*, 30-40. Edited by Charles H. Kirk. Philadelphia: Society of the Fifteenth Pennsylvania Cavalry, 1906.

Barringer, Rufus. "Ninth Regiment (First Cavalry)." In Clark, ed., Vol. 1, *Histories of the Several Regiments and Battalions from North Carolina*, 417-443.

Burgwyn, William H. S. "The Thirty-Fifth Regiment." In Clark, ed., Vol. 2, *Histories of the Several Regiments and Battalions from North Carolina*, 591-628.

Coles, David J., and Stephen D. Engle, eds. "'Powder, Lead, and Cold Steel': Campaigning in the Lower Shanandoah Valley with the Twelfth Pennsylvania

Cavalry – The Civil War Letters of John H. Black." *Magazine of the Jefferson County Historical Society* 55 (Dec. 1989): 17-114.

Conrad, D. B. "History of the First Battle of Manassas and the Organization of the Stonewall Brigade." *Southern Historical Society Papers* 19 (1891; reprint, 1977): 82-92.

Colston, W. B. "My Personal Reminiscences of the War." *The Berkeley Journal* 6, no. 2 (1977): 8-38.

Curry, James. "Narrative of James Curry, A Fugitive Slave." *The Liberator*, Jan. 10, 1840. http://docsouth.unc.edu/neh/curry/curry.html (accessed Nov. 25, 2010).

Duffey, J. W. "Capture of Generals Crook and Kelly." *Confederate Veteran* 33, no. 11 (Nov. 1925): 420-423, 437.

Early, Jubal A. "Early's March to Washington in 1864." In Vol. 4, *Battles and Leaders of the Civil War*, 492-499.

_____. "Winchester, Fisher's Hill, and Cedar Creek." In Vol. 4, *Battles and Leaders of the Civil War*, 522-530.

Evans, Thomas H. "The Enemy Sullenly Held on to the City." *Civil War Times Illustrated* 7, no. 1 (April 1968):32-40.

Fay, John B. "Daring Invasion of McNeill's Rangers, and Capture of Generals Crook and Kelly." James W. Thomas and T. J. C. Williams. *History of Allegany County, Maryland*. Vol. 1. 1923. Reprint, Baltimore: Regional Publishing, 1969, 389-398.

_____. "With M'Neill in Virginia." *Confederate Veteran* 15, no. 9 (Sept. 1907): 408-410.

Graham, James A. "Twenty-Seventh Regiment." In Clark, ed., Vol. 2, *Histories of the Several Regiments and Battalions From North Carolina*, 425-463.

"Historical Sketch of the Rockbridge Artillery, C. S. Army." *Southern Historical Society Papers* 23 (1895; reprint, 1977): 98-158.

Imboden, John D. "The Confederate Retreat from Gettysburg." In Vol. 3, *Battles and Leaders of the Civil War*, 420-429.

_____."Jackson at Harper's Ferry in 1861." In Vol. 1, *Battles and Leaders of the Civil War*, 111-125.

_____. "Stonewall Jackson in the Shenandoah." In Vol. 2, *Battles and Leaders of the Civil War*, 282-298.

Irwin, Richard B. "Ball's Bluff and the Arrest of General Stone." In Vol. 2, *Battles and Leaders of the Civil War*, 123-134.

"Journal of the First Maryland Regiment, May, 1861 to Sept. 1862." In Thomas V. Huntsberry and Joanne M. Huntsberry, Vol. 1, *Maryland in the Civil War*, 84-104.

McClellan, George B. "The Peninsular Campaign." In Vol. 2, *Battles and Leaders of the Civil War*, 160-187.

McNeill, Jesse C. "Capture of Generals Kelly and Crook." *Confederate Veteran* 14, no. 9 (Sept. 1906): 410-413.

Merritt, Wesley. "Sheridan in the Shenandoah Valley." In Vol. 4., *Battles and Leaders of the Civil War*, 500-521.

Nadenbousch, John Q. A. "A Memorandum of Occurrences and Events During the Service of Capt. John Q.A. Nadenbousch Commanding the Berkeley Border Guards From Martinsburg and Known as Company D 2nd Infantry Va. Vol." In Henshaw Gardiner & Henshaw Gardiner, *Chronicles of Old Berkeley*, 152-158.

Nesbitt, Otho. "Nesbitt's Civil War Memoirs." In *Windmills of Time*, edited by David E. Wiles, 181-209. [n.p.]: Clear Spring Alumni Association, 1981.

Phelps, Darwin E. "Reminiscences of Antietam." In *History of the Fifteenth Pennsylvania Cavalry, which was Recruited and Known as the Anderson Cavalry in the Rebellion of 1861-1865*, 49-55. Edited by Charles H. Kirk. Philadelphia: Society of the Fifteenth Pennsylvania Cavalry, 1906.

Riddle, Susan Nourse. "Diary." In Henshaw Gardiner & Henshaw Gardiner, *Chronicles of Old Berkeley*, 158-165.

Smith, James Ripley. "Civil War Diary." In *Hancock, 1776-1976* by Emily Mason Leatherman [Hagerstown?, Md.]: E.M. Leatherman, c1985, 20-32.

Waddell, J. M. "Forty-sixth Regiment." In Clark, ed., Vol. 3, *Histories of the Several Regiment and Battalions From North Carolina*, 63-82.

Walker, John G. "Jackson's Capture of Harpers Ferry." In Vol. 2, *Battles and Leaders of the Civil War*, 604-311

Weller, B. "Last Orders of Great Generals," *Confederate Veteran*, 23, no. 4 (April 1915): 174-175.

SECONDARY SOURCES

Books

Achenbach, Joel. *The Grand Idea: George Washington's Potomac and the Race to the West*. New York: Simon & Schuster, 2004.

Ackinclose, Timothy. *Sabres & Pistols: The Civil War Career of Colonel Harry Gilmor, C. S. A.* Gettysburg, Pa.: Stan Clark Military Books, 1997.

Anderson, Bern. *By Sea and By River: The Naval History of the Civil War*. New York: Alfred A. Knopf, 1962.

Andrews, Matthew Page. *Tercentenary History of Maryland*. 4 vols. Baltimore: S. J. Clarke Publishing, 1925.

Appleton's Cyclopaedia of American Biography. 6 vols. New York: D. Appleton, 1889.

Armstrong, Richard L. *7ᵗʰ Virginia Cavalry*. Virginia Regimental Histories Series. Lynchburg, Va.: H. E. Howard, 1992

Bacon-Foster, Corra. *Early Chapters in the Development of the Patomac Route to the West*. 1912. Reprint, New York: B. Franklin, 1971.

Bailey, Kenneth P. *The Ohio Company of Virginia and the Westward Movement, 1748-1792: A Chapter in the History of the Colonial Frontier*. Glendale, Calif.: Arthur H. Clark, 1939.

Baker, Jean H. *The Politics of Continuity: Maryland Political Parties From 1858 to 1870*. Baltimore: John Hopkins University Press, 1973.

Beachley, Charles E. *History of the Consolidation Coal Company, 1864-1934*. New York: Consolidation Coal Company, 1934.

Bean, W. G. *The Liberty Hall Volunteers: Stonewall's College Boys*. Charlottesville, Va.: The University Press of Virginia, 1964.

Boney, F. N. *John Letcher of Virginia: The Story of Virginia's Civil War Governor*. Southern Historical Publications 11. University, Ala.: University of Alabama Press, 1966.

Clark, Charles Branch. *Politics in Maryland During the Civil War*. Chestertown, Md., 1952.

Brown, Kent Masterson. *Retreat from Gettysburg: Lee, Logistics, and the Pennsylvania Campaign*. Chapel Hill: University of North Carolina Press, 2005.

Brown, Peter A. *Mosby's Fighting Parson: The Life and Times of Sam Chapman*. Westminster, Md.: Willow Bend Books, 2001.

Brugger, Robert J. *Maryland: A Middle Temperament, 1863-1980*. Baltimore: The Johns Hopkins University Press, 1988.

Burgess, John W. *The Civil War and the Constitution, 1859-1865*. 2 vols. New York: Charles Scribner's Sons, 1901.

Bushong, Millard, and Dean M. Bushong. *Fightin' Tom Rosser, C. S. A.* Shippensburg, Pa.: Beidel Printing House, 1983.

Camagna, Dorothy. *The C&O Canal: From Great National Project to National Historical Park*. Gaithersburg, Md.: Belshore Publications, 2006.

Canney, Donald L. *Lincoln's Navy: The Ships, Men and Organization, 1861-65*. Annapolis: Naval Institute Press, 1998.

Caudill, Harry M. *Theirs Be the Power: The Moguls of Eastern Kentucky*. Urbana and Chicago: University of Illinois Press, 1983.

Chambers, Lenoir. *Stonewall Jackson*. 2 vols. New York: William Morrow, 1959.

Cleaves, Freeman. *Rock of Chickamauga: The Life of General George H. Thomas*. Norman, Okla.: University of Oklahoma Press, 1948.

Coakley, Robert W. *The Role of Federal Military Forces in Domestic Disorders, 1789-1878*. Army Historical Series. Washington, D.C.: Center of Military History, United States Army, 1988.

Conrad, W. P., and Ted Alexander. *When War Passed This Way*. Revised Edition. 1982. Reprint, Shippensburg, Pa.: White Mane, 1987.

Cottom, Robert I., and Mary Ellen Hayward. *Maryland in the Civil War: A House Divided*. Baltimore: Maryland Historical Society, 1994.

Cozzens, Peter. *Shenandoah 1862: Stonewall Jackson's Valley Campaign*. Civil War America, ed. Gary W. Gallagher. Chapel Hill: University of North Carolina Press, 2008.

Crouch, Richard E. *"Rough-Riding Scout": The Story of John W. Mobberly, Loudoun's Own Civil War Guerrilla Hero*. Arlington, Va.: Elden Editions, 1994.

Cunz, Dieter. *The Maryland Germans*. Princeton, N. J.: Princeton University, 1948.

Davis, Burke. *They Called Him Stonewall: A Life of Lt. General T. J. Jackson, C. S. A.* 1954. Reprint, New York: Wings Books, 1988.

Davis, William C. *Duel Between the First Ironclads*. Garden City, N. Y.: Doubleday, 1975.

Delauter, Jr., Roger U. *McNeill's Rangers*. The Virginia Regimental Histories Series. Lynchburg, Va.: H. E. Howard, 1986.

Dilts, James D. *The Great Road: The Building of the Baltimore & Ohio, the Nation's First Railroad, 1828-1853*. Stanford: Stanford University Press, 1993.

Divine, John E. *35th Battalion Virginia Cavalry*. The Virginia Regimental Histories Series. Lynchburg, Va.: H. E. Howard, 1985.

Doherty, William Thomas. *Berkeley County, U.S. A.: A Bicentennial History of a Virginia and West Virginia County, 1772-1972*. Parsons, W. Va.: McClain Printing, 1972.

Dowdey, Clifford. *The Land They Fought For: The Story of the South as the Confederacy, 1832-1865*. Mainstream of America Series, ed. Lewis Gannett. Garden City, N. Y.: Doubleday, 1955.

Drago, Harry Sinclair. *Canal Days in America: The History and Romance of Old Towpaths and Waterways*. New York: Clarkson N. Potter, 1972.

Driver, Jr., Robert J. *The 1st and 2nd Rockbridge Artillery*. The Virginia Regimental Histories Series. Lynchburg, Va.: H. E. Howard, 1987.

Ecelbarger, Gary L. *Frederick W. Lander: The Great Natural American Soldier*. Baton Rouge: Louisiana State University Press, 2000.

Egerton, Douglas R. *Charles Fenton Mercer and the Trial of National Conservatism*. Jackson, Miss.: University Press of Mississippi, 1989.

Eisenberg, Gerson G. *Marylanders Who Served the Nation: A Biographical Dictionary of Federal Officials From Maryland*. Annapolis: Maryland State Archives, 1992.

Ernst, Kathleen A. *Too Afraid to Cry: Maryland Civilians in the Antietam Campaign*. Mechanicsburg, Pa.: Stackpole Books, 1999.

Everstine, Carl N. *The General Assembly of Maryland, 1850-1920*. Charlottesville: The Michie Company, 1984.

Evitts, William J. *A Matters of Allegiances: Maryland From 1850-1861*. The Johns Hopkins University Studies in Historical and Political Science, 92d ser. no. 1. Baltimore: The Johns Hopkins University Press, 1974.

Fairbanks, W. L., and W. S. Hamill. *The Coal-Mining Industry of Maryland*. Baltimore: Maryland Development Bureau of the Baltimore Association of Commerce, 1932.

Farber, Daniel. *Lincoln's Constitution*. Chicago: University of the Chicago Press, 2003.

Farwell, Byron. *Ball's Bluff: A Small Battle and Its Long Shadow*. McLean, Va.: E.P.M. Publications, 1990.

_____. *Stonewall: A Biography of General Thomas J. Jackson*. New York: W. W. Norton, 1992.

Fowler, Jr., William M. *Under Two Flags: The American Navy in the Civil War*. New York: W. W. Norton, 1990.

Franklin Cooling, III, Benjamin. *Jubal Early's Raid on Washington, 1864*. Second Edition. 1989. Reprint, Baltimore: Nautical & Aviation Publishing, 1990.

_____. *Symbol, Sword and Shield: Defending Washington During the Civil War*. Revised Second Edition. 1975. Reprint, Shippensburg, Pa.: White Mane, 1991.

Franklin Cooling, III, Benjamin, and Walton H. Owen, II. *Mr. Lincoln's Forts: A Guide to the Civil War Defenses of Washington*. Shippensburg, Pa.: White Mane, 1988.

Frye, Dennis E. *2nd Virginia Infantry*. The Virginia Regimental Histories Series. Lynchburg, Va.: H. E. Howard, 1984.

Furgurson, Ernest B. *Freedom Rising: Washington in the Civil War*. New York: Alfred A. Knopf, 2004.

Gardiner, Mabel Henshaw, and Ann Henshaw. *Chronicles of Old Berkeley: A Narrative History of a Virginia County From its Beginnings to 1926*. Durham, N. C.: The Seeman Press, 1938.

Gary, Keith O. *Answering the Call: The Organization and Recruiting of the Potomac Home Brigade, Maryland Volunteers, Summer and Fall, 1861*. Bowie, Md.: Heritage Books, 1996.

Gordon, Paul, and Rita Gordon. *Frederick County, Maryland: Never the Like Again*. Frederick, Md.: The Heritage Partnership, 1995.

_____. *Frederick County, Maryland: A Playground of the Civil War*. Frederick, Md.: The Heritage Partnership, 1994.

Gottfried, Bradley M. *Roads to Gettysburg: Lee's Invasion of the North, 1863*. Shippensburg, Pa.: White Mane Publishing, 2002.

Graham, Jr., Frank. *Potomac: The Nation's River*. Philadelphia & New York: J.B. Lippincott Co, 1976.

Green, Constance McLaughlin. *Washington: Village and Capital, 1800-1878.* Princeton: Princeton University Press, 1962.

Gutheim, Frederick. *The Potomac.* 1949. Reprint, Baltimore: The Johns Hopkins University Press, 1986.

Guzy, Dan. *Navigation on the Upper Potomac and its Tributaries.* Glen Echo, Md.: Chesapeake and Ohio Canal Association, 2008.

Hadfield, Charles. *The Canal Age.* New York: Frederick A. Praeger, 1968.

Hahn, Thomas F. *Towpath Guide to the C&O Canal, Georgetown (Tidelock) to Cumberland.* 1982. Revised combined edition, Shepherdstown, W. Va.: American Canal and Transportation Center, 1996.

_____. See also Hahn, Thomas Swiftwater

Hahn, Thomas F., and Emory L. Kemp. *Cement Mills Along the Potomac River.* Institute for the History of Technology and Industrial Archaeology Monograph Series 2, no. 1. Morgantown, W. Va.: West Virginia University Press, 1994.

Hahn, Thomas Swiftwater. *The Chesapeake & Ohio Canal Lock-Houses & Lock-Keepers.* Institute for the History of Technology and Industrial Archaeology Monograph Series 3. Morgantown, W. Va.: West Virginia University Press, 1996.

_____. See also Hahn, Thomas F.

Hahn, Thomas Swiftwater., and Emory L. Kemp. *The Alexandria Canal: Its History & Preservation.* Institute for the History of Technology and Industrial Archaeology Monograph Series 1, no. 1. Morgantown, W. Va.: West Virginia University Press, 1992.

Harsh, Joseph L. *Taken at the Flood: Robert E. Lee and Confederate Strategy in the Maryland Campaign of 1862.* Kent, Ohio: The Kent State University Press, 1999.

Hartzler, Daniel D. *Marylanders in the Confederacy.* [Silver Spring, Md.]: [Family Line Publications, c1986].

Harvey, Katherine A. *The Best-Dressed Miners: Life and Labor in the Maryland Coal Region, 1835-1910.* Ithaca, N. Y.: Cornell University Press, 1969.

Harwood, Jr., Herbert H. *Impossible Challenge: The Baltimore and Ohio Railroad in Maryland.* Baltimore: Barnard, Roberts and Co., 1979.

Hearn, Chester G. *Six Years of Hell: Harpers Ferry During the Civil War.* Baton Rouge: Louisiana State University Press, 1996.

Heitman, Francis B. *Historical Register and Dictionary of the United States Army, From its Organization, September 29, 1789, to March 2, 1903.* 2 vols. Washington, D.C.: Government Printing Office, 1903.

Henderson, G. F. R. *Stonewall Jackson and the American Civil War.* 1898. Reprint, New York: Longmans, Green & Co., 1955.

High, Mike. *The C&O Canal Companion*. Baltimore: The Johns Hopkins University Press, 1997.

Hoehling, A. A. *Damn the Torpedoes! Naval Incidents of the Civil War*. Winston-Salem, N. C.: John F. Blair, 1989.

_____. *Thunder at Hampton Roads: The U.S.S. Monitor, its Battle With the Merrimack and its Recent Discovery*. Englewood Cliffs, N. J.: Prentice-Hall, 1976.

Hollandsworth, Jr., James G. *Pretense of Glory: The Life of General Nathaniel P. Banks*. Baton Rouge: Louisiana State University Press, 1998.

Hollis, Jeffrey R., and Charles S. Roberts. *East End: Harpers Ferry to Cumberland, 1842-1992*. Baltimore: Barnard, Roberts & Co., 1992.

Hough, Walter S. *Braddock's Road Through the Virginia Colony*. Vol. 7, Winchester–Frederick County Historical Society Series. Winchester, Va.: Winchester–Frederick County Historical Society, 1970.

Hungerford, Edward. *The Story of the Baltimore & Ohio Railroad, 1827-1927*. 2 vols. Technology and Society Series. 1928. Reprint, New York: Arno Press, 1972.

Huntsberry, Thomas V., and Joanne M. Huntsberry. *Maryland in the Civil War*. 2 vols. Bunker Hill, W. Va.: J. Mart Publishers, 1985.

Imholte, John Quinn. *The First Volunteers: History of the First Minnesota Volunteer Regiment, 1861-1865*. Minneapolis: Ross & Haines, 1963.

Jacobs, Charles T. *Civil War Guide to Montgomery County, Maryland*. 1983. Revised edition, Rockville, Md.: Montgomery County Historical Society, 1996.

Johnston, II, Angus James. *Virginia Railroads in the Civil War*. Chapel Hill: University of North Carolina Press, 1961.

Jones, Virgil Carrington. *Gray Ghosts and Rebel Raiders*. 1956. Reprint, McLean, Va.: E.P.M. Publications, 1984.

_____. *Ranger Mosby*. 1944. Reprint, McLean, Va.: E. P. M. Publications, 1987.

Jordan, Philip D. *The National Road*. The American Trails Series, ed. Jay Monaghan. Indianapolis: Bobbs–Merrill, 1948.

Jordan, Jr., William B. *Red Diamond Regiment: The 17th Maine Infantry, 1862-1865*. Shippensburg, Pa.: White Mane, 1996.

Judge, Joseph. *Season of Fire: The Confederate Strike on Washington*. Berryville, Va.: Rockbridge, 1994.

Kapsch, Robert J. *Canals*. New York: W. W. Norton in association with the Library of Congress, 2004.

_____. *The Potomac Canal: George Washington and the Waterway West*. Morgantown: West Virginia University Press, 2007.

Kapsch, Robert J., and Elizabeth Perry Kapsch. *Monocacy Aqueduct on the Chesapeake & Ohio Canal*. Poolesville, Md.: Medley Press in association with Center for Historic Engineering & Architecture Research, 2005.

Katcher, Philip. *Building the Victory: The Order Book of the Volunteer Engineer Brigade, Army of the Potomac, October 1863–May 1865.* Shippensburg, Pa.: White Mane, 1998.

Keen, Hugh C., and Horace Mewborn. *43rd Battalion, Virginia Cavalry, Mosby's Command.* The Virginia Regimental Histories Series. Lynchburg, Va.: H. E. Howard, 1993.

Keller, S. Roger. *Events of the Civil War in Washington County, Maryland.* Shippensburg, Pa.: Burd Street Press, 1995.

_____. *Roster of Civil War Soldiers From Washington County, Maryland.* 1993. Revised edition, Baltimore: Clearfield Co., 1998.

Lamb's Biographical Dictionary of the United States. 8 vols. Boston: Federal Book Co. of Boston, 1903.

Larson, John Lauritz. *Internal Improvement: National Public Works and the Promise of Popular Government in the Early United States.* Chapel Hill: University of North Carolina Press, 2000.

Lash, Jeffrey N. *Destroyer of the Iron Horse: General Joseph E. Johnston and Confederate Rail Transport, 1861-1865.* Kent, Ohio: Kent State University Press, 1991.

Leech, Margaret. *Reveille in Washington, 1860-1865.* New York: Harper & Brothers Publishers, 1941.

Long, Priscilla. *Where the Sun Never Shines: A History of America's Bloody Coal Industry.* New York: Paragon House, 1989.

Lossing, Benson J. *Pictorial Field Book of the Civil War.* 3 vols. 1870-1876. Reprint, Baltimore: The Johns Hopkins University Press, 1997.

Lovell, Arthur. *Borden Mining Company: A Brief History.* Frostburg, Md.: [s.n.], 1938.

Lowdermilk, Will H. *History of Cumberland, From the Time of the Indian Town, Caiuctucuc, in 1728, up to the Present Day, Embracing an Account of Washington's First Campaign, and Battle of Fort Necessity, Together With a History of Braddock's Expedition.* Washington, D.C.: James Anglin, 1878.

Lowry, Thomas P. *Don't Shoot That Boy: Abraham Lincoln and Military Justice.* Mason City, Iowa: Savas, 1999.

Mason Leatherman, Emily. *Hancock, 1776-1976.* [Hagerstown?, Md.]: E.M. Leatherman, c1985.

Mackintosh, Barry. *C&O Canal: The Making of a Park.* Washington, D.C.: Department of the Interior, National Park Service, History Division, 1991.

Martin, David G. *Jackson's Valley Campaign, November 1861-June 1862.* Great Campaigns Series. 1988. Revised and expanded edition, Conshohocken, Pa.: Combined Books, 1994.

Mastrangelo, Mike. *Four Locks.* Washington, D.C.: Chesapeake and Ohio Canal National Historical Park, National Park Service, 1987.

McCardell, Lee. *Ill-Starred General: Braddock of the Coldstream Guards*. Pittsburgh: University of Pittsburgh Press, 1958.

McGrath, Thomas A. *Shepherdstown: Last Clash of the Antietam Campaign, September 19 – 20, 1862*. Lynchburg, Va.: Schroeder Publications, 2007.

McPherson, James M. *Battle Cry of Freedom: The Civil War Ear*. New York: Oxford University Press, 1988.

Mellander, Deane. *The Cumberland and Pennsylvania Railroad: Western Maryland's Historic Coal Carrier*. Newton: N. J.: Carstens Publications, 1981.

Miller, David W. *Second Only to Grant: Quartermaster General Montgomery C. Meigs*. Shippensburg, Pa.: White Mane, 2000.

Mitchell, Mary. *Divided Town: A Study of Georgetown, D.C. During the Civil War*. Barre, Mass.: Barre Publishers, 1968.

Moore, II, Robert H. *Chew's Ashby, Shoemaker's Lynchburg and the Newtown Artillery*. The Virginia Regimental Histories Series. Lynchburg, Va.: H. E. Howard, 1995.

Morgan, III, James A.. *A Little Short of Boats: The Fights at Ball's Bluff and Edwards Ferry, October 21-22, 1861*. Discovering Civil War America Series, vol. 2. Ft. Mitchell, Ky.: Ironclad Publishing, 2004.

Morse, Joseph E., and R. Duff Green, eds. *Thomas B. Searight's The Old Pike: An Illustrated Narrative of the National Road*. Orange, Va.: Green Tree Press.

Murfin, James V. *The Gleam of Bayonets: The Battle of Antietam and Robert E. Lee's Maryland Campaign, September 1862*. 1965. Paperback edition, Louisiana State University Press, 1982.

Murray, Robert Bruce. *Legal Cases of the Civil War*. Mechanicsburg, Pa.: Stackpole Books, 2003.

Musicant, Ivan. *Divided Waters: The Naval History of the Civil War*. New York: Castle Books, 1995.

Neely, Jr. Mark E. *The Fate of Liberty: Abraham Lincoln and Civil Liberties*. New York: Oxford University Press, 1991.

Nelson, John H. *"Bombard and Be Damned:" The Effects of Jackson's Valley Campaign on Hancock, Maryland and Fulton County, Pennsylvania*. McConnellsburg, Pa.: Fulton County Civil War Reenactment Advisory Committee, 1997.

Nesbitt, Mark. *Rebel Rivers: A Guide to Civil War Sites on the Potomac, Rappahannock, York, and James*. Mechanicsburg, Pa.: Stackpole Books, 1993.

Ogilvie, Philip Woodworth. *Along the Potomac*. Images of America. Charleston, S.C.: Arcadia Publishing, 2000.

Older, Curtis L. *The Braddock Expedition and Fox's Gap in Maryland*. Westminster, Md.: Family Line Publications, 1995.

Petrichick, Gary M. *Pocket Guide to the Chesapeake & Ohio National Historical Park*. Third Edition. N.P.: C&O Canal Association, 2004.

_____. *Pocket Guide to the Civil War on the Chesapeake & Ohio Canal*. Belmont, N.Y.: Gary M. Petrichick, 2003.

Phillips, David L. *Tiger John: The Rebel Who Burned Chambersburg*. Leesburg, Va.: Gauley Mount Press, 1993.

Powell, Allan. *Forgotten Heroes of the Maryland Frontier: Christopher Gist, Evan Shelby, Jr., Thomas Cresap*. Baltimore: Gateway Press, 2001.

_____. *Fort Cumberland*. Parsons, W. Va.: McClain Printing Co., 1989.

Proud, J. G. *Biographical Memoirs of Reverdy Johnson, LL.D., and Francis Thomas, A.M., Alumni of the St. John's College, Annapolis*. Baltimore: St. John's College Association of Alumni, 1879.

Radcliffe, George L. *Governor Thomas H. Hicks of Maryland and the Civil War*. Vol. 19, Johns Hopkins University Studies in Historical and Political Science, no. 11-12. 1901. Reprint, Baltimore: The Johns Hopkins University Press, 1965.

Raitz, Karl, ed. *The National Road*. The Road and American Culture, ed. Drake Hokanson. Baltimore: The Johns Hopkins University Press, 1996.

Ramage, James A. *Gray Ghost: The Life of Col. John Singleton Mosby*. Lexington: University Press of Kentucky, 1999.

Rankin, Thomas M. *Stonewall Jackson's Romney Campaign, January 1 – February 20, 1862*. The Virginia Civil War Battles and Leaders Series. Lychburg, Va.: H. E. Howard, 1994.

Reese, Timothy J. *Sealed With Their Lives: The Battle for Crampton's Gap, Burkittsville, Maryland, September 14, 1862*. Baltimore: Butternut and Blue, 1998.

Reidenbaugh, Lowell. *27th Virginia Infantry*. The Virginia Regimental Histories Series. Lynchburg, Va.: H. E. Howard, 1993.

_____. *33rd Virginia Infantry*. The Virginia Regimental Histories Series. Lynchburg, Va.: H. E. Howard, 1987.

Risch, Erna. *Quartermaster Support of the Army. A History of the Corps, 1775-1939*. Washington, D.C.: Quartermaster Historian's Office, Office of the Quartermaster General, 1962.

Robertson, Jr., James I. *4th Virginia Infantry*. The Virginia Regimental Histories Series. Lynchburg, Va.: H. E. Howard, 1982.

_____. *The Stonewall Brigade*. 1963. Reprint, Baton Rouge: Louisiana State University Press, 1991.

_____. *Stonewall Jackson: The Man, the Soldier, the Legend*. New York: MacMillan, 1977.

Rubin, Mary H. *The Chesapeake and Ohio Canal*. Images of America. Charleston, S.C., Chicago, Portsmouth, N.H., & San Francisco: Arcadia Publishing, 2003.

Ruffner, Kevin Conley. *Maryland's Blue & Gray: A Border State's Union and Confederate Junior Officer Corps*. Baton Rouge: Louisiana State University

Press, 1997.

Sanderlin, Walter S. *The Great National Project: A History of the Chesapeake and Ohio Canal.* Companies and Men: Business Enterprise in American. 1946. Reprint, n. p.: Arno Press, 1976.

Scharf, J. Thomas. *History of Western Maryland; Being a History of Frederick, Montgomery, Carroll, Washington, Allegany and Garrett Counties, From the Earliest Period to the Present Day; Including Biographical Sketches of their Representative Men.* 2 vols. 1882. Reprint, Baltimore: Regional Publishing, 1968.

Schildt, John W. *Roads from Gettysburg.* 1979. Second revised edition, Shippensburg, Pa.: Burd Street Press, 2000.

Schneller, Jr., Robert J. *A Quest For Glory: A Biography of Rear Admiral John A. Dahlgren.* Annapolis: Naval Institute Press, 1996.

Schuckers, J. W. *The Life and Public Services of Salmon Portland Chase.* 1874. Reprint, Miami: Mnemosyne Publishing, 1969.

Scott, Sr., Harold L. *The Civil War Era in Cumberland, Maryland and Nearby Keyser, West Virginia (1861-1865).* Cumberland, Md.: Harold L. Scott, Sr., 2000.

Thienel, Phillip M. *Mr. Lincoln's Bridge Builders: The Right Hand of American Genius.* Shippensburg, Pa.: White Mane, 2000.

Sears, Stephen W. *George B. McClellan: The Young Napoleon.* New York: Ticknor & Fields, 1988.

_____. *Landscape Turned Red: The Battle of Antietam.* New York: Ticknor & Fields, 1983.

_____. *To the Gates of Richmond: The Peninsula Campaign.* New York: Ticknor & Fields, 1992.

_____. *Gettysburg.* Boston: Houghton Mifflin, 2003.

Shaffer, Donald R. *"We Are Again in the Midst of Trouble": Flooding on the Potomac River and the Struggle for the Sustainability of the Chesapeake and Ohio Canal, 1828-1996.* College Park, Md.: University of Maryland, 1997.

Sheads, Scott Sumpter, and Daniel Carroll. *Baltimore During the Civil War.* Linthicum, Md.: Toomey Press, 1997.

Shriver, Samuel S. *History of the Shriver Family and Their Connections, 1684-1888.* Baltimore: Press of Guggenheimer, Weil & Co., 1888.

Siepel, Kevin H. *Rebel: The Life and Times of John Singleton Mosby.* New York: St. Martin's Press, 1983.

Stegmaier, Jr., Harry, David Dean, Gordon Kershaw, and John Wiseman. *Allegany County: A History.* Parsons, W. Va.: McClain Printing, 1976.

Stephenson, Darl L. *Headquarters in the Brush: Blazer's Independent Scouts.* Athens: Ohio University Press, 2001.

Stover, John F. *History of the Baltimore and Ohio Railroad.* West Lafayette, Ind.: Purdue University Press, 1987.

Summers, Festus P. *The Baltimore and Ohio in the Civil War*. c1939. Reprint, Gettysburg, Pa.: Stan Clark Military Books, 1993.

Sween, Jane C. *Montgomery County: Two Centuries of Change*. Woodland Hills, Calif.: Windsor Publications, 1984.

Swisher, Carl Brent. *Roger B. Taney*. Hamden, Conn.: Archon Books, 1961.

Symonds, Craig L. *Joseph E. Johnston: A Civil War Biography*. New York: W. W. Norton, 1992.

Tanner, Robert G. *Stonewall in the Valley: Thomas J. "Stonewall" Jackson's Shenandoah Valley Campaign, Spring 1862*. 1976. Revised edition, Mechanicsburg, Pa.: Stackpole Books, 1996.

Tate, Allen. *Stonewall Jackson, the Good Soldier*. 1928. Reprint, Ann Arbor: University of Michigan Press, 1965.

Taylor, George Rogers. *The Transportation Revolution, 1815-1860*. Vol. 4, The Economic History of the United States. New York: Rinehart, 1951.

Thomas, Clarence. *General Turner Ashby, the Centaur of the South: A Military Sketch*. Winchester, Va.: The Eddy Press Corp., 1907.

Thomas, Benjamin P., and Harold M. Hyman. *Stanton: The Life and Times of Lincoln's Secretary of War*. New York: Alfred A. Knopf, 1962.

Thomas, James W., and T. J. C. Williams. *History of Allegany County, Maryland, Including its Aboriginal History; the Colonial and Revolutionary Period; its Settlement by the White Race and Subsequent Growth; a Description of its Valuable Mining, Industrial and Agricultural Interests; Sketches of its Cities, Towns and Districts; Master Spirits; Character sketches of Founders; Military and Professional Men, etc.* 2 vols. 1923. Reprint, Baltimore: Regional Publishing, 1969.

Toomey, Daniel Carroll. *The Civil War in Maryland*. 1983. Seventh edition, Baltimore: Toomey Press, 1994.

Trout, Robert J. *Galloping Thunder: The Stuart Horse Artillery Battalion*. Mechanicsburg, Pa.: Stackpole Books, 2002.

Turner, George Edgar. *Victory Rode the Rails: The Strategic Place of the Railroads in the Civil War*. Indianapolis and New York: Bobbs-Merrill, 1953.

U.S. Congress. *Biographical Directory of the United States Congress, 1774-1989*. Washington: Government Printing Office, 1989.

U.S. Department of the Interior. National Park Service. *Chesapeake and Ohio Canal: A Guide to Chesapeake and Ohio Canal National Historical Park, Maryland, District of Columbia, and West Virginia*. Handbook 142. Washington, D.C.: Division of Publications, National Park Service, 1991.

Vandiver, Frank. *Mighty Stonewall*. New York: McGraw-Hill, 1957.

Van Every, Dale. *Forth to the Wilderness: The First American Frontier, 1754-1774*. New York: William Morrow, 1961.

Walker, Daniel. *Military Law*. New York: Prentice-Hall, 1954.

Wallace, Jr., Lee A. *5ᵗʰ Virginia Infantry*. The Virginia Regimental Histories Series. Lynchburg, Va.: H. E. Howard, 1988.

Walsh, Richard, and William Lloyd Fox, eds. *Maryland: A History – 1632-1974*. Baltimore: Maryland Historical Society, 1974.

Ward, George Washington. *The Early Development of the Chesapeake and Ohio Canal Project*. Johns Hopkins University Studies in Historical and Political Science, ed. Herbert B. Adams, vol. 17, no. 9-11. Baltimore: Johns Hopkins University Press, 1899.

Ware, Donna M. *Green Glades & Sooty Gob Piles: The Maryland Coal Region's Industrial and Architectural Past; A Preservation Guide to the Survey and Management of Historic Resources*. Crownsville, Md.: Maryland Historical & Cultural Publications, 1991.

Warner Harry, James. *The Maryland Constitution of 1851*. Vol. 20, Johns Hopkins University Studies in Historical and Political Science, nos. 7-8. Eds. J. M. Vincent, J. H. Hollander, & W.W. Willoughby. Baltimore: John Hopkins Press, 1902.

Warner, Ezra J. *Generals in Blue: Lives of the Union Commanders*. Baton Rogue: Louisiana State University Press, 1964.

Way, Peter. *Common Labor: Workers and the Digging of North American Canals, 1780-1860*. 1993. Reprint, Baltimore: Johns Hopkins Univeristy Press, 1997.

Weber, Thomas. *The Northern Railroads in the Civil War, 1861-1865*. 1952. Reprint, Westport, Conn.: Greenwood Press, 1970.

Weigley, Russell F. *Quartermaster General of the Union Army: A Biography of M.C. Meigs*. New York: Columbia University Press, 1959.

Welcher, Frank J. *The Union Army, 1861-1865: Organization and Operations*. Vol. 1, *The Eastern Theater*. Bloomington and Indianapolis: Indiana University Press, 1989.

Wert, Jeffry D. *From Winchester to Cedar Creek: The Shenandoah Campaign of 1864*. Carlisle, Pa.: South Mountain Press, 1987.

_____. *Mosby's Rangers: From the High Tide of the Confederacy to the Last Days at Appomattox – The Story of the Most Famous Command of the Civil War and its Legendary Leader, John S. Mosby*. New York: Simon and Schuster, 1990.

West, Jr., Richard S. *Mr. Lincoln's Navy*. New York: Longmans, Green & Co., 1957.

Williams, Thomas J. C. *A History of Washington County, Maryland, From the Earliest Settlements to the Present Time*. 2 vols. 1906. Reprint, Baltimore: Regional Publishing, 1968.

Wills, Mary Alice. *The Confederate Blockade of Washington, D.C., 1861-1862*. 1975. Reprint, Shippensburg, Pa.: Burd Street Press, 1998.

Wilmer, L. Allison, J. H. Jarrett, and Geo. W. F. Vernon. *History and Roster of Maryland Volunteers, War of 1861-5*. 2 vols. Baltimore: Press of Guggenheimer, Weil & Co.

Wilner, Alan M. *The Maryland Board of Public Works: A History*. Annapolis: Hall of
　　Records Commission, 1984.
Wittenberg, Eric J., and J. David Petruzzi. *Plenty of Blame Go Around: Jeb Stuart's
　　Controversial Ride to Gettysburg*. New York: Savas Beatie, 2006.
Woodward, Jr., Harold R. *Defender of the Valley: Brigadier General John Daniel
　　Imboden, C. S.A.* Berryville, Va.: Rockridge, 1996.
Worthington, Glenn H. *Fighting for Time: The Battle That Saved Washington*. 1932.
　　Reprint, Shippensburg, Pa.: White Mane, 1988.
Wright, William C. *The Secession Movement in the Middle Atlantic States*. Cranbury,
　　N. J.: Associated University Press, 1973.

Articles

Alexander, Ted. "Ten Days in July: The Pursuit to the Potomac." *North & South:
　　The Magazine of the Civil War Conflict* 2, no. 6 (August 1999): 10-34.
Armstrong, Alexander. "Reminiscences of Judge Richard Henry Alvey." *Maryland
　　Historical Magazine* 52, no. 2 (June 1957)" 124-141.
Atwood, Albert W. "Potomac, River of Destiny." *National Geographic Magazine*
　　88, no. 7 (July 1945): 33-70.
Barrett, Jason. "Stonewall Assaults Dam No. 5." *America's Civil War* 13, no. 4 (Sept.
　　2000): 50-56.
Bearss, Edwin C. "1862 Brings Hard Times to the Chesapeake and Ohio Canal." *West
　　Virginia History* 30, no. 2, (March 1969): 436-462.
＿＿＿＿. "War Comes to the Chesapeake and Ohio Canal." *West Virginia History* 29,
　　no. 3 (April 1968): 153-177.
Broadwater, Robert P. "To Catch a General–or Two." *America's Civil War* 16, no. 2
　　(May 2002): 46-52.
Brown, Kent Masterson. "A Golden Bridge: Lee's Williamsport Defense Lines and
　　His Escape Across the Potomac." *North & South: The Magazine of the
　　Civil War Conflict* 2, no. 6 (August 1999): 56-65.
Clark, Charles B. "Baltimore and the Attack on the Sixth Massachusetts Regiment,
　　April 19, 1861." *Maryland Historical Magazine* 56, no. 1 (March 1961): 39-
　　71.
＿＿＿＿. "Recruitment of Union Troops in Maryland, 1861-1865." *Maryland
　　Historical Magazine*, 53, no. 2 (June, 1958): 157-176.
＿＿＿＿. "Suppression and Control of Maryland, 1861-1865: A Study of Federal-
　　State Relations During Civil Conflict." *Maryland Historical Magazine* 54,
　　no. 3 (Sept. 1959): 241-271.
Curl, Donald Walter. "The Baltimore Convention of the Constitutional Union Party."
　　Maryland Historical Magazine 67, no. 3, (Fall 1972): 254-277.

Baird, W. David. "Violence Along the Chesapeake and Ohio Canal, 1839." *Maryland Historical Magazine* 66, no. 2 (Summer 1971): 121-134.

Droegemeyer, James R. "Stonewall Jackson's Battle for Dam Number 5." *The Berkeley Journal* 26 (2000): 81-114.

Duncan, Richard R. "The Era of the Civil War." *Maryland, A History, 1632-1974.* Edited by Richard Walsh and William Lloyd Fox. Baltimore: Maryland Historical Society, 1974.

_____. "Maryland's Reaction to Early's Raid in 1864: A Summer of Bitterness." *Maryland Historical Magazine* 64, no. 3 (Fall 1969): 248-279.

_____. "Marylanders and the Invasion of 1862." *Civil War History* 11, no. 4 (Dec. 1965): 370-383.

Franklin, William M. "The Tidewater End of the Chesapeake and Ohio Canal." *Maryland Historical Magazine* 81, no. 4 (Winter 1986): 289-304.

Frasure, Carl M. "Union Sentiment in Maryland, 1859-1861." *Maryland Historical Magazine* 24, no. 3 (Sept. 1929): 210-224.

French, Steve. "'Hurry was the Order of the Day:' Imboden and the Wagon Train of the Wounded. *North & South: The Magazine of the Civil War Conflict* 2, no. 6 (Aug. 1999): 35-42.

Frye, Dennis E. "Stonewall Attacks! – The Siege of Harpers Ferry." *Blue & Gray Magazine* 5, no. 1 (Aug.–Sept. 1987): 8-21, 24-27, 47-54.

Garrett, Wilbur E. "George Washington's Patowmack Canal." *National Geographic* 171, no. 6 (June 1987): 716-753.

Green, Fletcher M. "A People at War: Hagerstown, Maryland, June 15-August 31, 1863." *Maryland Historical Magazine* 40, no. 4 (Dec. 1945): 251-260.

Guzy, Dan. "Down the Monocacy—River Navigation and Canal Surveys in Frederick County, Maryland." *Catoctin History* 5 (Spring/Summer 2005): 33-41.

_____. "The Potomac River Survey of 1822." *Maryland Historical Magazine* 103, no. 4 (Winter 2008): 382-403.

Harvey, Katherine A. "The Civil War and the Maryland Coal Trade." *Maryland Historical Magazine* 62, no. 4 (Dec. 1967): 361-380.

Hearn, C. G. "The Great Locomotive March: Jackson's Railroad Campaign." *Civil War Times Illustrated* 25, no. 8 (Dec. 1986): 20-23, 28-31.

Kelly, Dennis P. "The Battle of Shepherdstown." *Civil War Times Illustrated* 20, no. 7 (Nov. 1981): 8-15, 32-35.

Mitchell, Charles W. "'The Whirlwind Now Gathering': Baltimore's Pratt Street Riot and the End of Maryland Secession." *Maryland Historical Magazine* 97, no. 2 (Summer 2002): 203-232.

Morris, Richard B. "Andrew Jackson, Strikebreaker." *American Historical Review* 55, no. 1 (Oct. 1949): 54-68.

Sanderlin, Walter S. "A House Divided – The Conflict of Loyalties on the Chesapeake and Ohio Canal, 1861-1865." *Maryland Historical Magazine* 42, no. 3 (Sept. 1947): 206-213.

_____. "The Maryland Canal Project – An Episode in the History of Maryland's Internal Improvements." *Maryland Historical Magazine* 41, no. 1 (March 1946): 51-65.

_____. "The Vicissitudes of the Chesapeake and Ohio Canal During the Civil War." *Journal of Southern History* 11, no. 1 (Feb. 1945): 51-67.

Snyder, Timothy R. "Border Strife on the Upper Potomac: Confederate Incursions from Harpers Ferry, April-June 1861." *Maryland Historical Magazine* 97, no. 1 (Spring 2002): 79-107.

_____. "The Chesapeake & Ohio Canal and the Underground Railroad." *Along the Towpath* 42, no. 1 (March 2010): 13-14.

_____. "Making No Child's Play of the Question: Governor Hicks and the Secession Crisis Reconsidered." *Maryland Historical Magazine* 101, no. 3 (Fall 2006): 304-331.

_____. "Securing the Potomac: Colonel Charles P. Stone and the Rockville Expedition, June–July 1861." *Catoctin History* 11 (2009): 9-17.

Stegmaier, Mark Joseph. "The Kidnapping of Generals Crook and Kelley by the McNeill Rangers." *West Virginia History* 29, no. 1 (1967): 13-47.

Wennersten, John R. "A Capital Waterfront: Maritime Washington, D.C., 1790–1880." National Maritime Heritage Foundation. Washington, D.C. http://www.nmhf.org/pdf/capital_waterfront.pdf (accessed Dec. 8, 2009).

Way, Peter. "Shovel and Shamrock: Irish Workers and Labor Violence in the Digging of the Chesapeake and Ohio Canal." *Labor History* 30, no. 4 (Fall 1989): 489-517.

Wood, Don C. "Honeywood Mills, Dam No. 5, the Colstons and the Civil War." *The Berkeley Journal* 6, no. 2 (1977): 60-66.

Wooster, Ralph A. "The Membership of the Maryland Legislature of 1861." *Maryland Historical Magazine* 56, no. 1 (March 1961): 94-102.

Internet Sites

Chesapeake and Ohio Canal. Western Maryland's Historical Library. Hagerstown, Md. http://www.whilbr.org/CandOCanal/index.aspx (accessed Dec. 8, 2009).

C&O Canal Association. Glen Echo, Md. http://www.candocanal.org/ (accessed Dec. 8, 2009).

Chesapeake and Ohio Canal National Historical Park. Hagerstown, Md. http://www.nps.gov/CHOH/index.htm (accessed Dec. 8, 2009).

Unpublished Sources

Bearss, Edwin C. "The Bridges. Chesapeake & Ohio Canal National Monument. Historic Structures Report, Part 2." 1968. Historical Data Section. Division of History. Office of Archeology and Historic Preservation. National Park Service. U.S. Department of the Interior.

French, Steve. Hedgesville, W. Va. "The Last Scout of Captain Burke."

"Morris Canal Fact Sheet." Canal Society of New Jersey. Morristown, N. J.

Sanderlin, Walter S. "A Study of the History of the Potomac River Valley, Prepared in Connection With a Report to Congress on the Proposed Parkway Along the Chesapeake and Ohio Canal Between Great Falls and Cumberland, Maryland." 1949. Historical and Cultural Resources Library, Chesapeake and Ohio Canal National Historical Park Headquarters, Hagerstown, Md.

Snyder, Timothy R. "'I Hope They Will Get Away Soon:' The Chesapeake and Ohio Canal and the Federal Authorities During the U.S. Civil War." Masters Thesis, Shippensburg University, Shippensburg, Pa., 1999.

_____. "Potomac River Fords Used by the Union and Confederate Armies." Revised, Oct. 11, 2009.

Unrau, Harlan D. "Historic Resource Study: Chesapeake & Ohio Canal." 2007. United States Department of the Interior, National Park Service, Chesapeake & Ohio Canal National Historical Park. Hagerstown, Md.

INDEX

canal boat bridges, 106-108,
115; military supply, 35, 54-55,
107, 110, 114, 138, 140, 143,
156, 164, 172, 212, 245, 246,
251; (photo) 116; seizure of
canal boats, 108-110, 112-117,
154; poor management, 122-
124; loyalty, 124, 157-158, 234-
235; Antietam Campaign, 125-
135; Union pursuit after
Antietam, 135-136, 138, 140-
144; Burnsides use of canal
boats, 144-145; Spates seeks
govt. post, 146-147; camps of
instruction, 149-150;
Gettysburg Campaign, 160-
171; Union pursuit after
Gettysburg, 169-172;
Confederates raids after
Gettysburg, 177-179; Spates's
arrest, 179-180, 186-187;
Rosser raid, 187; canal
improvements considered,
190-92; Monocacy Campaign,
192-201; McCausland raid,
202-204; Shenandoah Valley
Campaign (1864), 209, 211-212,
213, 223-224; Md.
Constitutional Convention
debates canal, 214-219;
capture of Gens. Crook and
Kelley, 228; coal market slump,
229-231; post-war condition of
canal, 237-238; Rock Creek
lots dispute, 238-239; Spates's
political career, 240, 244;
Spates's second term as
president, 241; incline plane,
242-243; Spates charged with
impropriety, 243-244; canal's
role in war, 245-247;
comparison with B&O

Railroad, 246, 247-249, 250;
relationship between army
and canal, 251-252; B&O
Railroad acquires canal, 254;
government purchases canal,
255; canal preserved as park,
255-256.
Clarke, Daniel, 218.
Clarke, James C., 242, 249.
Clear Spring Home Guard, 42, 43-44.
Coal, anthracite: 15, 18, 185, 190;
Cumberland Coal: 17-18, 60,
89, 230-231, 266n11, 270n13;
bituminous coal: 17-18, 28, 74,
89, 185, 191, 245, 262n11;
Broad Top Coal: 18, 24, 53,
112, 118; Nova Scotia coal: 18,
145; tariff: 28; gas coal: 68,
142, 145.
Coffee Raid, 228.
Cole, Henry, 178.
Confederate Military Units, Ashby's
Cavalry (7th Virginia Cavalry),
38, 79, 83; 2nd Virginia Infantry,
79; Carson's Militia, 79, 83;
Stonewall Brigade, 79, 83;
Rockbridge Artillery, 80;
Mosby's Rangers (43rd
Virginia Cav. Battalion), 157-
158, 192, 193-196, 204, 213,
220-221, 228; McNeill's
Rangers, 161, 192, 203, 220,
228, 240; 35th Virginia Cavalry,
163, 179, 227; 1st Virginia
Cavalry, 286n33.
Conococheague Aqueduct, 130, 132,
160, 171, illustration, 173; 200,
204, 228, 237.
Conrads Ferry, Md., 48.
Cook, Henry D., 232.
Cookus, Mortimer, 147-148.
Couch, Darius, 177,

damage reimbursement, 141; miners' departure, 142; new canal boats, 152; Williamsport Division damage, 174, 176; raids, 178, 220; robbed by Gilmor, 187; opposes toll hike, 188; Constitutional Convention delegate, 214; takes loyalty oath, 226.

Gutheim, Frederick, 3.

Hagerstown, Md., Franklin Railroad, 17, 53, 138; Spates trapped in, 169, 179, 186; military interference, 177; Brown's house, Confederate use of, 180; 233.

Halleck, Henry W., 126, 135-136, photo 139; 140, 149, 166, 167, 168, 170, 178, 198, 202, 211, 213.

Hampshire and Baltimore Coal Company, 185.

Hampshire Coal and Iron Company, 18.

Hampton Roads, Naval Battle of, 108, 109.

Hancock, Md., canal, use of, 17, 62; flood damage, 71, 99, 228; defense of canal, 79, 149; Jackson threatens, 92, 95; illustration, 93; Williams takes command, 97; claim against govt., 111; military interference, 153-154; Imboden occupies town 161; supply line 169-170; canal closed, 182, 224; McCausland occupies town, 202-203; Snively, early career, 233.

Harpers Ferry, Va. (W.Va.), 8, 11, 12, 13, 15, 17, 19, 26, 29; illustration 25; photo 27, 49; Wenner's canal boats, 30-31, 32; disable canal, Confederate plans, 35,

36, 38; interference with boating, Confederate 38, 41; damage to canal, 43-44, 45-46, 47; repairs to canal, 54-55; defense of canal 56, 58, 177; Herr's Mill, 62, 64; coal transferred to B&O, 68, 74, 142; canal boat bridge, 106-108; pontoon bridges, 106-107, 129, 136, 157, 171, 172, 189-190, 207, 292n1; damage, Antietam Campaign, 126-127, 132, 134, 282n30; pursuit after Antietam, 135-136, 140, 141, 142; military interference, 153-154, 224; Gettysburg Campaign, 168-169; pursuit after Gettysburg, 170-171, 172; Monocacy Campaign, 196; McCausland raid, 202, 204; Shenandoah Valley Campaign (1864), 212, 224; Greenback Raid, 228.

Hassett, Thomas, 98, 122, 170, 275n10.

Hebb, Hopewell, 218.

Heintzelman, Samuel, 167-168, 176, 177.

Herrs Mill, 62.

Hickel, Walter J., 256.

Hill, A.P., 131.

Hill, Daniel H., 102, 125-126, 129, 247.

Hoffman, Henry W., 179, 180, 262.

Holmes, Jr., Oliver Wendell, 66.

Holt, Joseph, 186-187.

Horsey, Outerbridge, 32, 33, 46.

Hotckiss, Jedediah, 130, 275n12.

Hollingsworth, J., 145.

Hunter, David, 192, 193, 198, 199, 201, 202, 208, 209.

Hunton, Eppa, 48, 276n22.

Imboden, John, 160-161, photo, 161; 192-193, 200, 204, 288n60.

Ingalls, Rufus, 135, 172.

CPSIA information can be obtained at www.ICGtesting.com
Printed in the USA
BVOW021448181211

278661BV00009B/19/P